The Michigan Model of World Production and Trade

The Michigan Model of World Production and Trade
Theory and Applications

Alan V. Deardorff and
Robert M. Stern

The MIT Press
Cambridge, Massachusetts
London, England

This book was set in Palatino by Asco Trade Typesetting Ltd., Hong Kong, and printed and bound by Halliday Lithograph in the United States of America.

Library of Congress Cataloging in Publication Data

Deardorff, Alan V.
The Michigan model of world production and trade.

Bibliography: p.
Includes index.
1. Commerce—Mathematical models. 2. Tariff—Mathematical models. 3. Nontariff trade barriers—Mathematical models. 4. Foreign exchange—Mathematical models.
I. Stern, Robert Mitchell, 1927– . II. Title.
HF1411.D314 1986 382′.0724 85-6639
ISBN 0-262-04081-6

Contents

List of Figures

List of Tables

Preface

This book is the culmination of more than a decade of research devoted to the development of our computational model of world production and trade and the application of the model to a variety of trade-policy and related issues. During this time we have learned a great deal about applied general-equilibrium modeling, and our efforts have in turn made more vivid for us many of the abstract concepts and relations that are central to trade theory and policy.

We describe in detail in the introduction the background of our research and its different phases over the years. Our efforts have of necessity required substantial amounts of computer time, and we are grateful to The University of Michigan and its Computing Center for providing us with such generous assistance and continuing access to its excellent computing facilities. We would certainly not have been able to implement, validate, and refine the model in the ways that we did had the assistance been unavailable.

We also wish to express our gratitude to a number of outside sponsors for their financial support and for facilitating our access to data. These include the U.S. Senate Committee on Finance, Office of External Research of the Department of State, Office of the U.S. Trade Representative, Bureau of International Labor Affairs of the Department of Labor, and most recently the Ford Foundation.

A research undertaking of this order of magnitude and duration has above all required substantial inputs of computer expertise, data gathering and editing, typing and revision of manuscripts, and administrative assistance. Over the years, Kit Baum, Mark Greene, Werner Riedl, and Deborah Laren have all been instrumental in developing and implementing many of the computational routines used. Mark Greene's assistance with the model's solution procedure was invaluable. We have also benefited from the assistance and collaboration of Drusilla Brown, who has developed her own bilateral version of our model. A large part of the typing and revision of manuscripts was done by Judy Jackson with her consummate skill, accuracy, and good humor. We would have been lost without her. Helene McCarren and the staff of the Institute of Public Policy Studies have provided in recent years the administrative support that has been essential for our efforts. In earlier years, we had administrative support from the Department of Economics.

Our final thanks are to our respective families not only for their endurance but especially for their continuous emotional support and encouragement. Our deepest gratitude is to our respective wives, Pat Deardorff and Lucetta Stern. It is to them that we dedicate this book.

April 1985

The Michigan Model of World Production and Trade

1 Introduction

The Development and Use of the Michigan Model

We began developing the Michigan model of world production and trade in 1974–1975 in response to an invitation from the Bureau of International Labor Affairs of the US Department of Labor. They asked us first to review some ongoing work on trade policy and employment being done in Washington, and then to submit proposals for research of our own. The purpose was to identify key issues and provide quantitative information on the trade and employment effects that might result from the Tokyo Round of Multilateral Trade Negotiations, which was then under way. Two proposals were prepared for submission. One involved econometric estimation of "tariff elasticities." The other proposed a disaggregated, computational model of production and trade covering the major producing sectors in the 18 advanced industrial countries that were the chief participants in the Tokyo Round negotiations. Funding was obtained for the first of these proposals, the results of which were later published in part in Leamer, Stern, and Baum (1977).

Although the second proposal was not funded, we decided to pursue on our own the conceptual development of a multicountry, multisector model that might eventually be used to analyze the employment and related effects of multilateral tariff reductions and other changes in policy. We wished to improve on existing methods of analysis, which at the time were exclusively partial equilibrium in nature, by taking into account such general-equilibrium effects as the interaction of foreign and domestic tariffs and the induced adjustment of exchange rates, as well as the interindustry interactions that had previously been captured through measurement of effective rates of protection. An early version of this model—Deardorff and Stern (1974)—was presented at the December 1974 meetings of the Econometric Society in San Francisco. It turned out that the data required to implement the model had already been assembled in large part in connection with the research on tariff elasticities. This was a fortunate occurrence because it enabled us to carry out a variety of computational experiments before settling on the version of the model reported in our 1974 paper.

We continued to work on the model thereafter in order to clarify and elaborate its theoretical structure, to explore alternative solution procedures, and to assess the likely employment impact by sector in the United States and the other major industrialized countries of various alternative formulas for tariff reductions that were being discussed in the Tokyo Round negotiations. While our modeling efforts have been guided all along by principles of pure trade theory, our primary concern was to devise a practical tool of analysis. We have therefore incorporated into the model those aspects of trade theory that we considered most relevant for the issues being considered. As a consequence, our model is not a fully general-equilibrium one in the purely theoretical sense, since it includes a certain amount of ad hoc modeling of particular policies and institutional features of different economies that we thought were important for purposes of analysis.

The theoretical structure of the model was first described at length in an unpublished working paper—Deardorff, Stern, and Baum (1976). The sectoral employment effects of alternative strategies for tariff reductions were then addressed in a series of subsequent papers in 1976–1978. These included Deardorff, Stern, and Baum (1977), Deardorff and Stern (1979a), Stern (1979), and Deardorff, Stern, and Greene (1979a). The estimates of job displacement for the United States in this latter paper were in turn used by Neumann (1979) in calculating the costs of adjustment assistance that might be required as a consequence of the Tokyo Round reductions in tariffs.

The first recognition of our model's potential usefulness as an input into the policy process came in the summer of 1978. We were asked at that time by the Senate Committee on Finance to undertake an analysis of the actual offers of tariff reductions and changes in nontariff barriers (NTBs) that were being tabled by the United States and the other major participants in the negotiations. This request was made in connection with the committee's responsibilities for evaluating the US offers prior to the conclusion of the negotiations and for preparing the groundwork for the ultimate approval or rejection of the Tokyo Round agreements by Congress. In order to carry out this analysis, it was necessary for us first to update the data base of the model from 1970 to 1976, which was the reference year being used in the negotiations, and also to obtain the detailed information on the negotiated tariff cuts and changes in NTBs. The results of our analysis were presented to the committee staff in April 1979 and later published in Deardorff and Stern (1979b) under the committee's auspices.

The next phase in the development of model was in 1979–1981. During this period, we received some assistance from the Office of External Research of the US Department of State. This enabled us to expand the model to include the 16 major developing countries. We subsequently used this 34-country version of the model to analyze a series of issues. These included further evaluation of the effects of the Tokyo Round, changes in trade and employment, the effects of tariffs and changes in exchange rates on the structure of protection, the effects of domestic taxes/subsidies and tariffs on the structure of protection, and the sectoral implications of changes in exchange rates. The results of these efforts were presented in a series of papers, in particular Deardorff and Stern (1981, 1983a,b,c,e). This phase in the model's development was thus instrumental in broadening its coverage and especially in demonstrating its adaptability to a variety of interesting and important issues in addition to those connected with trade liberalization.

The theoretical structure of the model has remained unchanged since 1981, except for a feature that we introduced in 1982 in an effort to represent some of the short-run lags in adjustment to exchange-rate changes. This feature of the model was pursued in response to a request from the Office of the US Trade Representative for some information on the sectoral employment effects within the United States of the appreciation of the US dollar that had occurred since 1980. The results appear in Deardorff and Stern (1982a,c). We also expanded the representation of national input-output tables in the model to include the United States, Japan, the individual member countries of the European Economic Community (EEC), and Brazil. This enabled us to undertake a more comprehensive analysis—see Deardorff and Stern (1984c)—of the effects of the Tokyo Round negotiations on the structure of protection in the United States and other major industrialized countries.

We are currently (early 1985) engaged in several additional lines of research using the model—see Deardorff and Stern (1984a,b,c, 1985) and Staiger, Deardorff, and Stern (1985a,b). These involve a comparison of the effects of unilateral and multilateral changes in tariffs, the sensitivity of model results to differences in national input-output tables, the effects of tariffs and NTBs on the structure of protection in the major industrialized countries, the terms-of-trade effects of protection by developing countries, and the effects of protection on the factor content of US and Japanese foreign trade. Our model has thus continued to be a useful way in which to address a variety of trade-related issues. In addition, we are planning a number of additional refinements and extensions of the model. These are discussed in our concluding chapter.

It is evident from the reference citations (at the back of the book) that our papers have been published or are forthcoming in a variety of professional journals and conference volumes and that some of our efforts are contained in unpublished working papers and special reports. We therefore welcomed the opportunity to bring together in a single volume the results of our research, which span about a decade of activity.

Comparison with Other Models

In the years since we began developing the Michigan model, a number of other efforts at empirical trade modeling have been underway elsewhere. These models differ greatly among themselves in terms of their industry and country coverage, the extent to which they incorporate general-equilibrium interactions, and the closeness with which they adhere to the theoretical paradigm of smoothly functioning, perfectly competitive markets. In many of these respects the assumptions of the Michigan model lie somewhere in the middle of the range of assumptions made by other models. The Michigan model is, for example, neither the most nor the least disaggregated, nor the most nor least "pure" in its assumptions of competition. If the Michigan model is unusual in any dimension, it is in the large number of countries that it covers and in its efforts to incorporate aspects of trade policy such as nontariff barriers (NTBs).[1]

Early efforts at empirical trade modeling were, like our own, directed primarily at the analysis of tariff reductions and were motivated by the Tokyo Round. At a conference held at the University of Western Ontario in 1979, we joined several of these other modeling teams in a comparison of the approaches we all were taking to the problem. These approaches ranged from the very disaggregated but largely partial equilibrium analyses of Baldwin (1976) and Cline et al. (1978), to the general-equilibrium model of Brown and Whalley (1980) that was built in the spirit of the Heckscher-Ohlin model of pure trade theory. Victor Ginsburgh even presented at the conference a computational rendering of the Arrow-Debreu general-equilibrium framework, in a paper that was evidently a precursor to Ginsburgh and Waelbroeck (1981).

Among these models, the Michigan model lay squarely in the middle in terms of its assumptions. With 29 industries and 34 countries, it was not as disaggregated as either Baldwin or Cline, yet it was more disaggregated than Brown-Whalley and Ginsburgh. At the same time, we included full general-equilibrium analysis of goods markets, unlike the partial-equilibrium efforts of Baldwin and Cline, but we held wages and expenditure fixed and permitted labor markets to be in disequilibrium, in contrast with the more complete equilibrium assumptions of the other authors. As we shall note again in our discussion of the Tokyo Round in chapter 4, in spite of these differences among the models, they were in agreement in their conclusion that the economic effects of likely tariff reductions would be relatively small.

In more recent years, empirical trade models have continued to evolve in two main directions. On the one hand, Whalley (1984) and a number of others have continued the development of full Walrasian general-equilibrium models. These Walrasian models are characterized computationally by their use of an algorithm to solve first for a benchmark equilibrium of the system, and then for a new equilibrium in the presence of the disturbance being analyzed. Such full solutions were made possible originally by an algorithm of Scarf (1967), though other algorithms have since been developed.

On the other hand, other models have also appeared that have taken the same approach as the Michigan model. That is, the equations of the model are first differentiated and then only the resulting linear system is solved computationally. This second approach is actually older, having been pioneered by Johansen (1960), and while it could easily be used to analyze a complete Walrasian system, it has more typically been applied to models in which some elements of disequilibrium are assumed. Though less accurate than the benchmark-equilibrium approach that has been used for Walrasian models, the Johansen approach has the advantage of permitting greater computational detail. As a result, the Michigan model and others like it tend to include a greater variety of policy parameters and other sometimes ad hoc institutional details than can be encompassed in models in which a full equilibrium solution is sought. Examples of both kinds of computational trade model will be discussed in chapter 2.

Another source of difference among models is the time frame that they attempt to represent. Since the models are typically static, their time dimension cannot be explicit, but it is nonetheless implicit in the assumptions that are made about what is and is not variable. In full equilibrium models, such as Whalley's, for example, it is assumed that both capital and labor are variable, and thus these models implicitly are directed at the fairly long run. In the Michigan model in contrast, capital is assumed to be fixed and labor is the only variable factor of production. Together with other of our assumptions, such as the fixity of money wages, this means that our model is directed more at the short run.

One final direction in modeling activity should also be mentioned. The Michigan model, despite its assumptions of disequilibrium in labor markets, holds otherwise to the assumption of perfect competition in all markets.

There has been growing interest in recent years among trade theorists in recasting trade theory to allow for imperfect competition. So far, this interest has carried over to computational trade models in only one instance. This is in the work by Harris—see Harris and Cox (1984). Harris allows both economies of scale and forms of non-price-taking behavior on the part of firms in models that otherwise follow the full equilibrium approach of Whalley. Harris is distinctive among computational modelers not only in his assumptions, but also in his conclusions about the welfare potential of trade liberalization. Because of the ability to exploit economies of scale in his models, he finds the welfare consequences of tariff reductions such as the Tokyo Round to be an order of magnitude larger than have typically been found by competitive model builders of all stripes. Harris's work is valuable in its effort to incorporate the reality of imperfect competition. However, there is as yet no consensus that his particular assumptions represent the best road one can take in this direction.[2]

The Michigan model, then, is distinguished among computable general-equilibrium trade models neither by its theoretical purity nor by its computational sophistication. Nor is it at the frontier in terms of efforts to incorporate undoubtedly important but still controversial representations of imperfect competition. Instead, the Michigan model has been designed more as a practical tool of analysis for trade policy. With that in mind, we have built in those features of trade policy that we felt were important, and we have been careful to allow for as complete a variety of general-equilibrium interactions among markets as we believe to be appropriate in the short run. As our description of our use of the model earlier in this chapter indicates, the resulting model has been successful in terms of its ability to provide numerical insights into important issues of trade policy.

Plan of the Book

In chapter 2, we begin with an overview of the model and then present its structure in equation form. Thereafter, we discuss the important technical and economic features of the model. The implementation of the model is discussed in chapter 3 in terms of its data requirements and parameters, method of solution, and applications to various issues. Chapters 4–9 deal with a number of different applications of the model, which were designed to analyze (1) the effects of the Tokyo Round of Multilateral Trade Negotiations and post-Tokyo Round negotiating alternatives; (2) the effects of tariffs on the structure of protection in the United States and other major industrialized countries; (3) the effects of domestic tax/subsidies on the structure of protection in the United States, the United Kingdom, and Japan; (4) the sectoral impact of real exchange-rate changes; and (5) the effects of trade on employment in the major industrialized countries. We conclude in chapter 10 with a discussion first of what we have learned from our efforts at computer modeling of trade, and then turn to directions for further research.

It should be evident from our introductory remarks that our model has undergone a variety of changes in structure and data since its inception. Rather than present the results of the different applications of the model as they appeared in the original papers, we have rerun everything using the most recent (June 1983) version of the model and data inputs. This should help to maintain consistency across chapters.

2 Theoretical Structure of the Model

We begin this chapter with a pictorial overview of one version of the model and a discussion of some of its relevant features that may be helpful in understanding how it works. We then present the detailed equations, including the notation for the endogenous and exogenous variables. Thereafter, we discuss how the supply and demand functions of consumers and firms are modeled, the substitution between imports and domestic goods, and the treatment of nontariff barriers, import licensing, rest-of-world net supply, and economic welfare. As an aid to understanding the significance of many of these features of the model, the last portion of the chapter provides a pair of simple theoretical models that illustrate how the more elaborate computational model works. The first of these simple models is a microeconomic, partial-equilibrium model, while the second is a simple Keynesian macroeconomic model. The latter also allows us to discuss briefly the issue of macroeconomic closure and how it is resolved in the Michigan model. The chapter closes with a short comparison of the Michigan model with others in the literature.

Overview of the Model[1]

The model is best thought of as composed of two parts: the country system and the world system. The country system is depicted in figure 2.1. It contains separate blocks of equations for each country, each one of which takes the form shown in the figure. The world system, sketched in figure 2.2, contains a single set of equations for the world as a whole. The country blocks are used first to determine each country's supplies and demands for goods and currencies on world markets as functions of exogenous variables and of world prices and exchange rates. These functions for each country are then combined to provide the input to the world system in figure 2.2, which permits world prices and exchange rates to be determined. These variables

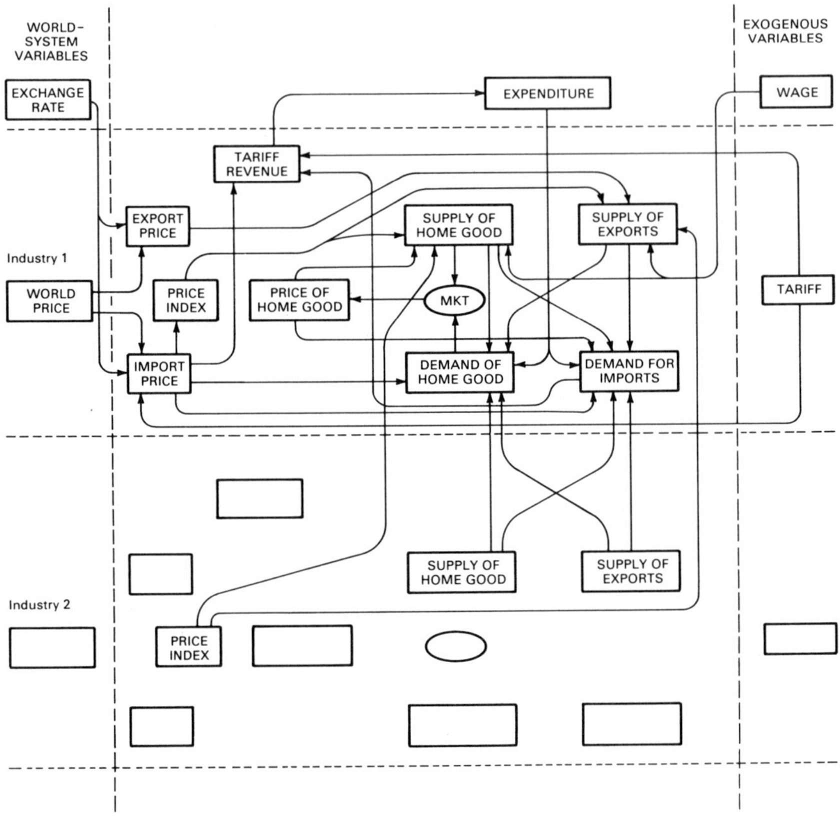

Figure 2.1
Country system.

are finally entered back into the separate country blocks to obtain values for other country-specific variables.

The most complicated economic interactions that are incorporated in the model are contained in the country blocks depicted in figure 2.1. The figure is divided into a number of parts, both horizontally and vertically. The horizontal divisions (finely dashed lines) separate industries, with those variables that pertain to the country as a whole listed across the top. As will be noted, each country included in the model has 29 industries. But since these industries are assumed to be identical in structure, we include only two of them in figure 2.1, with complete labels and arrows only in the first. The reader should thus imagine figure 2.1 extending a considerable distance beyond the page, with additional horizontal blocks for each of the remaining industries.

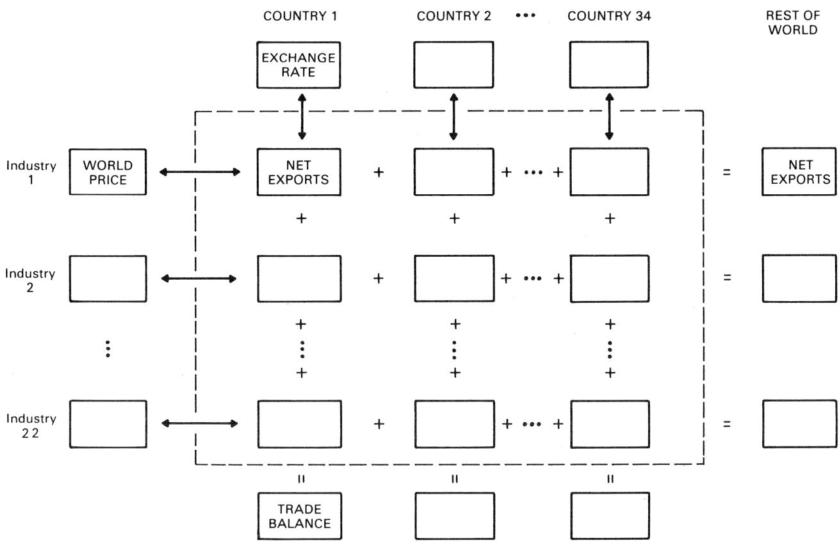

Figure 2.2
World system.

The vertical divisions in figure 2.1 (broadly dashed lines) separate exogenous variables on the right, country-specific endogenous variables in the middle, and variables to be determined in the world on the left. For illustrative purposes we include in the right-hand column only two exogenous variables: the country's tariff in each industry and its money wage, which we take here to be common to all industries. Other exogenous variables included in the model will be noted. The left-hand column contains the country's exchange rate and the world price for each industry. The variables in the center column reflect the complex demand and supply interactions of the consumers and firms represented in the model.

The world system in figure 2.2 is much simpler than the country system. We start with the export-supply and import-demand functions from the country equations, which depend on both world prices and exchange rates. To get world prices we simply add these supplies and demands for all countries (along rows in the figure) and set the difference equal to net demand from the rest of the world. To get exchange rates, when these are flexible, we likewise add the values of these excess supplies for a given country for all industries (along columns in the figure) and equate the resulting trade balances to exogenously given net capital flows. As mentioned, once we obtain the world prices for each traded-good industry and the exchange rate for each country, we can enter them into the separate country blocks in order to determine the rest of the relevant country-specific variables.

Figures 2.1 and 2.2 should provide the reader with some feel for the model. Let us now examine the structure of the model more formally and in greater detail.

Equations of the Model[2]

What we have described so far is a simple version of our model, without many of the complicating features, most of them optional, that we have built in over the years. The complete model, though without functional forms, is presented as equations (2.1)–(2.17)[3] (square brackets indicate variables that appear only with Cobb-Douglas specification of technology); functional forms appear in the technical appendix at the end of the book:

Country-system equations

Supply functions of products for export:

$$S_{ij}^{X} = S_{ij}^{X}(p_{ij}^{X}, p_{i1}^{H}, \ldots, p_{in'}^{H}, p_{i1}^{M}, \ldots, p_{in}^{M}, w_{ij}, K_{ij}^{X}), \quad i = 1, \ldots, m, \quad j = 1, \ldots, n. \tag{2.1}$$

Supply functions of products for home use:

$$S_{ij}^{H} = S_{ij}^{H}(t_{ij}^{H}\, p_{ij}^{H}, p_{i1}^{H}, \ldots, p_{in'}^{H}, p_{i1}^{M}, \ldots, p_{in}^{M}, w_{ij}, K_{ij}^{H}), \quad i = 1, \ldots, m, \quad j = 1, \ldots, n'. \tag{2.2}$$

Demand functions for imported goods:

$$D_{ij}^{M} = D_{ij}^{M}(p_{ij}^{M}, p_{ij}^{H}, E_i, [p_{i1}^{H}]\, S_{i1}^{H}, \ldots, [p_{in'}^{H}]\, S_{in'}^{H}, [p_{i1}^{X}] S_{i1}^{X}, \ldots, [p_{in}^{X}] S_{in}^{X}, G_{ij}), \quad i = 1, \ldots, m, \quad j = 1, \ldots, n. \tag{2.3}$$

Demand functions for home-produced goods:

Tradables:

$$D_{ij}^{H} = D_{ij}^{H}(p_{ij}^{H}, p_{ij}^{M}, E_i, [p_{i1}^{H}] S_{i1}^{H}, \ldots, [p_{in'}^{H}] S_{in'}^{H}, [p_{i1}^{X}] S_{i1}^{X}, \ldots, [p_{in}^{X}] S_{in}^{X}, G_{ij}), \quad i = 1, \ldots, m, \quad j = 1, \ldots, n. \tag{2.4a}$$

Nontradables:

$$D_{ij}^{H} = D_{ij}^{H}(p_{ij}^{H}, E_i, [p_{i1}^{H}] S_{i1}^{H}, \ldots, [p_{in'}^{H}] S_{in'}^{H}, [p_{i1}^{X}] S_{i1}^{X}, \ldots, [p_{in}^{X}] S_{in}^{X}), \quad i = 1, \ldots, m, \quad j = n + 1, \ldots, n'. \tag{2.4b}$$

Export prices:

$$p_{ij}^{X} = t_{ij}^{Xeq} R_i p_j^{W}, \qquad i = 1, \ldots, m, \qquad j = 1, \ldots, n. \tag{2.5}$$

Import prices:

$$p_{ij}^{M} = t_{ij}^{Meq} R_i p_j^{W}, \qquad i = 1, \ldots, m, \qquad j = 1, \ldots, n. \tag{2.6}$$

Consumer expenditure and tariff revenue:

With exogenous expenditure component:

$$E_i = E_i^0 + \sum_{j=1}^{n} (t_{ij}^{Meq} - 1) R_i p_j^W D_{ij}^M + \sum_{j=1}^{n} (1 - t_{ij}^{Xeq}) R_i p_j^W S_{ij}^X + \sum_{j=1}^{n'} (1 - t_{ij}^{H}) p_{ij}^H S_{ij}^H, \qquad i = 1, \ldots, m. \tag{2.7a}$$

Endogenous to hold employment constant:

$$\sum_{j=1}^{n'} D_{ij}^L = S_i^{L0}, \qquad i = 1, \ldots, m. \tag{2.7b}$$

Market equilibrium for home goods:

$$S_{ij}^H = D_{ij}^H, \qquad i = 1, \ldots, m, \qquad j = 1, \ldots, n'. \tag{2.8}$$

Tariff equivalents:

To reflect quantitative restrictions:

$$t_{ij}^{Meq} = t_{ij}^{Meq}(t_{ij}^M, D_{ij}^M, Q_{ij}^M), \qquad i = 1, \ldots, m, \qquad j = 1, \ldots, n. \tag{2.9a}$$

To reflect import licensing:

$$D_{ij}^M = L_{ij}\left(\sum_{k=1}^{n} p_k^W S_{ik}^X + B_i^{K0} \right), \qquad i = 1, \ldots, m, \qquad j = 1, \ldots, n. \tag{2.9b}$$

To determine exogenous imports:

$$D_{ij}^M = D_{ij}^{M0}, \qquad i = 1, \ldots, m, \qquad j = 1, \ldots, n. \tag{2.9c}$$

Export tax equivalents:

To reflect quantitative restrictions:

$$t_{ij}^{Xeq} = t_{ij}^{Xeq}(t_{ij}^{X}, S_{ij}^{X}, Q_{ij}^{X}), \qquad i = 1, \ldots, m, \qquad j = 1, \ldots, n. \tag{2.10a}$$

To determine exogenous exports:

$$S_{ij}^{X} = S_{ij}^{X0}, \qquad i = 1, \ldots, m, \qquad j = 1, \ldots, n. \tag{2.10b}$$

Demand for labor by industry:

Tradables:

$$D_{ij}^{L} = D_{ij}^{L}([w_{ij}], [p_{ij}^{X}], [p_{ij}^{H}], S_{ij}^{X}, S_{ij}^{H}, K_{ij}^{X}, K_{ij}^{H}), \qquad i = 1, \ldots, m, \qquad j = 1, \ldots, n. \tag{2.11a}$$

Nontradables:

$$D_{ij}^{L} = D_{ij}^{L}([w_{ij}], [p_{ij}^{H}], S_{ij}^{H}, K_{ij}^{H}), \qquad i = 1, \ldots, m, \qquad j = n + 1, \ldots, n'. \tag{2.11b}$$

Labour markets:

Exogenous wages:

$$w_{ij} = w_{i}^{0}, \qquad i = 1, \ldots, m, \qquad j = 1, \ldots, n'. \tag{2.12a}$$

Country-wide labor market:

$$\sum_{j=1}^{n'} D_{ij}^{L} = S_{i}^{L0}, \qquad w_{ij} = w_{ik}, \qquad i = 1, \ldots, m, \qquad j \neq k = 1, \ldots, n'. \tag{2.12b}$$

Industry labor market:

$$D_{ij}^{L} = S_{ij}^{L0}, \qquad i = 1, \ldots, m, \qquad j = 1, \ldots, n'. \tag{2.12c}$$

Net exports:

$$N_{ij}^{X} = S_{ij}^{X} - D_{ij}^{M}, \qquad i = 1, \ldots, m, \qquad j = 1, \ldots, n. \tag{2.13}$$

World-system equations

Market equilibrium for traded goods:

$$\sum_{i=1}^{m} N_{ij}^{X} + N_{j}^{row} = 0, \qquad j = 1, \ldots, n. \tag{2.14}$$

Trade balances:

$$B_i^T = \sum_{j=1}^{n} p_j^W N_{ij}^X, \qquad i = 1, \ldots, m. \tag{2.15}$$

Rest-of-world net supply:

$$N_j^{row} = N_j^{row}(p_1^W, \ldots, p_n^W, R_1, \ldots, R_m), \qquad j = 1, \ldots, n. \tag{2.16}$$

Exchange rates:

Fixed rates:

$$R_i = \prod_{j \neq i} R_j^{\theta_{ij}^R} R_i^0, \qquad i = 1, \ldots, m. \tag{2.17a}$$

Flexible rates:

$$B_i^T + B_i^{K0} = 0, \qquad R_m = R_m^0, \qquad i = 1, \ldots, m-1. \tag{2.17b}$$

Notation (m = number of countries; n = number of tradable goods; n' = number of goods total)

Endogenous variables:

S_{ij}^X, S_{ij}^H = supply of good j by country i, export and home sectors, respectively,

D_{ij}^M, D_{ij}^H = demand for good j in country i, imported and home-produced, respectively,

p_{ij}^X, p_{ij}^M = domestic price of good j in country i, exported and imported, respectively,

p_{ij}^H = home-sector price of good j in country i,

p_j^W = world price of good j,

E_i = consumer expenditure in country i,

B_i^T = balance of trade of country i,

R_i = exchange rate of country i, (domestic currency per unit of world currency),

D_{ij}^L = demand for labor in industry j in country i,

w_{ij} = wage of labor in industry j in country i,

$t_{ij}^{Xeq}, t_{ij}^{Meq}$ = export tax and tariff equivalents in industry j in country i, respectively,

N_{ij}^{X} = net exports of industry j in country i,

N_{j}^{row} = rest-of-world net supply in industry j.

Exogenous variables:

K_{ij}^{X}, K_{ij}^{H} = capital stock of industry j in country i, export and home sectors, respectively,

w_{i}^{0} = money wage in country i, if exogenous,

t_{ij}^{M} = 1 plus the ad valorem tariff on imports of good j into country i,

t_{ij}^{X}, t_{ij}^{H} = 1 minus the ad valorem tax on exports and home production, respectively, in industry j of country i,

G_{ij} = shift parameter representing government procurement in industry j in country i,

E_{i}^{0} = exogenous component of expenditure in country i,

R_{i}^{0} = exogenous exchange rate,

B_{i}^{K0} = exogenous capital inflow in country i,

Q_{ij}^{X}, Q_{ij}^{M} = shift parameter for quantitative restrictions on exports and imports, respectively, in industry j in country i,

D_{ij}^{M0}, S_{ij}^{X0} = imports and exports respectively, of industry j in country i, if exogenous,

S_{i}^{L0}, S_{ij}^{L0} = country i and industry j supplies of labor,

θ_{ij}^{R} = weight used in pegging currency of country i to that of country j.

The model includes m countries, $i = 1, \ldots, m$, producing and trading n goods, $j = 1, \ldots, n$, and producing an additional $(n' - n)$ nontradable goods, $j = n + 1, \ldots, n'$. A distinguishing characteristic of our model, however, is that both producers and consumers distinguish, within tradable industries, between home goods, which are produced and used domestically, and those that are either exported or imported. As a result there are really $2n$ goods produced by the n tradable industries, since each has both a home-market and an export product. Also, the number of markets for these goods is even greater than $2n$, since each country has its own home market in each industry.

Thus, within each country and tradable industry, producers are separated into a home sector and an export sector. Each has its own supply function, reflecting certain fixed factors of production that cannot easily be transferred between the sectors. This nontransferability may result from locational requirements or from the need to tailor products to national markets, though these features are not explicit in our model.

Demanders, too, differentiate between home-produced and imported products of a given tradable industry. Consumers and government, as well as producers who demand intermediate inputs and investment goods, are assumed to regard home-produced and imported goods as imperfect substitutes, but imports from various foreign countries as perfect substitutes.[4] The same elasticity of substitution is assumed to apply to all of these groups of demanders. Thus, demands for imports and home-produced goods are separate, but depend on the prices of both. On the other hand, a unit elasticity of substitution in final demand is assumed across industries, so that there are no direct cross-price effects in the demand functions of equations (2.3) and (2.4) except when there is a Cobb-Douglas specification of intermediate input technology.

Three separate prices obtain in each country, i, for each tradable industry, $j = 1, \ldots, n$. First, a home price, p_{ij}^{H}, is paid by users and received by producers in the home sector.[5] It is determined by the equality of home-sector supply and demand in equation (2.8). The second and third prices are those received for exports, p_{ij}^{X}, and those paid for imports, p_{ij}^{M}. All countries face a common world price, p_j^W, in each tradable industry, and it is determined in a world market to be described. Export and import prices are obtained from this in equations (2.5) and (2.6) by using exchange rates, R_i, and export tax and tariff-equivalent variables to be explained.

Equations (2.1)–(2.4), then, present supply and demand functions in terms of these prices, plus wages, expenditure levels, and various exogenous shift parameters. Supplies depend on all home and import prices, and demands depend on all supplies, both to reflect the use of intermediate inputs to production.

The aggregate behavior of the model depends crucially on the assumption made about aggregate expenditure, E_i. Our model is intended to focus on microeconomic and intersectoral issues, and we therefore wanted as neutral a characterization of macroeconomic policy as possible, one that would leave aggregates largely unaffected.[6] With this in mind we have, at various times, employed the two alternative assumptions shown in equations (2.7a) and (2.7b). In (2.7a) aggregate nominal expenditure is essentially exogenous. However, all tax and tariff revenue is assumed to be redistributed to consumers and spent, so that expenditure in (2.7a) equals this revenue plus an exogenous component. Alternatively, in (2.7b) we let aggregate expenditure vary endogenously so as to hold aggregate employment constant. One might think of the latter as assuming that macroeconomic policy is somehow successfully undertaken so as to stabilize the economy.

The remaining equations for each country, (2.9)–(2.13), determine tariff and export-tax equivalents, labor demands and wages, and net exports. The first of these include several cases to be explained. There are also three different assumptions made about labor markets, but these should be self-explanatory from the list of equations and variables. Net exports in each industry are just the difference between export supplies and import demands, and it is these that feed into the world-system equations (2.14)–(2.17), where world prices and exchange rates, if flexible, are determined.

Focusing on the world-system equations, note first that equilibrium in world markets for traded goods is required in equation (2.14), where the sum of these net exports plus net supply from the rest of the world is set equal to zero. This determines world prices, p_j^W. Next, the values of net exports are added over industries to form each country's balance of trade in equation (2.15). Rest-of-world net supply in each industry is determined in equation (2.16) as a simple and rather ad hoc function of world prices and exchange rates.

Finally, the exchange rates are determined in equations (2.17), with separate cases for fixed and flexible exchange-rate regimes. For any country with a pegged exchange rate, equation (2.17a) sets it equal to an index of other-country rates. Depending on the weights in this index, the peg may either be to a basket of currencies or to a particular currency. For any country with a flexible exchange rate, on the other hand, (2.17b) determines it by the requirement that its balance of trade plus an exogenous capital inflow be equal to zero.

Only $m - 1$ markets need to be cleared explicitly, due to Walras's law.[7] However, to determine absolute prices and exchange rates, we must then specify a numeraire. This is done in the last of equations (2.17b), where we fix the exchange rate of country m.

Since exogenous capital flows are specified in units of the numeraire, the selection of m is not trivial. In applying the model, we have chosen the U.S. dollar as the numeraire, with means that the dollar values of capital flows are assumed to be constant.

Supply and Demand Functions

We derived explicit supply and demand functions from utility and profit maximization of consumers and firms, assuming explicit utility and production functions. Details of these derivations are contained in Deardorff, Stern, and Baum (1976). Here we merely report the assumptions that were made, and the results themselves are listed in the appendix.

Since both producers and consumers demand goods, and since each tradable industry has both imported and home-produced goods available, we first characterized the choice between the two. This was done, for each industry, with functions that aggregate the services of home and imported goods. These then enter as arguments in both utility and production functions. To permit choice of the degree of substitution between home and imported goods, these aggregation functions were specified as Constant Elasticity of Substitution (CES) functions. The substitution elasticities for each industry were then inferred from published econometric estimates of import-demand elasticities.[8]

To obtain consumer demand functions, we used a Cobb-Douglas utility function. Its arguments were nontradable consumption levels plus these aggregates of home and imported tradable goods. By maximizing this utility function for a given level of expenditure, we obtained consumer demand functions for each industry.

It will be noted that the demands depend only on expenditure and on home and import prices of the own industry. Prices from other industries do not appear, since Cobb-Douglas utility forces cross elasticities of demand to be zero.

For firms, we assumed production functions whose arguments were again these home-import aggregates for each industry plus an aggregate of primary factors as well. The aggregate function for primary factors (labor and capital) was also specified as CES.[9] These aggregates were related by fixed coefficients in the primary version of the model, though we have also used a Cobb-Douglas technology, which permits more substitution among the inputs. The model can accommodate different input-output data for each country. However, we have so far been unable to gather and process that much data. Instead, we have used tables for only the United States, Japan, EEC member countries, and Brazil. The US table has been applied to the remaining 8 industrial countries and the Brazilian table to the other 13 developing countries included in the model.

By solving profit-maximization problems for firms, given their production technologies and capital stocks, we obtained supply functions for the export and home sectors, demand functions for home and imported intermediate inputs, and demand functions for labor. Unlike consumer demand functions, the firm-supply functions depend on prices in all industries, since all may provide intermediate inputs. Also, while firm-demand functions do not directly involve cross-price effects, they do have such effects indirectly, since they depend on supplies, which in turn depend on all prices.

The main difference between the two specifications of technology is that input-demand functions for Cobb-Douglas technology depend directly on output price and, for labor, on the wage. With fixed coefficients, output alone determines the demand for all inputs except for the division between home goods and imports. But with substitution allowed, the prices of inputs relative to output matter for input demands, even once the level of output is known.

A further difference is also worth noting. Own-price elasticities of supply and demand are all somewhat larger with Cobb-Douglas technology than with fixed coefficients, as one would expect with increased substitution.

The supply and demand functions of firms and consumers have been aggregated to get the explicit versions of equations (2.1)–(2.4) and (2.11) that appear as (A.4.1)–(A.4.4) and (A.4.11) in the appendix.

The Armington Assumption

In common with other empirically based trade models, we found early on that the traditional trade-theoretic assumption of perfect substitutability between domestic and foreign goods was not workable. On the one hand, such perfect substitutability is inconsistent with the empirical fact that countries have both exports and imports in any given industry. While such "cross hauling" may be dismissed as an artificial result of aggregation, an empirical model is necessarily aggregative and must be designed to be consistent with the data. Even more important, as we shall discuss further in chapter 10, perfect substitutability between domestic and foreign goods is inconsistent with the empirically observed elasticities that seem to prevail in international trade. It is difficult, if not impossible, to specify the parameters of behavior in such a way as to generate these observed elasticities and still maintain the assumption of perfect substitutability.

However, the size of our model in terms of countries has until recently made it impractical to implement fully the Armington (1969) assumption that goods are differentiated completely on the basis of country of origin. To implement the Armington assumption requires simultaneous solution for equilibrium in some 748 world markets (22 tradable goods times 34 countries). Such a task has been completed in Brown (1984), and it will be interesting in subsequent research to determine what differences may emerge between our model and Brown's. Some differences will be noted later. In any event, the assumptions that we have made instead—which separate production for export from production for the domestic market and which permit demanders to differentiate only between home-produced goods and imports—together enable us to represent the essence of the Armington assumption. That is, we have "home" markets for each tradable good, and in these home markets prices can vary independently of the prices of both exports and imports.

Although, as mentioned, it is now possible using Brown's model to implement the full Armington differentiation of imports by place of production, the model that accomplishes this is still very expensive to solve and therefore not practical for many of our purposes here, which require that multiple solutions be carried out. In addition, the Armington assumption as it is usually implemented dampens not only the substitution between a country's own goods and imports, but also the substitution in third-country markets between a country's exports and exports of its competitors. We remain unconvinced that this is necessarily the best assumption that can be made, and therefore believe that our own approach, even though it was originally motivated for computational reasons, has much to recommend it.

Nonetheless, the two alternative assumptions do have different implications for some of our results. For example, Brown (1985) has compared her results for the Tokyo Round with ours and has found a notable difference between the results of the two models in terms of which countries tend to benefit from multilateral tariff reductions. Thus, while the total effects of the Tokyo Round are very small in both models, the distribution of those effects across countries is different in the two. In our model, where efficiency effects seem to dominate the welfare calculations, those countries that reduce tariffs the most tend to gain the most from the Tokyo Round. In contrast, in Brown's model with the full Armington assumption, there are stronger terms of trade effects because of each country's greater influence over its own export prices. As a result, Brown's analysis of the Tokyo Round finds the greatest gainers to be those countries that reduce tariffs the least, including especially the LDCs (Less Developed Countries) that were not included in the negotiations.

Nontariff Barriers

We modeled the presence of quantitative restrictions (QRs) on imports by using tariff equivalents, t_{ij}^{Meq}, that vary endogenously to dampen the quantitative response of imports to changes in other variables. We also include a similar facility for handling QRs on exports, through an export-tax-equivalent variable, t_{ij}^{Xeq}, though we have not yet had much occasion to use this.

The tariff equivalent is defined as a weighted average of the nominal tariff variable, t_{ij}^{M}, and a second implicit tariff variable, t_{ij}^{QM}, that would reflect binding QRs for the entire industry. The weights are given by the fraction of the industry in which QRs are binding. The implicit tariff is defined as one that would, in a typical import demand equation, keep the quantity demanded equal to an exogenous value, Q_{ij}^{M}, set by a quota. The result, as shown in the appendix, is a simple expression relating the tariff equivalent to the nominal tariff and to the difference between the quota and import demand.

A rise in the quantity of permitted imports lowers the tariff equivalent and does in fact stimulate imports. On the other hand, changes (such as a fall in the world price) that would normally increase demand for imports will cause the tariff equivalent to rise and so cause the change in quantity to be smaller than it would otherwise be. Similar remarks apply to the export-tax equivalent, where it should be remembered that t_{ij}^{Xeq} is actually *one minus* the export-tax equivalent, which therefore varies inversely with t_{ij}^{Xeq}.

This formulation permits us to analyze problems other than nontariff barriers (NTBs) under the realistic and important assumption that NTBs are present and restrict the responsiveness of trade. This is accomplished by merely making the fractions θ_{ij}^{QM} and θ_{ij}^{QX} nonzero in industries where this is appropriate. In addition, by using the exogenous variables, Q_{ij}^{M} and Q_{ij}^{X}, we have been able to analyze the effect of changing a QR, so long as we know the volume of trade that is being released from a binding constraint. This is how we have treated the changes in agricultural quotas in our analysis of the Tokyo Round.

Import Licensing

A new feature of the model that we felt necessary with the addition of developing countries is the treatment of import licensing. Many of these countries have pegged exchange rates, but they are often unable to finance all of the imports that would be desired at that (or perhaps any) exchange rate and so resort to more direct regulation of import behavior.

We have modeled this again through the tariff-equivalent variable, t_{ij}^{Meq}. For countries where licensing is in effect, we suppress equation (2.9a) and assume instead that t_{ij}^{Meq} incorporates the shadow price of scarce foreign exchange to a particular sector. The government is assumed to allocate the foreign exchange that is earned from exports and capital inflows among importers in proportion to some base level of imports that is established. As a result, each sector's imports depend on the total value of exports and capital inflow as shown in the licensing function L_{ij} of equation (2.9b). What this specification does is to assure approximate balance-of-payments equilibrium even though the exchange rate is pegged.

Along with import licensing, we also modeled a subsidy to exports equal to the export sector's payment of any tariff equivalent on imported inputs. This was done to prevent import licensing from adversely affecting exports through its effect on input prices. Essentially, we are saying that exporters are exempt from licensing when what they import will contribute to production for export.[10]

Rest-of-World Net Supply

With the addition of 16 developing countries to our model, the importance of the sector representing the rest of the world is correspondingly reduced. In the past, we have experimented with several ways of specifying rest-of-world behavior, but for present purposes we have used only one.

We assume that rest-of-world exports in each industry respond positively to the world price with an elasticity, ε_j^r, that is typical of the included countries. Rest-of-world imports are assumed to be subject to import licensing and so are fixed at a constant fraction of the value of rest-of-world exports. Exchange rates in the rest of the world are assumed to be pegged to a basket of currencies of the included countries, with weights that depend primarily on their importance in trade. As a result, rest-of-world net exports in any particular industry depend upon all world prices and exchange rates.

There is one exception to this, however, that concerns the supply, and pricing, of oil. The major oil-producing countries are not part of our model, except as part of the aggregated rest-of-world. Normally this rest-of-world sector is modeled as pegging its exchange rate to a basket of currencies only about 60% of which is the US dollar. To reflect the fact that oil is priced in US dollars, however, we have made rest-of-world supply in the oil industry respond directly to the US dollar price. Since the elasticity of supply in this sector is quite large, this has the effect of essentially fixing that price.

Departures from General Equilibrium

We have already noted that ours is not a full general-equilibrium model. For example, because of our interest in effects on sectoral unemployment in the relatively short run, we do not ordinarily assume equilibrium in labor markets. This same motivation also accounts for our assumption of fixed sectoral stocks of capital. In the case of labor markets we implement our disequilibrium assumption in a rather Keynesian fashion by specifying money wages as fixed.

The model also departs from full general equilibrium in another fundamental way. The system is not "closed" in the sense of having the level of expenditure related directly to the level of earned income. Instead, as noted, we usually take aggregate expenditure to be essentially exogenous, except for a minor modification to permit tax and tariff revenues to be redistributed and spent by consumers. Or, alternatively, we sometimes allow aggregate expenditure to vary endogenously so as to hold aggregate employment constant.

Our treatment of money wages and expenditure together explains the role that exchange rates play in the model. If all nominal values were variable, presumably an exchange rate would play only a nominal role in the model. A devaluation, for example, would simply raise all wages and prices by the same percentage and leave real variables unchanged. With nominally fixed wages and expenditure, however, the exchange rate alters the values of these variables in one country relative to others. Thus, for example, a devaluation reduces the ratio of domestic to foreign wages and has real effects working through relative costs.

It is also important to note that our model is linearized in the neighborhood of an initial equilibrium, and thus yields only an approximation to comparative static changes in the neighborhood of that equilibrium, rather than old and new equilibria themselves. As a result of this linearization, solution of the model does not require any special algorithm. The advantage of this simplicity of solution is that we can include in the model somewhat more industries and countries than are typically present in computable general-equilibrium models, though not as many as have sometimes been included in partial equilibrium estimates of tariff effects.[11] The price we pay for this ability to deal with a large system is that our results are only approximate, and are good approximations depending on whether the changes we consider are relatively small.

Economic Welfare

Although our model provides information on changes in prices and changes in production, consumption, and trade, it does not readily lend itself conceptually to analysis of changes in economic welfare. We decided nonetheless to develop some ad hoc procedures for welfare calculations, and the ones we report in later chapters are based on the static, partial-equilibrium measures commonly used in the literature to calculate changes in consumer and producer surplus.

Theoretical Illustrations of the Model

As a further aid to the reader in understanding the model and how it works, it may be helpful to provide two simplified theoretical models that illustrate certain assumptions and behavior of the model. The first of these is based on conventional supply and demand analysis and is intended to illuminate the microeconomic workings of the Michigan model. The second simple model is based on a Keynesian framework and illustrates the macroeconomic assumptions that are implicit in the Michigan model.

The first of these simple models is shown in figure 2.3 and illustrates the case of a unilateral 50% tariff reduction in a small country with a fixed exchange rate and fixed level of expenditure. To simplify the illustration, suppose that there is only one industry in the economy, and that initial supplies and demands are as shown by the solid curves in the figure.

The world price of the good is p_W yielding an export price in domestic currency of $p_X = Rp_W$, where R is the exchange rate. The tariff, t, implies the somewhat higher import price, p_M^0. In figure 2.3a the home sector of this industry is shown, with supply and demand curves that both depend not only on the home-sector price, p_H, but on the import price, p_M^0, as well. The reasons are that demanders can substitute between home and imported goods, while suppliers rely partly on imported inputs. Together these supply and demand curves determine the equilibrium price, p_H^0, in the home sector.

Similarly, the supply of exports and the demand for imports depend, in figure 2.3b, not only on their respective own prices, p_X and p_M^0, but also on the home sector price p_H^0. Given p_H^0 these curves are determined and lead to quantities traded Q_M^0 and Q_X^0. Since this is the only industry, we have drawn these two quantities as equal, showing initially balanced trade.

Imagine now that the tariff is cut in half. This reduces the import price to p_M, which is easily determined since we assume that both R and p_W are fixed in this illustration. The lower import price shifts both curves in figure 2.3a as shown. The demand curve shifts down by the same proportion as p_M, since essentially only relative prices matter for demand. The supply curve shifts down by less than this, since imports constitute only a fraction of total costs. The result is a drop in both price and quantity in the home sector.

The fall in p_H in turn causes similar shifts in figure 2.3b. That is, both supply of imports and demand for imports are shifted vertically downward

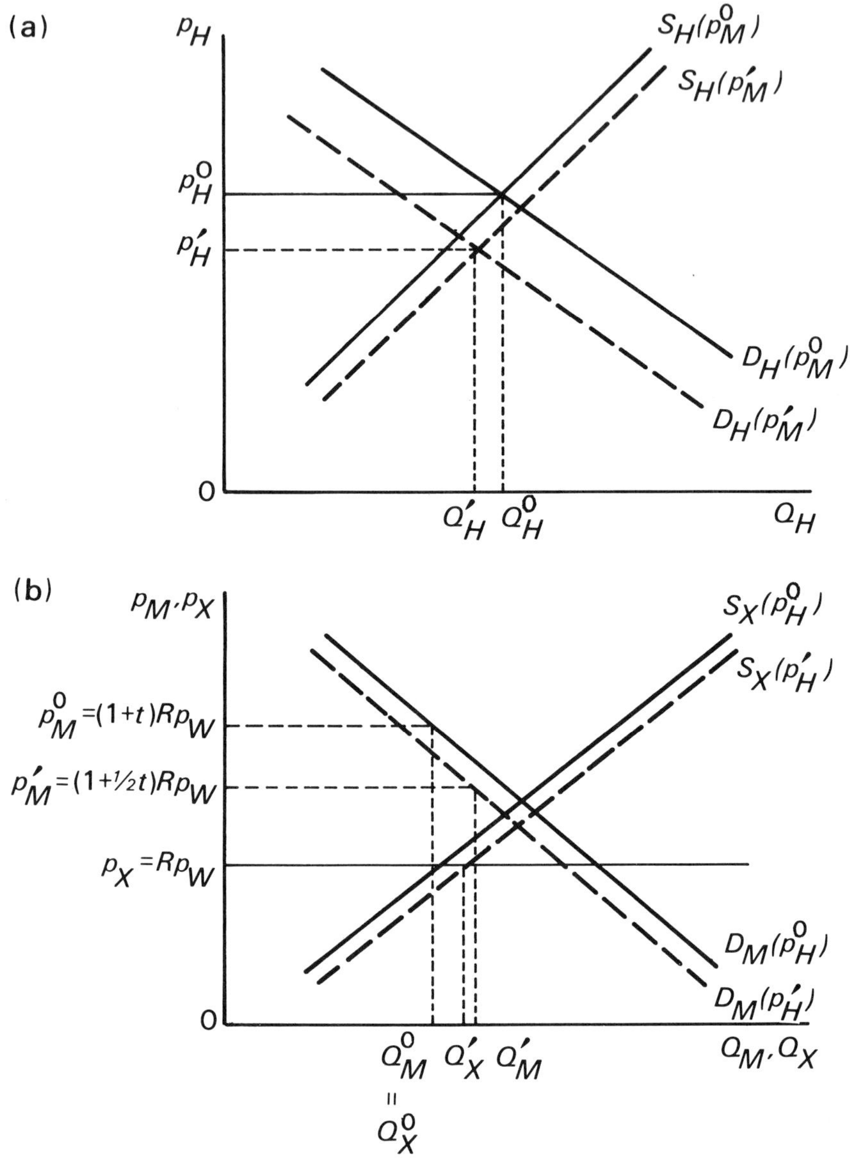

Figure 2.3
Microeconomic effects of a 50% tariff reduction: (a) home sector; (b) exports and imports.

by a small amount. Thus the new quantities traded are found at Q'_H and Q'_M, both above their initial levels. Exports have increased due to a reduction in their costs as input prices have fallen. Imports have increased as a more direct result of the tariff reduction, but the increase has been partially offset by the reduction in the price of home sector goods with which imports compete.

This is as far as the simple analysis of figure 2.3 can take us, but we can use it to sketch briefly some of the additional adjustments that take place in the model. First, we note that quantities produced have fallen in the home sector and risen in the export sector, entailing a movement of labor from the former to the latter. In the event that export expansion is insufficient to absorb all of the labor released from the home sector, then either there will be additional aggregate unemployment or total expenditure will have to be increased, expanding demand in both sectors. Similarly, it is likely as shown in figure 2.3 that a unilateral tariff reduction will expand imports more than exports, worsening the balance of trade. If the exchange rate is flexible, R will rise and both p_X and p_M will increase until trade balance is restored. Finally, if the tariff cut is multilateral, there will be tariff cuts abroad as well as at home, which will cause excess demand on the world market. Thus p_W will also rise somewhat, again causing further adjustments of domestic supplies and demands. Indeed the rise in p_W may eliminate or even reverse the need, in some countries, for the adjustments in expenditure and exchange rates just described.

We turn now to the second of our simple models, which is shown in figure 2.4 and is essentially the standard Keynesian model of income determination and the trade balance, such as may be found, for example, in Dornbusch (1980, chapter 3). The macroeconomic features of the Michigan model have been deliberately kept simple, with the intent of focusing attention more on microeconomic effects such as those we just discussed. Still, in a model where certain nominal values such as wages are held fixed, it is inevitable that some macroeconomic assumptions are being made, and it is as well to understand what they are.

If we imagine aggregating all of the domestic sectors of a country into one, then the Michigan model has the structure of an extremely simple Keynesian model. In goods-market equilibrium, income in a country must be equal to the country's expenditure plus its trade balance,

$$Y = E + (X - M),$$

and income will adjust to bring this about. The top panel of figure 2.4 describes how income is determined in this fashion, equating $(Y - E)$ and $(X - M)$.

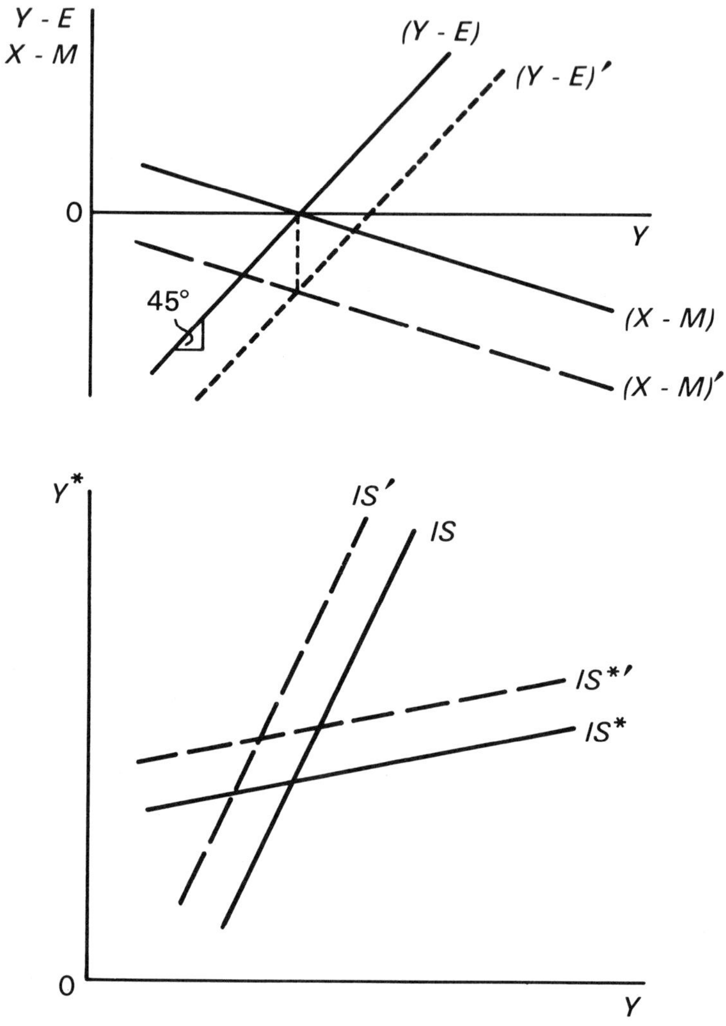

Figure 2.4
Macroeconomic effects of a tariff reduction and exchange-rate appreciation.

If expenditure (which includes all categories of final demand) is held fixed independently of income, as it is in one version of our model, then income net of expenditure ($Y - E$) will be an upward sloping 45° line as shown.[12] The other curve in the top panel is the trade balance, ($X - M$), which is downward sloping under the usual assumption of constant exports and a positive propensity to import. In the Michigan model, while exports are determined by domestic export suppliers rather than directly by foreign demand, it is still true that they depend on variables other than domestic income and can be taken as constant in this kind of analysis. The positive propensity to import is also a feature of the Michigan model, even when expenditure is held fixed, since imports are demanded as intermediate inputs to domestic production.

For a given country, then, income is determined by the intersection of these two curves, which depend in turn on a number of variables, such as aggregate expenditure, foreign income (which affects exports through world prices), and the exchange rate. Incomes in different countries are in turn interrelated, as shown in the bottom panel of figure 2.4 for a simple case of only two countries.

Let Y and Y^* be domestic and foreign incomes, respectively. Suppose first that foreign income, Y^*, falls. The foreign country will then demand fewer imports, causing prices to fall on world markets and inducing domestic firms to export less. This fall in X causes a downward shift in the ($X - M$) curve in the top panel, lowering equilibrium domestic income, Y. Thus a fall in foreign income causes a fall in domestic income, tracing out something like the curve *IS* in the bottom panel. By similar reasoning, changes in domestic income also lead to changes in foreign income, along a curve such as IS^*, and the two incomes together are determined by the intersection of these curves.

We are now in a position to examine how incomes in the countries, singly and together, are affected by various policy changes under various of the assumptions that we customarily make in the Michigan model. Consider first a unilateral tariff reduction by the domestic country, such as we considered above in figure 2.3. Such a tariff reduction will stimulate the country's imports, raising M and shifting the ($X - M$) curve down. If nothing else happens,[13] this will show up also as a shift of the *IS* curve in the lower panel to the left to IS'. In addition, the rise in imports will raise world prices of our imported goods, stimulating exports of the foreign country, and thus shifting the IS^* curve also to the left to $IS^{*\prime}$. Together these changes lead to a fall in domestic income and a rise in foreign income, as shown.[14]

However, as we normally use the Michigan model, it is not true that nothing else happens. First, in examining tariff reductions we customarily assume that aggregate expenditure is adjusted endogenously to maintain constant aggregate employment. In this simple model with only one good being produced, this is essentially the same as stabilizing national income.[15] Thus in the analysis of a unilateral tariff reduction, the $(Y - E)$ curve will also shift as this endogenous stabilization policy takes place. That is, while the tariff reduction shifts the $(X - M)$ curve down as shown, it also leads to a rise in expenditure, E, that shifts the $(Y - E)$ curve down as well by just enough to keep equilibrium income constant. This exacerbates the trade imbalance caused by the tariff cut. But if the stabilization policy is pursued in both countries, then it leaves both of the *IS* curves in the lower panel unchanged and thus prevents any change in either country's income. It is in this sense that we have used the assumption of endogenous stabilization policy to neutralize at least some of the aggregate effects of tariff reductions.

Another feature of the model for some countries, and one that reduces the need for this endogenous stabilization policy, is the flexibility of the exchange rate. If the exchange rate is flexible, then the increased trade deficit that would result from a tariff cut will lead instead to a depreciation. This will shift the $(X - M)$ curve back to its initial position without any need for E to change. Thus again, the tariff cut has no effect on equilibrium incomes in either country.

Finally, there may not even be a need for exchange-rate adjustment if the tariff cuts are multilateral rather than unilateral. If tariffs both at home and abroad are reduced, then both exports and imports will rise. Depending on the relative sizes of the tariff reductions and on various elasticities of supply and demand, $(X - M)$ may rise, fall, or remain unchanged. In any case, the need for induced changes in exchange rates and/or expenditure will be considerably reduced.

Thus for tariff reductions the assumptions that we make in applying the Michigan model do have important macroeconomic implications, but they are such as to neutralize, for the most part, the macroeconomic effects of the changes in tariffs.

In contrast, when we analyze exogenous exchange-rate changes in later chapters, we do allow more room for macroeconomic effects. Obviously, in order to examine such changes, we must assume that exchange rates are fixed, and thus one of the mechanisms just mentioned for neutralizing macroeconomic effects is absent. Aggregate expenditure could still be endogenous, of course, but we have preferred to follow the more Keynesian course of keeping it fixed in our analyses of exchange-rate changes. Thus we treat an exchange-rate change as altering not only relative wages across countries (since money wages are fixed), but also relative levels of expenditure.

The simple macroeconomic effects of an exchange rate change can also be seen in figure 2.4. An appreciation of the home country's currency, for example, leads to both a fall in exports and a rise in imports that together reduce $(X - M)$.[16] The downward shift in $(X - M)$, and its analogue abroad, again cause *IS* and *IS** in the lower panel to shift to the left, and once again we find a fall in domestic income and a rise in foreign income. These changes in turn translate into changes in aggregate employment in the two countries as a result of the appreciation.

Thus when we analyze exchange rate changes, we do allow them to have the familiar Keynesian multiplier effects on national incomes. It should be noted, however, that by holding expenditure constant rather than allowing it to rise with income, these multiplier effects are made smaller than would be the case in standard simple Keynesian models where the multiplier is made large by a marginal propensity to consume that is positive. We do not view this as a drawback of our model, however, since more elaborate Keynesian models include a number of features, not present in ours, that would dampen these multipliers considerably. For example, an IS-LM model includes feedback through money and interest rates that can reduce the multiplier even below unity. Short of building a complete macroeconomic model that would include these effects and others not present in the simple multiplier analysis, we feel it is better that the multiplier in the Michigan model is kept fairly small by the assumption of constant expenditure.

These macroeconomic results are not at all profound. Our purpose in presenting them here is to make the reader aware of what is being assumed in the Michigan model, as we go on in later chapters to analyze what it says for the effects of various policy changes. It is important to understand the model at this crude level, in order not to be misled into thinking that the macroeconomic results it generates are any more subtle or complicated than could be found in a much simpler model such as this.

The Closure Issue

There has been considerable discussion and confusion in the literature on computable general-equilibrium models concerning the issue of macroeconomic closure. From the simple macroeconomic model that we just presented, it should be clear what assumptions about closure are being used in the Michigan model, but it may be helpful to relate these to the alternatives that have been described in the closure literature.

The closure issue, as we would describe it, concerns the means that is chosen to determine aggregate expenditure in a general-equilibrium model. It derives its name from the method that is used in Walrasian general-equilibrium models, where expenditure is set equal to the total of factor incomes in the economy. This rule may be said to "close the loop," since factor incomes already equal the value of output from the supply side of the economy, and this rule assures that this same value of output will be demanded. This Walrasian closure rule serves a number of purposes, among which is to make disequilibrium in only one market of the economy impossible, since supply and demand are identically equal in the aggregate.

The Walrasian closure rule is unsatisfactory for a number of reasons, one of which is this strong association with equilibrium in all markets. If one wishes to allow at times for involuntary unemployment of labor, then the Walrasian closure rule is an awkward choice, since it means that one must explain not only why labor markets fail to clear (due perhaps to rigidity of wages in some form), but also why excess demand in some other market is allowed to persist.

The Walrasian closure rule is also unsatisfactory for another reason, however, even if one does not wish to allow for labor-market disequilibrium. The notion that all income should be spent is compelling only in a model that includes explicitly all of the things that income might be spent on, including not only financial assets but also demands for goods at all times. In a static model such as ours, which covers only the markets for goods (and perhaps factors), and which has no explicit time dimension but is directed implicitly at the short run, it seems quite inappropriate to assume that all income is spent. Therefore we have never tried to close the Michigan model in Walrasian fashion.

Alternatives to the Walrasian closure rule have been nicely described by Lysy (1983). In addition to the Walrasian, or neoclassical, closure rule, Lysy discusses three others. Of interest here are what he calls the Keynesian closure and the Johansen closure.[17]

The Keynesian closure is quite familiar, and consists of dropping the requirement of full employment and using instead an independent aggregate consumption function which permits desired expenditure to differ from income. In this sense our assumption of constant aggregate expenditure, which we use in some applications of the Michigan model, including our analyses of exchange-rate changes, constitutes a Keynesian closure. We differ from Keynes only in the form that we choose for our consumption function.

The Johansen closure is less familiar and consists, as Lysy describes it, of

Table 2.1
Summary of model characteristics of trade models

Model	Country(ies)	Demand side		Production side	
		Demand functions	Disaggregation	Production functions	Disaggregation
Multicountry models					
Cunning, Carrin, and Waelbroeck (with Burniaux and Mercenier) (1982)	11 groups of less developed countries and the rest of the world	Demand for CES import-export composite goods modeled as Extended Linear Expenditure System (ELES) for each consumer group	2 consumer groups (rural, urban) for each region, plus a rudimentary rest of the world	CES value-added functions plus fixed coefficient intermediate use of composite goods in the urban sectors; linear production functions in the rural sectors	6 production sectors (2 rural, 4 urban) in each regional model
Deardroff and Stern (1981)	18 major industralized countries, 16 major developing countries, and the rest of the world	Cobb-Douglas utility functions; CES between home and imported goods in the same industry	34 countries plus the rest of the world	CES value-added functions; fixed coefficient intermediate use of CES composites of home and imported goods[a]	22 tradable and 7 nontradable industries for each of the 34 countries plus a residual rest of the world
Manne and Preckel (1983)	3 regions: industrialized countries, oil-exporting developing countries, oil importing developing countries	Demand for energy and nonenergy imports derived from CES production functions	3 regions: industrialized countries, oil-exporting developing countries, oil-importing developing countries	Nested CES	Energy and aggregated nonenergy commodities for each region
Miller and Spencer (1977)	4 "countries": UK, (6-member) EEC, Australia and New Zealand, rest of the world	Derived from 2-stage CES utility functions	4 "countries": UK, (6-member) EEC, Australia and New Zealand, rest of the world	Cobb-Douglas	2 commodities per country (agriculture and nonagriculture)

Table 2.1 (continued)

		Demand side		Production side	
Model	Country(ies)	Demand functions	Disaggregation	Production functions	Disaggregation
Whalley (1982)	EEC, US, Japan, rest of the world	Derived from nested CES utility functions	41 consuming groups comprising households, government, investment (stratified by income in US and Japan and by region in EEC)	CES value-added functions; fixed coefficient intermediate use of CES domestic-import composites	33 commodities in each of 4 regions
Whalley (1984)	7 trade blocs: US, EEC, Japan, other developed countries, OPEC, newly industrialized countries, less developed countries	Derived from nested CES-LES utility functions	7 trade blocs	Nested CES value-added functions; fixed coefficient intermediate use of composite inputs	6 commodities in each of 7 trade blocs
Single-country models					
Boadway and Treddenick (1978)	Canada	Domestic final demand for each CES composite good is unit price and income elastic; import supply and export demand own price dependent only (constant elasticity)	Domestic demand for final goods, world demand for domestic exports	3 alternative specifications: fixed intermediate coefficients with Cobb-Douglas functions for labor and capital, fixed intermediate coefficients with CES functions for labor and capital, and variable coefficients Cobb-Douglas functions	2 alternate aggregations of industries: 1. 16 groups; 2. 56 groups

Dervis, de Melo, and Robinson (1982)	Turkey	Constant expenditure proportions for import-export composite goods	One aggregate household[b]	2-level CES production functions; fixed coefficient use of intermediate goods	19 industries, 3 labor types
Dixon, Parmenter, Sutton, and Vincent (1982)	Australia	Derived from Klein-Rubin utility functions with CES aggregration of comparable imported and domestic goods	Effectively one household	4-level input functions 1-Leontief between inputs of composite products 2-CES between imported and domestic products 3-CRESH between primary factors 4-CRESH between labor inputs CRESH output functions	114 commodities (112 industries)

a. Alternative assumptions are also used in other versions of this model.
b. In chapter 13 of this reference, the model is disaggregated to include 7 socioeconomic household groups in order to study income distribution effects.

Source: Shoven and Whalley (1984, pp. 1036–37).

keeping the requirement of full employment while dropping the consumption function. This means that consumption can be thought of as adjusting endogenously to assure full employment. Since in the Michigan model we do not distinguish consumption from other forms of final demand, our assumption that expenditure adjusts to maintain full employment may be thought of as analogous to this Johansen closure rule.

Thus the Michigan model handles the closure issue by rejecting, with cause, the Walrasian closure and using instead either the Keynesian closure or the Johansen closure, depending on the policy issue being addressed.

Comparison with Other Computational Models

Now that the details of the Michigan model have been laid out, it may be useful to compare them with several other models that have been constructed and used for a variety of purposes. Relevant details are summarized in table 2.1, which has been adapted from Shoven and Whalley (1984). It is evident that the models noted differ essentially based upon whether they are multicountry or single-country in character and the kinds of issues they are designed to analyze. The demand and production functions used in the various models apparently share many features, which is not surprising since the functional forms involved have many characteristics that make them tractable and convenient for computational work. Finally, the models differ noticeably in terms of the types and details of the disaggregation scheme used on the demand and production sides.

As we noted in chapter 1, the models can be further distinguished according to whether they are linearized and solved for approximations to comparative static equilibrium or whether they are fully general equilibrium in terms of their structure and solution. The former, in the Johansen (1960) tradition, include the Michigan model as well as the Boadway and Treddenick (1978) model of Canada and the Dixon et al. (1982) model of Australia.[18] The latter, which we shall refer to as Walrasian-type systems, include the others listed in table 2.1.

There is considerable debate, needless to say, about the advantages and limitations of these alternative approaches to computational modeling.[19] We have already mentioned that our choice of a Johansen-type model was dictated initially in large part by an interest in analyzing the employment and related effects of trade liberalization in a multicountry, multisector setting such as the Tokyo Round negotiations. This range of issues can also be analyzed using a Walrasian-type model, as Whalley (1982) has done, but the particular effects on employment, prices, and so forth, that we get in the Michigan model do not appear in the full Walrasian general equilibrium.

3 Implementation of the Model

In designing our model, the objective was to take into account as many as possible of the interconnections among industries and countries at the microeconomic level. This enables us to examine a variety of economic issues that other models cannot address, either because they are too highly aggregated or because they are specified only in partial-equilibrium terms. By the same token, however, our model is far too large to be able to say anything concrete without further specification of its parameters. Thus, to use the model, we must apply it to a realistic selection of countries and industries using, as far as possible, actual data to generate the parameters.

As noted earlier, we focused in our original model on the world's 18 major industrialized countries and treated the rest of the world as a residual to close the system.[1] We subsequently added 16 major developing countries, so that the model currently (early 1985) covers 34 countries plus a residual rest of world. The countries covered are listed in the following section.

Data and Parameters

As just indicated, our model includes 22 tradable and 7 nontradable industries in 34 countries, plus an aggregate sector representing the rest of the world. The current version of the model uses a base of 1976 data on trade, production, and employment for all 34 countries, plus tariffs and constructed measures of NTBs for the 18 major industrialized countries.

Major industrialized countries

Australia
Austria
Belgium-Luxembourg
Canada
Denmark
Italy
Japan
Netherlands
New Zealand
Norway

Finland
France
German Federal Republic (West Germany)
Ireland
Sweden
Switzerland
United Kingdom
United States

Major developing countries

Argentina
Brazil
Chile
Colombia
Greece
Hong Kong
India
Israel
South Korea
Mexico
Portugal
Singapore
Spain
Taiwan
Turkey
Yugoslavia

Our industry classification is based upon the International Standard Industrial Classification (ISIC), and is broken down by ISIC group (left column) into tradables and nontradables as follows (abbreviations in square brackets):[2]

Tradables

(1) Agriculture, hunting, forestry, and fishing [AGR., FOR., & FISH.]
(310) Food, beverages, and tobacco [FOOD, BEV., & TOB.]
(321) Textiles [TEXTILES]
(322) Wearing apparel, excluding footwear [WEARING APPAREL]
(323) Leather and leather and fur products [LEATHER PROD.]
(324) Footwear [FOOTWEAR]
(331) Wood products, excluding furniture [WOOD PROD.]
(332) Furniture and fixtures, excluding metal [FURN. & FIXT.]
(341) Paper and paper products [PAPER & PAPER PROD.]
(342) Printing, publishing [PRINT. & PUBL.]
(35A) Industrial chemicals (351); Other chemical products (352) [CHEMICALS]
(35B) Petroleum refineries (353); Miscellaneous production of petroleum and coal (354) [PETROL. & REL. PROD.]
(355) Rubber products [RUBBER PROD.]
(36A) Pottery, china and earthenware (361); Other nonmetallic mineral products (369) [NONMETAL. MIN. PROD.]
(362) Glass and glass products [GLASS & GLASS PROD.]
(371) Iron and steel basic industries [IRON & STEEL]
(372) Nonferrous metal basic industries [NONFERROUS METALS]
(381) Metal products, excluding machinery, etc. [METAL PROD.]

(382) Machinery, excluding electrical [NONELEC. MACH.]
(383) Electrical machinery, apparatus, etc. [ELEC. MACH.]
(384) Transport equipment [TRANSP. EQUIP.]
(38A) Plastic products, not elsewhere classified (356); Professional photographic goods, etc. (385); Other manufacturing industries (390) [MISC. MANUF.]

Nontradables

(2) Mining and quarrying [MIN. & QUARRY.]
(4) Electricity, gas, and water [ELEC., GAS, & WATER]
(5) Construction [CONSTRUCTION]
(6) Wholesale and retail trade, restaurants and hotels [WHOLE. & RET. TRADE]
(7) Transport, storage, and communication [TRANSP., STOR., & COMM.]
(8) Finance, insurance, real estate, etc. [FIN., INS., & REAL EST.]
(9) Community, social, and personal services [COMM., SOC., & PERS. SERV.]

The countries in the model are listed in table 3.1, together with their assumed exchange regimes, input-output coverage, the average pre-Tokyo Round (1976) tariff levels, and the average of trade covered by NTBs. The industries are listed in table 3.2, with the assumed elasticities of capital-labor substitution, import-home good substitution, and US import demand, as well as the pre-Tokyo Round average tariff levels and trade coverage of NTBs.

The import and export data used in the model were adapted from UN trade tapes. These trade data were concorded from the Standard International Trade Classification (SITC) to our ISIC industry categories. Information on the gross value of production and employment by ISIC sector were directly calculated or estimated from the United Nations *Yearbook of Industrial Statistics*, from the Organization for Economic Cooperation and Development (OECD) publications on national accounts and labor statistics, and from various national statistical sources.

Ad valorem tariff data were obtained from the Office of the US Trade Representative (USTR) based upon information compiled in machine readable form by the Secretariat of the General Agreement on Tariffs and Trade (GATT). The pre- and post-Tokyo Round ad valorem tariff rates were available on a line-item basis according to the detailed Brussels Tariff Nomenclature (BTN) together with import data for the major industralized countries for 1976, which was the reference year for the Tokyo Round negotiations. The BTN classification was concorded to SITC, and own-

Table 3.1
The countries of the model, their assumed exchange regimes, and the source and levels of input-output, tariff, and NTB data for each

Country	Country abbreviation	Flexible (F), pegged (P), or licensed (L), and country pegged to				Input-output table	Pre-Tokyo Round average tariff level[a] (%)	Assumed average coverage by NTB[a] (%)
		F	P	L	Pegged to			
Industrialized countries								
Australia	ALA		×		Basket[b]	US 1972	15.3	12.2
Austria	ATA	×				US 1972	14.1	6.7
Canada	CND	×				US 1972	6.4	11.7
European Economic Community (EEC)								
Belgium-Luxembourg (BEL-LUX)	BLX	×				BLX 1970	7.4	4.8
Denmark	DEN	×				DEN 1970	8.3	3.0
France	FR	×				FR 1970	6.6	30.1
German Federal Republic (West Germany)	GFR	×				GFR 1970	7.6	17.1
Ireland	IRE	×				IRE 1969	8.8	5.7
Italy	IT	×				IT 1970	5.9	13.3
Netherlands	NL	×				NL 1970	7.6	6.0
United Kingdom	UK	×				UK 1970	6.6	5.3
Finland	FIN		×		Basket	US 1972	8.0	4.0
Japan	JPN	×				JPN 1970	6.3	56.9
New Zealand	NZ			×	Basket	US 1972	15.6	13.6
Norway	NOR		×		Basket	US 1972	5.9	7.4
Sweden	SWD		×		Basket	US 1972	5.0	3.8
Switzerland	SWZ		×		GFR	US 1972	4.2	13.2
United States	US	×				US 1972	4.5	22.3

Developing countries								
Argentina	ARG			×	Basket	BRZ 1970	—	—
Brazil	BRZ			×	Basket	BRZ 1970	—	—
Chile	CHL			×	Basket	BRZ 1970	—	—
Colombia	COL			×	Basket	BRZ 1970	—	—
Greece	GRC			×	Basket	BRZ 1970	—	—
Hong Kong	HK	×				BRZ 1970	—	—
India	IND			×	Basket	BRZ 1970	—	—
Israel	ISR	×				BRZ 1970	—	—
South Korea	SK			×	Basket	BRZ 1970	—	—
Mexico	MEX	×				BRZ 1970	—	—
Portugal	POR			×	Basket	BRZ 1970	—	—
Singapore	SNG		×		Basket	BRZ 1970	—	—
Spain	SP			×	Basket	BRZ 1970	—	—
Taiwan	TWN			×	Basket	BRZ 1970	—	—
Turkey	TRK			×	Basket	BRZ 1970	—	—
Yugoslavia	YUG	×				BRZ 1970	—	—

a. Avaliable only for industrialized countries.
b. Pegged to a trade-weighted basket of currencies.

Table 3.2
The industries of the model, their assumed elasticities of substitution and demand and tariff and NTB data for each

Industry	(ISIC)	Elasticity of capital-labor substitution	Elasticity of import-home-good substitution	US import demand elasticity	Pre-Tokyo Round average tariff level[a] (%)	Assumed average coverage by NTBs[a] (%)
Traded goods						
AGR., FOR., & FISH.	(1)	0.787	1.139	1.130	7.8	18.4
FOOD, BEV., & TOB.	(310)	1.746	1.133	1.130	12.5	23.4
TEXTILES	(321)	0.963	1.147	1.140	10.8	29.1
WEARING APPAREL	(322)	1.191	4.269	3.920	20.7	46.5
LEATHER PROD.	(323)	1.230	1.810	1.580	4.4	1.1
FOOTWEAR	(324)	1.436	2.825	2.390	12.4	37.1
WOOD PROD.	(331)	0.852	1.757	1.690	2.7	0.0
FURN. & FIXT.	(332)	1.122	3.096	3.000	10.0	0.0
PAPER & PAPER PROD.	(341)	1.626	1.585	1.550	5.9	0.6
PRINT. & PUBL.	(342)	0.810	3.013	3.000	2.9	10.4
CHEMICALS	(35A)	1.098	2.612	2.530	9.1	4.1
PETROL. & REL. PROD.	(35B)	10.011	2.359	1.960	1.5	47.8
RUBBER PROD.	(355)	1.647	5.707	5.260	5.8	3.1
NONMETAL. MIN. PROD.	(36A)	1.246	2.784	2.700	5.8	8.4
GLASS & GLASS PROD.	(362)	1.267	1.628	1.600	10.5	0.0
IRON & STEEL	(371)	1.382	1.446	1.420	5.7	8.2
NONFERROUS METALS	(372)	1.350	1.430	1.380	2.0	6.9
METAL PROD.	(381)	0.943	3.674	3.590	9.0	2.5
NONELEC. MACH.	(382)	0.677	1.022	1.020	6.7	1.9
ELEC. MACH.	(383)	0.521	2.110	2.000	9.6	7.1
TRANSP. EQUIP.	(384)	0.344	3.585	3.280	7.5	10.4
MISC. MANUF.	(38A)	1.272	1.984	1.780	7.7	2.7

Nontraded goods						
MIN. & QUARRY	(2)	1.541	—	—	—	—
ELEC., GAS, & WATER	(4)	2.266	—	—	—	—
CONSTRUCTION	(5)	1.105	—	—	—	—
WHOLE. & RET. TRADE	(6)	2.266	—	—	—	—
TRANSP., STOR., & COMM.	(7)	1.457	—	—	—	—
FIN., INS., & REAL EST.	(8)	1.657	—	—	—	—
COMM., SOC., & PERS. SERV.	(9)	1.087	—	—	—	—

a. Available only for industrialized countries.

country imports were used in calculating the tariff rates. We then concorded from SITC to ISIC and aggregared to our ISIC categories used in the model. The resulting tariff rates entered in the model are thus own-country, import-weighted averages by ISIC sector.

The coverage of NTBs was measured in the form of indexes of the degree to which imports were subject to nontariff restrictions (for example, quotas and health regulations). A value of 100% indicates that all trade in a given sector/country was covered by NTBs; 0% denotes that no NTBs were present. The calculations were based on data in Murray and Walter (1978), who recorded the value of 1973 imports for a given country and SITC commodity category that was subject to some type of NTB, as identified in underlying documents prepared by the US Department of State and UNCTAD (United Nations Conference on Trade and Development). We in turn aggregated their results and concorded them with our ISIC classification. The indexes were updated to take into account more recent restrictions on such products as footwear, iron and steel, and television receivers. The indexes for textiles (ISIC 321) and wearing apparel (ISIC 322) were based upon the proportion of each country's 1976 imports in these sectors from all of the world's nonindustrialized countries. The resulting indexes thus represent the percentage of trade subject to NTBs of all kinds as of 1976.

As mentioned, we have data on trade, production, and employment by sector for the major developing countries covered in the model, but we were not able to compile data on tariffs and NTBs for these countries. We attempted, however, to capture elements of their existing NTBs by modeling a system of import licensing with exchange-rate pegging as characterizing the foreign exchange regime in most instances. The assumed exchange regimes for the various countries reflect our interpretation of individual country exchange practices in 1979–1980, based on information published in the International Monetary Fund (IMF) *International Financial Statistics.*

Our input-output coverage currently includes the 1972 input-output table for the United States and the 1970 national tables for the individual EEC-member countries and for Japan. The US table is applied to the remaining industrialized countries. We use the 1970 table for Brazil and apply this table to the other developing countries. Each of the national tables used had to be concorded to our ISIC classification. The fact that we do not have separate tables for each country in the model undoubtedly introduces some errors into our analysis, the size and importance of which cannot be assessed until the tables for all countries are included in the model.[3]

In general, the coefficients of explanatory variables that appear in the model are calculated from our data on production, trade, and employment by sector in each country, from the input-output matrices, and from relevant published estimates of demand and substitution elasticities. The import-demand elasticities used in the model were based upon the "best guesstimates" of US import-demand elasticities calculated by Stern, Francis, and Schumacher (1976). From these together with data on US trade we calculated the implied elasticities of substitution in demand between imports and home-produced goods in the United States.[4] These latter elasticities were then assumed to characterize the substitution between imports and home goods in all countries of the model. These elasticities of substitution are listed in table 3.2, together with the US import-demand elasticities from which they were calculated. The implicit import-demand elasticities in other countries are derivable from the common elasticities of substitution and differ across countries due to their differences in shares of trade. We used elasticities of substitution between capital and labor in each sector, based upon Zarembka and Chernicoff (1971). These were estimated from US data, but were assumed in our model to apply to all countries. It would be preferable, of course, to use estimates of these elasticities by sector for each country individually, but it would require a great amount of time and resources to obtain such estimates.[5]

Solution Procedure

Given appropriate data and parameter estimates for the countries and sectors noted, solution of the model should, in principle, be straightforward. By differentiating the equations of the model, we obtained a system of linear equations relating changes in all of the variables of the system. The coefficients in each of these linear equations were evaluated using the data and elasticity information we had collected. All that remained was to solve the system. Since the system was linear, it could in principle be solved by any of a variety of means.[6]

In fact, however, the size of the model made this difficult. With 34 countries and 29 industries, what we have represented here as single equations each become a large number of separate equations to be solved. Depending on how many of these equations were first eliminated by substitution, the number of equations in the model could run to several thousand. A system of this size strains the capacity of even high-speed, mainframe computers. And while the number of equations can be reduced substantially by prior substitutions, the substitutions themselves involve a tremendous amount of computation. It was to avoid these difficulties that, in our earliest applications of the model, we introduced a number of approximations to reduce the amount of simultaneity in the system.[7]

We have since been able to obtain exact solutions. To do so, we first devised several Fortran subroutines that process large partitioned matrices in which many of the partitioned blocks contain only zeros, and that avoids costly but meaningless computations involving these zeros. Second, we used a Fortran programming technique known as dynamic dimensioning to avoid wasting computer-memory space on these empty blocks, even as the contents of all blocks change during the course of the solution. And finally, we applied these techniques first to each of the 34 countries separately, using only equations (2.1)–(2.13) to solve for their net exports in terms of world prices, exchange rates, and exogenous variables, and then used equations (2.14)–(2.17) to complete the solution. The resulting computer program, when we first used it several years ago, was costly but within reason. Further improvements over the years in both the program and in the efficiency of available computers have reduced the cost even further.

Model Applications

Having described the theoretical structure of the model and various details concerning its implementation, we shall devote the next several chapters to particular applications of the model. Thus, in chapter 4, we analyze the economic effects of the Tokyo Round negotiations and the effects of complete elimination of Tokyo Round tariffs. In chapter 5, we consider the effects of pre- and post-Tokyo Round tariffs on the structure of protection in the United States and other major industrialized countries. In chapter 6, we examine the effects of domestic tax/subsidies on the structure of protection in the United States, the United Kingdom, and Japan. The sectoral impact of real exchange-rate changes is treated in chapters 7 and 8. Finally, in chapter 9, we analyze the employment effects of changes in trade during the 1970s and projections of future changes in trade between the major industrialized and developing countries.

4 Economic Effects of the Tokyo Round Negotiations

The conclusion of the Tokyo Round of Multilateral Trade Negotiations (MTN) in April 1979 was an important milestone in international commercial diplomacy. It marked the seventh round of multilateral reductions in international trade barriers negotiated under the General Agreement on Tariffs and Trade (GATT) since World War II. Tariffs on industrial products had last been reduced on a major scale in the Kennedy Round, which concluded in 1967 and was implemented over the ensuing 5 years. Tariffs are being reduced even further by the Tokyo Round, the reductions being phased in over 8 years beginning in 1980. An even more noteworthy accomplishment of the Tokyo Round is the negotiation of a series of codes covering nontariff barriers (NTBs). Depending on how these codes are interpreted and adhered to they will mean some significant reductions in NTBs and will clarify and harmonize government policies involving international trade.

This chapter provides an economic analysis of the effects of the Tokyo Round itself, as well as of the complete elimination of the tariffs that will remain once the Tokyo Round tariff reductions are completed.[1] We begin by examining the Tokyo Round negotiations, including the initial tariffs by country and sector, the tariff-cutting procedure and tariff offers, and the NTB codes. We then present calculations of the combined effects of the reductions in tariffs and NTBs using our model as it has been described in the preceding chapters. We consider thereafter the possible effects of NTB codes that we were unable to quantify and also look at trade policies that were excluded from the Tokyo Round. As will be noted momentarily, the Tokyo Round and preceding rounds of multilateral negotiations have had the effect of reducing tariff rates in the major industrailized countries to relatively low levels. It seems natural in this light to ask whether tariffs might not be eliminated altogether. We thus use our model in the final section of the chapter to provide estimates of the effects of complete elimination of post-

Tokyo Round tariffs. The chapter concludes with some summary comments on the effects of the Tokyo Round negotiations and implications for the future liberalization of world trade.

The Tokyo Round Negotiations

Tariff Offers in the Tokyo Round

Average post-Kennedy Round (1972) tariffs on industrial products appear in column (1) of table 4.1 for the 18 chief participants in the Tokyo Round negotiations.[2] The average rates negotiated, called the offer rates, are in column (2). Column (3) records the average depth of cut by country. A breakdown by major industrial sector and country is shown for the post-Kennedy Round tariffs in table 4.2 and for the offer rates in table 4.3.[3]

Negotiations on NTBs in the Tokyo Round

A great deal of attention was devoted in the Tokyo Round to the discussion and formulation of codes and agreements concerning nontariff measures. The principal items covered were as follows:

1. Customs valuation. This code sets up consistent valuation practices for trade based on a "transaction" price. The point is to limit arbitrary uplifts in valuing imports for duty purposes and to reduce uncertainty that traders face regarding the duty they will have to pay.

2. Government procurement. This code is designed to open up public procurement to competitive bidding by both domestic and foreign firms.

3. Import licensing procedures. This code encourages governments to simplify the administration of import licensing and to minimize practices that discriminate against foreign suppliers.

4. Subsidies and countervailing duties. This code states general principles that subsidies should not harm the trading interests of other countries and that countervailing duties, to offset foreign subsidies, should not impede trade unjustifiably. The United States has agreed to a test of "material injury" before imposing countervailing duties.

5. Product standards. Under this code, countries agree generally to follow international standards for health, safety, consumer and environmental protection, etc., and to refrain from establishing standards that impede trade.

In addition, there was an attempt to draft a safeguards code, governing policies to deal with market disruption due to sudden upsurges in imports.

Table 4.1
Average Post-Kennedy Round base rate tariffs on industrial products, Tokyo Round offer rate tariffs, and percentage depth of cut for the major industrialized countries in the Tokyo Round (weighted by own-country total imports)

Country	(1) Average post-Kennedy Round base rate (%)	(2) Tokyo Round offer rate (%)	(3) Average cut (%)
Australia[a]	17.0	16.5	2.8
Austria	15.4	12.1	21.5
Canada[a]	7.3	5.2	29.1
European Economic Community			
Belgium-Luxembourg	8.2	5.9	28.3
Denmark	9.0	6.6	25.8
France	8.3	6.0	27.8
German Federal Republic	8.7	6.3	27.1
Ireland	9.4	6.9	26.7
Italy	7.3	5.4	27.0
Netherlands	9.2	6.8	26.7
United Kingdom	7.3	5.2	27.7
Finland	9.6	7.1	25.2
Japan[a]	3.9	2.9	25.3
New Zealand	18.9	16.7	11.8
Norway	6.9	5.2	24.8
Sweden	6.4	5.0	23.0
Switzerland	3.9	3.1	21.2
United States	6.5	4.3	34.1
All countries	7.8	5.8	26.4

a. Based on prevailing rates, which include unilateral reductions in the Post-Kennedy round tariffs.

Source: Based on data supplied by Office of US Trade Representative.

Table 4.2
Post-Kennedy Round base rate tariffs on industrial products by sector in the major industrialized countries (percent; weighted by own-country imports, excluding petroleum)

Industry	ALA[a]	ATA	BLX	CND[a]	DEN	FIN	FR	GFR	IRE	IT	JPN[a]	NL	NZ	NOR	SWD	SWZ	UK	US	ALL
TEXTILES	21.5	18.7	9.5	18.9	12.1	24.1	9.8	10.3	10.7	7.5	3.3	11.8	14.2	16.2	10.9	8.2	9.2	14.4	10.7
WEARING APPAREL	61.8	36.3	16.7	25.4	16.4	37.2	16.7	16.8	16.4	16.6	13.8	16.8	58.7	22.8	14.4	15.5	16.9	27.8	20.7
LEATHER PROD.	25.7	9.1	4.1	8.2	3.6	12.6	3.3	5.1	5.4	1.7	3.0	5.2	15.3	6.6	4.8	2.8	2.8	5.6	4.5
FOOTWEAR	33.8	24.1	11.4	24.5	11.5	17.5	11.5	11.7	11.9	10.8	16.4	11.2	44.1	24.6	13.8	12.4	12.5	8.8	12.4
WOOD PROD.	13.6	4.8	3.2	5.8	4.4	0.5	3.3	3.9	3.2	1.0	0.3	3.6	11.7	2.0	0.9	5.0	4.0	3.6	2.7
FURN. & FIXT.	40.0	23.0	8.5	19.4	8.4	8.7[b]	8.5	8.5	8.5	8.5	7.8	8.5	40.3	7.6	5.4	13.2	8.5	8.1[b]	10.3
PAPER & PAPER PROD.	7.1	15.9	9.3	11.8	10.8	8.0	7.6	7.1	10.9	3.7	2.1	8.4	20.9	2.9	3.0	6.6	6.6	0.5	5.8
PRINT. & PUBL.	1.8	2.4	2.4	5.7	4.4	1.8	3.4	3.3	2.4	2.7	0.2	3.5	1.1	4.3	0.2	0.9	3.3	1.1	2.9
CHEMICALS	5.8	8.1	11.6	7.9	11.9	3.1	10.9	11.6	10.7	11.8	6.2	11.9	10.0	8.1	6.3	1.1	11.4	3.8	9.4
RUBBER PROD.	3.8	14.6	6.2	12.2	6.7	13.9	5.2	5.7	5.6	4.0	1.5	6.1	9.5	7.3	6.5	2.0	4.0	3.6	5.8
NONMETAL. MIN. PROD.	1.6	8.9	5.2	9.5	6.7	3.8	7.0	5.4	6.0	3.3	0.6	4.4	13.8	2.8	3.1	3.5	3.2	9.1	5.8
GLASS & GLASS PROD.	5.2	17.5	9.9	11.3	9.7	25.4	9.8	10.2	9.5	9.6	7.5	9.3	15.4	10.5	9.3	4.5	10.4	10.7	10.5
IRON & STEEL	0.8	6.2	6.1	6.7	7.2	5.7	6.6	6.3	7.5	4.7	3.3	7.1	6.0	2.2	4.7	2.1	6.3	4.7	5.8
NONFERROUS METALS	5.3	4.5	1.9	2.0	8.1	1.2	3.1	2.3	8.0	2.2	1.1	4.3	9.3	1.1	0.9	4.3	2.0	1.2	2.0
METAL PROD.	24.1	19.3	7.7	14.1	7.9	9.6	7.8	8.0	7.7	8.0	6.9	7.8	29.7	6.3	5.3	3.8	8.0	7.5	9.0
NONELEC. MACH.	14.2	10.8	6.4	6.1	6.4	8.7	6.4	6.6	6.1	6.5	9.1	6.4	28.1	8.8	4.9	1.5	6.4	5.0	6.7
ELEC. MACH.	21.6	18.7	9.6	12.9	9.3	11.0[b]	9.8	10.2	9.5	9.9	7.4	10.0	21.0	8.6	7.0	2.0	10.0	6.6	9.6
TRANSP. EQUIP.	22.1	24.5	11.1	2.4	8.5	6.0[b]	10.3	9.9	12.0	10.7	6.0	10.9	27.6	3.5	8.2	6.7	9.3	3.3	7.7
MISC. MANUF.	13.0	13.7	5.2	8.8	10.0	18.1	9.6	9.1	11.2	9.4	6.0	8.7	20.5	8.9	6.1	1.5	4.9	7.8	7.8
All industries	17.0	15.4	8.2	7.3	9.0	9.6	8.3	8.7	9.4	7.3	3.9	9.2	18.9	6.9	6.4	3.9	7.3	6.5	7.8

a. Prevailing rates, which include unilateral reductions in post-Kennedy round tariff rates.
b. Estimated from incomplete data.

Source: Based on data supplied by Office of US Trade Representative.

Table 4.3
Tokyo Round offer rate tariffs on industrial products by sector in the major industrialized countries (percent; weighted by own-country imports, excluding petroleum)

Industry	ALA[a]	ATA	BLX	CND[a]	DEN	FIN	FR	GFR	IRE	IT	JPN[a]	NL	NZ	NOR	SWD	SWZ	UK	US	ALL
TEXTILES	21.2	15.9	7.2	16.7	8.7	22.5	7.3	7.4	7.8	5.6	3.3	8.5	12.3	13.3	10.3	6.6	6.7	9.2	8.5
WEARING APPAREL	61.8	36.2	13.4	24.2	13.2	35.5	13.2	13.4	13.2	13.2	13.8	13.5	58.5	21.7	14.2	12.4	13.3	22.7	17.5
LEATHER PROD.	20.3	7.7	2.5	6.3	1.8	9.3	1.6	3.2	1.8	0.7	3.0	3.0	15.3	5.8	4.0	2.1	1.2	4.2	3.0
FOOTWEAR	33.8	23.4	11.4	21.9	11.5	17.4	11.3	11.7	11.9	10.4	15.7	11.2	40.7	21.7	13.7	9.0	12.5	8.8	12.1
WOOD PROD.	12.5	3.7	2.4	3.2	3.4	0.4	2.4	2.9	2.5	0.8	0.3	2.8	11.4	1.6	0.7	3.2	3.1	1.7	1.9
FURN. & FIXT.	31.2	22.1	5.6	14.3	5.5	5.5[b]	5.6	5.6	5.7	5.6	5.1	5.6	38.3	5.1	1.0	9.2	5.6	4.1[b]	7.3
PAPER & PAPER PROD.	7.1	12.3	6.9	6.7	7.9	4.5	5.5	5.2	8.0	2.6	2.1	6.2	20.5	1.9	2.4	4.3	4.9	0.2	4.2
PRINT. & PUBL.	1.8	1.5	1.5	1.0	2.8	1.1	2.2	2.1	1.5	1.8	0.1	2.2	1.1	4.3	0.2	0.7	2.1	0.7	1.5
CHEMICALS	5.4	4.7	8.0	7.5	8.5	1.8	7.6	8.0	7.6	8.1	4.8	8.1	8.1	6.2	4.8	0.9	7.9	2.4	6.7
RUBBER PROD.	11.2	9.9	4.2	6.7	4.4	13.5	3.5	3.8	3.7	2.7	1.1	4.1	9.5	6.6	6.1	1.7	2.7	2.5	4.1
NONMETAL. MIN. PROD.	11.5	5.9	3.7	6.4	5.0	2.9	4.7	3.6	4.5	2.8	0.5	3.3	12.7	2.4	2.8	2.5	2.4	5.3	4.0
GLASS & GLASS PROD.	15.2	12.9	8.0	7.2	7.5	22.3	7.4	7.9	7.3	7.6	5.1	7.5	13.5	8.0	7.1	3.1	7.9	6.2	7.9
IRON & STEEL	10.8	5.8	4.6	5.4	5.5	4.2	4.9	4.7	5.9	3.5	2.8	5.6	5.2	1.7	3.7	1.7	4.7	3.6	4.4
NONFERROUS METALS	4.2	3.3	1.6	2.0	6.6	0.8	2.6	1.9	6.5	1.8	1.1	3.6	4.1	0.9	0.7	2.4	1.7	0.7	1.6
METAL PROD.	23.7	10.4	5.4	8.5	5.5	7.7	5.4	5.5	5.4	5.5	5.2	5.4	26.5	4.4	4.0	2.8	5.6	4.8	6.3
NONELEC. MACH.	13.9	6.4	4.3	4.5	4.4	6.1	4.4	4.5	4.3	4.5	4.4	4.3	22.1	5.2	3.5	1.2	4.2	3.3	4.7
ELEC. MACH.	21.6	14.7	7.4	5.8	7.1	6.0[b]	7.7	8.3	7.2	8.0	4.3	7.8	19.6	6.9	4.5	1.6	8.1	4.4	7.1
TRANSP. EQUIP.	21.2	22.1	7.9	1.6	7.2	3.8[b]	7.9	7.7	10.2	8.8	1.5	9.0	26.8	2.2	5.1	6.1	7.2	2.5	6.0
MISC. MANUF.	12.8	8.7	3.0	5.4	6.1	12.6	5.8	5.6	6.5	5.8	4.6	5.2	18.2	7.4	4.6	1.1	3.0	4.2	4.7
All industries	16.5	12.1	5.9	5.2	6.6	7.1	6.0	6.3	6.9	5.4	2.9	6.8	16.7	5.2	5.0	3.1	5.2	4.3	5.8

a. Prevailing rates, which include unilateral reductions in post-Kennedy round tariff rates.
b. Estimated from incomplete data.

Source: Based on data supplied by Office of US Trade Representative.

The EEC in particular wanted the authority to use safeguards selectively by product and supplying country, whereas developing countries opposed such discrimination among countries. Discussions on this code are still in progress.

Besides these NTB codes, the Tokyo Round agreement contains provisions for reform of the GATT framework and reductions in NTBs on specific products. It was suggested that the GATT allow more flexible trade preferences for developing countries and that it be made easier for developing countries to use trade restrictions for balance-of-payments and development objectives. Bilateral agreements were also reached to encourage trade in selected agricultural products, and there was an agreement to remove trade impediments on civil aircraft.

We have noted the failure to negotiate a safeguards code. This was not the only failure, for the Tokyo Round also left intact the NTBs on imports of agricultural products and foodstuffs, textiles and wearing apparel, footwear, iron and steel products, consumer electronic products, and shipbuilding. These barriers are substantial in many industrialized countries and the Tokyo Round may therefore be of only limited significance for the developing countries that export in these industries.

Estimates of the Economic Effects of the Tokyo Round

We mentioned earlier that the Senate Committee on Finance had commissioned us to do a study of the economic effects of the Tokyo Round in connection with their mandate to review the negotiating offers made by the United States and the other major participating countries. For this purpose, we used our original 18-country version of the model. The results of our study were published in Deardorff and Stern (1979b). Since there was interest in the possible effects of the Tokyo Round negotiations on the developing countries, we subsequently expanded the model to include the 16 major developing countries listed in the preceding chapter. We have used this 34-country version of the model for the analysis of the Tokyo Round negotiations to be presented here.

To obtain tariff reductions for use in the model, we began with tariff changes at the line-item level of the Brussels Tariff Nomenclature (BTN). These changes were aggregated using own-country total imports as weights, for each of our 22 tradable industries in each country.[4] The resulting changes in tariffs were then entered into the model as changes in exogenous tariff variables, and the model was solved simultaneously for the resulting changes in all endogenous variables.

The only changes in NTBs that we could quantify in the Tokyo Round were those involving agricultural concessions and the code liberalizing nondefense government procurement. The bilateral agricultural concessions were treated as a relaxation of import quotas in each of the countries. For government procurement, we had information on the amounts of nondefense procurement that governments had tentatively agreed to open to foreign bidding. We assumed these amounts would be spent in proportion to the sector breakdown of each government's expenditure. Estimated amounts of government imports by sector were then determined by applying import shares from the private sector.[5]

All the foregoing exogenous changes in tariffs and NTBs were entered at once into the model, which was then solved for percentage changes in the endogenous variables. Absolute changes were found by multiplying these by initial 1976 levels taken as the reference point for all calculations. In addition, we calculated the changes in economic welfare by country from changes in consumer and producer surplus and total expenditure. The former were calculated from changes in supplies and demands estimated by the model, together with the price changes that would be needed to bring them about, given the assumed price elasticities of supply and demand.[6]

The results, which have been calculated using 1976 as the reference year, are summarized in table 4.4. The principal findings are as follows:[7]

1. Compared with 1976 levels, exports will rise in total by about $13 billion for all the countries listed, or 1.6%. All of this increase is accounted for by the industrialized countries, since the exports of the major developing countries hardly change.

2. Regarding employment, we have prevented any aggregate change in employment by endogenizing expenditure to assure this.[8] To indicate labor-market dislocation, we have therefore calculated the "Gross change in employment" in table 4.4; this is the sum of all positive sectoral employment changes, also shown as percentage of the labor force. It represents the workers in each country who change jobs due to the Tokyo Round. It includes those who move only between export and home sectors of their industries, but nonetheless is only a fraction of a percent in each country. It should presumably be possible therefore to accommodate these changes to the extent that they occur within industries and also with respect to normal labor-market turnover that may occur between industries both nationally and within regions. Since the Tokyo Round reductions will be phased in between 1980 and 1987, the required adjustments will be spread over several years and in any event will be small in comparison with the adjustments that are occurring in a dynamically changing economy.

Table 4.4
Summary of effects of reductions in tariffs and selected nontariff barriers in the Tokyo Round on the major industrialized and developing countries

Country	Change in		Gross change in employment[a]		Change in welfare		Change in effective exchange rate[c] (%)	Change in prices[d] (%)
	Exports ($ × 10^6)	Imports ($ × 10^6)	Workers (× 10^3)	%	$ × 10^6	% GDP[b]		
Industrialized countries								
Australia	64.4	32.4	4.02	0.07	−18.5	−0.02	0.00	−0.06
Austria	305.6	293.6	18.64	0.63	−118.0	−0.29	0.28	−0.84
Canada	1,031.7	1,007.7	26.99	0.28	371.9	0.19	−0.01	−0.23
European Economic Community								
Belgium-Luxembourg	707.7	710.3	29.76	0.77	296.2	0.42	0.52	−1.06
Denmark	258.5	249.4	16.31	0.68	−6.0	−0.01	−0.05	−0.64
France	1,346.1	1,381.1	59.71	0.29	253.0	0.07	−0.32	−0.31
German Federal Republic	1,961.1	2,155.4	108.58	0.44	126.3	0.03	0.01	−0.60
Ireland	59.2	56.1	3.81	0.37	8.4	0.10	0.33	−0.69
Italy	697.4	723.2	45.61	0.24	258.1	0.15	−0.05	−0.28
Netherlands	726.3	744.1	23.98	0.53	184.9	0.21	0.33	−0.82
United Kingdom	1,101.9	1,125.8	54.69	0.22	433.8	0.20	−0.10	−0.25
Total EEC	6,858.1	7,145.3	342.44	0.34	1,554.6	0.11	−0.05	−0.47
Finland	223.8	266.8	11.36	0.53	111.0	0.39	0.00	−0.38
Japan	388.0	572.1	35.95	0.07	245.3	0.04	0.11	−0.12
New Zealand	−26.3	−34.0	1.05	0.09	−6.9	−0.05	0.00	0.15
Norway	206.8	367.9	8.86	0.50	337.7	1.09	0.00	−0.25
Sweden	532.3	770.3	21.77	0.53	606.1	0.82	0.00	−0.42
Switzerland	277.4	434.3	14.28	0.51	427.6	0.75	0.07	−0.24
United States	2,886.1	2,441.0	122.75	0.14	694.9	0.04	−0.21	−0.07
Total industrialized	12,747.9	13,297.3	608.11	0.22	4,205.7	0.10	−0.08	−0.24

Developing countries								
Argentina	−0.9	7.1	3.05	0.03	7.8	0.02	0.00	−0.04
Brazil	−5.0	−10.9	10.33	0.03	−10.9	−0.01	0.00	−0.01
Chile	−60.5	−63.3	42.45	1.52	198.2	2.35	0.00	44.80
Colombia	2.8	5.9	4.69	0.06	0.2	0.00	0.00	−0.09
Greece	−9.1	−23.9	2.01	0.05	−2.9	−0.01	0.00	0.09
Hong Kong	0.1	−2.0	2.45	0.19	−1.6	−0.02	0.38	−0.06
India	3.8	4.2	30.31	0.01	7.4	0.01	0.00	−0.02
Israel	1.8	−1.6	0.69	0.06	5.4	0.04	0.25	0.01
South Korea	22.4	25.3	13.74	0.11	3.8	0.01	0.00	−0.16
Mexico	21.6	19.1	27.38	0.16	44.1	0.06	−0.06	−0.04
Portugal	−3.1	−14.3	2.20	0.07	−9.2	−0.06	0.00	0.09
Singapore	3.4	−16.5	4.48	0.17	−8.9	−0.15	0.00	0.04
Spain	−9.2	−31.8	5.00	0.04	−15.3	−0.01	0.00	0.02
Taiwan	24.9	31.0	6.49	0.11	30.4	0.18	0.00	−0.24
Turkey	−8.2	−19.7	4.02	0.03	−5.1	−0.01	0.00	0.04
Yugoslavia	−3.6	−10.4	2.49	0.05	8.8	0.03	0.05	0.02
Total LDCs	−18.7	−102.0	158.78	0.04	252.2	0.04	0.01	0.54
All countries	12,729.1	13,195.3	766.89	0.12	4,457.8	0.09	−0.07	−0.13

a. Refers to sum of changes in the home and export sectors within industries.
b. GDP = gross domestic product.
c. Positive = appreciation.
d. Index of import and home prices.

Table 4.5

Net changes in employment by ISIC sector in the major industrialized and developing countries due to the effects of reductions in tariffs and selected nontariff barriers in the Tokyo Round (man-years × 1,000)

Industry	(ISIC)	ALA	ATA	BLX	CND	DEN	FIN	FR	GFR	IRE	IT	JPN	NL	NZ	NOR	SWD	SWZ	UK
Traded goods																		
AGR., FOR., & FISH.	(1)	0.324	0.286	0.095	2.654	1.742	1.558	1.076	-12.019	-0.099	-6.454	-4.929	2.536	0.053	1.545	0.907	0.735	-1.664
FOOD, BEV., & TOB.	(310)	0.240	0.275	1.225	0.485	1.663	0.391	2.173	3.425	0.400	1.022	1.180	3.176	-0.044	0.290	0.091	0.306	-1.660
TEXTILES	(321)	-0.341	3.829	3.693	-0.215	0.361	0.172	4.448	3.087	0.374	1.832	-0.511	3.847	-0.497	0.080	-0.281	0.412	-0.147
WEARING APPAREL	(322)	0.081	2.602	1.220	0.374	0.439	2.648	4.194	-0.869	-0.048	2.778	1.113	0.966	0.057	0.228	0.335	0.123	-1.554
LEATHER PROD.	(323)	0.294	0.310	-0.017	0.837	0.086	0.284	1.028	-2.057	0.054	-0.649	-0.132	0.153	-0.171	-0.002	-0.012	-0.222	-0.068
FOOTWEAR	(324)	0.087	0.431	0.042	0.093	0.062	0.460	0.694	0.524	0.025	-0.200	-0.151	0.116	-0.010	0.026	0.048	-0.276	0.040
WOOD PROD.	(331)	-0.114	0.287	-0.442	1.546	-0.007	0.261	-0.690	-0.634	-0.015	-0.450	0.724	-0.716	0.000	-0.056	0.307	-0.361	-0.504
FURN. & FIXT.	(332)	-0.221	0.286	0.796	0.345	1.500	0.167	-0.344	1.947	-0.020	1.841	-0.158	-0.247	0.006	-0.047	0.154	-0.246	0.651
PAPER & PAPER PROD.	(341)	0.011	0.636	-0.160	3.900	-0.502	0.981	-1.269	-4.334	-0.091	-1.255	-0.024	-0.837	-0.047	0.040	0.670	-0.558	-2.124
PRINT. & PUBL.	(342)	0.060	0.024	0.204	-1.705	0.061	-0.118	0.439	-0.255	0.024	0.247	0.112	0.214	0.040	-0.111	-0.130	0.047	0.144
CHEMICALS	(35A)	0.239	-0.193	3.039	0.492	0.033	0.557	-1.210	7.161	0.129	-3.409	-0.702	2.328	0.093	-0.396	-1.189	0.536	-0.244
PETROL. & REL. PROD.	(35B)	-0.253	-0.073	-1.763	0.167	-0.381	-0.055	0.091	-1.152	-0.091	-3.058	-2.058	-0.185	-0.009	-0.055	-0.142	-0.127	-0.539
RUBBER PROD.	(355)	-0.523	-0.264	0.083	-1.156	-0.130	-0.160	0.405	-1.040	0.005	1.525	1.234	0.236	0.021	-0.110	-0.085	-0.168	1.076
NONMETAL. MIN. PROD.	(36A)	0.041	-0.474	-0.182	0.189	0.320	-0.215	-0.358	-0.560	0.482	2.266	0.688	-0.894	0.013	-0.098	-0.188	-0.286	1.763
GLASS & GLASS PROD.	(362)	0.005	-0.039	0.578	-0.143	0.032	0.028	0.201	0.348	0.156	0.238	-0.036	0.235	0.007	-0.032	0.007	-0.027	0.332
IRON & STEEL	(371)	-0.131	-0.145	2.501	0.187	0.015	-0.078	1.224	3.697	-0.062	0.894	-2.246	-0.349	0.032	0.114	0.571	-0.090	0.632
NONFERROUS METALS	(372)	0.694	0.216	-0.826	0.584	-0.003	0.052	-0.065	-0.963	0.025	-1.295	0.747	-0.051	-0.076	0.288	0.256	0.050	0.281
METAL PROD.	(381)	0.233	-2.484	-0.579	-1.798	0.296	-0.180	1.565	0.991	0.075	2.141	2.116	-0.289	0.055	-0.445	0.624	0.322	2.236
NONELEC. MACH.	(382)	0.122	1.977	-0.325	1.121	1.048	-0.674	4.642	8.093	0.079	4.357	-0.744	-0.147	0.034	-0.988	-0.995	-0.506	7.109
ELEC. MACH.	(383)	0.273	0.841	-0.176	-1.408	-0.238	-0.893	2.547	11.650	0.020	1.965	3.390	0.461	0.059	-0.620	-0.405	0.635	1.541
TRANSP. EQUIP.	(384)	-0.124	0.199	4.090	2.089	0.315	-0.624	0.419	6.442	-0.032	5.973	1.333	0.413	0.075	-0.627	-0.377	-1.364	-0.443
MISC. MANUF.	(38A)	0.584	1.682	2.131	-2.249	1.468	-0.765	0.978	11.108	0.631	4.298	3.992	3.107	0.142	-0.690	-0.833	1.103	13.431
Total traded		1.582	10.207	15.229	6.387	8.182	2.983	22.186	34.561	2.021	14.607	4.936	14.074	-0.168	-1.665	-0.670	-0.784	20.292
Nontraded goods																		
MIN. & QUARRY.	(2)	-0.154	-0.248	-0.026	1.097	-0.143	-0.412	0.024	-0.942	0.073	-0.562	-0.261	-0.185	-0.012	-0.057	-0.470	-1.664	0.170
ELEC., GAS, & WATER	(4)	0.007	-0.302	-0.135	-0.136	-0.238	-0.079	-0.426	-0.490	-0.040	-0.068	-0.025	-0.166	-0.009	0.029	0.034	0.164	-0.282
CONSTRUCTION	(5)	-0.170	-0.466	-0.839	0.428	-0.535	-0.078	-2.037	-3.960	-0.116	-2.376	0.175	-0.292	-0.056	0.496	0.521	0.599	-1.213
WHOLE. & RET. TRADE	(6)	-0.481	-3.285	-6.070	-2.100	-2.015	-0.799	-8.205	-4.412	-0.810	-5.780	-2.408	-3.864	0.060	0.305	-0.014	0.421	-5.882
TRANSP., STOR., & COMM.	(7)	-0.084	-0.812	-0.518	0.048	-0.564	-0.162	-1.487	-2.368	-0.126	-0.237	0.001	-1.117	-0.027	0.079	0.079	0.037	-0.575
FIN., INS., & REAL EST.	(8)	-0.249	-1.284	-1.720	-0.912	-0.926	-0.444	-3.385	-5.476	-0.159	-2.232	-0.995	-1.737	0.055	0.065	-0.157	0.451	-2.470
COMM., SOC., & PERS. SERV.	(9)	-0.451	-3.810	-5.921	-4.812	-3.761	-1.010	-6.670	16.913	-0.843	-3.353	-1.424	-6.713	0.157	0.748	0.676	0.777	-10.039
Total nontraded		-1.582	-10.207	-15.229	-6.387	-8.182	-2.983	-22.186	34.561	-2.021	-14.607	-4.936	-14.074	0.168	1.665	0.670	0.784	-20.292
Total, all industries		-0.000	-0.000	-0.000	-0.000	-0.000	-0.000	-0.000	-0.000	-0.000	-0.000	-0.000	-0.000	0.000	-0.000	-0.000	0.000	-0.000

Table 4.5 (continued)

Industry	(ISIC)	US	ARG	BRZ	CHL	COL	GRC	HK	IND	ISR	SK	MEX	POR	SNG	SP	TWN	TPK	YUG
Traded goods																		
AGR., FOR., & FISH.	(1)	55.760	1.430	6.126	16.869	2.052	0.646	0.003	-1.243	0.053	-5.442	-15.388	0.224	0.105	0.938	-1.029	0.445	0.059
FOOD, BEV., & TOB.	(310)	-2.398	-0.257	-0.707	-0.444	-0.165	-0.266	-0.068	-1.406	-0.139	-0.332	8.190	-0.123	-0.224	-0.588	0.179	-0.110	-0.177
TEXTILES	(321)	2.199	-1.295	-0.225	1.241	-0.127	-0.066	-1.015	-2.989	-0.097	-0.374	0.319	-0.062	-0.099	-0.116	-0.304	-0.746	-0.313
WEARING APPAREL	(322)	-2.632	0.096	0.010	0.260	0.092	0.013	-0.686	0.402	-0.018	1.944	0.325	0.149	0.129	0.064	0.400	0.014	0.061
LEATHER PROD.	(323)	1.638	-0.133	-0.222	-0.271	-0.017	-0.761	-0.083	-0.840	-0.029	-0.020	0.034	-0.044	-0.019	-0.325	-0.014	-0.245	-0.216
FOOTWEAR	(324)	0.169	0.046	-0.319	-0.172	-0.059	-0.214	-0.119	-0.404	-0.008	-0.382	-0.011	-0.313	-0.034	-0.632	-0.203	-0.009	-0.417
WOOD PROD.	(331)	-0.575	0.055	0.025	-0.311	0.021	0.085	-0.018	0.111	-0.006	-0.013	0.463	0.025	-0.010	0.190	0.247	-0.001	0.063
FURN. & FIXT.	(332)	-0.813	0.067	0.015	0.057	0.040	-0.049	0.076	0.841	0.007	0.474	-0.076	-0.039	0.054	-0.033	0.242	-0.002	0.200
PAPER & PAPER PROD.	(341)	0.960	-0.029	-0.017	-0.389	-0.053	0.050	-0.082	0.056	-0.011	-0.104	0.079	-0.062	-0.016	0.025	-0.075	0.029	-0.055
PRINT. & PUBL.	(342)	0.175	0.025	-0.025	-0.517	-0.004	0.002	0.010	0.022	0.004	-0.055	0.010	-0.002	0.044	0.084	-0.008	-0.001	0.030
CHEMICALS	(35A)	3.252	-0.051	0.134	0.045	-0.233	0.139	0.001	0.333	0.017	-0.212	3.173	0.092	0.035	0.317	-0.495	0.370	0.214
PETROL. & REL. PROD.	(35B)	0.575	-0.171	-0.082	-0.090	-0.007	-0.017	0.0	-0.112	-0.016	-0.011	0.025	-0.021	-0.012	-0.040	-0.001	-0.024	-0.123
RUBBER PROD.	(355)	0.013	0.009	0.015	0.308	-0.086	0.046	0.004	0.228	0.012	0.429	0.498	0.021	0.048	0.276	0.038	0.091	0.177
NONMETAL. MIN. PROD.	(36A)	-2.042	-0.002	-0.105	0.169	-0.003	0.080	-0.004	0.515	-0.000	0.081	0.595	-0.011	0.016	0.113	0.020	0.055	0.066
GLASS & GLASS PROD.	(362)	-0.322	-0.002	-0.004	-0.272	-0.016	0.017	-0.018	0.051	-0.004	-0.006	0.108	0.002	-0.000	0.033	0.007	0.001	-0.001
IRON & STEEL	(371)	0.377	-0.392	-0.028	-3.307	-0.321	0.012	-0.023	-1.912	-0.017	-0.374	0.103	0.301	-0.012	0.122	-0.916	1.314	-0.162
NONFERROUS METALS	(372)	0.339	-0.102	-0.051	0.308	-0.100	-0.013	-0.015	-0.458	-0.017	-0.085	0.107	0.283	-0.002	0.140	-0.077	0.167	-0.128
METAL PROD.	(381)	0.637	0.054	0.010	-11.327	0.126	0.052	0.446	4.492	0.125	0.937	2.539	0.008	0.150	0.458	0.355	0.013	0.364
NONELEC. MACH.	(382)	5.174	0.059	0.111	-1.680	0.036	0.018	-0.020	0.441	0.001	0.042	1.712	-0.015	0.033	0.327	0.213	-0.017	0.079
ELEC. MACH.	(383)	1.663	0.017	0.120	-9.134	-0.004	0.030	0.297	0.643	0.049	2.009	1.145	0.002	0.368	0.111	1.113	0.010	0.364
TRANSP. EQUIP.	(384)	3.207	0.098	0.071	-2.195	-0.026	0.051	0.006	0.511	0.022	0.236	0.301	-0.034	0.092	0.174	0.090	0.007	0.215
MISC. MANUF.	(38A)	-7.256	0.096	0.562	-0.056	0.517	0.109	1.602	7.779	0.261	5.221	0.395	0.567	0.408	0.556	0.802	0.062	0.255
Total traded		60.101	-0.384	5.416	-10.907	1.662	-0.036	0.293	3.561	0.187	3.962	4.645	0.949	1.053	2.192	0.585	1.421	0.555
Nontraded goods																		
MIN. & QUARRY.	(2)	1.884	-0.127	0.535	-3.133	-0.028	-0.174	-0.000	-2.498	-0.308	-0.084	0.616	-0.053	-0.010	-0.317	-0.009	-0.351	-0.817
ELEC., GAS, & WATER	(4)	-1.078	-0.030	-0.224	0.763	-0.054	0.023	-0.011	-0.062	0.001	-0.061	-0.022	-0.004	-0.021	-0.029	-0.027	0.006	-0.006
CONSTRUCTION	(5)	-1.471	0.099	-0.616	-3.363	-0.002	-0.107	0.005	0.129	0.038	-0.095	-0.977	-0.343	-0.092	-0.504	0.336	-0.336	0.071
WHOLE. & RET. TRADE	(6)	-21.577	-0.078	-1.390	10.684	-1.127	0.159	-0.157	-1.311	0.053	-2.756	-0.242	-0.111	-0.369	-0.559	-0.523	-0.028	0.167
TRANSP., STOR., & COMM.	(7)	-2.037	-0.036	-0.406	3.686	-0.242	0.012	-0.016	-0.166	0.017	-0.416	-0.296	-0.065	-0.164	-0.141	-0.165	-0.047	0.047
FIN., INS., & REAL EST.	(8)	-9.455	-0.042	-1.393	5.264	-0.137	0.225	-0.077	-0.094	0.006	-0.243	-0.095	-0.008	-0.071	-0.200	-0.450	0.019	0.031
COMM., SOC., & PERS. SERV.	(9)	-26.368	0.599	-0.852	-2.995	-0.072	-0.103	-0.037	0.440	0.006	-0.308	-3.630	-0.366	-0.327	-0.443	0.253	-0.685	-0.048
Total nontraded		-60.101	0.384	-5.416	10.907	-1.662	0.036	-0.293	-3.561	-0.187	-3.962	-4.645	-0.949	-1.053	-2.192	-0.585	-1.421	-0.555
Total, all industries		-0.000	-0.000	-0.000	-0.000	-0.000	-0.000	0.000	0.000	0.000	0.000	-0.000	-0.000	-0.000	-0.000	0.000	-0.000	-0.000

3. Our assessment of economic welfare is based upon partial-equilibrium estimates of the changes in consumer surplus, producer surplus, and total expenditure. Depending on the changes in tariffs and NTBs and the composition of trade, individual countries may experience either increases or declines in welfare. Our results indicate that welfare will increase in all major industrialized countries except Australia, Austria, Denmark, and New Zealand. The total welfare gain for industrialized countries is an estimated $4.2 billion per annum, approximately 0.1% of their combined gross domestic product. Developing countries will experience small changes in economic welfare, some positive and some negative. The developing countries with the largest gains are Argentina, Chile, Mexico, and Taiwan, while the biggest losers are Brazil, Portugal, Spain, and Turkey. All of these changes are extremely small, however, except for Chile, which we have reason to believe is anomalous.[9]

4. Exchange rates will change very little. The US dollar will depreciate very slightly as will such currencies as the French franc and British pound. The German mark and the yen will appreciate very slightly.[10]

5. Import and therefore consumer prices will fall somewhat in all industrialized countries except New Zealand. Prices decline in eight of the developing countries listed, but these changes and the increases elsewhere are extremely small, again with the anomalous exception of Chile.

All of these changes, small as they are, relate to the entire changes in tariffs and NTBs that were negotiated. Since they will be phased in over a period of up to 7 years, the effects in any one year will be even smaller.

The country results in table 4.4 mask much industry detail. An important feature of our model is that it yields employment effects by sector and country. The net changes in employment across all sectors and countries are recorded in table 4.5. It is evident that there are both increases and reductions in particular sectors. In the United States, for example, the largest increases are recorded, in thousands of workers, for agriculture (56), nonelectrical machinery (5), chemicals (3), transport equipment (3), and textiles (2). Employment falls in food, beverages, and tobacco (−2), wearing apparel (−3), nonmetallic mineral products (−2), miscellaneous manufactures (−7), and in all nontradable industries except mining and quarrying.[11] These changes are very small in absolute terms and also in percentage terms, except in agriculture and leather products, where employment rises by 1.7 and 1.8%, respectively, of the 1976 level.

The sectoral effects in other countries can be similarly discerned from table 4.5. It is noteworthy how many negative employment changes in developing countries appear in agriculture, textiles, and wearing apparel. NTBs in these sectors were left intact in the Tokyo Round. With tariffs being reduced in other sectors, world prices (exclusive of tariffs) in these other sectors tend to rise and consumer prices (inclusive of tariffs) tend to fall. World demand thus shifts away from the exempted sectors and toward those where tariffs fall. This fall in demand occurs in important export sectors of developing countries, and is further worsened by the rise in prices of other manufactures which may serve as inputs to these sensitive sectors. It is specialization in these sectors by developing countries that largely accounts for their loss of welfare due to the Tokyo Round. By the same token, certain developing countries that have succeeded in exporting durable manufactures are free riders in the Tokyo Round.

The smallness of our results is not surprising if we consider the reasons for it. First, the Tokyo Round tariff reductions are themselves quite small. As noted in table 4.1, average tariffs are to be cut from approximately 8 to 6%. Even if tariffs were reflected fully in import prices, these would fall by only 2%. But even this will not happen since tariff cuts in many industries and countries simultaneously cause world prices to rise and exchange rates to move to reduce effects on domestic prices. Finally, what price changes do occur have only limited effects on output and employment since their roles as output prices and input prices counteract. All things considered, then, it is to be expected that the effects of the Tokyo Round on trade, employment, and welfare should be measured in tenths, or even hundredths, of a percent.[12]

Sensitivity of Results to Changes in Parameters

The question naturally arises as to how sensitive our results are to key parameters. To test this, we ran three experiments. We first doubled all supply elasticities, then doubled all elasticities of substitution between home and imported goods, and finally doubled both supply and substitution elasticities.

Doubling supply elasticities enlarges employment changes, but the effects are still comparatively small. Effects on welfare are not very sensitive to increased supply elasticities. Doubling elasticities of substitution has a negligible effect on changes in employment, but there is a sizable increase in effects on economic welfare because higher elasticities imply a shift of a more elastic schedule. Doubling both supply and substitution elasticities has a minor effect on the employment results, but the welfare calculation as just noted is larger.

The elasticities of supply and substitution used in our model are empirically based. Still, our confidence in the model is enhanced by the stability of the employment results. By the same token, our welfare calculation is more ad hoc since it is not rigorously derived from the model. It is apparently fairly sensitive to the elasticity parameters and should be interpreted cautiously therefore.

Comparison with Other Studies

In order to provide additional perspective, it would be useful if we could compare our results with other studies. The two most comparable studies to our own are Whalley (1982) and Brown (1984), who both used the reductions in tariff rates actually negotiated in the Tokyo Round. Baldwin (1976), Deardorff, Stern, and Baum (1977), Cline et al. (1978), Deardorff, Stern, and Greene (1979a), Baldwin, Mutti, and Richardson (1980), and Brown and Whalley (1980) all used hypothetical rather than actual tariff reductions, and their results are thus not strictly comparable to those reported above. Further, the fact that the various studies differ among themselves in terms of their conceptual framework may also make comparisons difficult.

Despite these qualifications, it is nevertheless the case that all of these studies of the Tokyo Round negotiations have reached the same conclusion regarding their overall economic effects, namely, that the effects on trade, employment, and economic welfare are likely to be small.[13] The main differences in results involve the distribution of the changes across the major countries/regions and industries. These differences stem mainly from whether the models used are partial or general equilibrium in nature, whether and how the Armington assumption is implemented, and the level of aggregation used for countries/regions and industries. This suggests that our detailed country and industry results reported previously may not agree in terms of magnitude and possibly sign with the results in other studies.

When it comes to deciding which detailed results are to be preferred, we would argue in favor of those based on models such as ours that make allowance for the variety of interactions among and within countries and industries. The detailed results of partial-equilibrium studies such as Baldwin (1976), Cline et al. (1978), and Baldwin, Mutti, and Richardson (1980) are thus potentially misleading. Results derived from Walrasian-type models like Whalley's emphasize welfare effects in the aggregate and do not provide industry detail because all markets are permitted to clear. Brown's model, which is an adaptation of our Michigan model but with the full Armington assumption, provides the same country and industry detail that we report.

As mentioned in chapter 1, Brown's results differ somewhat from ours insofar as they reflect strong terms of trade effects due to the Armington assumption; it is not obvious in this light that her results are necessarily preferable to those that we report.[14]

Effects of NTB Codes and Remaining NTBs

We have noted that agreements were reached in the Tokyo Round on several NTB codes. The only changes in NTBs that we could quantify in our analysis were certain agricultural concessions and the liberalization of government procurement. While the remaining codes do not lend themselves to quantification, they are not unimportant. We therefore examine them qualitatively to determine their possible future impact. Also of interest are the NTBs not covered by the Tokyo Round.

Effects of the NTB Codes

Just as it is difficult to measure NTBs, it is also difficult to assess the effects of the codes intending to liberalize them. The codes themselves are stated in advisory, rather than quantitative, terms. One cannot predict, therefore, how well participating governments will adhere to them. Several years' experience must precede judgments on some of the codes, and even then definitive evaluation may be impossible. The principal significance of the codes may be that they signal the willingness and intent of governments to reduce interference with trade. The success of the codes ultimately depends on whether that attitude continues.

Even if a liberal attitude is maintained, the success of the codes will also depend on an effective mechanism of enforcement. This is necessary if only to define what the codes mean so that countries can abide by them. And it is here that the Tokyo Round codes may run into trouble. The negotiations themselves were facilitated by discussing each issue in a separate forum and producing a separate code on each. Likewise, separate mechanisms for administration and enforcement were created in each of the codes. The result could be a bureaucratic nightmare, as each nation may also have to set up a separate institution to deal with each code. The diverse interpretations that may be reached, on such broad issues as national sovereignty and individual and corporate rights, may prevent the codes from ever forming the nucleus of a coherent body of international trade law.

These reservations aside, let us now consider the individual codes and see what can be said about their likely effects.

1. Customs valuation. This code is intended to make customs-valuation procedures more uniform and rational than in the past. It defines five alternative methods of valuation, all of which use or approximate the transactions price as the base on which duties are to be levied. By specifically prohibiting procedures such as the American Selling Price method that raise the duty collected, this code might be expected to lower the level of tariffs. However, most such implications of the code were accounted for in the tariff changes themselves, so that this effect is really not important.

The significant effect of the code will be that it reduces uncertainty in international trade. Customs-valuation procedures can constitute nontariff barriers to trade, not because they raise the level of duties, but because they impose a nonmonetary uncertainty cost on engaging in international trade. This is a cost to traders and a benefit to no one. If the code succeeds in reducing this uncertainty, it will be a benefit to all.

2. Government procurement. This code is intended to reduce discrimination against foreign suppliers in the purchase of nonstrategic goods by governments. The signatories have each listed specific government agencies that will be subject to the code, and there are rules for all stages of the procurement process. We have included this code in our previous estimates. Separate estimates of the effects of the procurement code alone are comparable to those of the tariff reductions themselves. The effect on US economic welfare is positive.

A side effect of the code is that it requires an elaborate bureaucratic mechanism for procurement in each country. The United States already has such a mechanism, but in many countries the bureaucratic cost of implementing this code may be substantial. Of course, one could also argue that these countries will benefit if the code reduces discrimination among domestic suppliers as well.

3. Import-licensing procedures. This code is intended to minimize the nuisance aspects of import-licensing requirements. Requirements for obtaining licenses should be published and involve a minimum of red tape, and licenses are to be granted on a nondiscriminatory basis. The code provides a deadline for approval of automatic licenses. As with customs-valuation procedures, it is not so much the licenses themselves that impede trade as the uncertainty, confusion, and delay surrounding their administration. If the code regularizes import-licensing procedures, the costs of trade should go down.

4. Subsidies and countervailing duties. This code prohibits export subsidies on nonprimary products and discourages domestic subsidies where these

will harm trade. Also, it establishes an injury test for the use of duties to countervail against such subsidies. In both aspects, the code should discourage the process of subsidy and retaliation that has recently characterized trade policy. The inclusion of domestic subsidies in the code is a notable achievement, though the weak provisions regarding them will cause little change in behavior.

5. Product standards. This code discourages the use of product standards as barriers to trade. When national standards are being drafted or revised, it encourages the use of existing international standards and otherwise requires that countries publish proposed measures and accept comments from all concerned. Where particular goods must be certified, access to the certification process is to be granted equally to foreign and domestic suppliers. This should remedy particular current practices which have been the source of complaint. The code itself contains no standards and does not apply to existing standards or certification systems except through the dispute-settlement mechanism. Thus, its effects will be felt only gradually over many years. Still there can be no doubt of its ultimate beneficial effects.

NTBs Not Covered in the Tokyo Round

A number of sectors were explicitly exempted from the Tokyo Round. The few bilateral concessions on agricultural products were limited and most existing agricultural protection arrangements will remain. Trade in textiles and wearing apparel is still controlled by the Multifibers Arrangement and there are also special measures regulating imports of footwear, iron and steel products, consumer electronic products, and shipbuilding. Many of these were adopted while the Tokyo Round was being negotiated. They involved voluntary export restraints and orderly marketing arrangements, sanctioned in US trade legislation, as well as trigger and reference price schemes, which are executive measures designed ostensibly to forestall dumping. These measures appear to be beyond the control of GATT.

The NTBs not covered in the Tokyo Round may be considerably more important than the tariff and NTB concessions that were included. Brown and Whalley (1980) have estimated the ad valorem equivalents of these NTBs crudely by sector. Using a model that is somewhat similar to ours, they have calculated that eliminating these NTBs would increase world welfare by $16 billion (in 1973 prices). This contrasts with their estimates of the gains from assumed tariff reductions of about $1.5 billion. While these estimates are subject to a wide margin of error, it appears nonetheless that the Tokyo Round has dealt with a relatively limited part of all interferences with international trade.

Estimated Effects of Complete Elimination of Post-Tokyo Round Tariffs

It is evident from tables 4.1 and 4.3 that tariff rates in the major industrialized countries have now been reduced to relatively low rates as a consequence of the Tokyo Round and preceding rounds of multilateral negotiations. It seems natural in this light to ask whether tariffs might not be eliminated altogether by mutual agreement sometime in the near future. In order to evaluate this question, we need estimates of the important economic effects involved by sector and country. Our model is well suited for this purpose.

Before presenting the results of our calculations of the effects of eliminating all post-Tokyo Round tariffs, it is useful to reiterate what the Tokyo Round negotiations accomplished and what was left undone and to discuss the political economy of post-Tokyo Round negotiating options. As discussed previously, the Tokyo Round negotiations were concluded in 1979. Beginning in 1980, the process of implementation has been under way, with the tariff reductions being phased in over a period of 8 years and some liberalization of agricultural trade and government procurement instituted. In addition, a series of codes covering particular NTBs was established under GATT auspices, and these codes are currently operational.

In table 4.3, we provided an indication of the average post-Tokyo Round nominal tariff levels by major industrial country and sector. These are the tariffs that will exist once the annually phased reductions have been completed in 1987. It can be seen that the weighted post-Tokyo Round average tariff on industrial products is 4.3% for the United States, 5.2–6.9% for the 9-member EEC, and 2.9% for Japan. Canada, Finland, Norway, Sweden, and Switzerland have comparably low average tariffs, while those for Australia, Austria, and New Zealand are significantly higher. There is a fair amount of dispersion across sectors, with the highest rates generally in wearing apparel, footwear, and textiles. This in turn suggests that tariff escalation is still present in the tariff structures of the major industrialized countries.

We have already noted that the Tokyo Round was devoted in large part to the discussion and formulation of codes and agreements concerning nontariff measures. The principal items negotiated included codes covering customs valuation, government procurement, import-licensing procedures, subsidies and countervailing duties, and standards. There was an attempt to draft a safeguards code governing policies to deal with market disruption due to sudden upsurges in imports, but agreement could not be reached on the principle of applying safeguards selectively by product and supplying country. Besides these NTB codes, the Tokyo Round agreement contained provisions for reform of the GATT framework, arrangements designed to encourage more trade in selected agricultural products, and a sectoral agreement to remove trade impediments affecting civil aircraft.

The failure to negotiate an acceptable safeguards code was not the only omission, however, for the Tokyo Round left intact a wide variety of NTBs governing imports of agricultural products and foodstuffs, textiles and wearing apparel, footwear, iron and steel products, consumer electronic products, and shipbuilding. These NTBs are especially important in the United States and many of the other industrialized countries. To the extent that imports especially from developing countries are affected by existing NTBs, our calculations suggested that the Tokyo Round may be of relatively little significance to these countries. We shall return to this point.

The Political Economy of Protection and Post-Tokyo Round Negotiating Options

The post-Tokyo Round tariff rates for the particular sectors and countries listed in table 4.3 reflect a variety of historical circumstances involving protection and the changes that countries have negotiated multilaterally in successive GATT rounds. It is of interest in this regard to note the work by Baldwin (1981) on the political economy of protection in order to obtain some insight into the forces that shaped the US negotiating position in the Tokyo Round. According to Baldwin, the demand for protection by an industry will depend upon various industry characteristics that determine the extent of its lobbying efforts and the size of the losses that may be experienced if existing protection is reduced. The supply of protection reflects the government's perceptions of voter support and the pressures brought to bear by the interested public on their elected representatives.

Baldwin estimated empirically the determinants of several variants of the Tokyo Round tariff reductions, including the actual average tariff cuts, the average percentage reduction in the prices of domestically produced goods, the difference between the Swiss formula and the rates proposed by the United States, and the proportion of Swiss-formula cuts actually offered. In general, his regression results suggested that the demand for protection across industries in the United States reflected already high tariff rates, a small ratio of exports to shipments, a high import-penetration ratio, a low ratio of value added to shipments, and a high labor share of value added. On the supply side, the proportion of unskilled labor in an industry, the level of industry employment, and the level of import penetration were apparently instrumental in shaping government responses. There was also evidence that industries tended to be protected by both tariffs and NTBs.[15]

These results are indicative of the forces at work in the United States that shaped the outcome of the Tokyo Round negotiations. Presumably, similar forces would be present in the other major industrialized countries, although allowance would have to be made for differences in industry structure and in the mode and responsiveness of government officials to protectionist pressures. If post-Tokyo Round tariffs were to be eliminated, a major effort would be required by governments to withstand the pressures from those sectors that might lose the most. It would be necessary furthermore to prevent countries from using NTBs to make up for what they might lose from tariff elimination.

The question of NTBs is one perhaps that should be addressed in its own right. While some noteworthy progress was made in the Tokyo Round in terms of the various NTB codes that were negotiated, the fact remains that practically nothing was done to reduce or eliminate existing NTBs covering a wide variety of agricultural and industrial products. The domestic interest groups that benefit from NTBs are obviously politically very important and deeply entrenched, and governments have been, it seems, increasingly responsive to these pressures. The stakes involved may indeed be substantial, as the calculations of Brown and Whalley (1980) cited earlier suggest.

It will be recalled from chapter 2 that NTBs are represented in our model in terms of the fraction of trade covered by NTBs in a given sector. Unfortunately, we do not have sufficient information available at present to encompass the economic effects of NTBs in our model. We shall not consider accordingly the negotiating options for reducing or eliminating NTBs, but instead we shall concentrate on the effects of tariff elimination. In this connection, we shall abstract from the measures that governments might find necessary to engender support domestically for the elimination of tariffs. By the same token, our results for individual sectors could be helpful in devising policies for adjustment for those sectors that will be affected adversely and in seeking support from the ones that will benefit from tariff elimination.

Results

Since tariffs constitute exogenous variables in our model, we solved the model for the changes in other variables that would be realized from the complete elimination of the tariffs in all sectors in the major industrialized countries. The elimination was assumed to occur all at once rather than being phased in over a period of years. As noted, the trade coverage of NTBs is assumed to remain intact, so that the sectors subject to NTBs will not respond as fully as might otherwise be the case. We have already mentioned that there are no systematic and easily accessible data on tariffs and NTBs for the developing countries. This may not be much of a drawback if we can assume that these countries would make few, if any, changes in their existing policies in response to complete elimination of post-Tokyo Round tariffs by the major industrialized countries.

The overall results are summarized in table 4.6 for the major industrialized and developing countries. As before, these results are measured using 1976 as the reference year. The principal findings are as follows:

1. Based upon 1976 levels, exports will rise by about $28 billion for all the countries listed, which is about a 3.7% increase. The major industrialized countries account for practically all of the increase. US exports rise by $3.4 billion and imports by $4.2 billion.[16]

2. We have already noted that expenditure has been endogenized to prevent any aggregate change in employment from occurring. As an indicator of labor-market dislocation, we have therefore calculated the "Gross change in employment" in table 4.6. This is the sum of all positive sectoral employment changes, and is also shown as a percentage of each country's 1976 labor force. The former figure represents the total number of workers in each country who would have to change jobs if post-Tokyo Round tariffs were eliminated. It includes those who might have to move only between the export and home sectors of their industries. For the United States, the gross change in employment is 131 thousand workers, which is 0.15% of the 1976 US labor force. The total for the European Economic Community is 792 thousand workers, which is 0.79% of 1976 employment. For individual EEC-member countries, the percentages range from 0.55 for the United Kingdom to 1.66 for Belgium-Luxembourg. The total for Japan is 130 thousand workers, which is 0.25% of the 1976 labor force.[17] It will be recalled that we have assumed that tariffs will be eliminated all at once. If instead the elimination were phased in over a period of several years, the adjustment of employment might not add materially to normal labor-market turnover within and between industries, so that any serious disruptions in labor markets would be less likely to occur. This would also be the case to the extent that adjustment occurred in the context of a growing world. However, as will be noted, our disaggregated results by sector do not fully support such a conclusion since there are numerous sectors in which the

Table 4.6
Summary of effects of elimination of tariffs remaining after the Tokyo Round on the major industrialized and developing countries

Country	Change in		Gross change in employment[a]		Change in welfare		Change in effective exchange rate[b] (%)	Change in prices[c] (%)
	Exports ($ × 10⁶)	Imports ($ × 10⁶)	Workers (× 10³)	%	$ × 10⁶	% GDP		
Industrialized countries								
Australia	1,321.8	1,945.9	47.45	0.82	647.1	0.63	0.00	−0.95
Austria	1,322.0	1,292.0	86.29	2.93	−501.9	−1.21	0.65	−2.91
Canada	1,735.7	1,731.4	50.59	0.53	261.6	0.13	0.51	−0.70
European Economic Community								
Belgium-Luxembourg	1,328.7	1,301.9	64.10	1.66	−13.3	−0.02	1.60	−2.75
Denmark	531.7	538.4	36.15	1.51	−289.2	−0.70	0.52	−1.99
France	2,956.9	3,031.8	139.14	0.67	−70.4	−0.02	−0.59	−0.82
German Federal Republic	4,399.1	4,430.1	231.38	0.94	1,530.1	−0.34	−0.25	−1.43
Ireland	167.9	172.7	12.18	1.19	8.9	0.11	0.88	−1.98
Italy	1,572.6	1,571.0	117.87	0.62	193.3	0.11	−0.21	−0.75
Netherlands	1,658.6	1,718.0	58.19	1.28	52.5	0.06	1.00	−2.16
United Kingdom	2,716.8	2,635.2	133.11	0.55	825.4	0.37	−0.67	−0.62
Total EEC	15,332.4	15,399.1	792.12	0.79	−822.9	−0.06	−0.20	−1.20
Finland	861.0	363.8	49.12	2.29	−522.7	−1.83	0.00	−1.64
Japan	1,474.1	1,565.1	129.61	0.25	317.1	0.06	−0.41	−0.41
New Zealand	87.8	86.4	8.81	0.73	−65.2	−0.48	0.00	−0.58
Norway	432.7	346.0	17.09	0.96	−99.0	−0.32	0.00	−0.81
Sweden	1,091.6	615.9	41.58	1.09	−597.7	−0.81	0.00	−1.01
Switzerland	543.6	411.9	21.07	0.75	−243.6	−0.43	0.00	−0.66
United States	3,397.7	4,248.1	130.75	0.15	1,720.1	0.10	−0.35	−0.11
Total industrialized	27,600.4	28,005.6	1,377.47	0.51	92.9	0.00	−0.23	−0.63

Developing countries								
Argentina	34.4	90.0	23.43	0.23	30.3	−0.06	0.00	−0.50
Brazil	107.8	189.7	60.91	0.15	−41.2	−0.03	0.00	−0.21
Chile	−187.5	−197.8	130.48	4.68	614.8	7.30	0.00	138.10
Colombia	13.3	41.2	23.40	0.29	4.8	0.03	0.00	−0.51
Greece	−0.3	−13.1	6.25	0.16	−11.6	−0.05	0.00	0.00
Hong Kong	−1.9	−5.6	6.32	0.48	−30.9	−0.33	1.09	−0.24
India	27.5	28.3	141.73	0.06	−39.1	−0.05	0.00	−0.11
Israel	−1.9	−5.6	1.54	0.14	4.1	0.03	0.48	0.03
South Korea	123.8	149.5	49.16	0.39	55.0	0.20	0.00	−0.78
Mexico	−34.3	−17.7	27.86	0.16	−73.6	−0.09	0.59	−0.11
Portugal	1.4	−21.2	6.94	0.22	−38.1	−0.25	0.00	0.05
Singapore	8.2	−35.5	3.50	0.40	−23.9	−0.41	0.00	0.17
Spain	35.2	20.9	15.60	0.13	−49.5	−0.05	0.00	−0.09
Taiwan	108.5	128.7	30.10	0.53	78.3	0.45	0.00	−1.03
Turkey	−2.9	0.1	10.87	0.07	−5.1	−0.01	0.00	−0.05
Yugoslavia	−9.0	−7.2	5.67	0.12	22.2	0.07	0.30	0.01
Total LDCs	222.5	345.0	543.76	0.15	436.1	0.06	0.11	1.53
All countries	27,822.8	28,350.6	1,921.23	0.30	529.0	0.01	0.18	−0.33

a. Refers to sum of changes in the home and export sectors within industries.
b. Positive = appreciation.
c. Index of import and home prices.

Table 4.7
Net changes in employment by ISIC sector in the major industrialized and developing countries due to the elimination of Post-Tokyo Round tariffs (man-years × 1,000)

Industry	(ISIC)	ALA	ATA	BLX	CND	DEN	FIN	FR	GFR	IRE	IT	JPN	NL	NZ	NOR	SWD	SWZ	UK
Traded goods																		
AGR., FOR., & FISH.	(1)	14.319	−4.916	2.617	10.692	6.611	−8.011	17.035	−5.579	3.632	−10.004	−62.588	12.242	4.837	2.361	0.496	−0.614	0.410
FOOD, BEV., & TOB.	(310)	4.275	−0.850	1.123	0.256	3.595	−0.573	5.890	−0.585	1.271	1.142	10.315	7.731	1.682	−0.062	−0.932	0.159	−4.437
TEXTILES	(321)	10.355	18.161	10.519	−1.744	1.176	5.576	9.059	11.674	0.972	3.974	15.273	9.630	0.125	1.960	3.356	1.362	0.881
WEARING APPAREL	(322)	−3.178	25.248	5.131	−2.606	1.324	26.108	14.135	−4.051	−0.112	13.869	2.638	3.204	0.889	1.377	7.810	1.914	−2.223
LEATHER PROD.	(323)	2.815	1.644	−0.018	1.591	0.112	1.696	1.766	0.564	0.060	0.996	0.354	0.210	−0.153	0.499	0.638	0.002	0.292
FOOTWEAR	(324)	−0.241	6.680	0.124	0.059	0.089	2.777	3.785	−2.222	−0.047	17.415	0.017	0.514	0.131	0.357	1.281	0.505	−1.798
WOOD PROD.	(331)	−1.465	0.889	−0.555	0.541	0.048	0.989	−0.990	−0.834	−0.069	−0.024	5.052	−0.847	−0.026	−0.018	0.672	−0.317	−1.262
FURN. & FIXT.	(332)	−0.598	−2.000	1.290	−0.020	2.931	0.904	−0.759	4.012	−0.039	2.913	0.013	−0.249	0.003	0.144	1.327	−0.482	1.906
PAPER & PAPER PROD.	(311)	−0.671	2.513	1.097	2.134	−0.457	2.629	−1.091	−3.793	−0.260	−0.751	0.509	−0.266	0.094	0.690	2.095	−0.185	−3.684
PRINT. & PUBL.	(342)	−0.183	−0.378	0.305	−0.585	0.018	−0.612	−0.008	−0.994	−0.016	−0.237	0.226	−0.096	−0.166	−0.646	−0.422	−0.271	−0.442
CHEMICALS	(35A)	0.798	0.976	7.680	−2.260	0.496	0.737	2.231	23.215	0.327	−6.528	2.199	5.007	−0.521	0.353	0.566	2.535	3.367
PETROL. & REL. PROD.	(35B)	0.059	−0.263	−3.934	−0.380	−1.112	0.016	0.935	−1.537	−0.574	−1.170	−1.878	−0.409	0.050	0.035	0.016	0.001	−0.348
RUBBER PROD.	(355)	−2.269	−0.678	0.150	−0.975	−0.103	−1.222	1.284	2.488	0.010	3.386	4.622	0.337	−0.068	−0.040	−0.519	−0.035	2.892
NONMETAL. MIN. PROD.	(36A)	−1.001	−1.449	−1.490	−0.660	0.264	−0.539	−1.173	−0.369	0.721	2.933	1.829	−0.843	−0.087	−0.086	−0.500	−0.304	4.701
GLASS & GLASS PROD.	(362)	−0.529	−0.160	1.694	−0.361	0.009	−0.032	0.067	0.883	0.284	0.337	0.205	0.996	−0.004	−0.087	−0.007	−0.032	1.632
IRON & STEEL	(371)	−1.259	0.781	7.534	−0.606	−0.040	−0.050	1.301	14.766	−0.233	0.582	8.398	−1.265	−0.110	0.367	1.047	−0.076	5.240
NONFERROUS METALS	(372)	4.327	0.433	−2.676	11.076	0.075	0.087	−0.614	0.573	0.124	−1.231	0.304	−0.359	0.059	0.570	0.490	−0.061	1.005
METAL PROD.	(381)	−4.965	−2.046	−1.663	−2.342	1.218	−0.590	3.097	3.706	0.230	4.069	5.468	−0.210	−0.093	0.060	2.037	1.457	5.566
NONELEC. MACH.	(382)	−0.587	3.150	1.114	1.810	2.925	0.526	8.599	19.022	0.169	4.233	4.471	0.905	−0.104	0.292	3.583	1.267	13.904
ELEC. MACH.	(383)	−4.428	−0.112	1.110	−0.094	0.489	0.422	3.384	18.960	0.004	1.127	13.763	1.333	−0.185	0.230	4.195	2.561	2.260
TRANSP. EQUIP.	(384)	−7.770	−1.826	11.217	4.978	3.566	1.061	2.716	16.602	−0.242	14.173	15.208	0.609	−0.270	2.279	4.895	−0.269	1.660
MISC. MANUF.	(38A)	−2.317	2.393	2.528	0.070	2.965	−0.617	0.766	16.105	0.970	4.854	10.241	4.270	−0.058	0.224	1.940	4.076	21.783
Total traded		5.486	48.192	44.899	20.575	26.201	31.281	66.950	112.606	7.181	56.057	36.637	42.447	6.024	10.861	34.063	13.191	53.307
Nontraded goods																		
MIN. & QUARRY.	(2)	2.625	−0.874	−0.010	0.383	−0.636	−0.107	−0.017	1.252	0.039	−1.095	−0.070	−0.449	−0.029	0.167	0.087	−0.209	2.239
ELEC., GAS, & WATER	(4)	−0.137	−1.286	−0.454	−0.477	−0.725	−0.901	−1.309	−1.217	−0.184	−0.609	0.138	−0.535	−0.197	−0.229	−0.569	−0.616	−0.368
CONSTRUCTION	(5)	1.692	−5.288	−2.778	0.953	−1.689	−3.693	−6.291	−15.721	−0.464	−8.796	−7.335	−1.546	−0.388	−0.893	−3.115	−1.347	−3.961
WHOLE. & RET. TRADE	(6)	−4.514	−14.835	−17.398	−5.723	−6.399	−7.847	−24.667	−21.086	−2.694	−22.634	−16.526	−11.912	−1.688	−3.049	−7.861	−2.992	−15.233
TRANSP., STOR., & COMM.	(7)	−0.354	−3.606	−2.124	−1.423	−1.834	−2.039	−4.331	−6.885	−0.433	−2.231	−2.739	−3.303	−0.601	−0.779	−1.769	−1.144	−0.743
FIN., INS., & REAL EST.	(8)	−1.755	−5.779	−4.991	−2.904	−2.996	−4.038	−9.984	−17.860	−0.564	−8.712	−4.990	−5.169	−0.959	−1.128	−4.346	−2.830	−6.582
COMM., SOC., & PERS. SERV.	(9)	−3.043	−16.524	−17.144	−11.384	−11.921	−12.656	−20.351	−51.089	−2.881	−11.981	−5.115	−19.533	−2.161	−4.949	−16.492	−4.052	−28.658
Total nontraded		−5.486	−48.192	−44.899	−20.575	−26.201	−31.281	−66.950	−112.606	−7.181	−56.058	−36.637	−42.447	−6.024	−10.861	−34.063	−13.191	−53.307
Total, all industries		−0.000	−0.000	−0.000	−0.000	−0.000	−0.000	−0.000	−0.000	−0.000	−0.000	0.000	−0.000	−0.000	−0.000	−0.000	−0.000	−0.000

Table 4.7 (continued)

Industry	(ISIC)	US	AGR	BRZ	CHL	COL	GRC	HK	IND	ISR	SK	MEX	POR	SNG	SP	TWN	TRK	YUG
Traded goods																		
AGR., FOR., & FISH.	(1)	51.449	9.304	41.849	53.425	11.910	2.459	0.091	27.436	0.652	−15.749	18.768	0.321	0.615	5.258	−0.036	6.185	0.588
FOOD, BEV., & TOB.	(310)	1.062	4.513	7.018	−1.074	−0.163	0.196	−0.279	22.235	−0.408	0.320	−1.691	−0.001	−0.491	1.662	5.447	−0.003	−0.071
TEXTILES	(321)	−8.771	−3.996	−0.935	3.784	−0.604	0.007	−2.468	−9.378	−0.250	0.115	−3.662	0.091	−0.338	−0.648	−0.142	−1.872	−0.851
WEARING APPAREL	(322)	−15.514	1.179	0.214	0.787	0.657	1.298	5.440	3.092	0.229	13.419	0.710	2.860	0.994	0.916	2.506	0.303	1.082
LEATHER PROD.	(323)	−1.652	−0.386	−0.440	−0.824	0.010	−1.968	−0.421	−3.373	−0.097	0.045	−0.179	0.022	−0.121	−0.013	−0.030	−0.699	−0.217
FOOTWEAR	(324)	−1.403	0.604	0.972	−0.397	0.269	0.265	0.142	2.046	0.025	2.098	−0.004	0.524	0.114	1.717	1.213	−0.000	0.568
WOOD PROD.	(331)	−0.329	0.415	−0.323	−0.993	0.011	−0.033	−0.137	0.042	−0.038	−1.660	−0.456	−0.209	−0.156	−0.113	−0.061	−0.016	−0.292
FURN. & FIXT.	(332)	−0.022	0.721	−0.076	0.168	0.066	−0.089	0.009	0.532	0.008	1.660	0.035	−0.138	0.096	0.619	0.620	0.001	0.421
PAPER & PAPER PROD.	(341)	0.642	−0.457	−0.573	−1.189	−0.402	0.008	−0.246	−0.324	−0.038	−0.680	−0.351	−0.152	−0.037	−0.188	−0.426	−0.033	−0.211
PRINT. & PUBL.	(342)	−0.241	−0.126	−0.315	−1.623	−0.202	−0.027	−0.143	−0.361	−0.009	−0.142	−0.127	−0.030	−0.023	−0.174	−0.085	−0.013	0.002
CHEMICALS	(35A)	4.519	−1.310	−2.973	0.093	−1.968	0.062	−0.028	−1.694	0.024	−1.806	1.147	0.100	0.072	−0.110	−3.014	−0.099	0.251
PETROL. & REL. PROD.	(35B)	0.180	−0.387	−0.106	−0.257	0.035	−0.014	0.0	0.019	−0.026	0.195	−0.169	−0.022	−0.005	−0.041	1.018	−0.029	−0.252
RUBBER PROD.	(355)	−1.489	−0.141	−0.462	0.944	−0.689	0.014	−0.082	0.076	−0.014	−0.123	−0.022	0.015	0.050	0.176	0.260	−0.023	0.045
NONMETAL. MIN. PROD.	(36A)	−2.995	−0.525	−0.814	0.499	−0.289	0.022	−0.020	−0.853	−0.013	0.079	−0.559	−0.086	0.018	−0.211	−0.073	−0.011	−0.045
GLASS & GLASS PROD.	(362)	−0.272	−0.054	−0.141	−0.833	−0.145	0.007	−0.045	0.089	−0.008	−0.067	−0.123	0.002	0.005	−0.016	0.023	−0.003	−0.017
IRON & STEEL	(371)	−2.015	−5.245	−3.301	−10.238	−2.296	−0.065	−0.066	−6.846	−0.040	−1.769	−0.890	0.284	−0.025	−0.559	−5.010	−0.273	−0.565
NONFERROUS METALS	(372)	−1.174	−1.479	−0.662	0.855	−0.756	−0.077	−0.049	−2.490	−0.058	−1.772	−0.645	0.289	−0.008	−0.218	−1.179	−0.677	−0.714
METAL PROD.	(381)	1.023	0.026	−0.249	−34.970	0.497	0.085	0.400	3.050	0.195	2.288	2.087	−0.008	0.267	0.664	0.822	0.003	0.526
NONELEC. MACH.	(382)	5.404	−0.109	−1.182	−5.191	0.009	−0.022	−0.193	−0.354	−0.025	−0.042	−2.563	−0.222	−0.027	−0.324	0.214	−0.032	−0.342
ELEC. MACH.	(383)	9.629	−0.058	−0.536	−28.157	−0.019	0.031	0.227	2.208	0.081	4.853	0.890	0.002	0.680	0.065	2.457	−0.004	0.519
TRANSP. EQUIP.	(384)	7.197	0.555	−0.059	−6.765	−0.165	0.044	0.009	1.137	0.062	0.711	0.308	−0.085	0.241	0.374	0.276	−0.014	0.450
MISC. MANUF.	(38A)	−5.333	−0.020	−0.553	−0.362	0.273	0.038	−0.500	8.023	0.062	7.161	−0.057	0.424	0.346	0.170	1.010	−0.003	0.064
Total traded		39.896	3.023	36.341	−32.320	6.039	2.241	1.643	44.312	0.315	9.134	12.447	3.982	2.267	9.013	5.290	2.690	0.640
Nontraded goods																		
MIN. & QUARRY.	(2)	−0.268	−0.348	−0.839	−9.108	0.054	−0.158	−0.004	−0.013	−0.503	1.309	−4.038	−0.058	−0.004	−0.358	0.752	−0.448	−1.768
ELEC., GAS, & WATER	(4)	−0.844	−0.707	−2.008	2.313	−0.280	−0.072	−0.059	−1.205	−0.005	−0.234	−0.209	−0.068	−0.047	−0.319	−0.188	−0.104	−0.067
CONSTRUCTION	(5)	0.908	0.157	−2.509	−10.563	0.326	−0.290	−0.033	−1.227	0.087	1.298	−0.681	−0.929	−0.199	−1.084	1.490	−0.224	0.444
WHOLE. & RET. TRADE	(6)	−14.894	−4.125	−11.618	32.352	−5.600	−0.575	−0.767	−27.755	−0.003	−9.639	−2.894	−0.963	−0.878	−3.772	−3.781	−0.701	0.268
TRANSP., STOR., & COMM.	(7)	−1.453	−1.562	−2.985	11.163	−1.124	−0.381	−0.129	−5.362	0.007	−1.364	−0.845	−0.446	−0.356	−0.844	−1.210	−0.330	0.077
FIN., INS., & REAL. EST.	(8)	−6.279	−1.130	−13.397	16.073	−0.694	−0.399	−0.472	−1.501	−0.003	−0.906	−0.546	−0.209	−0.158	−1.600	−2.731	−0.139	0.053
COMM., SOC., & PERS. SERV.	(9)	−17.066	4.691	−2.985	−9.911	1.279	−0.366	−0.179	−7.250	0.105	0.403	−3.233	−1.308	−0.624	−0.946	0.379	−0.744	0.354
Total nontraded		−39.896	−3.023	−36.342	32.320	−6.039	−2.241	−1.643	−44.312	−0.315	−9.134	−12.447	−3.982	−2.267	−9.013	−5.290	−2.690	−0.640
Total, all industries		−0.000	−0.000	−0.000	−0.000	−0.000	−0.000	−0.000	−0.000	−0.000	0.000	−0.000	−0.000	−0.000	−0.000	−0.000	−0.000	0.000

relative changes in employment are sufficiently large to suggest that there could indeed be difficulties in adjustment. As for the major developing countries, the employment changes recorded in table 4.6 are all comparatively small.

3. Economic welfare will be increased in the United States, Japan, Australia, Canada, Ireland, Italy, the Netherlands, and the United Kingdom and reduced in the remaining industrialized countries.[18] It will be recalled that the welfare effects are based on partial-equilibrium estimates of the changes in consumer surplus, producer surplus, and total expenditures, and that countries may experience either an increase or decline in welfare. That is, when tariffs are eliminated, world prices (exclusive of tariffs) will rise and consumer prices will fall. Depending upon the composition of a country's trade, it is possible that the former effect may predominate. Excluding Chile, 5 of the developing countries experience a small increase in welfare and the remaining 10 a reduction.

4. The US dollar will depreciate on an effective basis by 0.35%, as will the French franc (0.59%), German mark (0.25%), Italian lira (0.21%), British pound (0.67%), and Japanese yen (0.41%). The remaining industrial-country currencies will appreciate, with the changes most notable for Belgium-Luxembourg (1.60%), Ireland (0.88%), and the Netherlands (1.00%).[19] The exchange rates of most developing countries will remain more or less constant because of controls over foreign exchange licensing.

5. Import and therefore consumer prices fall by a small 0.1% in the United States while the declines for most other industrialized countries are significantly greater, ranging from around 0.5 to nearly 3%.[20] Prices fall in 10 of the developing countries, ranging from 0.05% in Turkey to 1.03% in Taiwan.

The country results in table 4.6 again mask much industry detail that our model is well able to calculate. The net changes in employment across the 22 tradable and 7 nontradable sectors in each of the 34 countries are recorded in table 4.7. It is evident that there are net increases as well as reductions in particular sectors. In the United States, for example, the largest increases are recorded, in thousands of workers, for agriculture (51), electric machinery (10), transport equipment (7), nonelectric machinery (5), and chemicals (5). There are negative employment effects in wearing apparel (−16), textiles (−9), miscellaneous manufactures (−5), nonmetallic mineral products (−3), and leather products (−2). All of the nontradable sectors except construction show net declines in employment. This result is prevalent in most of the countries in the model, as it was for the Tokyo Round calculations. It can again be explained by the general substitution toward tradable goods and away from nontradables due to the reduction in the prices of tradable goods that would result from the elimination of tariffs.

The effects on the individual sectors in the other countries can be similarly discerned from the detailed results in table 4.7. In West Germany, for example, the increases are concentrated in textiles, chemicals, and durable manufactures and the declines in agriculture, footwear, paper and paper products, and to a small extent in some other tradable sectors. France has increases in agriculture and food products, textiles and wearing apparel, leather products, footwear, and durable manufactures, and small declines in some other tradable sectors. The United Kingdom has increases in furniture and fixtures, chemicals, rubber products, nonmetallic mineral products, and durable manufactures and declines especially in food, beverages, and tobacco, clothing, and paper and paper products. Japan has increases in all sectors except agriculture and petroleum products. It thus appears that there are some notable differences across the industrial countries in terms of the industries that would experience net employment increases or declines as the result of tariff elimination.

In discussing the overall gross-employment results in table 4.6, we noted that there were several cases in which these changes represented sizable percentages of total 1976 employment. In table 4.8, we present the results in terms of the net percentage changes in employment by sector for all the countries. In the United States, for example, agriculture shows a net percentage increase of 1.6, electric machinery of 0.5, and transport equipment of 0.4, whereas leather products shows a decline of 1.8, wearing apparel of 1.3, and textiles of 0.7. The United States is clearly on the low side, as inspection of table 4.8 clearly indicates. Indeed, some of the positive and negative percentage changes are sufficiently large that they might signal sectors in which labor adjustment may present difficulties.[21] This is particularly the case if there are problems of labor mobility and if there is a mismatch in labor skills between the industries that would expand or contract in response to tariff elimination. Again, if tariff elimination were staged over a period of years, the difficulties would be lessened, but they might not be fully resolved in certain individual sectors. The large percentage changes in net employment are not so prevalent for the developing countries, reflecting the fact that those countries will in general be less materially affected by tariff elimination in terms of their production and trade. If, on the other hand, NTBs were to be reduced or eliminated, the developing countries would show much greater responses in their sectors of specialization.

Table 4.8

Net percentage changes in employment by ISIC sector in the major industrialized and developing countries due to the elimination of Post-Tokyo round tariffs

Industry	(ISIC)	ALA	ATA	BLX	CND	DEN	FIN	FR	GER	IRE	IT	JPN	NL	NZ	NOR	SWD	SWZ	UK
Traded goods																		
AGR., FOR., & FISH.	(1)	3.829	−1.351	1.912	1.889	2.964	−2.697	0.752	−0.320	1.495	−0.342	−0.973	4.150	3.406	1.406	0.195	0.253	0.062
FOOD, BEV., & TOB.	(310)	2.099	−1.018	1.016	0.096	3.779	−0.801	0.953	−0.105	2.343	0.274	0.674	4.303	2.302	−0.118	−1.051	0.226	0.571
TEXTILES	(321)	17.108	23.817	10.063	−1.622	4.776	20.277	2.477	2.839	4.631	0.658	1.291	19.835	0.668	13.900	11.788	2.125	0.169
WEARING APPAREL	(322)	−5.164	55.921	9.029	−2.234	6.305	74.938	5.272	−1.221	−0.828	3.851	0.452	10.237	4.391	12.157	28.991	6.449	−0.657
LEATHER PROD.	(323)	45.695	26.695	−0.276	16.401	4.558	50.931	3.812	1.255	2.701	2.032	0.646	7.228	−4.793	33.291	20.006	0.061	0.695
FOOTWEAR	(324)	−2.139	33.910	1.037	0.295	2.530	45.746	4.638	−3.444	−1.292	11.976	0.042	9.089	2.207	17.162	30.643	4.393	−2.118
WOOD PROD.	(331)	−2.726	8.010	−2.190	0.445	0.313	2.553	−0.577	−0.426	−1.749	−0.024	0.796	−2.326	−0.149	−0.072	0.944	−1.332	−0.991
FURN. & FIXT.	(332)	−2.225	−6.676	8.494	−0.037	14.626	8.668	−0.737	3.417	−0.967	2.149	0.006	−1.277	0.044	1.408	6.698	−3.745	1.586
PAPER & PAPER PROD.	(341)	−2.208	7.943	3.539	1.472	−3.399	4.732	−0.871	−1.932	−4.345	−0.570	0.131	−0.908	0.902	2.578	3.058	−0.824	−1.625
PRINT. & PUBL.	(342)	−0.247	−1.364	0.692	−0.570	0.049	−1.842	−0.004	−0.457	−0.146	−0.156	0.038	0.123	−0.873	−1.559	−0.846	−0.500	−0.132
CHEMICALS	(35A)	1.373	1.846	8.916	−2.377	1.700	2.998	−0.566	3.430	3.260	−1.357	0.370	6.624	−3.678	1.712	1.225	2.816	0.765
PETROL. & REL. PROD.	(35B)	0.984	−4.347	−29.509	−1.896	−33.608	0.494	0.663	−4.293	−30.882	−3.477	−3.440	−4.100	5.575	1.254	0.510	0.056	−0.934
RUBBER PROD.	(355)	−11.922	−5.321	1.839	−3.221	−2.346	−21.740	1.446	1.873	0.468	2.834	2.992	1.835	−1.191	−1.132	−3.201	−0.566	2.433
NONMETAL. MIN. PROD.	(36A)	−2.252	−3.291	−2.738	−1.408	0.942	−2.778	−0.594	−0.130	8.002	0.944	0.344	−2.663	−1.041	−0.695	−1.513	−1.497	2.129
GLASS & GLASS PROD.	(362)	−6.398	−1.277	5.304	−2.537	0.248	−0.725	0.090	0.856	8.387	0.368	0.238	9.894	−0.161	−3.465	−0.106	−0.771	2.483
IRON & STEEL	(371)	−1.754	0.929	6.950	−0.826	−0.480	−0.286	0.567	2.428	−3.859	0.138	1.290	−2.443	−3.516	2.212	1.406	−0.451	1.335
NONFERROUS METALS	(372)	16.459	3.023	−9.637	19.993	2.103	1.396	−0.993	0.508	6.951	−1.268	0.164	−2.340	1.803	4.688	3.067	−0.356	0.926
METAL PROD.	(381)	−4.448	−2.289	−1.455	−1.545	2.970	−1.917	0.619	0.602	2.906	1.090	0.535	0.300	−0.370	0.206	1.955	2.000	0.967
NONELEC. MACH.	(382)	−0.531	4.759	1.687	1.630	4.105	0.795	1.794	1.426	3.498	0.801	0.329	0.909	−0.889	0.902	2.254	0.967	1.611
ELEC. MACH.	(383)	−5.387	−0.129	1.113	−0.069	1.271	1.283	0.603	1.584	0.033	0.188	0.930	1.477	−1.039	0.897	4.339	2.154	0.813
TRANSP. EQUIP.	(384)	−5.392	−5.045	14.793	2.664	7.773	2.701	0.391	1.946	−1.792	2.101	1.248	0.756	−1.379	3.981	3.285	−2.032	0.184
MISC. MANUF.	(38A)	−3.998	6.593	6.940	0.088	10.094	−3.913	0.246	3.574	7.796	1.518	1.169	7.237	−0.507	1.424	5.642	3.517	5.544
Total traded		0.334	3.896	3.557	0.819	3.438	3.706	0.837	1.095	1.606	0.618	0.184	3.177	1.369	1.863	2.516	1.154	0.660
Nontraded goods																		
MIN. & QUARRY.	(2)	3.366	−3.800	−0.027	0.263	−1.790	−0.342	−0.010	0.338	0.390	−0.336	−0.039	−2.158	−0.584	1.520	0.415	−0.351	0.651
ELEC., GAS, & WATER	(4)	−0.160	−3.897	−1.266	−0.426	−2.060	−3.217	−0.719	−0.529	−1.314	−0.247	0.042	−1.189	−1.233	−1.208	−1.724	−1.016	−0.107
CONSTRUCTION	(5)	0.342	−2.090	−3.871	0.148	−0.866	−2.308	−0.339	−0.815	−0.610	−0.501	−0.149	−0.354	−0.417	−0.603	−1.059	−0.687	−0.239
WHOLE. & RET. TRADE	(6)	−0.338	−3.071	−2.431	−0.345	−1.813	−2.460	−0.702	−0.592	−1.594	−0.859	−0.144	−1.462	−0.875	−1.030	−1.328	−0.876	−0.372
TRANSP., STOR., & COMM.	(7)	−0.080	−1.831	−0.764	−0.197	−1.105	−1.266	−0.367	−0.461	−0.676	−0.203	−0.080	−1.065	−0.537	−0.484	−0.643	−0.455	−0.048
FIN., INS., & REAL EST.	(8)	−0.388	−4.249	−2.068	−0.580	−2.011	−3.481	−0.794	−1.327	−2.016	−0.636	−0.288	−1.700	−1.230	−1.376	−1.803	−1.025	−0.468
COMM., SOC., & PERS. SERV.	(9)	−0.239	−2.825	−1.758	−0.347	−1.690	−2.611	−0.432	−0.956	−1.353	−0.495	−0.048	−1.533	−0.800	−1.012	−1.292	−0.831	−0.416
Total nontraded		−0.132	−2.818	−1.725	−0.291	−1.599	−2.406	−0.520	−0.789	−1.251	−0.569	−0.112	−1.324	−0.785	−0.901	−1.247	−0.788	−0.327
Total, all industries		−0.000	−0.000	−0.000	−0.000	−0.000	−0.000	−0.000	−0.000	−0.000	−0.000	−0.000	−0.000	−0.000	−0.000	−0.000	−0.000	−0.000

Table 4.8 (continued)

Industry	(ISIC)	US	ARG	BRZ	CHL	COL	GRC	HK	IND	ISR	SK	MEX	POR	SNG	SP	TWN	TRK	YUG
Traded goods																		
AGR., FOR., & FISH.	(1)	1.560	0.580	0.275	8.024	0.386	0.161	0.903	0.017	0.897	−0.284	0.268	0.038	3.123	0.198	−0.002	0.065	0.237
FOOD, BEV., & TOB.	(310)	0.061	0.973	0.636	−1.123	−0.066	0.118	−3.132	0.572	−1.122	0.093	−0.186	−0.001	−3.384	0.363	2.967	−0.001	0.047
TEXTILES	(321)	0.747	−1.088	−0.143	6.615	−0.254	0.006	−2.130	−0.195	−1.101	0.025	−1.359	0.057	−2.266	−0.213	−0.043	−0.519	0.386
WEARING APPAREL	(322)	−1.333	5.357	0.060	5.700	0.619	1.967	2.046	4.650	0.977	5.909	0.257	3.095	5.096	0.671	5.557	1.307	1.278
LEATHER PROD.	(323)	−1.837	−4.436	−0.917	−16.821	0.054	−7.600	17.534	−4.853	10.782	0.282	−0.519	0.374	−12.128	−0.030	−0.631	−5.589	−1.027
FOOTWEAR	(324)	−0.802	7.749	0.843	−3.032	1.084	1.381	2.847	3.228	0.895	6.597	−0.022	1.509	5.194	1.871	6.250	−0.000	1.296
WOOD PROD.	(331)	−0.062	0.557	−0.125	−7.302	0.054	−0.080	−1.776	0.027	−0.562	−1.407	−0.667	−0.271	−1.431	−0.171	−0.082	−0.060	−0.338
FURN. & FIXT.	(332)	−0.005	2.486	−0.044	4.101	0.344	−0.263	0.100	0.841	0.215	6.511	0.064	−0.389	3.084	0.277	7.944	0.013	0.151
PAPER & PAPER PROD.	(311)	0.096	−0.693	−0.383	−11.776	−1.309	0.064	−2.735	−0.122	−0.744	−1.078	−0.537	−0.793	−0.943	−0.230	−0.692	−0.092	0.920
PRINT. & PUBL.	(312)	−0.022	−0.179	−0.170	−12.880	−0.411	−0.116	−0.638	−0.072	−0.100	−0.202	−0.128	−0.231	−0.234	0.154	−0.321	−0.056	0.003
CHEMICALS	(35A)	0.416	−0.797	−0.935	0.345	−1.855	0.210	−0.513	0.144	0.204	−1.752	0.233	0.394	1.217	−0.048	1.444	0.106	0.200
PETROL. & REL. PROD.	(35B)	0.102	−0.376	−0.186	−6.758	0.282	−0.389	−2.440	0.023	−1.511	0.677	−0.943	−0.363	−0.129	−0.223	0.688	−0.248	−1.148
RUBBER PROD.	(355)	−0.570	−0.286	−0.527	11.951	−2.609	0.223	−1.306	0.039	−0.267	−0.075	−0.041	0.286	0.969	0.258	−0.887	−0.088	0.134
NONMETAL. MIN. PROD.	(36A)	−0.683	−0.312	−0.180	2.291	−0.414	0.049	−1.419	−0.108	−0.155	0.076	−0.281	−0.326	0.350	−0.101	−0.148	−0.011	−0.062
GLASS & GLASS PROD.	(362)	0.153	−0.196	−0.180	−13.020	−0.754	0.142	−1.782	0.044	−0.396	−0.399	−0.216	0.031	0.388	−0.036	0.330	−0.011	−0.099
IRON & STEEL	(371)	−0.258	−3.181	−0.923	−51.970	−6.306	−0.610	−2.537	−0.429	−1.329	−2.632	−0.837	0.973	−1.585	−0.400	−6.959	−0.183	−0.907
NONFERROUS METALS	(372)	−0.384	−7.430	−1.875	7.007	−12.396	−1.710	−4.083	−1.450	−2.008	−8.770	−2.079	2.515	−1.645	−0.596	−5.359	−1.039	−1.634
METAL PROD.	(381)	0.067	0.077	−0.085	−111.724	0.591	0.113	0.573	0.398	0.716	2.153	0.587	−0.017	2.051	0.187	4.153	0.005	0.509
NONELEC. MACH.	(382)	0.238	−0.270	−0.199	−31.463	0.021	−0.087	−1.604	−0.034	−0.210	−0.042	−0.954	−0.409	−0.235	−0.218	0.379	−0.045	−0.356
ELEC. MACH.	(383)	0.525	−0.214	−0.159	−225.257	−0.051	0.122	0.258	0.264	0.331	1.886	0.689	0.021	1.223	0.032	1.710	−0.009	0.335
TRANSP. EQUIP.	(384)	0.402	0.169	−0.017	−28.788	−0.319	0.171	0.073	0.071	0.262	0.507	0.198	−0.105	0.761	0.162	0.448	−0.015	0.257
MISC. MANUF.	(38A)	−0.414	−0.024	−0.172	−4.164	0.424	0.126	−0.428	2.517	0.359	3.510	−0.083	0.772	1.792	0.143	3.267	−0.009	0.158
Total traded		0.179	0.077	0.169	−2.987	0.137	0.097	0.212	0.025	0.097	0.111	0.116	0.236	0.891	0.151	0.162	0.024	0.033
Nontraded goods																		
MIN. & QUARRY.	(2)	−0.034	−0.701	−0.328	−9.836	0.212	−0.564	−0.653	−0.001	−2.061	1.036	−1.596	−0.525	−0.227	−0.358	0.989	−0.403	−1.437
ELEC., GAS & WATER	(4)	−0.115	−0.434	−0.333	9.000	−0.623	−0.175	−0.568	−0.168	−0.043	−0.631	−0.275	−0.314	−0.416	−0.204	−0.695	−0.120	−0.077
CONSTRUCTION	(5)	0.025	0.024	−0.089	−5.898	0.143	−0.120	−0.064	−0.044	0.101	0.245	−0.085	−0.355	−0.474	−0.095	0.422	−0.042	0.089
WHOLE. & RET. TRADE	(6)	0.072	−0.249	−0.299	8.854	−0.523	−0.152	−0.435	−0.168	−0.002	−0.513	−0.214	−0.312	−0.436	−0.185	−0.501	−0.111	0.041
TRANSP., STOR., & COMM.	(7)	−0.040	−0.216	−0.182	5.957	−0.286	0.125	−0.282	−0.110	0.008	−0.350	−0.165	−0.251	−0.350	−0.129	−0.362	−0.068	0.021
FIN., INS., & REAL EST.	(8)	−0.081	−0.305	−0.243	10.084	−0.457	−0.115	−0.347	−0.146	−0.004	−0.577	−0.145	−0.244	−0.279	−0.152	−0.636	−0.075	0.039
COMM., SOC., & PERS. SERV.	(9)	−0.061	0.164	−0.075	−1.424	0.077	−0.105	−0.137	−0.038	0.027	0.033	−0.101	−0.240	−0.310	−0.077	0.087	−0.046	0.034
Total nontraded		−0.061	−0.047	−0.194	1.895	−0.169	−0.132	−0.298	−0.095	−0.039	−0.211	−0.190	−0.282	−0.368	−0.140	−0.220	−0.073	−0.022
Total, all industries		−0.000	−0.000	−0.000	−0.000	−0.000	−0.000	−0.000	−0.000	0.000	−0.000	−0.000	−0.000	−0.000	−0.000	−0.000	−0.000	0.000

Conclusion

We have examined in this chapter the economic effects of reductions in tariffs and NTBs negotiated in the Tokyo Round as well as the possible effects of the NTB codes that were negotiated. We have also analyzed the economic effects of complete elimination of the tariffs that will remain once the Tokyo Round reductions have been fully implemented.

The calculations based on our model suggested that the Tokyo Round negotiations will have small but beneficial overall effects on trade, prices, and economic welfare in the United States and in practically all other major industrialized countries. Employment will change by small amounts in various sectors, industries, and countries, but the total labor-market dislocation will be negligible for all countries. There will be small gains for some but not all developing countries. There are also many aspects of the Tokyo Round, particularly in the NTB codes, that could not be quantified but may be important. By the same token, from the standpoint of developing countries, important NTBs were left intact in the Tokyo Round. The Tokyo Round may thus be of limited significance to some developing countries and for many it may be detrimental.

If post-Tokyo Round tariffs in the major industrialized countries were to be eliminated, our findings are that the exports of these countries would increase by 3.7% over 1976 levels, there would be relatively small gross-employment effects in the United States and Japan and somewhat larger effects in the European Economic Community especially (which might signal some adjustment difficulties in particular sectors), economic welfare would increase in the United States and Japan but decline in the EEC except for Ireland, Italy, the Netherlands, and the United Kingdom, the US dollar and other major currencies would depreciate somewhat, and consumer prices would fall to a small extent in the United States but to a much greater extent in most other industrialized countries. The effects on the major developing countries would in general be comparatively small. It should be emphasized that these results are based on the assumption that existing NTBs are left unchanged. If both tariffs and NTBs were to be eliminated, the effects would be significantly larger and presumably much more beneficial to the developing countries.

It should be emphasized that the foregoing conclusions must be interpreted in the light of the particular model that we have constructed, the behavioral parameters that determine the responses involved, and the available data.

We should mention finally that we have abstracted from the domestic political environment in the United States and other countries. This environment has a great bearing on the nature and determinants of changes in trade policies. Our model has the merit of identifying the particular sectors that may expand or contract in response to policy changes. Accordingly, results such as those presented can help to shape policy options for trade liberalization and the associated measures that may be implemented domestically to facilitate adjustment within or between sectors.

5 Effects of Tariffs and Exchange Rates on the Structure of Protection in the United States and Other Major Industrialized Countries

There has been considerable interest in the theory and measurement of the structure of protection since the mid-1960s. Most of the early theoretical work and practically all of the actual calculations of effective protection have been conducted in a partial-equilibrium framework. On the theoretical side, these early developments have been followed by more rigorous and complete theoretical examination of the general-equilibrium properties of effective protection, and much of the partial-equilibrium analysis has been questioned on grounds of ignoring interactions and feedback effects among different sectors in an economy. At the same time, substantial efforts have also been devoted to the construction of computational general-equilibrium models for different countries for the purpose of analyzing changes in government policies including tariffs. It is somewhat surprising, therefore, that these more sophisticated computational models have been used comparatively so little in measuring the levels of protection arising from the structure of tariffs and changes in exchange rates.[1] In this chapter we use our own computational model for these purposes in order to assess the empirical significance of pre- and post-Tokyo Round tariffs and exchange-rate changes on the structure of protection.[2]

Treating tariffs in this context is imporant also when we consider how a country's trading partners may be affected by the instruments of protection. That is, tariffs themselves can represent a significant international disturbance or a means of transmitting the effects of a domestic disturbance abroad. For precisely this reason, a proper measure of the effects of protection should encompass foreign as well as domestic tariffs, and we shall provide such a measure. Further, exchange-rate movements—both those that are induced by other protective devices and those that are used deliberately as instruments of protection—should be accounted for in the assessment of protection internationally.

Following Corden (1966, p. 22), the level of protection afforded by the structure of tariffs may be defined as "the percentage increase in value added per unit in an economic activity which is made possible by the tariff structure." Our computational model is designed specifically to analyze the effects of tariff changes and so can be used to compute the effects of removal or imposition of a particular set of tariffs. In the previous chapter, we focused attention on the economic effects of changes in tariffs and NTBs negotiated in the Tokyo Round. But our model also solves for effects on prices and is therefore well suited to the measurement of value added. We can therefore use our model's computation of the change in per unit value added to measure the effects of the structure of protection across sectors for the major industrialized countries of the world.

In what follows, we first discuss some conceptual issues regarding the measurement of effective protection. The simple partial-equilibrium formula that has most often been used for this purpose is shown to be inadequate for general-equilibrium reasons and in addition because of the only moderate degree of substitution between imports and home-produced goods that appears to characterize behavior in international trade.[3] Our computational model, which incorporates both of these considerations, can therefore give a more realistic indication of the degree to which industries are protected.

Problems of definition remain, however, since one can examine tariff changes under a variety of assumptions about which tariffs are allowed to change and whether exchange rates are allowed to adjust in response. We therefore proceed to evaluate and compare measures of protection afforded by the structure of tariffs under both fixed and flexible exchange-rate regimes and for both unilateral and multilateral changes in tariffs. In all cases our experiment consists of assuming complete elimination of the pre-Tokyo Round 1976 tariffs and using our model to work out the resulting effects on per unit value added by country and industry. Results are then reported with their signs reversed to indicate what would have been the effects of imposing the 1976 structure starting from a zero base. These measures of the 1976 structure of protection are compared with both nominal tariffs and a partial-equilibrium measure of effective protection for the following selected countries: Canada, West Germany, Japan, the Netherlands, and the United States.

The role that exchange rates play in determining the structure of protection is partially indicated by the comparison of fixed and flexible rate estimates to be noted. We then also look at this issue more directly by using our model to compute, for each country, the effects of a 1% exogenous devaluation. The solution, again focusing on changes in per unit value added, gives us a measure of the structure of protection that would be provided by such an exchange-rate change.

Using this same methodology, the remainder of this chapter is devoted to analysis of the structure of protection in the United States and abroad as it was altered by reductions in tariffs and selected NTBs negotiated in the Tokyo Round. In this connection, we also examine how our measures of protection correspond to alternative specifications of our data inputs and assumed technology and to a number of economic variables and other characteristics of our model, including the resource flows that are calculated directly by the model.

Conceptual Framework

To proceed more formally, let us define the value added per unit of an activity that produces a good j as

$$v_j = p_j^O - \sum_{i=1}^{n} a_{ij} p_i^I, \tag{5.1}$$

where v_j is value added per unit in production of good j, p_j^O is the price that producers receive for their output of good j, p_i^I is the price they must pay for intermediate inputs of good i, and a_{ij} is the number of units of good i used in producing one unit of good j. Our objective is to calculate the change in this variable—that is, the "change in per unit value added" (CPVA)—that will result from the implementation or change of some measure of protection. From (5.1), in proportional terms, this is

$$\text{CPVA}_j \equiv \frac{\Delta v_j}{v_j} = \left(\frac{1}{1 - \sum_{i=1}^{n} b_{ij}}\right)\left[\frac{\Delta p_j^O}{p_j^O} - \sum_{i=1}^{n} b_{ij} \frac{\Delta p_i^I}{p_i^I}\right], \tag{5.2}$$

where

$$b_{ij} = \frac{p_i^I a_{ij}}{p_j^O} \tag{5.3}$$

is the share of input i in the value of production of a unit of good j. The changes (Δs) in equation (5.2) can refer to the results of any protective policy one wishes to examine. Most often, they refer to the results of implementing an entire structure of tariffs, starting from a base of free trade. But they could just as easily be used to measure the effects of changing particular tariffs or groups of tariffs, installing or removing a system of nontariff barriers, or changing the exchange rate.

Calculation of all of the price changes that appear on the right-hand side of (5.2) would normally be very difficult, though, of course, that is what our computational model is designed to do. In most previous studies of the structure of protection, however, the problem has been considerably simplified by assuming that all traded goods are infinitely elastically supplied at given world prices p_i^W. It follows, for imported goods, that the domestic prices p_i^D of both outputs and inputs are given by the world price plus the tariff. For ad valorem tariffs τ_i, this gives us

$$p_i^D = (1 + \tau_i)p_i^W. \tag{5.4}$$

The price changes that result when these tariffs are levied, starting from tariffs of zero, are just the tariffs themselves, since the world prices are constant. Equation (5.2) then provides the following simpler measure of protection:

$$\mathrm{ERP}_j \equiv \frac{\Delta v_j}{v_j} = \frac{\tau_j - \sum_{i=1}^{n} b_{ij}\tau_i}{1 - \sum_{i=1}^{n} b_{ij}}. \tag{5.5}$$

This is the formula used by Corden (1966) and many others to measure the protection due to a tariff structure. For convenience, we shall use the term "effective rate of protection" to refer only to this simple calculation, and reserve the term "change in per unit value added," or CPVA, for the more accurate measure of protection defined in (5.2).[4]

As our derivation of (5.5) indicates, and as Corden himself acknowledges, the validity and usefulness of (5.5) depend upon a number of assumptions, of which the following three will be of particular interest to us here:[5]

1. Goods are infinitely elastically supplied or demanded on world markets, so that tariff-exclusive prices are independent of the tariffs themselves.
2. Exchange rates are held constant.
3. Foreign tariffs are either constant or irrelevant.

Each of these assumptions plays an identifiable role in causing differences between ERP and CPVA. Since the assumptions noted are important for interpreting the results to be presented, it is useful to review them in more detail.

Exogeneity of Tariff-Exclusive Prices

For this to be true, two further assumptions are necessary. First, the country must be sufficiently small, as a participant in world markets, so that its changes in supply and demand do not affect world prices. For some countries this may be approximately true, but for the United States it most certainly is not. Thus, if the United States were to levy tariffs and consequently reduce its demand for imports, the world prices in affected sectors would fall and the US domestic price would not rise by the full amount of the tariff. The precise implication of this phenomenon for calculation of protection in (5.2) depends upon how the country's importance to world markets is distributed among outputs and inputs. But we would expect in general that by dampening the domestic price changes that occur, country size would tend to reduce somewhat the levels of protection.

The second assumption needed for price exogeneity is that domestic and foreign goods are perfect substitutes. If they are not, then even if the price of an import rises by the full amount of the tariff, the price of a corresponding domestic good will not. Thus imperfect substitutability will further dampen the price changes in (5.2) and reduce levels of protection below what would be calculated by the ERP.

Imperfect substitutability is also what warrants the distinction we made in (5.1) and (5.2) between input and output prices. Outputs are, by definition, domestically produced, while inputs will in general come from both imported and domestic sources. If the two are imperfect substitutes, with the prices of domestic goods varying by less than the prices of imports as just suggested, then the prices of outputs will also vary by less than the prices of inputs. When, as we impose a structure of tariffs, all are tending to rise, this means that the positive term in (5.2) is dampened by more than the negative terms, and the level of effective protection is reduced algebraically compared with (5.5).

All prices are endogenous in our computational model. World prices are determined simultaneously by the interaction of all countries together, and no country is assumed ex ante to be small. Further, domestic and traded goods are distinct, with finite elasticities of substitution between them based on empirically estimated import elasticities. Thus from what we have said so far, we would expect our calculations of CPVA based on (5.2) to be both smaller in absolute value and more often negative than the effective rate of protection based on the Corden formula (5.5)

Exogeneity of Exchange Rates

While Corden defined effective protection under the assumption of a fixed exchange rate, he recognized the inevitability of an eventual exchange-rate change in response to the imposition or elimination of a complete structure of tariffs. He thus suggested a simple adjustment of all effective rates to take this into account. Such an ad hoc procedure is not necessary for us here, since our computational model can be solved for endogenous exchange rates along with everything else. Nor need the effect of the exchange-rate change be quite so trivial as it was for Corden, since different sectors can be affected differently by exchange rates in our model.[6]

In general terms, both we and Corden expect exchange-rate adjustment to alter the protection calculation as follows. When a country imposes tariffs in most industries, its trade balance is expected to improve. If the exchange rate is flexible, its currency will appreciate to restore equilibrium, and this will reduce the domestic prices of both imports and exports, leading to negative protection in those sectors that were least protected by the tariffs themselves. Thus, exchange-rate flexibility reduces and makes more negative our measures of CPVA based on (5.2) as compared with analogous rates based on fixed currency values. Naturally, the opposite is true of the CPVA due to a general tariff reduction rather than an increase.

Exogeneity of Foreign Tariffs

There is nothing in the concept of effective protection that limits it to a country's own tariffs, though these are obviously the only policies that can be taken into account in the simplified formula (5.5). Industries also experience protective and antiprotective effects from the tariffs levied by other countries, and one might want to include them with own-country tariffs in a complete analysis of the structure of protection worldwide. Whether to do so is largely a matter of choice, depending less on economic reasoning than on the question one wishes to answer. But given that tariffs today are almost never reduced unilaterally, but only by multilateral negotiation, the world view is clearly the most appropriate.

Presumably a country's own tariffs tend to protect its industries and foreign tariffs tend to play the opposite role. Therefore, we expect levels of protection to be even smaller and more negative when allowance is made for foreign tariffs. It thus appears that the modifications of the simple analysis that we have discussed here—endogenizing prices and exchange rates and allowing for foreign tariffs—all tend to reduce, either absolutely or algebraically, the levels of protection that we should expect.

Traded versus Nontraded Goods

The treatment of nontraded goods has always been a source of difficulty in calculations of effective protection. The problem is that the prices of nontraded goods are not pegged to any world prices as in equation (5.4). Corden (1966) describes two alternative procedures for handling them, neither of which is wholly satisfactory. One alternative is to include them with the traded inputs in both summations of equation (5.5), letting their tariffs in the numerator be zero. This would be valid only if the nontraded goods were themselves infinitely elastically supplied, so that their prices would be unaffected by the tariffs on traded goods. Since this is manifestly implausible, especially if the nontraded goods are themselves produced with traded inputs, Corden prefers the second alternative of including nontraded goods with value added, and thus excluding them from both summations in (5.5). This second alternative, which differs from the first only in the denominator, leaves us with no clear idea of which sectors are actually being protected by the levels of effective protection that we measure.

An important advantage of using our computational model to estimate protection via (5.2) instead of (5.5) is that none of this difficulty arises. From the model we have estimates of how all prices are affected by tariffs, and these include the prices of nontraded goods. Thus, we can include nontraded with traded goods in calculating (5.2), and the results refer clearly to the protection of value added actually employed directly in each sector. Protection of value added in nontraded sectors is handled in the same way.

Using the simple formula (5.5) to estimate effective protection of nontraded sectors, one would of course find their levels of protection to be negative. This results from the rise in the prices of traded inputs that are used in the nontraded sectors. In a general-equilibrium context, however, this can be reversed. Tariffs on most tradable goods, especially if levied by all countries at once, tend to act like a consumption tax on tradables, raising their prices relative to nontradables. As demanders substitute toward nontradables their prices also tend to rise, and since the output price in (5.2) gets a larger weight than even the combined prices of the inputs, the nontradables in general may be protected positively. This phenomenon, that tariffs may afford positive protection to nontradable industries, is an important implication of a general-equilibrium model that deserves to be studied further.

The Structure of Pre-Tokyo Round Tariff Protection

In this section we report the results of three experiments, each designed to measure the structure of protection due to the pre-Tokyo Round tariffs that existed in 1976. Results are reported in columns (3)–(5) of tables 5.1–5.5 for five representative countries: Canada, West Germany, Japan, the Netherlands, and the United States.[7]

All three of these columns contain values calculated from equation (5.2) for the various industries and countries, with price changes determined by

Table 5.1
Protection measures in Canada

Industry	(ISIC)	(1) Nominal tariffs		(2) Effective protection (Corden)		(3) Change in value added (fixed-own) (%)		(4) Change in value added (flex-own) (%)		(5) Change in value added (flex-all) (%)	
		Level	Rank	Level	Rank	Level	Rank	Level	Rank	Level	Rank
Traded goods											
AGR., FOR., & FISH.	(1)	3.4	19	3.5	19	0.24	14	−0.04	19	−3.08	28
FOOD, BEV., & TOB.	(310)	6.9	14	11.8	12	−0.12	21	−0.14	20	−0.02	19
TEXTILES	(321)	18.9	4	35.5	4	0.40	12	0.32	11	0.50	8
WEARING APPAREL	(322)	25.4	1	41.4	2	0.87	6	0.84	4	0.52	6
LEATHER PROD.	(323)	8.2	12	9.6	15	−4.91	29	−5.37	29	−2.59	26
FOOTWEAR	(324)	24.5	2	45.4	1	0.42	11	0.39	10	0.19	12
WOOD PROD.	(331)	5.8	17	7.3	16	−0.87	23	−1.16	23	−0.63	23
FURN. & FIXT.	(332)	19.4	3	35.9	3	0.04	18	−0.03	18	−0.13	20
PAPER & PAPER PROD.	(341)	11.8	8	19.7	6	−1.03	24	−1.25	24	−0.95	24
PRINT. & PUBL.	(342)	5.7	18	6.3	18	0.50	8	0.46	8	0.53	4
CHEMICALS	(35A)	7.9	13	12.5	11	1.15	3	0.91	3	0.51	7
PETROL. & REL. PROD.	(35B)	0.2	22	−1.5	27	−0.15	22	−0.24	22	−0.01	18
RUBBER PROD.	(355)	12.2	7	16.6	8	1.80	1	1.65	1	1.56	1
NONMETAL. MIN. PROD.	(36A)	9.5	10	15.6	10	0.49	9	0.30	12	0.27	11
GLASS & GLASS PROD.	(362)	11.3	9	16.4	9	0.91	4	0.78	6	0.81	2
IRON & STEEL	(371)	6.7	15	10.9	14	−0.06	20	−0.20	21	0.06	16
NONFERROUS METALS	(372)	2.0	21	1.8	20	−3.96	28	−4.33	28	−2.72	27
METAL PROD.	(381)	14.1	5	25.2	5	1.19	2	1.10	2	0.75	3
NONELEC. MACH.	(382)	6.1	16	6.4	17	−1.41	25	−1.67	25	−1.19	25
ELEC. MACH.	(383)	12.9	6	19.1	7	0.91	5	0.83	5	0.52	5
TRANSP. EQUIP.	(384)	2.4	20	−4.0	28	−1.64	27	−1.94	26	−3.37	29
MISC. MANUF.	(38A)	8.8	11	11.0	13	0.73	7	0.48	7	−0.27	21
Average traded		7.7		11.0		−0.11		−0.29		−0.92	

Nontraded goods									
MIN. & QUARRY.	(2)	−1.1	26	−1.45	26	−2.09	27	−0.49	22
ELEC., GAS, & WATER	(4)	−0.2	21	0.33	13	0.26	13	0.33	10
CONSTRUCTION	(5)	−7.2	29	0.00	19	0.01	17	0.01	17
WHOLE. & RET. TRADE	(6)	−1.0	25	0.14	15	0.14	14	0.14	13
TRANSP., STOR., & COMM.	(7)	−0.7	24	0.11	16	0.07	15	0.11	14
FIN., INS., & REAL EST.	(8)	−0.3	22	0.48	10	0.43	9	0.49	9
COMM., SOC., & PERS. SERV.	(9)	−0.5	23	0.07	17	0.07	16	0.07	15
Average nontraded		−1.8		0.07		−0.01		0.16	
Average, all industries		2.0		0.01		−0.10		−0.17	

Table 5.2
Protection measures in West Germany

Industry	(ISIC)	(1) Nominal tariffs		(2) Effective protection (Corden)		(3) Change in value added (fixed-own) (%)		(4) Change in value added (flex-own) (%)		(5) Change in value added (flex-all) (%)	
		Level	Rank	Level	Rank	Level	Rank	Level	Rank	Level	Rank
Traded goods											
AGR., FOR., & FISH.	(1)	7.5	12	9.5	14	1.97	1	1.63	1	0.12	9
FOOD, BEV., & TOB.	(310)	13.4	2	27.1	2	−0.75	20	−0.75	18	−0.23	15
TEXTILES	(321)	10.3	5	14.9	8	−3.69	29	−4.27	29	−2.58	28
WEARING APPAREL	(322)	16.8	1	28.3	1	1.60	2	1.37	2	0.29	6
LEATHER PROD.	(323)	5.1	18	−0.7	24	−2.17	28	−2.74	28	−0.89	21
FOOTWEAR	(324)	11.7	3	19.8	4	0.77	3	0.63	3	0.32	4
WOOD PROD.	(331)	3.9	19	3.6	19	−0.08	15	−0.48	16	0.05	12
FURN. & FIXT.	(332)	8.5	10	13.1	9	−1.19	23	−1.51	22	−1.61	25
PAPER & PAPER PROD.	(341)	7.1	13	10.6	12	0.56	4	0.13	7	0.74	1
PRINT. & PUBL.	(342)	3.3	20	3.1	20	0.08	13	−0.05	12	0.12	8
CHEMICALS	(35A)	11.6	4	19.9	3	−1.11	22	−1.71	23	−2.27	26
PETROL. & REL. PROD.	(35B)	1.8	22	4.6	17	0.34	6	0.05	10	0.57	2
RUBBER PROD.	(355)	5.7	16	4.5	18	−0.25	17	−0.75	19	−0.74	20
NONMETAL. MIN. PROD.	(36A)	5.4	17	8.1	15	0.10	11	−0.07	13	−0.03	14
GLASS & GLASS PROD.	(362)	10.2	7	14.9	7	−0.20	16	−0.45	15	−0.33	17
IRON & STEEL	(371)	6.3	15	10.3	13	−1.32	26	−1.84	24	−0.93	22
NONFERROUS METALS	(372)	2.3	21	2.6	21	−0.89	21	−1.39	21	−0.25	16
METAL PROD.	(381)	8.0	11	12.2	10	0.32	7	0.06	9	−0.50	19
NONELEC. MACH.	(382)	6.6	14	8.1	16	−1.35	27	−1.87	26	−1.20	23
ELEC. MACH.	(383)	10.2	6	15.0	6	−0.38	18	−0.66	17	−1.25	24
TRANSP. EQUIP.	(384)	9.9	8	15.6	5	−1.28	25	−1.91	27	−2.83	29
MISC. MANUF.	(38A)	9.1	9	11.8	11	−1.26	24	−1.87	25	−2.51	27
Average traded		8.6		13.4		−0.60		−1.00		−1.05	

Nontraded goods									
MIN. & QUARRY.	(2)	−1.0	27	−0.63	19	−1.35	20	−0.38	18
ELEC., GAS, & WATER	(4)	−0.3	23	0.11	10	−0.10	14	−0.00	13
CONSTRUCTION	(5)	−5.0	29	0.28	8	0.35	5	0.30	5
WHOLE. & RET. TRADE	(6)	−1.5	28	0.08	14	0.06	8	0.07	10
TRANSP., STOR., & COMM.	(7)	−0.8	26	0.09	12	0.04	11	0.07	11
FIN., INS., & REAL EST.	(8)	−0.2	22	0.53	5	0.51	4	0.53	3
COMM., SOC., & PERS. SERV.	(9)	−0.7	25	0.24	9	0.24	6	0.25	7
Average nontraded		−1.8		0.20		0.15		0.20	
Average, all industries		5.8		−0.20		−0.42		−0.43	

Table 5.3
Protection Measures in Japan

Industry	(ISIC)	(1) Nominal tariffs		(2) Effective protection (Corden)		(3) Change in value added (fixed-own) (%)		(4) Change in value added (flex-own) (%)		(5) Change in value added (flex-all) (%)	
		Level	Rank	Level	Rank	Level	Rank	Level	Rank	Level	Rank
Traded goods											
AGR., FOR., & FISH.	(1)	18.4	2	27.7	3	2.62	1	2.10	1	1.87	1
FOOD, BEV., & TOB.	(310)	25.4	1	51.1	1	−0.67	27	−0.47	18	−0.34	18
TEXTILES	(321)	3.3	14	0.8	16	−0.80	28	−1.47	27	−0.74	24
WEARING APPAREL	(322)	13.8	4	27.1	4	0.74	3	0.47	3	−0.20	14
LEATHER PROD.	(323)	3.0	15	−10.2	29	−0.55	26	−1.30	26	−0.46	21
FOOTWEAR	(324)	16.4	3	33.6	2	0.47	5	0.30	5	0.13	6
WOOD PROD.	(331)	0.3	21	−4.8	28	−0.49	25	−0.74	20	−0.59	22
FURN. & FIXT.	(332)	7.8	6	15.1	5	−0.00	19	0.07	9	0.06	9
PAPER & PAPER PROD.	(341)	2.1	17	2.2	15	0.01	18	−0.47	17	−0.25	15
PRINT. & PUBL.	(342)	0.2	22	−0.9	24	0.06	14	−0.01	11	0.02	11
CHEMICALS	(35A)	6.2	10	9.8	10	0.61	4	−0.75	21	−0.70	23
PETROL. & REL. PROD.	(35B)	2.8	16	9.4	11	2.05	2	0.85	2	1.66	2
RUBBER PROD.	(355)	1.5	18	−0.4	21	−0.37	24	−0.92	24	−1.03	25
NONMETAL. MIN. PROD.	(36A)	0.6	20	−0.0	18	−0.05	21	−0.30	16	−0.26	16
GLASS & GLASS PROD.	(362)	7.5	7	11.5	8	0.07	12	−0.13	14	−0.14	13
IRON & STEEL	(371)	3.3	13	4.8	14	−1.09	29	−3.01	29	−1.45	28
NONFERROUS METALS	(372)	1.1	19	0.5	17	0.05	16	−1.14	25	−0.30	17
METAL PROD.	(381)	6.9	9	12.0	7	0.09	10	−0.10	13	−0.37	19
NONELEC. MACH.	(382)	9.1	5	13.8	6	−0.17	22	−0.84	22	−0.43	20
ELEC. MACH.	(383)	7.4	8	11.0	9	−0.02	20	−0.73	19	−1.31	26
TRANSP. EQUIP.	(384)	6.0	12	8.6	12	−0.29	23	−1.64	28	−2.39	29
MISC. MANUF.	(38A)	6.0	11	8.1	13	0.40	7	−0.87	23	−1.33	27
Average traded		8.4		13.2		0.18		−0.57		−0.54	

Nontraded goods									
MIN. & QUARRY.	(2)	−0.9	25	0.42	6	−0.18	15	0.22	4
ELEC., GAS, & WATER	(4)	−0.4	20	0.07	11	−0.06	12	−0.01	12
CONSTRUCTION	(5)	−3.2	27	0.06	15	0.20	6	0.16	5
WHOLE. & RET. TRADE	(6)	−2.3	26	0.10	9	0.09	7	0.08	7
TRANSP., STOR., & COMM.	(7)	−0.6	23	0.07	13	0.05	10	0.05	10
FIN., INS., & REAL EST.	(8)	−0.2	19	0.39	8	0.34	4	0.34	3
COMM., SOC., & PERS. SERV.	(9)	−0.6	22	0.04	17	0.07	8	0.07	8
Average nontraded		−1.8		0.14		0.14		0.14	
Average, all industries		4.9		0.16		−0.18		−0.16	

Table 5.4
Protection measures in the Netherlands

Industry	(ISIC)	(1) Nominal tariffs		(2) Effective protection (Corden)		(3) Change in value added (fixed-own) (%)		(4) Change in value added (flex-own) (%)		(5) Change in value added (flex-all) (%)	
		Level	Rank	Level	Rank	Level	Rank	Level	Rank	Level	Rank
Traded goods											
AGR., FOR., & FISH.	(1)	6.6	14	7.9	14	−4.95	25	−2.83	25	−5.70	28
FOOD, BEV., & TOB.	(310)	13.0	2	26.8	2	−2.15	21	−1.82	22	−1.32	22
TEXTILES	(321)	11.8	4	18.1	5	−17.31	29	−15.54	29	−12.84	29
WEARING APPAREL	(322)	16.8	1	27.2	1	−2.85	23	−1.90	23	−4.20	25
LEATHER PROD.	(323)	5.2	17	−0.5	24	−7.63	28	−5.77	28	−2.54	24
FOOTWEAR	(324)	11.2	5	18.3	4	−1.21	14	−0.56	20	−1.28	20
WOOD PROD.	(331)	3.6	20	3.2	19	0.74	1	1.59	1	2.19	2
FURN. & FIXT.	(332)	8.5	10	12.9	10	−0.14	11	0.70	6	0.77	6
PAPER & PAPER PROD.	(341)	8.4	11	13.2	9	−1.35	16	−0.22	16	0.60	10
PRINT. & PUBL.	(342)	3.5	21	3.1	20	−0.14	10	0.08	14	0.20	15
CHEMICALS	(35A)	11.9	3	20.4	3	−5.25	27	−3.61	27	−4.35	27
PETROL. & REL. PROD.	(35B)	1.0	22	1.5	21	−0.50	12	0.15	13	0.74	8
RUBBER PROD.	(355)	6.1	16	4.9	18	−1.37	17	−0.54	19	−0.44	18
NONMETAL. MIN. PROD.	(36A)	4.4	18	6.2	17	0.27	9	1.07	3	1.14	5
GLASS & GLASS PROD.	(362)	9.3	8	13.3	8	−4.34	24	−2.58	24	−2.17	23
IRON & STEEL	(371)	7.1	13	11.8	11	−0.58	13	0.41	11	1.26	4
NONFERROUS METALS	(372)	4.3	19	7.4	16	−1.78	20	−0.49	18	1.27	3
METAL PROD.	(381)	7.8	12	11.1	12	0.56	4	1.30	2	0.55	12
NONELEC. MACH.	(382)	6.4	15	7.5	15	−2.78	22	−1.34	21	−0.39	17
ELEC. MACH.	(383)	10.0	7	14.4	7	−1.63	19	−0.44	17	−1.30	21
TRANSP. EQUIP.	(384)	10.9	6	17.6	6	−1.61	18	−0.16	15	−1.23	19
MISC. MANUF.	(38A)	8.7	9	10.9	13	−5.17	26	−3.59	26	−4.33	26
Average traded		8.3		13.5		−2.62		−1.52		−1.80	

Nontraded goods									
MIN. & QUARRY.	(2)	−1.0	27	−1.26	15	0.70	7	2.31	1
ELEC., GAS, & WATER	(4)	−0.3	23	0.68	3	0.72	5	0.65	9
CONSTRUCTION	(5)	−4.8	29	0.30	8	0.21	12	0.17	16
WHOLE. & RET. TRADE	(6)	−1.4	28	0.54	5	0.56	8	0.57	11
TRANSP., STOR., & COMM.	(7)	−0.8	26	0.48	7	0.52	9	0.54	13
FIN., INS., & REAL EST.	(8)	−0.2	22	0.72	2	0.74	4	0.75	7
COMM., SOC., & PERS. SERV.	(9)	−0.8	25	0.49	6	0.49	10	0.50	14
Average nontraded		−1.7		0.52		0.53		0.54	
Average, all industries		4.6		−0.78		−0.32		−0.43	

Table 5.5
Protection measures in the United States

Industry	(ISIC)	(1) Nominal tariffs Level	Rank	(2) Effective protection (Corden) Level	Rank	(3) Change in value added (fixed-own) (%) Level	Rank	(4) Change in value added (flex-own) (%) Level	Rank	(5) Change in value added (flex-all) (%) Level	Rank
Traded goods											
AGR., FOR., & FISH.	(1)	2.2	18	2.1	18	0.18	12	−0.58	28	−2.56	29
FOOD, BEV., & TOB.	(310)	6.3	10	13.4	5	−0.02	27	−0.05	17	0.02	16
TEXTILES	(321)	14.4	2	28.3	2	0.14	15	−0.19	21	0.22	4
WEARING APPAREL	(322)	27.8	1	50.6	1	0.60	2	0.53	1	0.43	1
LEATHER PROD.	(323)	5.6	11	5.6	14	−0.35	29	−0.96	29	0.02	15
FOOTWEAR	(324)	8.8	5	13.1	6	0.24	6	0.19	4	0.17	5
WOOD PROD.	(331)	3.6	16	4.6	15	0.22	8	−0.16	19	0.06	9
FURN. & FIXT.	(332)	8.1	6	12.3	8	0.07	19	0.03	9	0.02	13
PAPER & PAPER PROD.	(341)	0.5	22	−1.1	28	0.01	25	−0.20	22	−0.09	24
PRINT. & PUBL.	(342)	1.1	21	1.3	20	0.04	21	−0.00	14	0.01	18
CHEMICALS	(35A)	3.8	14	5.8	13	0.23	7	−0.26	23	−0.33	26
PETROL. & REL. PROD.	(35B)	1.4	19	4.3	16	0.03	22	−0.04	16	−0.01	21
RUBBER PROD.	(355)	3.6	15	2.4	17	0.35	4	0.09	6	0.11	7
NONMETAL. MIN. PROD.	(36A)	9.1	4	15.9	4	0.39	3	0.23	3	0.29	2
GLASS & GLASS PROD.	(362)	10.7	3	16.9	3	0.19	10	−0.02	15	0.04	11
IRON & STEEL	(371)	4.7	13	7.8	11	0.10	17	−0.10	18	0.01	19
NONFERROUS METALS	(372)	1.2	20	1.0	21	0.02	23	−0.29	24	−0.01	20
METAL PROD.	(381)	7.5	8	12.7	7	0.21	9	0.02	10	−0.06	23
NONELEC. MACH.	(382)	5.0	12	6.3	12	−0.10	28	−0.51	27	−0.26	25
ELEC. MACH.	(383)	6.6	9	9.4	10	0.11	16	−0.18	20	−0.33	27
TRANSP. EQUIP.	(384)	3.3	17	1.8	19	0.16	14	−0.36	26	−0.63	28
MISC. MANUF.	(38A)	7.8	7	11.1	9	0.74	1	0.26	2	0.26	3
Average traded		5.2		8.1		0.14		−0.18		−0.35	

Nontraded goods									
MIN. & QUARRY.	(2)	−0.7	26	0.33	5	−0.33	25	−0.05	22
ELEC., GAS, & WATER	(4)	−0.2	23	0.17	13	0.06	7	0.11	8
CONSTRUCTION	(5)	−4.7	29	0.00	26	0.01	13	0.01	17
WHOLE. & RET. TRADE	(6)	−0.8	27	0.05	20	0.04	8	0.04	10
TRANSP., STOR., & COMM.	(7)	−0.5	25	0.08	18	0.02	12	0.04	12
FIN., INS., & REAL EST.	(8)	−0.1	22	0.19	11	0.11	5	0.13	6
COMM., SOC., & PERS. SERV.	(9)	−0.4	24	0.02	24	0.02	11	0.02	14
Average nontraded		−0.9		0.11		0.04		0.07	
Average, all industries		1.8		0.12		−0.03		−0.06	

our computational model. The ordinal rankings of the values within columns are also reported. In each case the experiment consisted of reducing tariffs from their 1976 levels to zero and then using the negative of the resulting price changes in equation (5.2). Since our model distinguishes production for export from production for home use, with different prices for each, our calculation is based on an appropriately weighted average of the two sectors. In order to focus attention exclusively on the structures of tariffs, all three experiments are done assuming that nontariff barriers do not exist in the industrialized countries. Our model calculates results for all 34 of the countries, with interaction among all of them taken into account. However, we have data on tariffs for only the 18 most industrialized countries, and it was therefore only for these that we analyzed the tariff structure.

For tables 5.1–5.5, column (3) for each country reports the protection due to own-country tariffs alone with fixed exchange rates for all countries; in column (4), exchange rates of all industrialized countries are allowed to fluctuate, but it is still only the own-country tariffs that are analyzed; finally, in column (5), tariffs in all 18 industrialized countries are analyzed simultaneously, so that the results indicate the protection provided by the tariff structure of the developed world as a whole—again, like column (4), with flexible exchange rates. These results are compared, in columns (1) and (2), with nominal tariffs and levels of effective protection as computed from the simplified formula (5.5).[8] For the latter, we use the first of Corden's alternatives for handling nontraded goods. That is, they are included in both summations in equation (5) but with zero tariffs.

The most noticeable feature of these results is that all of our own calculations of effective protection are an order of magnitude smaller than both the nominal tariffs and the effective tariffs calculated from the Corden formula. Also there are a great many more industries with negative protection in our calculations. We have already listed a number of reasons why we expect smaller and more negative values for protection than have traditionally been calculated, and we see now that our expectations have been borne out with a vengeance.

Of the reasons discussed, the most important—based on our model—appears to be the imperfect substitutability between domestic and foreign goods. The damping of effective protection due to country size does not appear to be significant, and the effects of exchange-rate flexibility and foreign tariffs do not appear until columns (4) and (5), while low values appear already in column (3). Since the role of imperfect substitution appears so important, it is wroth recapitulating how it works.

When tariffs are increased, they raise the prices of imports. If domestic goods were perfect substitutes for imports, their prices too would rise by the same amount. But if substitution is imperfect, an equal rise in domestic prices would leave demand unchanged while increasing supply. Equilibrium requires instead that domestic prices rise by less than import prices so as to stimulate both supply and demand by equal amounts. This smaller rise in domestic prices means that protection, as calculated from equation (5.2), is reduced from what it would be if substitution were perfect.

Note further that domestic prices are only part of what appears in the numerator of (5.2). Import prices also enter, but negatively, to the extent that imports are used as inputs. Thus imperfect substitution reduces substantially the protective effect of tariffs on output prices, but does not reduce by nearly as much the antiprotective effect of tariffs on input prices. Together these two mechanisms can account for much of the reduction in effective rates going from columns (2) to (3) in tables 5.1–5.5. Note incidentally that a more open economy will experience the antiprotective effect on input prices more severely than will an economy in which most of demand is for domestic goods. This may account for much of the negative protection measured for small countries like the Netherlands.

A related phenomenon, not mentioned so far, is the effect of tariffs on exports. If domestic and foreign goods were perfect substitutes, then a given industry could not both export and import. But with imperfect substitution such two-way trade can and does take place. Now, producers for export enjoy no increase at all in their output price when tariffs are raised and, if anything, suffer a fall in price if world markets weaken. Thus producers for export experience only antiprotective effects of tariffs. Producers for export should be included with producers for the domestic market in calculating the effects of protection, since they often draw on the same pool of resources. When the two are averaged together, as they are in the calculations we report, they account still further for the smallness of effective protection. They may also account for the largely negative rates that we get for West Germany in table 5.2, since exports in West Germany are so important.

Finally we should note that our other expectations have also been borne out. Looking at average rates of protection, we see that exchange-rate flexibility [compare columns (3) and (4)] does indeed reduce protection in all countries but the Netherlands. And allowing for foreign tariffs [compare columns (4) and (5)] reduces protection still further in all five countries. The reason for the anomalous result in the case of the Netherlands is that its currency actually depreciates when it levies tariffs, according to our model. The Netherlands is so small and open that protection mainly raises the prices of inputs to its export sectors, and worsens its balance of trade.

Regarding nontraded goods, we find that they tend to be protected positively rather than negatively in a general-equilibrium model. This is to be expected, for reasons discussed previously in the section on nontraded goods.

So far we have looked only at the levels of protection overall and have ignored the comparisons among industries that are provided by the ordinal rankings that are also reported in the tables. Yet it is precisely such comparisons that constitute the major rationale for measurements of protection. The concept is intended to indicate how resources are reallocated due to tariffs, with movement being from the lowest to the highest industries in terms of the level of protection.

If one examines the detailed rankings of industries in the tables for the particular measures of protection used, the rankings are fairly similar in most cases. Yet there are also particular examples of industries whose rankings change substantially as we move across the tables from less to more sophisticated measures of protection. Thus the use of a general-equilibrium model, as well as the complications introduced by flexible exchange rates and foreign tariffs, can have significant implications for the position in the tariff structure of particular industries. To cite some examples, agriculture (ISIC 1) in Canada changes from about average protection to nearly the most antiprotected sector when exchange rate are flexible and foreign tariffs are taken into account. This is the case as well for agriculture in the United States. In Japan, there are notable shifts in rankings for wearing apparel (ISIC 322), chemicals (ISIC 35A), and miscellaneous manufactures (ISIC 38A). In the United States, besides agriculture, textiles (ISIC 321), leather products (ISIC 324), chemicals (ISIC 35A), and metal products (ISIC 381) exhibit substantial changes in rankings. These results suggest that it is important to know exactly what environment one is dealing with in assessing whether a particular industry is being protected.

The Protective Effects of Exchange-Rate Changes

Our next experiment was to analyze the effects of a 1% devaluation for each country, assuming that the exchange rates for all other countries remain unchanged. The devaluation was treated as an exogenous change and the model was then solved for the changes in the endogenous variables. As before, we are interested in the percentage changes in value added by sector, as calculated in equation (5.2).

The effect of a devaluation will be to increase the domestic prices of exportable and important goods. This in turn will stimulate both production for exports and for the home market so that the value added can be expected to rise. There will be some offset, however, to the extent that the prices of imported intermediates will be increased as the result of the devaluation. The nontradable industries may be affected favorably insofar as they provide inputs into the expanding home and export sectors. The nontradables should also benefit by a shift in demand since they will become relatively cheaper compared with tradable goods due to the devaluation. Finally, depending upon the size of an industry in world markets, the benefits of the devaluation in terms of price changes may be diminished to some extent as world prices fall. We may expect therefore that the effects of a devaluation will be positive depending upon the degree to which an industry expands and its output is used in the expansion of other industries. The effects of a devaluation will be diminished depending upon the degree to which an industry uses imported inputs and the larger the industry is in world markets.

The results of our experiment are summarized in table 5.6. For Canada, the greatest percentage increases in value added are in mining and quarrying, leather products, nonferrous metals, wood products, transport equipment, agriculture, and paper products. For West Germany, the greatest increases are in mining and quarrying, transport equipment, chemicals, miscellaneous manufactures, textiles, leather products, and iron and steel. For Japan, the greatest increases are in iron and steel, chemicals, transport equipment, miscellaneous manufactures, nonferrous metals, leather products, and fuel products. For the Netherlands, the greatest increases are in agriculture, mining and quarrying, leather products, glass products, textiles, chemicals, and miscellaneous manufactures. Finally, for the United States, the greatest increases are in agriculture, leather products, mining and quarrying, transport equipment, chemicals, miscellaneous manufactures, and nonelectric machinery. The effects on the other sectors in each of the countries can of course be gauged from the rankings indicated in the table. By the same token, if we had assumed an appreciation of the exchange rate, the effects would be the opposite of those shown.

If we compare the results in table 5.6 with those for the individual countries in tables 5.1–5.5, there is of course a similarity with our second experiment, in which each country was assumed to impose its tariff structure and permit its exchange rate to adjust to restore the initial trade balance. In the country tables, the industries with the highest numerical rankings had the least protection or the greatest antiprotection. These are the industries generally that are stimulated the most by the assumed devaluations whose effects are summarized in table 5.6. Presumably, if tariff removal were coupled with exchange-rate flexibility, the industries with the least protec-

Table 5.6
Protection due to 1% devaluation

Industry	(ISIC)	(1) Canada		(2) West Germany		(3) Japan		(4) Netherlands		(5) U.S.	
		Level	Rank	Level	Rank	Level	Rank	Level	Rank	Level	Rank
Traded goods											
AGR., FOR., & FISH.	(1)	0.90	6	0.50	13	0.26	14	1.43	1	0.59	1
FOOD, BEV., & TOB.	(310)	0.05	26	0.01	27	−0.11	29	0.22	22	0.03	25
TEXTILES	(321)	0.26	18	0.91	5	0.47	8	1.12	5	0.26	9
WEARING APPAREL	(322)	0.05	25	0.29	20	0.15	17	0.62	14	0.04	22
LEATHER PROD.	(323)	1.60	2	0.90	6	0.52	6	1.27	3	0.54	2
FOOTWEAR	(324)	0.07	24	0.20	22	0.10	20	0.34	21	0.02	26
WOOD PROD.	(331)	0.98	4	0.63	12	0.18	15	0.58	15	0.31	8
FURN. & FIXT.	(332)	0.22	20	0.50	14	−0.05	27	0.58	16	0.04	23
PAPER & PAPER PROD.	(341)	0.86	7	0.66	11	0.32	13	0.78	12	0.17	13
PRINT. & PUBL.	(342)	0.11	23	0.19	23	0.04	22	0.15	23	0.03	24
CHEMICALS	(35A)	0.81	10	0.94	3	0.91	2	1.12	6	0.38	5
PETROL. & REL. PROD.	(35B)	0.31	15	0.40	17	0.51	7	0.44	20	0.05	20
RUBBER PROD.	(355)	0.50	12	0.78	10	0.37	11	0.56	17	0.20	12
NONMETAL. MIN. PROD.	(36A)	0.61	11	0.27	21	0.16	16	0.53	18	0.12	17
GLASS & GLASS PROD.	(362)	0.43	14	0.39	18	0.14	18	1.20	4	0.16	14
IRON & STEEL	(371)	0.45	13	0.82	7	1.33	1	0.67	13	0.16	15
NONFERROUS METALS	(372)	1.30	3	0.79	9	0.82	5	0.88	10	0.26	10
METAL PROD.	(381)	0.31	16	0.40	16	0.12	19	0.49	19	0.15	16
NONELEC. MACH.	(382)	0.86	8	0.80	8	0.43	10	0.98	9	0.31	7
ELEC. MACH.	(383)	0.27	17	0.43	15	0.45	9	0.82	11	0.22	11
TRANSP. EQUIP.	(384)	0.93	5	0.97	2	0.88	3	0.99	8	0.40	4
MISC. MANUF.	(38A)	0.82	9	0.94	4	0.84	4	1.07	7	0.37	6
Average traded		0.60	18	0.61	5	0.49	8	0.74	5	0.25	9

Nontraded goods											
MIN. & QUARRY.	(2)	2.16	1	1.10	1	0.34	12	1.34	2	0.50	3
ELEC., GAS, & WATER	(4)	0.22	19	0.32	19	0.09	21	0.03	24	0.08	18
CONSTRUCTION	(5)	−0.02	29	−0.10	29	−0.09	28	−0.06	29	−0.01	29
WHOLE. & RET. TRADE	(6)	0.02	27	0.02	25	0.01	25	0.01	27	0.01	27
TRANSP., STOR., & COMM.	(7)	0.13	22	0.08	24	0.01	24	0.02	25	0.05	21
FIN., INS., & REAL EST.	(8)	0.17	21	0.02	26	0.01	23	0.02	26	0.06	19
COMM., SOC., & PERS. SERV.	(9)	0.00	28	0.00	28	−0.03	26	0.00	28	−0.00	28
Average nontraded		0.27	28	0.07	28	−0.00	26	0.01	28	0.06	28
Average, all industries		0.37	18	0.34	5	0.22	8	0.31	5	0.11	9

tion would expand the most and those with the greatest protection would expand the least. Assuming that there are not other distortions in the economies, these changes would foster an improved allocation of resources among the industries.

The Effects of the Tokyo Round on the Structure of Protection

In the first part of this chapter, we analyzed the effects of pre-Tokyo Round tariff protection on the structure of protection in the United States and other selected industrial countries. We now turn to analysis of the effects of the Tokyo Round on the structure of protection. For this purpose, we used the same data on nominal tariffs as in the preceding chapter. These tariff rates are shown in columns (1) and (4) of tables 5.7–5.9 for the United States, the EEC, and Japan.[9] Along with these changes in tariffs, we also consider the changes in agricultural concessions and the liberalization of government procurement which were negotiated in the Tokyo Round.

Levels of the effective rate of protection based upon equation (5.5) for the pre- and post-Tokyo Round are shown in the columns (2) and (5) of tables 5.7–5.9, together with the sector rankings. These calculations include nontraded goods in both summations in (5), but with zero tariffs.

In columns (3) and (6) of tables 5.7–5.9 we report the "change in per unit value added" (CPVA) for the pre- and post-Tokyo Round based upon our model, using equation (5.2). These calculations were obtained by reducing the tariffs from their given levels to zero and then using the negative of the resulting price changes in equation (5.2) to calculate the CPVAs by sector. The calculations in column (6) reflect as well the agricultural concessions and liberalization of government procurement. Since the results in columns (3) and (6) are based upon a full model solution, they take into account all of the interactions both within the among all 34 of the countries in the model.

We have already seen that our model calculations of CPVA are an order of magnitude smaller than the nominal tariffs and the simple effective tariffs based upon the Corden formula. Also, there are many more sectors with negative protection in our calculations. We discussed earlier several reasons why we expect smaller and more negative values for our measure of protection than have traditionally been calculated. The most important of these reasons, based on our model, appears to be the imperfect substitutability between domestic and foreign goods.

Finally, in columns (7) to (9) of tables 5.7–5.9, we report the *changes* due to the Tokyo Round in nominal tariffs, simple effective tariffs based on equation (5.5), and our model calculations of CPVA based on equation (5.2). The

Table 5.7
Protection measures in the United States: percentage levels and changes in protection[a]

Industry	(ISIC)	Pre-Tokyo Round			Post-Tokyo Round			Change due to Tokyo Round		
		(1) Nominal tariffs	(2) Effective rate of protection (Corden)	(3) CPVA (change per unit value added)	(4) Nominal tariffs	(5) Effective rate of protection (Corden)	(6) CPVA (change per unit value added)	(7) Nominal tariffs	(8) Effective rate of protection (Corden)	(9) CPVA (change per unit value added)
Traded goods										
AGR., FOR., & FISH.	(1)	2.20(18)	2.09(18)	−1.96(29)	1.80(17)	1.91(18)	−0.21(27)	−0.40(4)	−0.18(12)	1.74(1)
FOOD, BEV., & TOB.	(310)	6.30(10)	13.41(5)	−0.01(20)	4.70(7)	10.16(4)	−0.05(24)	−1.60(12)	−3.26(22)	−0.04(23)
TEXTILES	(321)	14.40(2)	28.33(2)	0.12(5)	9.20(2)	18.02(2)	0.16(3)	−5.20(22)	−10.31(29)	0.04(7)
WEARING APPAREL	(322)	27.80(1)	50.63(1)	0.14(4)	22.70(1)	43.30(1)	0.12(5)	−5.10(21)	−7.33(28)	−0.02(21)
LEATHER PROD.	(323)	5.60(11)	5.62(14)	0.11(6)	4.20(9)	4.95(12)	0.30(1)	−1.40(10)	−0.67(16)	0.19(2)
FOOTWEAR	(324)	8.80(5)	13.14(6)	0.06(9)	8.80(3)	15.37(3)	0.07(7)	0.0 (1)	2.23(1)	0.01(13)
WOOD PROD.	(331)	3.60(16)	4.58(15)	0.10(7)	1.70(18)	1.72(19)	0.05(9)	−1.90(14)	−2.86(20)	−0.05(26)
FURN. & FIXT.	(332)	8.10(6)	12.33(8)	0.02(14)	4.10(11)	5.52(11)	−0.01(22)	−4.00(19)	−6.81(26)	−0.04(22)
PAPER & PAPER PROD.	(341)	0.50(22)	−1.14(28)	−0.02(23)	0.20(22)	−0.86(28)	0.00(14)	−0.30(3)	0.27(4)	0.03(9)
PRINT. & PUBL.	(342)	1.10(21)	1.32(20)	−0.00(18)	0.70(21)	0.90(20)	0.00(15)	−0.40(5)	−0.43(14)	0.00(15)
CHEMICALS	(35A)	3.80(14)	5.76(13)	−0.24(26)	2.40(16)	3.66(15)	−0.12(26)	−1.40(11)	−2.11(18)	0.12(4)
PETROL. & REL. PROD.	(35B)	1.40(19)	4.27(16)	−0.02(22)	1.40(19)	4.69(13)	−0.00(20)	0.0 (2)	0.42(3)	0.02(11)
RUBBER PROD.	(355)	3.60(15)	2.37(17)	0.15(3)	2.50(14)	1.95(16)	0.15(4)	−1.10(9)	−0.42(13)	0.00(16)
NONMETAL. MIN. PROD.	(36A)	9.10(4)	15.93(4)	−0.31(1)	5.30(5)	9.23(6)	0.18(2)	−3.80(18)	−6.70(25)	−0.13(28)
GLASS & GLASS PROD.	(362)	10.70(3)	16.87(3)	0.08(8)	6.20(4)	9.77(5)	0.03(11)	−4.50(20)	−7.10(27)	−0.04(24)
IRON & STEEL	(371)	4.70(13)	7.81(11)	0.04(12)	3.60(12)	6.18(9)	0.05(10)	−1.10(8)	−1.63(17)	0.01(14)
NONFERROUS METALS	(372)	1.20(20)	1.03(21)	0.03(13)	0.70(20)	0.50(21)	0.05(8)	−0.50(6)	−0.53(15)	0.02(10)
METAL PROD.	(381)	7.50(8)	12.70(7)	−0.02(21)	4.80(6)	7.86(7)	−0.01(21)	−2.70(16)	−4.84(23)	0.01(12)
NONELEC. MACH.	(382)	5.00(12)	6.25(12)	−0.16(25)	3.30(13)	4.06(14)	−0.08(25)	−1.70(13)	−2.20(19)	0.08(6)
ELEC. MACH.	(383)	6.60(9)	9.38(10)	−0.26(27)	4.40(8)	6.34(8)	−0.22(28)	−2.20(15)	−3.04(21)	0.03(8)
TRANSP. EQUIP.	(384)	3.30(17)	1.80(19)	−0.43(28)	2.50(15)	1.94(17)	−0.28(29)	−0.80(7)	0.14(8)	0.15(3)
MISC. MANUF.	(38A)	7.80(7)	11.11(9)	0.34(1)	4.20(10)	5.79(10)	0.11(6)	−3.60(17)	−5.32(24)	−0.23(29)
Average		5.22	8.11	−0.25	3.59	5.75	−0.06	−1.63	−2.36	0.19

Table 5.7 (continued)

Industry	(ISIC)	Pre-Tokyo Round (1) Nominal tariffs	(2) Effective rate of protection (Corden)	(3) CPVA (change per unit value added)	Post-Tokyo Round (4) Nominal tariffs	(5) Effective rate of protection (Corden)	(6) CPVA (change per unit value added)	Change due to Tokyo Round (7) Nominal tariffs	(8) Effective rate of protection (Corden)	(9) CPVA (change per unit value added)
Nontraded goods										
MIN. & QUARRY.	(2)		−0.70(26)	−0.09(24)		−0.47(26)	0.02(12)		0.23(5)	0.10(5)
ELEC.,GAS, & WATER	(4)		−0.20(23)	0.50(10)		−0.16(23)	0.01(13)		0.04(11)	−0.05(25)
CONSTRUCTION	(5)		−4.69(29)	−0.01(19)		−2.88(29)	−0.02(23)		1.81(2)	−0.01(17)
WHOLE. & RET. TRADE	(6)		−0.77(27)	0.02(15)		−0.55(27)	0.00(16)		0.21(6)	−0.02(20)
TRANSP., STOR., & COMM.	(7)		−0.52(25)	0.01(16)		−0.35(25)	−0.00(18)		0.17(7)	−0.02(19)
FIN., INS., & REAL EST.	(8)		−0.14(22)	0.05(11)		−0.09(22)	−0.00(19)		0.05(10)	−0.05(27)
COMM., SOC., & PERS. SERV.	(9)		−0.41(24)	0.01(17)		−0.28(24)	−0.00(17)		0.13(9)	−0.01(18)
Average			−0.71	0.02		−0.47	−0.00		0.24	−0.02
Average, all goods			1.19	−0.04		0.87	−0.01		−0.32	0.03

a. Numbers in parentheses are column ranks. Averages shown are weighted using value added.

Table 5.8
Protection measures in the European Economic Community: percentage levels and changes in protection[a]

Industry	(ISIC)	Pre-Tokyo Round			Post-Tokyo Round			Change due to Tokyo Round		
		(1) Nominal tariffs	(2) Effective rate of protection (Corden)	(3) CPVA (change per unit value added)	(4) Nominal tariffs	(5) Effective rate of protection (Corden)	(6) CPVA (change per unit value added)	(7) Nominal tariffs	(8) Effective rate of protection (Corden)	(9) CPVA (change per unit value added)
Traded goods										
AGR., FOR., & FISH.	(1)	7.10(13)	6.18(17)	−0.44(18)	4.86(12)	4.10(17)	−0.53(22)	−2.24(14)	−2.08(14)	−0.09(23)
FOOD, BEV., & TOB.	(310)	12.44(2)	20.96(2)	−0.20(14)	10.06(3)	17.83(3)	−0.07(13)	−2.38(16)	−3.13(21)	0.13(8)
TEXTILES	(321)	9.78(8)	11.42(11)	−1.52(28)	7.17(8)	8.79(10)	−1.14(29)	−2.62(18)	−2.63(17)	0.38(3)
WEARING APPAREL	(322)	16.77(1)	23.49(1)	−0.50(19)	13.37(1)	19.26(2)	−0.41(19)	−3.40(21)	−4.23(26)	0.09(11)
LEATHER PROD.	(323)	3.65(18)	1.35(21)	−0.70(22)	2.01(21)	−2.19(28)	−1.07(28)	−1.63(8)	−3.54(23)	−0.37(28)
FOOTWEAR	(324)	11.67(3)	17.90(4)	−0.74(23)	11.63(2)	20.08(1)	−0.64(24)	−0.04(2)	2.17(1)	0.10(10)
WOOD PROD.	(331)	3.31(19)	2.00(20)	0.38(3)	2.51(18)	1.68(20)	0.11(6)	−0.79(4)	−0.32(10)	−0.27(27)
FURN. & FIXT.	(332)	8.50(9)	18.20(3)	−0.83(24)	5.60(9)	11.30(8)	−0.52(21)	−2.90(19)	−6.90(29)	0.31(5)
PAPER & PAPER PROD.	(341)	7.32(12)	11.13(12)	0.54(1)	5.37(11)	8.29(12)	0.11(7)	−1.95(10)	−2.85(20)	−0.43(29)
PRINT. & PUBL.	(342)	3.23(20)	−0.64(22)	0.07(11)	2.06(20)	−1.03(26)	0.09(10)	−1.17(5)	−0.39(11)	0.02(15)
CHEMICALS	(35A)	11.49(4)	17.00(5)	−0.88(25)	7.95(5)	11.71(6)	−0.67(25)	−3.55(22)	−5.29(27)	0.20(7)
PETROL. & REL. PROD.	(35B)	1.16(22)	3.11(19)	0.37(4)	1.16(22)	3.39(18)	0.11(8)	0.0 (1)	0.28(4)	−0.26(26)
RUBBER PROD.	(355)	5.28(16)	3.76(18)	−0.63(20)	3.54(17)	2.29(19)	−0.52(20)	−1.74(9)	−1.47(12)	0.10(9)
NONMETAL. MIN. PROD.	(36A)	5.19(17)	8.95(15)	0.03(12)	3.66(16)	6.52(15)	0.02(11)	−1.53(6)	−2.43(16)	−0.01(16)
GLASS & GLASS PROD.	(362)	9.89(7)	15.30(7)	−0.29(17)	7.70(7)	12.16(5)	−0.20(17)	−2.19(13)	−3.14(22)	0.09(12)
IRON & STEEL	(371)	6.21(15)	15.43(6)	−0.25(15)	4.67(14)	11.59(7)	−0.18(15)	−1.54(7)	−3.84(25)	0.08(13)
NONFERROUS METALS	(372)	2.56(21)	9.92(14)	0.07(10)	2.13(19)	8.29(11)	−0.04(12)	−0.43(3)	−1.63(13)	−0.11(24)
METAL PROD.	(381)	7.88(10)	10.75(13)	−0.26(16)	5.46(10)	7.07(13)	−0.19(16)	−2.42(17)	−3.68(24)	0.07(14)
NONELEC. MACH.	(382)	6.45(14)	7.35(16)	−0.88(26)	4.37(15)	4.71(16)	−0.57(23)	−2.07(12)	−2.64(18)	0.31(4)

Table 5.8 (continued)

Industry	(ISIC)	Pre-Tokyo Round (1) Nominal tariffs	Pre-Tokyo Round (2) Effective rate of protection (Corden)	Pre-Tokyo Round (3) CPVA (change per unit value added)	Post-Tokyo Round (4) Nominal tariffs	Post-Tokyo Round (5) Effective rate of protection (Corden)	Post-Tokyo Round (6) CPVA (change per unit value added)	Change due to Tokyo Round (7) Nominal tariffs	Change due to Tokyo Round (8) Effective rate of protection (Corden)	Change due to Tokyo Round (9) CPVA (change per unit value added)
ELEC. MACH.	(383)	9.92(6)	13.51(9)	−0.66(21)	7.89(6)	10.79(9)	−0.40(18)	−2.03(11)	−2.72(19)	0.26(6)
TRANSP. EQUIP.	(384)	10.23(5)	14.65(8)	−1.38(27)	7.95(4)	12.31(4)	−0.99(26)	−2.27(15)	−2.34(15)	0.39(2)
MISC. MANUF.	(38A)	7.70(11)	12.13(10)	−1.88(29)	4.67(13)	6.55(14)	−1.02(27)	−3.03(20)	−5.58(28)	0.86(1)
Average		8.82	11.63	−0.54	6.09	8.82	−0.42	−2.14	−2.81	0.13
Nontraded goods										
MIN. & QUARRY.	(2)		−0.72(24)	−0.10(13)		−0.51(22)	−0.14(14)		0.22(5)	−0.04(18)
ELEC., GAS, & WATER	(4)		−0.80(25)	0.20(7)		−0.61(23)	0.14(4)		0.19(9)	−0.05(21)
CONSTRUCTION	(5)		−4.10(29)	0.21(6)		−2.96(29)	0.17(3)		1.14(2)	−0.04(20)
WHOLE. & RET. TRADE	(6)		−1.76(28)	0.26(5)		−1.37(27)	0.20(2)		0.39(3)	−0.06(22)
TRANSP., STOR., & COMM.	(7)		−0.94(27)	0.12(9)		−0.74(25)	0.09(9)		0.20(7)	−0.03(17)
FIN., INS., & REAL EST.	(8)		−0.66(23)	0.45(2)		−0.46(21)	0.34(1)		0.19(8)	−0.11(25)
COMM., SOC., & PERS. SERV.	(9)		−0.83(26)	0.18(8)		−0.61(24)	0.13(5)		0.21(6)	−0.04(19)
Average			−1.41	0.22		−1.05	0.17		0.36	−0.06
Average, all goods			2.68	−0.02		2.05	−0.02		−0.63	0.00

a. Numbers in parentheses are column ranks. Averages shown are weighted using value added.

Protection measures in Japan: percentage levels and changes in protection[a]

Industry	(ISIC)	Pre-Tokyo Round			Post-Tokyo Round			Change due to Tokyo Round		
		(1) Nominal tariffs	(2) Effective rate of protection (Corden)	(3) CPVA (change per unit value added)	(4) Nominal tariffs	(5) Effective rate of protection (Corden)	(6) CPVA (change per unit value added)	(7) Nominal tariffs	(8) Effective rate of protection (Corden)	(9) CPVA (change per unit value added)
Traded goods										
AGR., FOR., & FISH.	(1)	18.40(2)	21.17(4)	0.86(1)	18.40(2)	21.40(4)	0.77(1)	0.0 (1)	0.23(14)	−0.08(26)
FOOD, BEV., & TOB.	(310)	25.40(1)	49.80(2)	−0.18(20)	25.40(1)	50.31(1)	−0.14(20)	0.0 (2)	0.51(7)	0.03(10)
TEXTILES	(321)	3.30(14)	−3.55(24)	−0.37(24)	3.30(12)	−2.41(24)	−0.39(24)	0.0 (3)	1.14(2)	−0.02(18)
WEARING APPAREL	(322)	13.80(4)	41.62(3)	−0.13(18)	13.80(4)	42.20(3)	−0.09(16)	0.0 (4)	0.58(4)	0.04(9)
LEATHER PROD.	(323)	3.00(15)	−15.56(28)	−0.05(16)	3.00(13)	−14.75(28)	−0.12(19)	0.0 (5)	0.81(3)	−0.07(24)
FOOTWEAR	(324)	16.40(3)	51.99(1)	0.06(4)	15.70(3)	50.02(2)	−0.02(13)	−0.70(14)	−1.98(21)	−0.08(27)
WOOD PROD.	(331)	0.30(21)	−30.94(29)	−0.32(22)	0.30(21)	−30.59(29)	−0.27(22)	0.0 (6)	0.35(11)	0.05(8)
FURN. & FIXT.	(332)	7.80(6)	16.45(5)	0.03(8)	5.10(7)	10.26(5)	0.00(10)	−2.70(19)	−6.18(27)	−0.02(20)
PAPER & PAPER PROD.	(341)	2.10(17)	1.22(15)	−0.04(14)	2.10(16)	1.75(14)	−0.05(14)	0.0 (7)	0.53(6)	−0.00(14)
PRINT. & PUBL.	(342)	0.20(22)	−1.58(23)	−0.01(12)	0.10(22)	−1.51(23)	−0.01(12)	−0.10(9)	0.07(17)	0.01(11)
CHEMICALS	(35A)	6.20(10)	8.69(11)	−0.04(13)	4.80(8)	6.39(11)	−0.11(17)	−1.40(15)	−2.31(22)	−0.07(25)
PETROL. & REL. PROD.	(35B)	2.80(16)	5.21(13)	0.51(2)	2.20(15)	4.14(13)	0.17(2)	−0.60(13)	−1.08(20)	−0.34(29)
RUBBER PROD.	(355)	1.50(18)	−5.17(27)	−0.78(26)	1.10(18)	−4.99(27)	−0.60(25)	−0.40(11)	0.18(16)	0.18(3)
NONMETAL. MIN. PROD.	(36A)	0.60(20)	−0.92(19)	−0.16(19)	0.50(20)	−0.54(19)	−0.11(18)	−0.10(10)	0.38(10)	0.05(7)
GLASS & GLASS PROD.	(362)	7.50(7)	12.02(9)	−0.05(15)	5.10(6)	8.10(7)	−0.07(15)	−2.40(18)	−3.92(25)	−0.02(19)
IRON & STEEL	(371)	3.30(13)	4.77(14)	−0.48(25)	2.80(14)	4.34(12)	−0.65(27)	−0.50(12)	−0.43(19)	−0.17(28)
NONFERROUS METALS	(372)	1.10(19)	1.18(16)	−0.08(17)	1.10(19)	1.73(15)	0.09(4)	0.0 (8)	0.55(5)	0.17(4)
METAL PROD.	(381)	6.90(9)	12.52(7)	−0.33(23)	5.20(5)	9.23(6)	−0.23(21)	−1.70(17)	−3.29(24)	0.10(6)
NONELEC. MACH.	(382)	9.10(5)	15.57(6)	−0.23(21)	4.40(10)	6.74(9)	−0.27(23)	−4.70(22)	−8.83(29)	−0.04(22)
ELEC. MACH.	(383)	7.40(8)	12.49(8)	−1.10(28)	4.30(11)	6.73(10)	−0.86(28)	−3.10(20)	−5.76(26)	0.24(2)
TRANSP. EQUIP.	(384)	6.00(12)	8.42(12)	−1.73(29)	1.50(17)	0.03(16)	−1.58(29)	−4.50(21)	−8.39(28)	0.15(5)
MISC. MANUF.	(38A)	6.00(11)	10.00(10)	−0.87(27)	4.60(9)	7.30(8)	−0.62(26)	−1.40(16)	−2.70(23)	0.25(1)
Average		9.70	13.28	−0.22	8.28	10.88	−0.20	−1.41	−2.40	0.02

Table 5.9 (continued)

Industry	(ISIC)	Pre-Tokyo Round (1) Nominal tariffs	(2) Effective rate of protection (Corden)	(3) CPVA (change per unit value added)	Post-Tokyo Round (4) Nominal tariffs	(5) Effective rate of protection (Corden)	(6) CPVA (change per unit value added)	Change due to Tokyo Round (7) Nominal tariffs	(8) Effective rate of protection (Corden)	(9) CPVA (change per unit value added)
Nontraded goods										
MIN. & QUARRY.	(2)		−1.49(22)	0.06(5)		−0.99(22)	0.01(9)		0.50(9)	−0.05(23)
ELEC., GAS, & WATER	(4)		−1.11(21)	−0.00(11)		−0.79(21)	−0.00(11)		0.33(12)	−0.00(15)
CONSTRUCTION	(5)		−5.07(26)	0.06(6)		−3.64(25)	0.06(5)		1.43(1)	0.00(12)
WHOLE. & RET. TRADE	(6)		−0.59(18)	0.04(7)		−0.39(18)	0.03(6)		0.21(15)	−0.00(17)
TRANSP., STOR., & COMM.	(7)		−1.04(20)	0.02(10)		−0.54(20)	0.02(7)		0.50(8)	0.00(13)
FIN., INS., & REAL EST.	(8)		−0.21(17)	0.16(3)		−0.16(17)	0.14(3)		0.05(18)	−0.03(21)
COMM., SOC., & PERS. SERV.	(9)		−3.96(25)	0.02(9)		−3.69(26)	0.02(8)		0.27(13)	−0.00(16)
Average			−2.09	0.05		−1.72	0.04		0.38	−0.01
Average, all goods			3.11	−0.04		2.55	−0.04		−0.57	0.00

a. Numbers in parentheses are column ranks. Averages shown are weighted using value added.

calculations in column (9) are of most immediate interest since they provide an indication of which sectors will tend to expand or contract relatively in response to the tariff reductions and NTB concessions that were negotiated among the major industrialized countries.

Thus, in the United States, the largest percentage increases in value added due to the Tokyo Round were recorded in agriculture, leather products, transport equipment, chemicals, and mining and quarrying, while the largest percentage declines were in miscellaneous manufactures, nonmetallic minerals, finance, insurance, and real estate, wood products, and electricity, gas, and water. For the EEC, the largest percentage increases in value added due to the Tokyo Round were in miscellaneous manufactures, transport equipment, textiles, nonelectric machinery, and furniture and fixtures, and the largest declines in paper and paper products, leather products, wood products, petroleum and related products, and finance, insurance, and real estate. For Japan, the largest increases were in miscellaneous manufactures, electrical machinery, rubber products, nonferrous metals, and transport equipment, and the largest declines in petroleum and related products, iron and steel, footwear, agriculture, and chemicals.

In order to make comparisons involving the columns in these tables, we calculated both simple and rank correlations for each pair of columns in each table. Based on these correlations, which are not reported here, it does not seem to matter very much whether one uses nominal tariffs or effective tariffs to measure protection. The two are highly correlated for each group of columns. On the other hand, our measure of CPVA is generally not significantly correlated with either of the other two measures of protection. Thus, one needs something like the approach based on our model in order correctly to evaluate the positions of individual sectors due to protection or changes therein. Otherwise, the effects of general equilibrium and imperfect substitution are not taken into account. Corden's simple formula does not even provide a poor approximation for this purpose.

The similarity of pre- and post-Tokyo Round structures of protection also is apparent from the correlations, regardless of how protection is measured. This can be seen by comparing columns (1) and (4), (2) and (5), and (3) and (6). Likewise, the change in protection due to the Tokyo Round is for the most part strongly negatively correlated with the levels of protection, again regardless of how both are measured. This is evident by comparing columns (1) and (4) with (7), (2) and (5) with (8), and (3) and (6) with (9). Thus, the effects of the Tokyo Round were in the direction of undoing the protection that previously existed, but were not strong enough to cause the overall pattern of protection to change significantly.

Besides calculating the effects of the Tokyo Round as just noted, we made several additional calculations of interest. These involved alternative measures of CPVA, correlation analysis designed to explain the nature of tariff reductions in the Tokyo Round, evaluation of indicators of resource pull, some further comparisons of the structures of protection in the pre- and post-Tokyo Round, and the effects of the Tokyo Round on the developing countries. Let us consider each of these in turn.

Alternative Measures of CPVA

Our basic measure of the CPVA due to the Tokyo Round is calculated from our model assuming simultaneous changes in both tariffs and quantifiable NTBs in all (developed) countries at once. Also, our basic solution assumes a technology of fixed coefficients among intermediate inputs. In order to investigate the importance of these assumptions, we conducted alternative runs of the model in which we calculated CPVA for tariff changes only, for own-country tariff and NTB changes only, and for a version of the model with a Cobb-Douglas technology. The results were as follows.

For most developed countries, it made little difference whether the tariff and NTB changes for all countries were accounted for or only the own-country effects were calculated. This may be a surprise, since one might expect the effects of foreign tariff reductions to be quite different from one's own. The reason that this is not the case is that the patterns of tariff reduction were quite similar in most countries. This means that foreign tariff reductions do tend to offset the effects of domestic ones, but in the same industries, thus merely dampening their effects and not changing their pattern very much.[10] This pattern of correlated tariff reductions may bear out earlier observations of previous negotiations, namely, that trade liberalization has usually been balanced, presumably in order to avoid major industry dislocation.

Further, it does not seem to matter very much for the structure of protection whether negotiated changes in NTBs are or are not included in calculating the effects of the Tokyo Round. All correlations between the two sets of results are large and quite significant except for Norway and Sweden, where correlations are negative, and to a lesser extent Finland, Switzerland, and Mexico. These are all countries where NTB concessions were substantial, especially compared with country size.

Finally, the introduction of a Cobb-Douglas technology into the model in place of fixed coefficients made virtually no difference for the results, especially in the major industrialized countries.[11] Both simple and rank correlations were above 0.90 and highly significant for CPVA measures from the two runs, except in a few developing countries.

Explanations of the Pattern of Changes in Tariffs and Protection

We correlated both nominal tariff changes and CPVA with a number of variables that we thought might help to explain *why* tariffs were reduced as they were in the Tokyo Round. The ideas here stem from the recent interest in the political economy of protection. Ideally, policymakers and their constituents understand the economy well enough so that it is the actual *effects* of protection that guide their lobbying and policy choices. These effects are what we try to capture in our CPVA measure. However, if either our measure is inaccurate or, more likely, if policymakers are unable to perceive where true economic interest lies, then they may view nominal tariffs as the more appropriate indicator of protection, and it is this that will be correlated with the variables explaining protection.

One problem here is that the variables we look at are likely to influence both the level of protection and its change. Thus, for example, import penetration seems a likely source of protectionist pressure, and this could show up as small Tokyo Round tariff reductions and hence a large protective effect of the Tokyo Round. On the other hand, this same import penetration would also account for high pre-Tokyo Round tariffs and, if in general tariffs are reduced by some across-the-board proportion, would also show up as large tariff reductions and a small or negative protective effect. Therefore, we do not know a priori whether a determinant of protection will show up in our results as a large or as a small protective effect due to the Tokyo Round. Our results are important in indicating the pattern of changes that are likely to have occurred, but they do not tell us anything about the validity or otherwise of various political theories of protection.

A final problem with the interpretation of these correlations concerns the mechanism of causation. The CPVA is calculated endogenously in our model and depends on everything in it. It is not at all an exogenous indicator of the results of the Tokyo Round negotiations. Thus it may be, as we have found before, that virtually *any* pattern of tariff reductions will tend to benefit traded sectors at the expense of nontraded ones, and thus give us a positive correlation between CPVA and import or export shares independently of whether the negotiations in fact favored sectors with large trade shares. Again, our results telling who has benefited are valid. But whether this benefit was the deliberate outcome of the political process or instead a built-in economic effect of the way an economy responds to trade liberalization, we cannot say.

With these remarks as caveats, let us turn now to our findings. The patterns we report are based on correlations that were run between pairs of variables, both for individual countries and industries, across groups of countries and industries, and overall.

Initial Tariffs: As just explained, an across-the-board tariff reduction would reduce large tariffs the most, and a harmonization formula (for example, the Swiss formula) should have this effect to an even greater extent. When we correlated nominal tariff changes with initial (pre-Tokyo Round) nominal tariff levels, this was confirmed. That is, the correlation between the two was negative and significant, although not terribly large. Thus, tariffs in the Tokyo Round were in fact reduced the most in those sectors where they were initially highest.[12] Interestingly, this relation does *not* carry over to the estimated effects of the Tokyo Round as measured by the CPVA. Here the only significant correlations are positive, but these are few enough so as not to be particularly meaningful. Thus, it appears that initial tariffs are a poor guide to the protective effects that actually occurred as the general-equilibrium implications of the Tokyo Round worked themselves out.

Initial Protection: When we correlated CPVA due to the Tokyo Round with the CPVA due to initial tariffs, we did find a strong relation. The simple correlation is negative and significant (−0.61). Previously protected sectors appear therefore to be the greatest losers from the Tokyo Round. It may well be that this result is the automatic bias in favor of traded goods that we normally observe for trade liberalization. Presumably those sectors that were initially the most protected were also rather lightly involved with trade as a result.

Trade Shares: We correlated both tariff changes and CPVA due to the Tokyo Round with various import and export shares. Since trade shares are zero for nontraded sectors and since tariff changes were zero for the developing countries, the only meaningful correlations here are those for the traded sectors of the developed countries. We looked first at each sector's share of its country's imports and exports. We found nothing significant for import shares, yet small but significant correlations with export shares. The latter were negative for tariff changes, but positive for CPVA. This indicates that tariffs tended to be reduced most in sectors with large export shares, but that these sectors were also the most likely to benefit from reductions overall. This suggests that it is not really the country's own tariff reductions that are providing the benefit here, but rather those of its trading partners.

We have already seen how the tariff changes tend to be correlated across countries, so this makes some sense. The failure of the import shares to show a significant correlation is somewhat surprising, given our expectation of benefits from relying on trade. Indeed when nontraded sectors are included, the correlation does become positive and significant, making it clear that traded sectors benefit more than nontraded ones, but within the traded-sector group we find no such relation.

Looking at countries' shares of *world* exports and imports by sector, similar results were found. No significant correlations appeared for import shares, but significant correlations were noted for export shares of world markets. Again though, they are small and of opposite sign for tariff changes and CPVA. These indicate that tariff reductions were largest where they were also presumably the least meaningful, that is, in those sectors and countries with the most dominant export positions in world markets. Furthermore, since the benefits of general trade liberalization go substantially to exporters, it is the dominant export sectors and countries that benefit the most.

Net Exports: We also looked for correlations with net export positions, and found results that parallel those for exports just discussed.

Final Demand Shares: In light of the observation that tariffs are highest on final goods and lowest on primary and semiprocessed goods, we might then expect some relation between our results and the shares of final demand in total demand by industry. However, we did not find anything significant here either, except for a slight tendency for tariffs to be reduced most in sectors with large final demand shares. Thus, we find no evidence that protection has become any more or less cascaded against imports of final goods as the result of the Tokyo Round.

Labor Shares: To see whether the Tokyo Round favored labor-intensive industries, we correlated tariff changes and CPVA with shares of labor in both value added and gross output. Nothing meaningful was found.

Employment: As another check on the connection between protection and labor, we correlated our results with employment, both levels and shares. While nothing much significant was found, the results had one odd feature. Simple correlations were not significant, but in several instances rank correlations, though small, were. These rank correlations show some evidence, admittedly weak, that tariffs were reduced most in those sectors where both employment levels and shares were large, while at the same time the Tokyo Round had its most beneficial effects, measured by CPVA, in these same sectors.

NTBs: We correlated CPVA with our data on quantitative restrictions on trade and found nothing significant.

Indicators of Resource-Pull Effects of Protection

Corden's formula in equation (5.5) for the effective rate of protection was intended to provide a better indicator of the effect of protection on resource allocation than was provided by nominal tariffs. Our measure of CPVA in intended to be ever better. To check that the various measures do in fact perform this way, we correlated them with estimates calculated from the model of changes in employment, changes in outputs, and changes in the returns to capital by sector and country. The results of these correlations demonstrate clearly the superiority of our measure of CPVA over both nominal and effective tariffs in determining resource flows.[13]

Looking first at employment changes, in percentage terms, we found a strong positive relation between these and our CPVA measure. The rank correlation across developed-country traded sectors was 0.97, and was almost as high when developing countries and nontraded goods were included. Simple correlations were smaller, but still significant at the 99% level. Corden's effective tariff changes showed no significant correlation with employment changes in developed-country traded sectors. Nominal tariff changes did even worse, since they showed a small but significant *negative* correlation with employment changes, even for developed-country traded goods. The reason, again, is the similarity of tariff reductions among the developed countries, which leads employment to expand in precisely those sectors where tariffs are being reduced the most. Here, presumably, it is the fact that our measure of protection captures worldwide tariff changes that makes it work so well.

Output changes, again in percentage terms by sector and country, were similarly well explained by our CPVA measure and not at all by nominal and effective tariff changes. The only difference in comparison with the employment-change results just noted is that nominal tariffs no longer showed any significant correlation of any sign.

Finally, we calculated the change in the return to capital by sector and country due to the Tokyo Round as an indicator of the incentives for longer-run resource movement. This was calculated as the change in value added net of wages, as a percentage of the (fixed) value of the capital stock. From this definition it may not be surprising that the CPVA will be related to it, since their definitions overlap. However, the relation is not at all trivial, since changes in employment change the wage bill in a direction that could conceivably cancel out improvements in the return to capital. Nonetheless, our correlations showed the strongest connection yet between CPVA and changes in the return to capital, both simple and rank correlations being close to unity wherever we measured them. Once again, both nominal and effective tariffs failed to show any significant correlations with this variable worth noting.

We conclude therefore that our measure provides a vastly superior indicator of resource flows than the alternatives. Given that our basis for comparison is the pattern of resource flows calculated by our own model, the success of our measure may not be surprising. But the failure of even the Corden measure to correspond at all with these calculated flows is surprising indeed, since the Corden formula is intended to yield an approximation to the same economic magnitude of the change in per unit value added. Nonetheless, the Corden measure seems to provide no guidance at all, and nominal tariffs are actually misleading, as to the pattern of resource flows as we have calculated them.

Further Comparison of the Pre- and Post-Tokyo Round Structures of Protection

We have already noted that changes in protection were negatively correlated with their levels prior to the Tokyo Round. This was also true with respect to the structure of protection remaining after completion of the Tokyo Round. Both of these results are consistent with the view that the Tokyo Round tended to reduce tariffs across the board, without much effect on the cross-industry and cross-country pattern of protection. This was verified even more strongly when we correlated the structures of protection for the pre- and post-Tokyo Round with each other. Here both simple and rank correlations were in the 90% range throughout, and highly significant.

It was also of interest to examine whether the efforts to "harmonize" the tariff reductions using the Swiss formula had the desired effect of making structures of protection more uniform. To check this we calculated coefficients of variation of our CPVA measures of pre- and post-Tokyo Round protection, both across industries, across countries, and overall. These turned out to have remained roughly the same before and after the Tokyo Round, suggesting that if levels of protection are indeed more uniform, it is only because they are closer to zero. This is in marked contrast, incidentally, to the pattern of nominal tariffs. The coefficients of variation for these fell consistently due to the Tokyo Round, for all countries, almost all industries, and overall. Thus, while the general adherence to the Swiss formula resulted in some harmonization of nominal tariffs, this may not be particularly meaningful in terms of harmonizing levels of protection.[14]

The Terms of Trade of the Major Developing Countries

Our final concern was to investigate whether the structure of changes in tariffs and NTBs in the Tokyo Round was biased in favor of, or against, the major developing countries. As an indicator of this, we correlated the changes in world prices that our model ascribes to the Tokyo Round with various measures of trade performance of the developing countries. These measures were import shares, export shares, and trade balances. None of the results was significant, with some minor exceptions. This suggests that the effects of the Tokyo Round were *not* significantly biased either for or against the major developing countries as far as changes in world prices are concerned.[15]

Conclusion

In this chapter, we have analyzed the effects of pre-Tokyo Round tariffs and changes in exchange rates on the structure of protection. We also analyzed the effects of the Tokyo Round negotiations themselves. Since prices are endogenous in our model, we are able to calculate the changes in per unit value added by sector for all the major industrialized and developing countries included in the model. We take into account the direct effects of levels of and changes in both domestic and foreign tariffs and NTBs as well as the indirect effects of changes in exchange rates.

Our findings demonstrate clearly that a general-equilibrium model like ours is needed in order to analyze how individual sectors may be affected by the existing structure of protection as well as changes in the structure of protection. It will *not* be very helpful in this regard to look at changes in nominal tariffs or even effective rates of protection calculated under simplified conditions. As our results show, calculations from the model of changes in value added by sector are very good indicators of the sectoral resource shifts that tend to take place within a general-equilibrium model.

There were many findings noted in this chapter. The following are the most noteworthy with regard to the analysis of the structure of protection:

1. Imperfect substitutability between imports and home goods has an important bearing on how individual sectors will respond to changes in prices.

2 The ranking of industries by the degree of protection should take account of any exchange-rate changes that would have to accompany changes in tariffs. Exchange-rate flexibility tends to moderate the protective effect of a tariff structure, bringing the average level of protection closer to zero.

3. Protection and antiprotection are provided not only by a country's own tariffs, but also by the tariffs of its trading partners. Rankings of protection should take these foreign tariffs into account if the net effect on resource allocation is to be understood. Our rankings based on tariff removal by all countries simultaneously indicate that the presence of foreign tariffs lowers the average level of protection in all countries considered.

4. Changes in exchange rates by themselves can be an effective instrument of protection. A 1% devaluation has effects on per unit value added that are comparable in size to those of existing tariffs. The effects vary among industries, however, depending upon each good's use as an intermediate input, the industry's reliance upon imported inputs, and the size of the industry in world markets.

The major findings concerning the effects of the Tokyo Round negotiations on the structure of protection were as follows:

1. The Tokyo Round reduced protection most in those sectors that were previously most protected. Nonetheless, the pattern of protection remains substantially unaltered from what it was before.

2. The greatest benefits of the Tokyo Round will tend to be felt in those sectors with the greatest export interests. This is true even though these are also the sectors in which nominal tariffs tended to be reduced the most, and reflects the fact that the pattern of tariff reductions was quite similar across most countries.

3. There was no evidence that levels of protection have become more uniform as a result of the Tokyo Round. Nor did we find, within the constraints of our model and the level of aggregation of our data, any significant evidence that protection is becoming any more or less cascaded against imports of final goods, or that the Tokyo Round has been biased against the exports of the major developing countries.

6 Effects of Domestic Tax/Subsidies on the Structure of Protection in the United States, the United Kingdom, and Japan

It has been long recognized that differential taxes and subsidies may have a significant impact on the composition of a country's trade in conjunction with existing tariffs and nontariff barriers. Calculations by Melvin (1979) have suggested a sizable impact of the US corporate income tax on its most capital-intensive industries, while Whalley (1980) has shown that domestic factor taxes, particularly on capital, are highly distortionary especially in the United States and to a lesser extent in the European Economic Community (EEC). In this chapter, we continue this line of research, using the Michigan model to investigate the protective implications of domestic tax/subsidies, as well as tariffs, for three selected industrialized countries: the United States, the United Kingdom, and Japan.[1]

Our focus will be on the allocative effects of the various policy measures across sectors in each country, based on model calculations of the percentage change in value added per unit by sector that may be associated with the imposition or removal of particular measures. This idea is familiar from the literature on effective protection and has formed the basis of our analysis of the structure of protection in the preceding chapter.

We begin this chapter by discussing the domestic tax/subsidy data that we have used for the three countries. We then discuss some conceptual issues concerning the effects of domestic tax/subsidies and the nature of our calculations. In this connection, we ran a series of experiments involving the successive removal of domestic commodity and excise taxes on output, taxes on labor, taxes on capital, and all three combined.[2] In each case, we report the percentage changes in net value added per unit and the rankings of these changes by sector for each country. For purposes of comparison, we also report the results of complete tariff removal.[3] Some concluding remarks are noted in the final section of the chapter.

Table 6.1
1973 net tax/subsidy rates and Pre-Tokyo Round nominal tariffs for the United States, Japan, and the United Kingdom by ISIC sector[a]

		United States				Japan				United Kingdom			
		Factor Taxes		Sales and excise	Nominal	Factor Taxes		Sales and excise	Nominal	Factor Taxes		Consumer taxes on domestic	Nominal
Industry	(ISIC)	Capital	Labor	taxes	tariffs	Capital	Labor	taxes	tariffs	Capital	Labor	products	tariffs
Traded goods													
AGR., FOR., & FISH.	(1)	9.0	7.0	0.0	2.2	13.6	3.7	0.0	18.4	6.4	8.2	0.6	6.3
FOOD, BEV., & TOB.	(310)	178.2	11.0	13.9	6.3	76.8	9.1	7.1	25.4	183.4	9.8	38.5	13.1
TEXTILES	(321)	138.9	13.1	14.0	14.4	25.4	9.9	0.0	3.3	121.4	11.5	10.2	9.2
WEARING APPAREL	(322)	138.9	13.1	14.0	27.8	25.4	8.1	0.0	13.8	240.2	11.1	8.5	16.9
LEATHER PROD.	(323)	138.9	13.1	14.0	5.6	25.4	9.4	0.0	3.0	276.5	12.8	10.2	2.8
FOOTWEAR	(324)	138.9	13.1	14.0	8.8	25.4	9.4	0.0	16.4	276.5	12.8	10.2	12.5
WOOD PROD.	(331)	49.6	12.5	6.0	3.6	28.4	10.5	1.0	0.3	116.6	7.9	10.1	4.0
FURN. & FIXT.	(332)	49.6	12.5	6.0	8.1	28.4	10.5	1.0	7.8	116.6	7.9	10.1	8.5
PAPER & PAPER PROD.	(341)	96.8	10.3	2.0	0.5	28.4	9.6	0.0	2.1	96.9	8.7	3.8	6.6
PRINT. & PUBL.	(342)	96.8	10.3	2.0	1.1	28.4	9.2	0.0	0.2	96.9	8.7	3.8	3.3
CHEMICALS	(35A)	99.0	10.5	2.4	3.8	31.9	10.5	0.7	6.2	116.0	8.4	8.2	11.4
PETROL. & REL. PROD.	(35B)	19.7	8.4	19.0	1.4	31.9	11.9	20.0	2.8	230.6	12.0	215.5	1.1
RUBBER PROD.	(355)	144.7	10.5	6.0	3.6	31.9	9.0	0.0	1.5	120.3	9.2	10.1	4.0
NONMETAL. MIN. PROD.	(36A)	81.0	10.3	0.0	9.1	30.2	9.8	0.0	0.6	120.3	9.2	10.1	3.2
GLASS & GLASS PROD.	(362)	81.0	10.3	0.0	10.7	30.2	9.8	0.0	7.5	120.3	9.2	10.1	10.4
IRON & STEEL	(371)	81.0	10.3	0.0	4.7	27.8	11.0	0.0	3.3	6.3	9.8	0.0	6.3
NONFERROUS METALS	(372)	81.0	10.3	0.0	1.2	24.7	11.5	0.0	1.1	6.3	9.8	0.0	2.0
METAL PROD.	(381)	81.0	10.3	0.0	7.5	35.0	9.9	0.0	6.9	6.3	9.8	0.0	8.0
NONELEC. MACH.	(382)	103.5	10.5	5.0	5.0	28.9	9.6	19.0	9.1	390.2	9.0	0.0	6.4
ELEC. MACH.	(383)	131.2	10.7	0.0	6.5	39.0	9.7	0.0	7.4	285.5	10.5	0.0	10.0
TRANSP. EQUIP.	(384)	86.8	9.6	14.0	3.3	34.1	9.9	48.0	6.0	282.5	8.2	28.0	9.3
MISC. MANUF.	(38A)	86.6	10.5	12.7	7.8	33.2	9.4	30.0	6.0	144.1	9.1	9.1	4.9

Nontraded goods													
MIN. & QUARRY.	(2)	34.3	9.6	11.1		40.4	19.0	4.9		−55.9	9.7	3.7	
ELEC., GAS, & WATER	(4)	45.7	2.6	18.0		12.8	16.2	4.0		−7.2	8.1	0.0	
CONSTRUCTION	(5)	133.3	10.4	0.0		29.3	10.7	0.0		43.9	9.2	0.0	
WHOLE. & RET. TRADE	(6)	112.0	10.5	20.0		19.9	8.7	0.0		275.5	9.7	10.2	
TRANSP., STOR., & COMM.	(7)	186.6	11.3	3.6		27.4	10.3	1.9		−47.4	7.3	0.0	
FIN., INS., & REAL EST.	(8)	135.2	9.7	0.0		31.5	11.0	2.0		144.9	6.5	5.0	
COMM., SOC., & PERS. SERV.	(9)	21.2	9.6	0.8		17.9	8.5	5.0		42.9	12.9	5.9	
Coefficient of variation		0.48	0.19	1.00	0.89	0.36	0.24	2.16	0.94	0.87	0.17	2.67	0.55

a. All data are in percentages.

Source: The US tax rates were adapted from Whalley (1980); the tax rates for Japan were calculated by Gary Saxonhouse, following the procedures and data sources in Whalley (1980); the UK tax/subsidy rates were adapted from Piggott and Whalley (1981); and the data on nominal tariffs were taken from table 4.2.

Tax/Subsidy Rates by Sector

The domestic tax data that we have used for the United States are based upon the 33-sector estimates for 1973 that underly the 5-sector aggregation used in Whalley (1980). The estimates for Japan were calculated by Gary Saxonhouse, following Whalley's procedures and data sources.[4] Separate tax rates were calculated for capital and labor and for final demand.[5] We then concorded these rates to our ISIC sector classification noted earlier.[6] The data for the United Kingdom were drawn from Piggott and Whalley (1981), whose estimates include both domestic taxes and subsidies, so that the rates used for the United Kingdom are thus not strictly comparable to those for the United States and Japan.[7]

The tax/subsidy rates by ISIC sector are listed for the three countries in table 6.1. These are average effective rates and are expressed on a net basis.[8] Each country's pre-Tokyo Round (1976) nominal tariff rates are also shown. Coefficients of variation are indicated in the last row of the table. It is evident that capital-use taxes are substantial in all countries and vary considerably across sectors. The United Kingdom has the highest tax rates on capital use in the tradable sectors compared with the United States and Japan, particularly in wearing apparel, leather products, footwear, petroleum products, machinery, and transportation equipment. However, UK tax rates on capital in agriculture, iron and steel, nonferrous metals, and metal products are relatively low.[9] The United States has the highest tax rates on labor use, while the rates for the United Kingdom and Japan are somewhat lower. The tax rates on labor use are clearly much lower and more uniform than the rates on capital. Finally, the selectivity of the sales and excise taxes on final demand across sectors is evident in each country.

Modeling the Effects of Tax/Subsidies

The variations in the tax rates in table 6.1 across countries and sectors clearly reflect differences in institutional practices and objectives of policy. It would take us too far afield to consider how and why these differences have arisen and to assess the margins of error that may exist in the rates listed.[10] It is also not possible to determine how omitted elements of the tax/subsidy systems interact with the rates shown. We shall proceed accordingly to use the rates as given.

Our purpose is to determine the extent to which the structure of these taxes "protects" the various industries within the countries. Protection, as the term has been used in the literature on effective protection, has come to mean the change in value added per unit of output that is caused by the structure of tariffs. We shall therefore use the term here to mean the percentage of value added per unit that is attributable to the structure of certain taxes. To measure protection in this sense, we use our model to calculate the effects on value added of removing certain taxes. The results, with their signs reversed, provide a measure of relative industry protection that is comparable to measures of the structure of protection such as we examined in the preceding chapter. The precise calculation will be described in a moment.

Our model includes directly three tax variables: an export tax, an import tax, and a "home" tax that is applied to goods that are both produced and used domestically. Sales and excise taxes apply to both domestically produced and imported goods. We therefore modeled the sales and excise taxes of table 6.1 as a reduction in both the import-tax and home-tax variables by the percentages indicated.

To model labor taxes, we used the version of our model in which wage rates paid by industries are exogenous. Assuming that labor taxes are passed on to employers, we then reduced these wages by the percentage labor taxes recorded in table 6.1.[11] This pass-through of labor taxes is questionable, of course, but is justified to the extent that labor is mobile among industries.

Capital in our model is assumed fixed in each sector. Competitive assumptions, such as made by Whalley (1980), would therefore assure that any capital tax should be borne entirely by capital. However, in the long run, if capital is mobile, then differences in capital taxes among industries must be passed through to prices. It might be argued furthermore that elements of monopoly and administered pricing cause such pass-through even in the short run. We therefore attempt to follow Melvin (1979) in assuming that capital taxes are fully reflected in commodity prices. Since prices are endogenous in our model, we made them reflect capital taxes by shifting the supply functions in both home and export sectors by amounts that would, at constant outputs, reduce supply prices by appropriate amounts. These price reductions were calculated in turn as the amounts of capital tax paid per unit of output in each sector.[12]

Tax changes cannot, in general equilibrium, be considered alone, but must be accompanied either by changes in government expenditure or by changes in other taxes to balance the budget. In the trade literature, tariff revenues are customarily assumed to be redistributed in some nondistorting fashion and spent like all other consumption. We make the same assumption here about all taxes. In effect, then, the exercises that we shall be reporting are ones in which certain taxes from table 6.1 are replaced by lump-sum taxes of equal revenue.[13]

In practice, certain inaccuracies in our data seem to have prevented us from finding lump-sum taxes that exactly offset the tax reductions. As a result, for some of the runs there seems to be an upward or downward bias to the overall results for certain countries. This is not of great consequence, however, since there are already theoretical reasons for focusing only on relative degrees of protection across industries and for ignoring the absolute levels across the board. Two such reasons arise from the rationales for pass-through of labor and capital taxes discussed. In both cases, it is only differences in taxes across industries that should be reflected in commodity prices. A third and more basic reason, however, is that the concept of protection itself is intended to provide an indicator of incentives for resources to move among sectors. Such incentives can only be relative, since resources can move into one sector only after having moved out of another.

Let us now describe the measure of protection that we use in this chapter. Consider an industry, j, whose output price is p_j and that requires, per unit of output, a_{ij} units of intermediate inputs with prices p_i. Per unit value added in the industry is then conventionally defined as follows:

$$\mathrm{VA}_j \equiv p_j - \sum_{i=1}^{n} a_{ij} p_i. \tag{6.1}$$

It is the percentage change in this variable (CPVA) that is the customary measure of the effects of the structure of protection, with price changes being those that would arise from tariffs. In the preceding chapter, we have examined alternative versions of this CPVA measure that are valid under various assumptions about exchange-rate flexibility and about the scope of the tariffs (own country or all country) being considered.

In the present chapter, we again calculated CPVA measures of protection. In this connection, the above formula is inappropriate for measuring the protective effects of factor taxes. In the presence of factor taxes, the entirety of the value added just defined is not available to the owners of the factors and thus cannot serve as an incentive for resource allocation. Instead we need to net out the factor taxes paid per unit of output in defining the following measure of *net value added*:

$$\mathrm{NVA}_j = \mathrm{VA}_j(1 - \theta_j^L \tau_j^L - \theta_j^K \tau_j^K), \tag{6.2}$$

where θ_j^L and θ_j^K are the labor and capital shares of (gross) value added in industry j and τ_j^L and τ_j^K are the fractions of payments to labor and capital that go to factor taxes in the industry.[14] In what follows we use the percentage change in NVA_j due to removal of the various good and factor taxes as our basic measure of their protective effects. With their signs reversed, as will be reported, the results tell us the percentage of net value added in an industry that can be attributed to the structure of taxes being examined.[15]

Effects of Tax/Subsidies on the Structure of Protection

We ran a series of experiments for the countries individually, which involved the successive removal of taxes/subsidies on output, labor, capital, and all these combined. In each case, import tariffs were assumed to be unchanged. We then ran one final experiment involving the removal of tariffs. Lacking adequate data on NTBs, we assumed that they would remain intact. The results are shown in tables 6.2–6.4.

Several conclusions emerge from these results. First, the amount of protection attributable to domestic taxes, either separately [columns (1)–(3)] or in combination [column (4)] is substantially larger than that due to tariffs. This is evident, not from the absolute levels of protection in the tables, which mean little, but rather from the variation among these levels across industries.[16] Except for labor taxes, the difference in protection between most and least protected industries is always greater than 10%, and in combination these differences [computed from column (4)] are 49% for Japan, 142% for the United Kingdom, and 29% for the United States. In contrast, the difference between the largest and smallest levels of tariff protection in column (5) are no greater than about 5%. Since these and other differences among levels of protection in the tables indicate the pull on resources that the taxes and tariffs exert, it is clear that domestic taxes are a more important influence on resource allocation than are tariffs, at least given the assumptions that underlie our calculations.

This is consistent with the results of Whalley (1980), who found the welfare effects of domestic taxes to dominate those of tariffs. It should not be surprising in view of the substantial sizes of the taxes reported in table 6.1 and their variation across industries. In addition, it should be noted that the pre-Tokyo Round tariffs whose protective effects we have calculated are themselves quite low as a result of successive rounds of trade negotiations since World War II. Further, the particular countries examined here are economically quite large, so that trade and tariffs might be expected to be less important for them than for much smaller countries that depend more heavily on trade.

The relative importance of domestic taxes compared with tariffs is also, in part, a result of the fact that domestic taxes apply to all domestic product,

Table 6.2
The protective effects of domestic taxes and import tariffs for the United States[a]

Industry	(ISIC)	(1) Sales and excise taxes		(2) Labor tax		(3) Capital tax		(4) All domestic taxes		(5) Import tariffs	
		% of net value added	Rank	% of net value added	Rank	% of net value added	Rank	% of net value added	Rank	% of net value added	Rank
Traded goods											
AGR., FOR., & FISH.	(1)	−1.8	22	1.4	6	2.0	3	3.8	8	−0.58	28
FOOD, BEV., & TOB.	(310)	−2.4	25	1.9	4	−10.2	28	−7.7	28	−0.05	17
TEXTILES	(321)	−3.1	27	−0.3	27	−0.6	14	−2.5	25	−0.19	21
WEARING APPAREL	(322)	−1.9	23	−0.0	25	−0.1	11	−1.0	23	0.53	1
LEATHER PROD.	(323)	−4.0	28	−1.5	29	−1.3	20	−5.8	27	−0.96	29
FOOTWEAR	(324)	−1.0	19	0.2	24	−0.4	13	−0.1	20	0.19	4
WOOD PROD.	(331)	2.7	5	1.1	10	0.2	10	5.5	5	−0.16	19
FURN. & FIXT.	(332)	0.4	18	0.9	14	0.6	7	2.8	12	0.03	9
PAPER & PAPER PROD.	(341)	0.6	17	1.1	11	−1.7	21	1.4	17	−0.20	22
PRINT. & PUBL.	(342)	1.8	9	0.3	23	−0.2	12	3.1	10	−0.00	14
CHEMICALS	(35A)	2.1	7	1.3	7	−4.1	25	1.5	16	−0.26	23
PETROL. & REL. PROD.	(35B)	−1.7	21	3.4	1	−2.3	22	−0.1	21	−0.04	16
RUBBER PROD.	(355)	1.0	16	1.0	12	−3.6	24	0.6	18	0.09	6
NONMETAL. MIN. PROD.	(36A)	2.7	6	1.1	9	−0.6	15	4.6	6	0.23	3
GLASS & GLASS PROD.	(362)	1.0	14	1.2	8	−0.7	16	3.0	11	−0.02	15
IRON & STEEL	(371)	1.1	12	1.0	13	0.3	9	3.4	9	−0.10	18
NONFERROUS METALS	(372)	1.1	13	0.6	18	−0.9	18	1.9	15	−0.29	24
METAL PROD.	(381)	1.9	8	0.8	15	0.3	8	4.3	7	0.02	10
NONELEC. MACH.	(382)	2.8	4	0.6	19	2.2	2	6.9	3	−0.51	27
ELEC. MACH.	(383)	3.8	3	−0.0	26	1.9	4	6.9	2	−0.18	20
TRANSP. EQUIP.	(384)	−2.0	24	0.4	21	5.2	1	5.5	4	−0.36	26
MISC. MANUF.	(38A)	4.8	2	2.0	2	1.5	5	10.1	1	0.26	2
Average		0.6		1.1		−0.6		2.7		−0.18	

Nontraded goods											
MIN. & QUARRY.	(2)	−9.3	29	−0.7	28	−9.7	27	−19.0	29	−0.33	25
ELEC., GAS, & WATER	(4)	−2.7	26	0.8	16	−1.1	19	−2.0	24	0.06	7
CONSTRUCTION	(5)	1.7	10	0.3	22	−0.9	17	2.5	14	0.01	13
WHOLE. & RET. TRADE	(6)	−1.2	20	1.7	5	−3.2	23	−0.7	22	0.04	8
TRANSP., STOR., & COMM.	(7)	1.6	11	0.7	17	−4.6	26	0.6	19	0.02	12
FIN., INS., & REAL EST.	(8)	6.4	1	1.9	3	−16.3	29	−3.9	26	0.11	5
COMM., SOC., & PERS. SERV.	(9)	1.0	15	0.5	20	0.8	6	2.6	13	0.02	11
Average		1.3		1.0		−4.6		−0.5		0.03	
Overall average		1.1		1.0		−3.7		0.2		−0.01	
Standard deviation		3.1		0.9		4.2		5.4		0.29	
Range		15.7		4.9		21.5		29.1		1.49	

a. Averages shown are weighted using value added.

Table 6.3
The protective effects of domestic taxes and import tariffs for Japan[a]

Industry	(ISIC)	(1) Sales and excise taxes: % of net value added	Rank	(2) Labor tax: % of net value added	Rank	(3) Capital tax: % of net value added	Rank	(4) All domestic taxes: % of net value added	Rank	(5) Import tariffs: % of net value added	Rank
Traded goods											
AGR., FOR., & FISH.	(1)	1.8	2	−0.1	29	−3.2	24	−0.7	20	2.10	1
FOOD, BEV., & TOB.	(310)	−3.8	25	3.5	3	−9.5	29	−8.2	26	−0.47	18
TEXTILES	(321)	0.8	9	1.5	20	1.3	2	4.2	2	−1.47	27
WEARING APPAREL	(322)	0.5	12	1.0	25	0.6	3	2.5	8	0.47	3
LEATHER PROD.	(323)	−1.6	20	1.7	15	0.0	7	0.7	17	−1.30	26
FOOTWEAR	(324)	0.6	10	1.6	19	0.2	5	2.9	6	0.30	5
WOOD PROD.	(331)	1.2	6	1.7	17	−0.2	10	3.4	5	−0.74	20
FURN. & FIXT.	(332)	0.6	11	1.6	18	−0.8	14	2.0	12	0.07	9
PAPER & PAPER PROD.	(341)	−0.1	15	2.7	5	−1.1	16	2.3	10	−0.47	17
PRINT. & PUBL.	(342)	0.3	13	0.9	26	0.2	6	2.0	11	−0.01	11
CHEMICALS	(35A)	−1.4	19	2.5	7	−2.9	23	−0.7	21	−0.75	21
PETROL. & REL. PROD.	(35B)	−5.8	26	2.0	12	−6.2	28	−9.2	27	0.85	2
RUBBER PROD.	(355)	−1.9	22	2.0	13	−0.2	11	0.6	19	−0.92	24
NONMETAL. MIN. PROD.	(36A)	1.0	7	1.4	21	−1.4	19	2.0	13	−0.30	16
GLASS & GLASS PROD.	(362)	−0.7	18	2.2	10	−1.8	21	0.6	18	−0.13	14
IRON & STEEL	(371)	−3.0	23	2.3	9	−4.1	25	−3.9	25	−3.01	29
NONFERROUS METALS	(372)	−3.7	24	2.2	11	−2.3	22	−3.0	24	−1.14	25
METAL PROD.	(381)	1.2	5	1.2	23	−1.5	20	1.8	14	−0.10	13
NONELEC. MACH.	(382)	−13.8	28	1.0	24	−0.9	15	−12.6	28	−0.84	22
ELEC. MACH.	(383)	1.2	4	0.4	27	−4.2	26	−1.4	22	−0.73	19
TRANSP. EQUIP.	(384)	−42.9	29	0.3	28	−1.2	18	−42.8	29	−1.64	28
MISC. MANUF.	(38A)	−7.9	27	2.4	8	2.7	1	−1.4	23	−0.87	23
Average		−5.7		1.2		−2.5		−6.0		−0.20	

Nontraded goods											
MIN. & QUARRY.	(2)	−1.8	21	4.6	2	−0.6	13	4.0	3	−0.18	15
ELEC., GAS, & WATER	(4)	−0.6	17	6.3	1	−0.0	8	6.3	1	−0.06	12
CONSTRUCTION	(5)	1.5	3	1.7	16	−1.2	17	2.9	7	0.20	6
WHOLE. & RET. TRADE	(6)	0.9	8	2.6	6	−0.1	9	3.9	4	0.09	7
TRANSP., STOR., & COMM.	(7)	0.2	14	1.8	11	−0.3	12	2.3	9	0.05	10
FIN., INS., & REAL EST.	(8)	2.8	1	2.9	4	−5.9	27	1.0	16	0.34	4
COMM., SOC., & PERS. SERV.	(9)	−0.4	16	1.2	22	0.4	4	1.6	15	0.07	8
Average		0.7		2.2		−0.9		2.6		0.12	
Overall average		−1.5		1.8		−1.5		−0.3		0.01	
Standard deviation		8.5		1.3		2.5		9.0		0.91	
Range		45.7		6.4		12.2		49.1		5.11	

a. Averages shown are weighted using value added.

Table 6.4
The protective effects of domestic taxes and import tariffs for the United Kingdom

Industry	(ISIC)	(1) Sales and excise taxes		(2) Labor tax		(3) Capital tax		(4) All domestic taxes		(5) Import tariffs	
		% of net value added	Rank	% of net value added	Rank	% of net value added	Rank	% of net value added	Rank	% of net value added	Rank
Traded goods											
AGR., FOR., & FISH.	(1)	2.4	16	3.5	5	−36.8	28	−28.0	28	1.21	2
FOOD, BEV., & TOB.	(310)	−14.4	29	3.6	4	7.3	5	0.4	24	0.69	4
TEXTILES	(321)	0.3	25	0.9	17	−2.5	21	0.9	22	−0.42	24
WEARING APPAREL	(322)	3.5	11	−0.1	27	−2.3	20	2.9	18	1.39	1
LEATHER PROD.	(323)	−0.1	27	−0.8	29	−21.1	27	−18.0	27	−1.52	29
FOOTWEAR	(324)	2.3	17	0.2	24	−6.2	21	−0.5	25	0.68	5
WOOD PROD.	(331)	5.5	7	0.8	18	0.5	12	8.2	10	0.61	6
FURN. & FIXT.	(332)	0.3	24	0.6	19	0.0	14	1.7	20	−0.17	19
PAPER & PAPER PROD.	(341)	4.0	9	1.6	10	−1.0	17	6.0	14	0.51	7
PRINT. & PUBL.	(342)	6.0	5	0.4	22	−1.5	18	6.1	13	0.16	14
CHEMICALS	(35A)	0.4	23	1.7	9	−2.9	22	1.0	21	0.29	11
PETROL. & REL. PROD.	(35B)	−4.2	28	4.7	2	62.4	1	63.7	1	−0.08	18
RUBBER PROD.	(355)	1.7	19	1.0	15	1.1	11	4.9	16	−0.27	22
NONMENTAL. MIN. PROD.	(36A)	1.6	20	0.4	21	5.0	7	7.6	11	−0.22	20
GLASS & GLASS PROD.	(362)	0.9	22	0.3	23	4.1	8	5.9	15	−0.26	21
IRON & STEEL	(371)	1.0	21	1.2	13	10.7	4	12.8	4	−0.41	23
NONFERROUS METALS	(372)	0.0	26	1.1	14	18.0	3	19.0	3	−0.69	26
METAL PROD.	(381)	3.2	14	1.5	11	2.6	9	7.3	12	0.10	16
NONELEC. MACH.	(382)	5.6	6	0.1	26	1.6	10	8.7	9	−0.89	27
ELEC. MACH.	(383)	10.0	2	−0.3	28	−2.1	19	10.2	6	0.43	9
TRANSP. EQUIP.	(384)	2.4	15	0.1	25	5.1	6	8.8	8	0.49	8
MISC. MANUF.	(38A)	3.4	12	1.5	12	−6.3	25	0.8	23	−1.38	28
Average		0.1		1.7		2.3		6.0		0.18	

Nontraded goods											
	(2)	3.9	10	5.0	1	−92.3	29	−78.2	29	−0.49	25
ELEC., GAS, & WATER	(4)	7.1	4	3.9	3	0.0	13	10.9	5	0.25	12
CONSTRUCTION	(5)	7.3	3	1.8	8	0.4	15	9.5	7	0.31	10
WHOLE. & RET. TRADE	(6)	3.4	13	1.0	16	−4.0	23	3.1	17	0.20	13
TRANSP., STOR., & COMM.	(7)	4.3	8	3.1	6	−10.5	26	−3.4	26	0.15	15
FIN., INS., & REAL EST.	(8)	18.7	1	2.4	7	22.7	2	39.7	2	0.91	3
COMM., SOC., & PERS. SERV.	(9)	1.9	18	0.5	20	−0.8	16	2.1	19	0.10	17
Average		5.7		1.5		−0.6		6.7		0.26	
Overall average		4.2		1.5		0.1		6.5		0.24	
Standard deviation		5.2		1.5		23.5		22.2		0.68	
Range		33.1		5.8		154.7		141.9		2.92	

Table 6.5
Coefficients of rank correlation for the sectoral rankings of protection associated with different types of taxes in the United States, Japan, and the United Kingdom[a]

Country	(1)	(2)	(3)	(4)	(5)
United States					
(1)	1.00	0.30	0.21	0.64*	0.23
(2)	0.30	1.00	−0.23	0.12	0.24
(3)	0.21	−0.23	1.00	0.79*	−0.10
(4)	0.64*	0.12	0.79*	1.00	−0.06
(5)	0.23	0.24	−0.10	−0.06	1.00
Japan					
(1)	1.00	−0.27	0.00	0.56*	0.52*
(2)	−0.27	1.00	−0.15	0.14	−0.08
(3)	0.00	−0.15	1.00	0.58*	−0.02
(4)	0.56*	0.14	0.58*	1.00	0.35
(5)	0.52*	−0.08	−0.02	0.35	1.00
United Kingdom					
(1)	1.00	0.02	−0.18	0.26	0.35
(2)	0.02	1.00	0.06	−0.01	0.12
(3)	−0.18	0.06	1.00	0.78*	−0.00
(4)	0.26	−0.01	0.78*	1.00	0.05
(5)	0.35	0.12	−0.00	0.05	1.00

*Significant at the .01 level.

a. (1), sales and excise taxes; (2), labor tax; (3), capital tax; (4), all domestic taxes; (5), import tariffs. Based upon sector rankings in tables 6.2–6.4.

while tariffs apply only to that portion that is traded. This would not by itself explain the result, since in a small country domestic prices can theoretically be totally determined by world prices and tariffs, so that the leverage of tariffs on the domestic economy can be quite large. However, as already noted in chapter 5, imperfect substitution between domestic goods and imports causes domestic prices even in small countries to be relatively independent of world prices. Thus to some extent, this result concerning the relative effects of domestic taxes compared with tariffs is also a product of that imperfect substitutability.

A second observation from the tables concerns the rankings of protection among industries and how these rankings compare as between columns (1)–(4) and column (5). We calculated coefficients of rank correlation, and the results, which are shown in table 6.5, were only moderately suggestive overall. Thus, for the United States, the only statistically significant relations were positive between all domestic taxes vis-a-vis sales and excise taxes and capital taxes. For Japan, there was a positive and statistically significant correlation between the rankings for sales and excise taxes vis-a-vis all domestic taxes and import tariffs, and between capital taxes and all domestic taxes. For the United Kingdom, the only statistically significant relation of rankings was a positive one between capital taxes and all domestic taxes. These comparisons of overall rankings thus suggest that, in order to understand the results in the tables, it is important to examine how protection is related to the levels of the particular kinds of domestic taxes being considered.

The relation is most straightforward for sales and excise taxes. These taxes raise prices to demanders and lower them to suppliers. This reduces value added as measured in equation (6.1). Thus, we expect—and find—that high sales and excise taxes will be associated with low or negative levels of protection and vice versa. The effects of these taxes can be quite pronounced. See, for example, the −43% anti protection of the transportation-equipment industry in Japan that arises from a tax of 48%. On the other hand, the effect of a tax can be considerably reduced if its incidence falls more on demanders, or if the industry also benefits from low taxes in other industries with which it has input-output interactions. Thus, one cannot predict levels of protection from levels of sales and excise taxes without exception.

The effects of capital taxes tend to be similar to those of sales and excise taxes. To the extent that sellers succeed in passing them through to prices, there would be no direct effect on net value added. However, those sectors with larger than average taxes would need larger than average price increases to maintain net value added, and substitution by demanders away from such sectors will therefore dampen their price increases. We therefore expect levels of protection to be negatively correlated with capital taxes, as they were with sales and excise taxes.

This pattern does show up in the tables. See, for example, the harsh effects of relatively high taxes on capital in the food, beverages, and tobacco industries in the United States and Japan. On the other hand, the pattern is again by no means universal. Exceptions arise partly due to interindustry relations, and partly because the taxes alone do not determine how much prices will rise, even for complete pass-through. The price increase depends also on the share of capital in the industry, which varies considerably across industries.

It is clear from table 6.1 that both the size and the interindustry variation of capital tax rates are large compared with the other domestic taxes. This is especially true in the United Kingdom, where subsidies are also taken into account. Nonetheless, the size and variation of protection as reported in column (3) for the United States and Japan seem not to be noticeably larger than in column (1) for sales and excise taxes. This is not the case, however, for the United Kingdom, where the column (3) results are quite substantial in many sectors. Thus, depending on the country and the size of its capital tax rates, there are instances in which the price changes that would result from complete pass-through are usually only a few percent. This is because capital's share in the value of output may be quite small. But in the case of the United Kingdom, capital tax rates more than compensate for the small capital shares.

Finally, labor taxes require an even more subtle explanation, as even the sign of their effects on net value added cannot be predicted a priori. The reason for this ambiguity is that, because labor is the variable primary factor in the model, its wage determines marginal cost and therefore price. At a constant output, a tax on labor raises both marginal cost and price by the percentage of the tax and thus, since labor's share is only a fraction, raises price by more than needed to pay the tax. If demand is inelastic, so that quantity can be maintained close to constant, it follows that a labor tax *increases* net value added. Only if elastic demand prevents price from rising enough to pay the tax will net value added fall. Thus, labor taxes may appear either to protect or to anti protect the industries in which they are applied, depending both on elasticities of demand and on labor shares.

On comparing the labor taxes in table 6.1 with column (2) in tables 6.2–6.4, the taxes seem usually to be anti protective in both the United States and the United Kingdom. Agriculture in both countries, for example, is seen to benefit from a relatively low tax on labor. In Japan, however, the pattern seems to be reversed. Japanese agriculture is also lightly taxed but is the *least* protected of all Japanese industries by the structure of labor taxes. In contrast, the most protected Japanese industries are mining and quarrying and electricity, gas, and water, where labor taxes are extremely high.

This difference between Japan and the other two countries may be due to a difference that exists among the input-output tables of the three countries. By and large, labor shares are reported as substantially smaller in the Japanese table than in the others, and this, as explained earlier, reduces the burden of a labor tax without reducing its effect on price. Alternatively—and this may be especially relevant for agriculture—Japanese nontariff barriers are somewhat higher and more restrictive of changes in quantities imported in Japan than elsewhere. This reduces the elasticity of demand and again permits taxes to be more easily shifted onto consumers.

Comparison with Import Tariffs

When we consider the protective effects of all domestic taxes in comparison with tariffs, there are some striking effects for particular sectors, especially in the United States. Thus, for example, the wearing apparel and footwear industries are among the most highly tariff-protected industries in the United States. But these same industries are among the most highly taxed domestically, and therefore are subject to negative, or anti-, protection from that source. Net value added in these industries would therefore rise perceptibly if domestic taxes were removed. By the same token, the wood products industry in the United States is one of the least protected industries in terms of tariffs. Yet the structure of domestic taxes is biased strongly in its favor, so that we calculate a level of domestic tax protection for that industry of 5.5%. In the United Kingdom, agriculture is indicated to be the second most highly protected tariff sector, but it is subject to considerable antiprotection from domestic taxes.

Conclusion

We have attempted in this chapter to analyze the effects of domestic tax/subsidies and import tariffs on the structure of protection in three major industrialized countries. A number of conclusions have emerged from our calculations.

1. Domestic taxes in general provide significant incentives for resource allocation among industries, and these incentives are much larger than those provided by tariffs.

2. The tax rates themselves are often not an accurate indication of the incentives for resource allocation. The incentives will depend upon the incidence of the taxes and variations of the rates across sectors, input-output interactions, producer and consumer responses to changes in relative prices, and the shares of labor and capital in the value of output. Among the taxes considered, sales and excise taxes and capital taxes appear to be the most important. Labor taxes are more uniform across industries and are therefore comparatively less important.

3. There is some evidence, particularly in the United States, that certain industries with relatively high tariffs may be antiprotected by relatively high domestic taxes.[17]

Our results are derived of course from rather crude data on tax rates. We have also made some assumptions about the pass-through of various taxes that may not appeal to everyone.[18] Despite all these caveats, there is little doubt that domestic tax/subsidies have a significant impact on trade. It would be worthwhile accordingly to examine other countries besides the three here and to determine to what extent our results may be corroborated.

7 The Sectoral Impact of Uniform Exchange-Rate Changes

The experience of recent years has demonstrated to the United States what has long been known by other countries: that the rest of the world matters. This has become especially true in the last decade for exchange rates, which provide one major channel through which dependence on the rest of the world is transmitted. Changes in exchange rates among national currencies have been frequent and pronounced since the move to greater flexibility beginning in 1971, and the importance of these changes for the performance of domestic economies is becoming impossible to ignore even in such a relatively closed economy as the United States. It is important, therefore, that we try to understand the role of exchange rates in the world's major economies. In this and the following chapter we make an effort in this direction by examining several aspects of the role of exchange rates using our model of world production and trade.

We begin the chapter with a simple theoretical discussion of how exchange rates may be expected to affect outputs and prices in an economy. The first empirical part of this chapter is then devoted to an examination of the effects of exchange-rate changes on outputs by industry. The purpose is to provide some indication of the size of these effects and also how they are distributed across sectors in individual countries. We then shift attention to the price effects of exchange-rate changes, both at the disaggregated level and as summarized in the aggregate by various price indices and measures of real exchange rates. Here the object is to determine the extent to which exchange-rate changes are passed through, in our model, to changes in domestic prices, under various assumptions about wage flexibility and about the nature of the exchange-rate change.

Throughout this chapter it will be assumed that exchange-rate changes are uniform. That is, we shall analyze the effects of a given country undergoing a devaluation of a common percentage relative to all other countries' currencies, the relative prices among these other currencies remaining fixed.

In chapter 8 we shall analyze some of the consequences of exchange-rate changes that are not uniform in this respect.

In addition, our analysis in this chapter, like all that has appeared before now in this volume, will be strictly comparative static in nature. That is, exchange-rate changes will be analyzed on a once and for all basis, their effects being calculated for some rather short-run time horizon that is implicit in our assumptions about factor mobility and wage rigidity. In chapter 8 this assumption too will be changed, and we shall attempt a more explicitly dynamic analysis of the very short-run effects of exchange-rate changes over several periods of time.

Conceptual Issues

The first question that needs to be addressed is why an exchange rate should have any real effect on the economy at all. In a purely Walrasian model in which all supplies and demands depend only on relative prices, the exchange rate, if it is mentioned at all, serves only to set the relative prices of the numeraires in different countries. A devaluation of one country's currency relative to the others in such a model serves only to raise all nominal values—prices, wages, and whatever else is specified in nominal terms—in that country by the amount of the devaluation and leaves all real values unchanged.

The Michigan model is not purely Walrasian in this sense, however, in part because of our view, as discussed in chapter 2, that the world is not Walrasian, in the short run at least. Instead, depending on the particular assumptions chosen for a run of the model, several economic variables are held fixed in nominal terms and the exchange rate of a country does matter.

The two most important variables that are sometimes fixed in nominal terms are wages and expenditure. To the extent that either or both of these are held fixed, a devaluation by one country, which reduces the value of its nominal variables relative to those abroad, has effects by reducing either its relative wages or its relative expenditure or both. It is these changes that lie at the heart of the sectoral effects of devaluation that we shall report in this chapter.

In earlier chapters, as we have examined changes in tariffs and other trade barriers, we have chosen to hold money wages fixed in each country but have allowed each country's total expenditure to vary endogenously so as to stabilize aggregate employment. This was done because we wished to focus our analysis on the real effects that trade barriers could have independently of any macroeconomic effects on total expenditure. In this chapter, however, we recognize that exchange rates are really macroeconomic variables. To allow endogenous stabilization via expenditure would be to assume away one of the main channels through which, we believe, exchange rates have their effects. Thus, we now assume that aggregate levels of expenditure are essentially fixed in nominal terms.[1] All of our results in this chapter, then, arise at least in part from the effects of exchange rates in altering relative levels of expenditure in different countries.

For most of our analysis we shall also continue to assume that money wages are fixed as well. So long as this is the case, exchange rates will work through changes in relative wages in addition to relative expenditures. However, near the end of this chapter, in connection with the price effects of devaluation, we also explore the implications of allowing wages to adjust to clear either national or industry-specific labor markets. In these calculations, then, relative national expenditure levels provide the only channel for the effects of exchange rates.

We are now in a position to discuss conceptually how exchange rates affect the individual sectors of an economy. This can be done easily, up to a point, using the conventional partial-equilibrium supply and demand curves of figures 7.1–7.3. In this context the roles of nominal wages and expenditure are that they, among other variables, serve to determine the positions of the supply and demand curves, respectively. Naturally, this partial-equilibrium analysis can only provide a start toward understanding what the sectoral effects of exchange-rate changes will be. The full effects must include a host of general-equilibrium interactions that only something like the computational Michigan model can take into account. Still, it is useful for understanding the empirical results to begin with an idea of what is to be expected in simple theoretical terms.

Figures 7.1–7.3 show the effect of a devaluation in an export market and in the home-sector markets for a tradable good and a nontradable good, respectively. In all three figures it is assumed for simplicity that the country is a price taker on world markets.

To begin, a 1% devaluation raises the prices of both exports and imports by, as a first approximation, 1% also. The major effect of the export price increase, which shifts the horizontal demand curve facing exports in figure 7.1 upward, is that it causes movement up and to the right along the export supply curve, S_X. Thus the output of the good in the export sector of the industry increases, the amount of the increase depending on the industry elasticity of supply. This outcome will be modified slightly in a moment by other changes in the economy, but this increase from Q_X^0 to Q_X' will still be the main effect that one expects to find on exports from the devaluation.

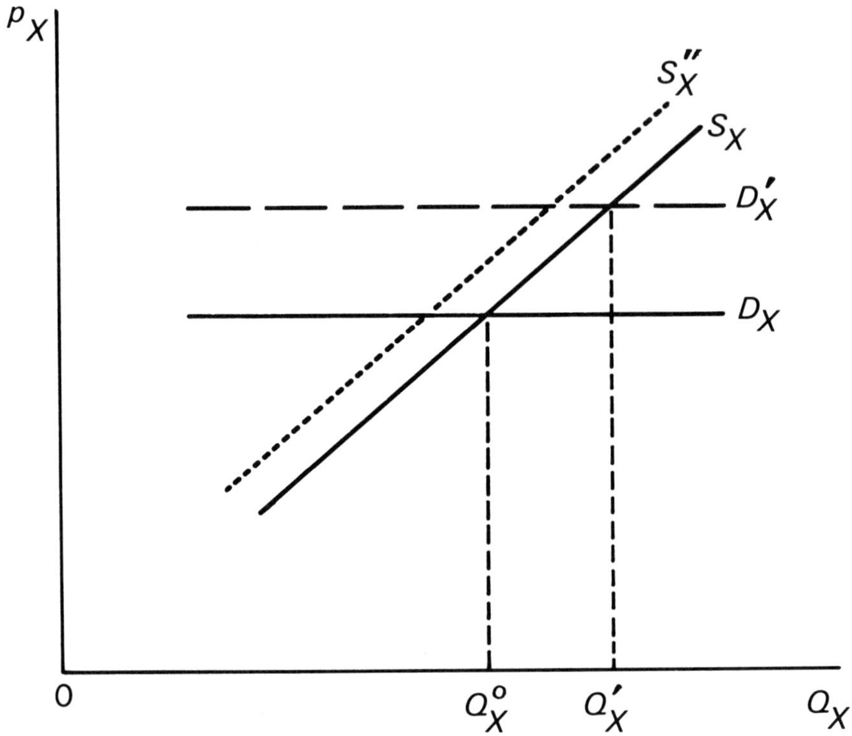

Figure 7.1
Effect of a devaluation on an export sector.

The major effect of the import price increase is on corresponding home-sector markets, where it causes substitution by demanders away from the more expensive imports and toward domestically produced versions of the same goods. This shifts up demand curves in home-sector markets, as shown in the dashed demand curve of figure 7.2, and provides an important reason for increases in both home-sector prices and home-sector quantities produced. These increases will be larger, the greater is the import share and the greater is the elasticity of substitution between imports and home goods in the industry in question, since these parameters determine the size of the upward shift in demand. Whether this shift then results primarily in increases in outputs or increases in prices then depends on the elasticity of supply in the industry. The smaller is this elasticity, the steeper is the supply curve and the more will the effect of the devaluation be absorbed in increases in domestic prices.

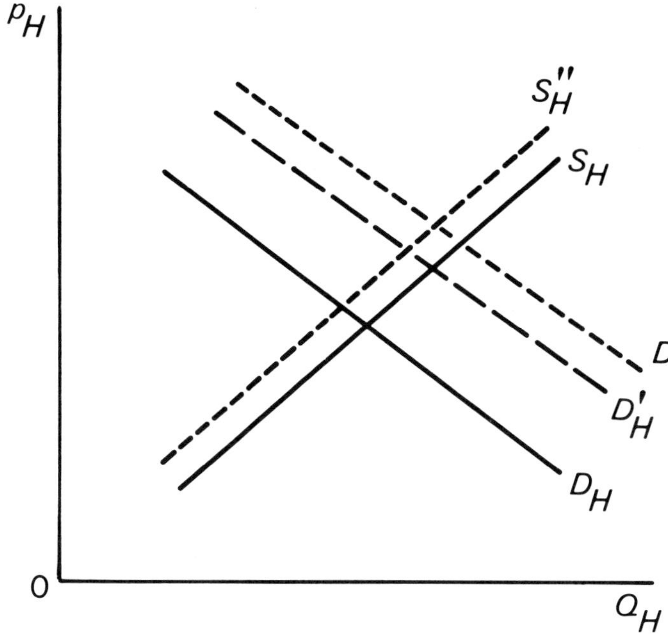

Figure 7.2
Effect of a devaluation on the home-sector market for a tradable good.

This import substitution effect operates, however, only in tradable industries, where there is direct competition with imports. Two additional and somewhat weaker effects also operate, and these apply to both tradables and nontradables.

First, the increased prices of imports raise costs in all industries to the extent that imports are used as inputs in their production. This shows up as an upward shift in each of the supply curves in all three figures. Second, to the extent that production in both export and home sectors of tradable industries does expand, and to the extent also that this production uses intermediate inputs from other domestic industries, there will be an additional upward shift of demand in these industries, both tradable and nontradable. These shifts are also shown by the dotted demand curves D''_H in figures 7.2 and 7.3. These two secondary effects tend to dampen the increase in quantity of exports, while having an ambiguous effect on quantities in home markets. However, they act together to increase prices in nontradables, and to increase prices further than before in home-sector tradables.

The end result of all of this is that quantities may be expected to rise as a

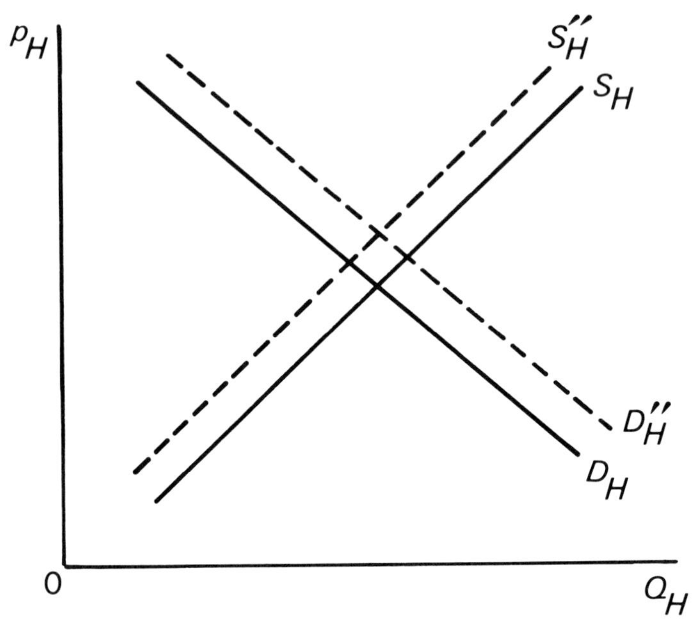

Figure 7.3
Effect of a devaluation on the market for a nontradable good.

result of a devaluation in both export and home sectors of tradable industries, while outputs may either rise or fall in nontradables. As for prices, these may be expected to rise generally in all industries, with the larger increases being found in tradables. Generally, too, the price increases are less than the 1% of the devaluation itself, for the reason that, for the import substitution effect to operate at all, imports must become more expensive relative to domestically produced goods. In figure 7.2 this mans that the first shift of the demand curve is upward by 1%. It is possible for the secondary shifts of supply and demand to raise the price beyond 1%, but it should not happen often.

All of the effects just described would be dampened somewhat if export and import prices do not rise by the full amount of the devaluation. This would be most true for large countries, where increased net supply to world markets would drive down the price.

In addition, these results can be altered considerably if markets are not allowed to function freely. We shall see that countries that are assumed to use import licensing turn out to behave quite differently, and this is easily understood.

As we model import licensing, all imports of a country are rationed to exhaust the available foreign exchange that has been obtained from exports. The means of implementing the rationing is that each industry is charged, either by its government or by a market for import licenses, a premium over the exchange rate for its use of foreign exchange. This premium adjusts with changes in market conditions so as to keep imports in the industry at the permitted level, and it shows up exactly like a tariff in the prices of imported goods to demanders.

A devaluation in this situation raises, as before, the domestic prices received for exports and so raises their quantity and the resulting pool of foreign exchange. This permits an expansion of the value of imports at world prices and requires that the domestic prices of imports fall. Since domestic import prices would otherwise rise from the devaluation, this means that the exchange premia must fall substantially—by more than the devaluation—in order to give rise to the necessary rise in imports. Thus the import substitution effect operates in reverse in a country with import licensing, shifting demand for home-sector tradables down instead of up, as shown in figure 7.4. There are also secondary effects that occur here as well, though they are not shown in the figure. On the one hand, the drop in imports prices reduces costs of intermediate inputs in all sectors that use imports, and this shifts supply curves down. At the same time, with outputs rising in export sectors and falling in home sectors, the secondary effect on intermediate goods demand is ambiguous. Suffice it to say that the overall effects of a devaluation are made quite different by the presence of import licensing.

One final modification in these results should also be mentioned. If, as will be assumed briefly, wages are not held fixed but are permitted to adjust to conditions in labor markets, then supply curves in all of these diagrams will shift further as changes in wages cause changes in labor costs. For example, in figures 7.1–7.3 where outputs tended to rise with a devaluation, labor demand would also increase, causing a rise in wages and a further upward shift in supply curves. This will dampen the increases in outputs in many sectors, while causing outputs necessarily to fall in others, especially nontradables. At the same time they will cause prices in all sectors to rise more than they would have if wages were fixed.

Output Effects of Exchange-Rate Changes[2]

We turn now to our empirical analysis of the effects of exchange rates on outputs. Experience with flexible exchange rates has demonstrated that the rates do in fact move substantially when they are allowed to and, as some observers believe, may overshoot their dynamic equilibrium paths. If, in fact,

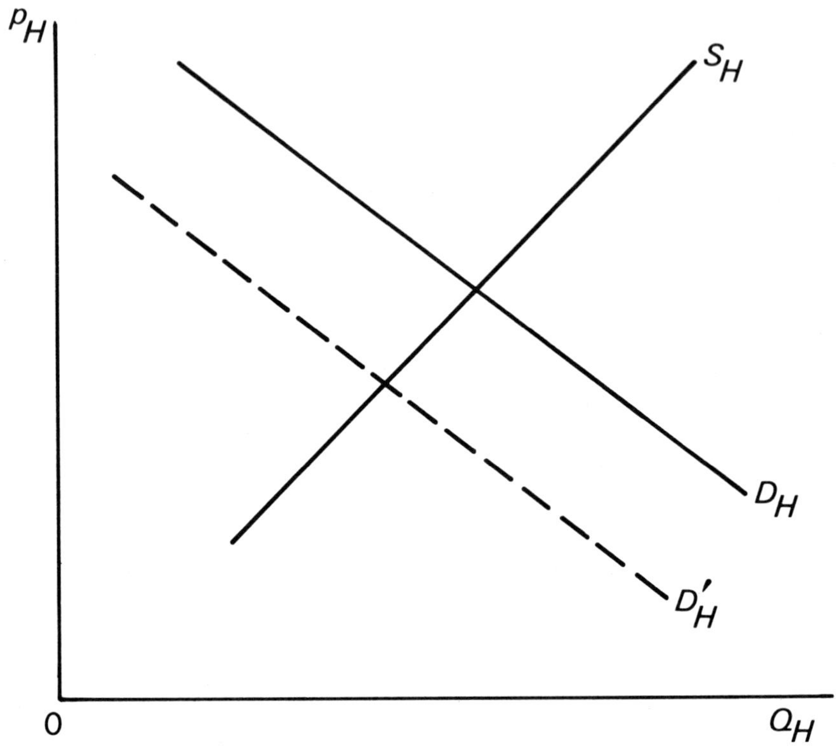

Figure 7.4
Primary effect of a devaluation on a home-sector tradable in a country with import licensing.

overshooting of an exchange rate does occur, it is a cause for concern to the extent that it gives rise to misleading price signals and thus to unnecessary real adjustments. In order to provide some perspective on this issue, we analyze and attempt to quantify the sensitivity of a country or industry to exchange-rate changes. It will not be possible to give a precise indication of the adjustment costs involved because we lack the knowledge of what equilibrium exchange rates are and of how the various goods and factor markets in fact adjust. Nevertheless, a beginning can be made toward placing some boundaries on these costs by a reasonably realistic modeling of the output and employment effects that may occur when exchange rates change in the major industrialized countries.

The costs associated with exchange-rate fluctuations have been discussed in the literature primarily under the heading of "false trading." The concern is that exchange rates may depart from their dynamic equilibrium values and thus cause trade to take place in a way that runs counter to underlying comparative advantage. For example, if "unwarranted" speculative pressures cause a country's currency to be overvalued compared with its true equilibrium, then that country may find itself importing products from abroad that can be produced more cheaply, in real terms, at home. At the same time, the country's trading partners may be deprived of certain products that the country would normally export, as the real costs of those products are masked by the overvalued currency. As a result, all countries fail to capture a portion of the traditional gains from trade, since these gains require that trade be determined solely by comparative advantage.

Whatever the merits of this argument, however, the phenomenon of false trading cannot be regarded as exclusively the product of a system of flexible exchange rates. False trading may occur whenever exchange rates are misaligned, and government intervention to peg the exchange rate is surely as likely a cause of misalignment as is unwarranted private speculation. To evaluate the alternative systems of pegged versus flexible exchange rates in terms of the false trading that they would induce would therefore require an assessment of the relative abilities of governments and speculators as predictors and enforcers of the equilibrium exchange rate.

This discussion of false trading misses, however, what may be a much more important cost of exchange-rate flexibility. Whenever an exchange rate changes, it alters the structure of prices faced by producers and consumers in all countries and induces them to alter, in turn, the pattern of production and consumption. While these changes are reflected in changes in trade, the costs of adjusting to the new prices will likely be borne by all producers and consumers, whether or not they engage directly in trade.

It is possible, of course, for exchange-rate changes to be caused by internal developments in the underlying economies. Indeed, a principal advantage of flexible exchange rates is the capacity of this system rapidly to reconcile international variations in productivity, inflation, and aggregate demand. Thus, we would not argue that *any* exchange-rate change that we observe is the cause of adjustment costs that should be avoided. But when exchange rates first move one way, then the other, the presumption is that the resulting real adjustments serve no useful purpose. When an industry contracts due to an exchange-rate change, only to expand later when that movement is reversed, it is hard to see how the adjustment costs borne by capital and labor in that industry during the interim can have been offset by benefits elsewhere in the system.

It is in this context, then, that we have chosen to examine the industry responsiveness to exchange-rate changes in the major industrialized and

Table 7.1
Exchange-rate elasticities of output by industry and country[a]

Industry	(ISIC)	ALA	ATA	BLX	CND	DEN	FIN	FR	GFR	IRE	IT	JPN	NL	NZ*	NOR	SWD	SWZ	UK
Traded goods																		
AGR., FOR., & FISH.	(1)	0.29	0.20	0.05	0.17	0.24	0.22	0.11	0.06	0.10	0.07	0.03	0.20	1.55	0.18	0.16	0.20	0.10
FOOD, BEV., & TOB.	(310)	0.43	0.13	0.18	0.08	0.51	0.09	0.22	0.00	0.23	0.08	−0.08	0.51	3.50	0.16	0.02	0.07	0.03
TEXTILES	(321)	4.12	4.11	1.25	1.10	0.85	3.72	2.05	0.84	1.13	1.19	0.88	1.53	35.08	2.83	3.15	3.84	1.03
WEARING APPAREL	(322)	0.05	5.31	2.34	0.49	1.83	8.06	2.33	0.66	1.60	1.59	0.46	2.42	5.84	2.69	4.38	2.84	0.90
LEATHER PROD.	(323)	14.03	9.18	1.32	13.40	1.75	13.61	4.51	1.29	2.53	1.66	1.20	3.20	65.92	14.37	13.89	9.55	1.46
FOOTWEAR	(324)	0.03	5.54	0.16	0.62	1.59	5.34	1.88	0.40	0.93	2.13	0.31	1.43	4.53	2.20	5.53	2.63	0.34
WOOD PROD.	(331)	0.40	1.85	0.59	1.35	0.94	1.71	0.36	0.43	0.45	0.46	0.25	0.48	0.32	0.99	1.60	1.06	0.50
FURN. & FIXT.	(332)	−0.03	0.49	0.91	0.92	3.06	2.72	0.57	1.09	0.54	0.88	−0.10	1.53	−1.10	1.02	3.05	0.79	0.74
PAPER & PAPER PROD.	(341)	0.71	3.92	2.11	3.33	1.13	4.76	1.23	0.70	0.93	0.91	0.43	1.78	7.76	3.57	4.54	2.06	0.87
PRINT. & PUBL.	(342)	0.22	1.14	0.84	0.35	0.21	0.52	0.47	0.18	0.44	0.28	0.06	0.32	−5.43	0.30	0.45	0.72	0.32
CHEMICALS	(35A)	1.29	1.59	1.30	1.14	1.06	1.55	0.88	1.14	1.06	1.05	0.57	0.99	−11.67	1.58	1.57	1.78	1.20
PETROL. & REL. PROD.	(35B)	4.19	0.94	1.97	2.33	0.22	1.17	0.87	0.89	0.12	0.35	0.49	0.67	10.92	1.86	1.22	2.76	1.08
RUBBER PROD.	(355)	0.87	2.09	1.34	1.42	1.03	1.47	1.58	1.50	0.75	1.61	1.00	0.89	−6.64	1.77	1.84	1.78	1.82
NONMETAL. MIN. PROD.	(36A)	0.36	1.22	1.74	1.52	1.88	0.58	0.32	0.94	2.00	1.42	0.19	1.45	−4.91	1.05	0.78	0.98	1.60
GLASS & GLASS PROD.	(362)	0.71	2.12	5.52	1.23	2.91	2.49	1.07	1.60	2.73	1.94	0.18	3.94	−3.65	1.31	2.21	1.63	2.83
IRON & STEEL	(371)	1.70	4.26	2.89	2.12	1.62	2.87	2.15	2.12	0.97	1.67	0.93	1.41	−20.86	4.87	4.20	3.32	2.60
NONFERROUS METALS	(372)	6.14	3.52	2.78	5.02	1.73	4.20	1.60	1.90	2.00	1.80	0.82	1.82	37.75	5.37	5.63	3.54	3.26
METAL PROD.	(381)	0.43	1.64	0.89	0.82	0.84	1.24	0.53	0.65	1.37	0.83	0.14	0.85	−3.36	1.44	1.42	1.63	0.95
NONELEC. MACH.	(382)	0.49	2.40	1.01	1.84	1.30	1.40	1.18	1.04	1.11	1.18	0.30	0.94	−4.47	1.29	2.13	2.54	1.56
ELEC. MACH.	(383)	0.38	1.45	0.65	0.59	0.64	1.32	0.71	0.70	0.29	0.52	0.20	0.56	−7.34	1.26	1.95	1.50	0.56
TRANSP. EQUIP.	(384)	0.21	0.69	0.81	0.79	1.87	0.86	0.55	0.67	0.19	0.96	0.33	0.40	−8.34	0.98	0.97	0.59	0.80
MISC. MANUF.	(38A)	0.65	1.47	1.11	0.97	1.81	0.99	0.52	1.04	1.20	0.98	0.47	1.27	−4.90	1.15	1.47	1.44	1.72
Average		0.99	1.77	1.08	1.09	0.85	1.57	0.76	0.81	0.56	0.80	0.34	0.77	2.34	1.31	1.69	1.57	0.98
Nontraded goods																		
MIN. & QUARRY.	(2)	1.64	1.24	1.26	1.66	0.33	1.21	0.68	0.81	0.31	0.80	0.44	0.59	−0.04	1.70	1.47	1.31	1.18
ELEC., GAS, & WATER	(4)	0.19	0.37	0.28	0.19	0.07	0.40	0.18	0.25	0.07	0.48	0.09	0.03	−1.71	0.32	0.30	0.27	0.32
CONSTRUCTION	(5)	−0.08	−0.13	−0.23	−0.10	−0.18	−0.11	−0.14	−0.14	−0.23	−0.11	−0.13	−0.23	−1.75	−0.11	−0.15	−0.16	−0.07
WHOLE. & RET. TRADE	(6)	0.07	0.16	−0.01	0.07	0.02	0.20	−0.02	0.04	−0.01	0.02	0.01	0.02	−3.09	0.12	0.14	0.14	0.14
TRANSP., STOR., & COMM.	(7)	0.23	0.51	0.23	0.30	0.12	0.56	0.19	0.17	0.07	0.27	0.02	0.05	−1.77	0.40	0.47	0.41	0.33
FIN., INS., & REAL EST.	(8)	0.11	0.16	0.04	0.12	−0.01	0.17	0.05	0.02	0.03	0.10	0.01	0.04	−2.34	0.16	0.13	0.17	0.14
COMM., SOC., & PERS. SERV.	(9)	0.02	0.04	0.01	0.00	−0.03	0.06	−0.01	0.00	0.02	0.06	−0.06	0.00	−4.64	0.04	0.02	0.00	0.01
Average		0.15	0.14	0.02	0.14	−0.03	0.14	0.00	0.03	−0.01	0.08	−0.03	−0.02	−2.78	0.22	0.09	0.13	0.13
Overall average		0.43	0.84	0.43	0.43	0.32	0.81	0.32	0.40	0.22	0.42	0.15	0.32	−1.12	0.60	0.76	0.83	0.44

Table 7.1 (continued)

Industry	(ISIC)	US	ARG*	BRZ*	CHL*	COL*	GRC*	HK	IND*	ISR	SK*	MEX	POR*	SNG	SP*	TWN*	TRK*	YUG
Traded goods																		
AGR., FOR., & FISH.	(1)	0.11	0.05	0.01	0.33	0.02	−0.03	0.11	−0.01	0.07	−0.21	0.02	−0.05	0.16	−0.03	−0.24	−0.01	0.03
FOOD, BEV., & TOB.	(310)	0.04	0.26	0.19	0.55	0.01	0.12	−0.08	0.19	0.00	−0.15	0.02	0.09	0.28	0.16	1.00	−0.01	0.03
TEXTILES	(321)	1.10	0.89	0.05	0.70	0.20	0.25	0.58	0.27	0.29	0.40	0.41	0.32	0.59	0.08	0.70	0.32	0.28
WEARING APPAREL	(322)	0.39	1.40	0.02	0.84	0.15	0.77	0.71	1.46	0.24	2.01	0.07	1.20	0.73	0.24	2.08	0.44	0.38
LEATHER PROD.	(323)	4.53	4.76	1.41	0.49	1.09	4.88	1.38	4.81	2.15	8.85	0.14	1.08	1.23	1.37	10.30	3.59	0.90
FOOTWEAR	(324)	0.18	2.09	0.32	0.86	0.30	0.77	0.86	1.26	−0.04	1.47	−0.01	0.73	0.87	0.74	1.62	0.01	0.54
WOOD PROD.	(331)	0.42	0.18	0.00	0.84	0.18	−0.30	0.41	0.16	0.22	−0.58	0.51	0.28	0.55	−0.34	0.57	−0.07	0.35
FURN. & FIXT.	(332)	0.16	0.90	0.01	0.75	0.22	0.05	0.93	0.85	−0.05	5.05	−0.28	−0.13	0.69	0.78	6.95	0.01	0.22
PAPER & PAPER PROD.	(341)	0.67	−0.11	−0.12	0.69	−0.02	−0.42	0.69	−0.05	0.30	−0.59	0.20	0.86	0.81	−0.07	−0.59	−0.13	0.28
PRINT. & PUBL.	(342)	0.09	0.01	−0.07	0.89	−0.03	−0.14	0.13	0.01	0.02	−0.40	−0.01	−0.16	0.42	0.02	−0.80	−0.06	−0.00
CHEMICALS	(35A)	0.53	−0.09	−0.25	0.53	−0.13	−0.16	0.29	−0.07	0.31	−0.71	0.21	−0.16	0.30	−0.14	−0.75	−0.22	0.21
PETROL. & REL. PROD.	(35B)	0.40	0.66	1.03	0.85	1.42	1.53	1.28	1.02	1.24	1.65	1.02	1.38	0.99	1.21	2.04	0.83	1.28
RUBBER PROD.	(355)	0.56	−0.02	−0.15	1.03	−0.24	−0.49	0.43	0.03	0.39	−0.24	0.32	−0.30	0.55	0.01	−0.79	−0.27	0.43
NONMETAL. MIN. PROD.	(36A)	0.31	−0.06	−0.07	1.15	−0.01	0.12	0.51	−0.05	0.11	−0.13	0.22	−0.09	0.52	−0.06	−0.65	0.03	0.15
GLASS & GLASS PROD.	(362)	0.47	−0.01	−0.08	0.95	0.04	−0.36	0.71	0.08	0.32	−0.43	0.19	0.06	0.77	−0.13	0.54	0.07	0.27
IRON & STEEL	(371)	0.73	−0.49	−0.21	0.92	−0.69	0.08	0.45	0.15	0.35	−0.66	0.23	−0.67	0.61	−0.10	−3.24	−0.68	0.31
NONFERROUS METALS	(372)	0.99	−1.55	0.48	0.37	−1.40	0.73	0.76	0.92	0.56	−4.06	0.65	−0.97	0.76	−0.56	−2.93	0.05	0.53
METAL PROD.	(381)	0.40	0.06	−0.05	1.55	0.09	−0.03	0.46	0.23	0.22	0.70	0.25	0.18	0.49	0.05	1.98	−0.06	0.15
NONELEC. MACH.	(382)	0.66	0.27	−0.05	1.12	0.12	−0.13	0.54	0.08	0.08	−0.08	0.61	0.28	0.53	0.40	0.86	−0.02	0.24
ELEC. MACH.	(382)	0.49	−0.04	−0.11	1.90	−0.03	−0.10	0.32	0.21	0.11	0.74	0.36	0.17	0.32	−0.04	0.75	−0.07	0.12
TRANSP. EQUIP.	(384)	0.34	0.05	−0.02	0.57	−0.06	−0.14	0.09	0.05	0.11	0.10	0.09	−0.01	0.20	0.05	0.03	−0.04	0.10
MISC. MANUF.	(38A)	0.43	0.06	−0.04	0.73	0.28	−0.02	0.63	1.04	0.68	1.50	0.18	0.28	0.63	−0.09	1.64	−0.05	0.31
Average		0.41	0.11	0.06	0.61	0.04	0.11	0.51	0.06	0.22	0.01	0.23	0.12	0.62	0.09	0.22	0.03	0.18
Nontraded goods																		
MIN. & QUARRY.	(2)	0.38	0.53	0.83	0.79	1.12	1.17	0.10	0.80	0.96	1.47	0.98	1.07	0.98	1.00	1.73	0.74	0.90
ELEC., GAS, & WATER	(4)	0.07	−0.05	−0.07	0.93	−0.08	−0.16	0.03	−0.01	0.01	−0.50	0.02	−0.16	0.03	−0.11	−0.83	−0.07	0.05
CONSTRUCTION	(5)	−0.04	0.01	−0.06	1.13	−0.04	−0.15	−0.24	0.03	−0.17	−0.16	−0.15	−0.11	−0.26	−0.07	−0.34	−0.02	−0.13
WHOLE. & RET. TRADE	(6)	0.03	−0.02	−0.07	0.93	−0.07	−0.15	0.06	−0.03	−0.01	−0.47	−0.01	−0.15	−0.01	−0.10	−0.76	−0.07	0.01
TRANSP., STOR., & COMM.	(7)	0.11	−0.05	−0.08	1.15	−0.10	−0.18	−0.04	−0.03	−0.05	−0.58	−0.03	−0.20	−0.01	−0.13	−0.98	−0.08	−0.02
FIN., INS., & REAL EST.	(8)	0.04	−0.08	−0.12	1.34	−0.13	−0.29	−0.02	−0.07	−0.01	−0.87	−0.01	−0.28	−0.01	−0.18	−1.41	−0.12	−0.00
COMM., SOC., & PERS. SERV.	(9)	−0.00	0.11	−0.02	1.17	−0.01	−0.12	−0.10	0.06	−0.09	−0.26	−0.11	−0.13	−0.09	−0.01	−0.53	−0.02	−0.04
Average		0.04	0.03	−0.07	1.08	−0.04	−0.14	−0.03	0.02	−0.04	−0.43	0.03	−0.16	−0.05	−0.08	−0.77	−0.03	0.01
Overall average		0.16	0.08	−0.01	0.91	0.01	−0.02	0.16	0.05	0.07	−0.18	0.11	−0.01	0.21	−0.00	−0.22	0.00	0.11

a. Countries assumed to use import licensing are marked with an asterisk. Averages are weighted using value of production.

developing countries. Our analysis may make it possible to form some judgment regarding the costs of adjustment to exchange-rate changes when these changes are not warranted by underlying movements in real economic variables.

The procedure that we followed was to solve the model with positive exchange-rate changes for each country separately. As defined, an exchange-rate increase represents a devaluation of the currency in question. From the solution, we took the ratio of the percentage change in output, by industry, to the percentage change in the exchange rate. These ratios are reported for each country and industry in table 7.1, and are referred to as the exchange-rate elasticity of output (EREO). Each column represents the solution of the model for a devaluation of the currency of the country indicated, with all other exchange rates held fixed. The output changes include both home-sector and export-sector production in the case of tradable industries.

It is clear from the table that the vast majority of industries in the industrialized countries are affected positively by a devaluation of their individual currencies, but there is also considerable variation across both countries and industries in the size of this response. In several cases, the expansion is considerably larger than the exchange-rate change that causes it (the elasticity is larger than one), but the responses vary all the way down to near zero and a few are even negative. In nontradable industries, the values are generally smaller than in tradable industries, and there is a higher proportion of negative entries. Again, this is to be expected.

Dramatically different results are reported for New Zealand and for many of the developing countries. The reason is that these countries, which are marked with an asterisk in the table, are the ones that are assumed to use import licensing. As noted previously, when they devalue, their imports are allowed to rise, and this causes output to fall in many tradable sectors that compete heavily with imports.

Our primary objective here is to find what it is about a country and industry that determines the size of the exchange-rate response. To do so, we shall look at the problem first in theoretical terms, within the context of our model. Then, we shall examine the numerical results to see to what extent they confirm our theoretical expectations.[3]

The Export Effect

The first channel through which a devaluation would be expected to affect output is via the price responsiveness of the export sector of each tradable industry, as was shown in figure 7.1. By assuming, for the moment, that a devaluation causes export prices to rise by the same percentage as the exchange rate, the effect on the export sector of each industry will depend upon its elasticity of supply. In addition, this effect on the export sector will be reflected in an increase in output for the entire industry that will be larger, in percentage terms, the larger is the export sector as compared to the home sector. *These considerations, then, suggest that the EREO of each industry should be positively related to both the elasticity of supply of the industry and the share of exports in total production.*

The Import Substitution Effect

The rise in import prices also should have an effect on output, as noted in figure 7.2. As the import price rises, demanders will substitute away from imports and toward domestically produced goods. As they do so, they will bid up the home price in the industry and thus stimulate production in the home sector as well. This effect is limited, both by the importance of imports in demand and by the willingness of demanders to substitute between imports and home goods. *We would therefore expect two additional determinants of the EREO to be the share of imports in total demand and the elasticity of substitution between imported and home-produced goods.*[4]

The World Price Effect

Both the export effect and the import substitution effect depend on the devaluation raising the domestic prices of exports and imports. However, to the extent that these prices do rise, the increased supply of exports and the reduced demand for imports will both tend to depress the world price in the industry. This fall in the world price will to some extent offset both of the direct effects previously mentioned and thus reduce the size of the EREO. Now the decline in the world price will be greater, the greater are the country's exports and imports in the industry as shares of the corresponding world supply and demand. Thus, we would expect the EREO to be negatively related to these shares. *In addition, since both of these shares are likely to depend heavily on the size of the industry as a whole, we would expect the EREO to be negatively related to the value of production.*

The Interindustry Sales Effect

So far in this section, we have considered each industry in isolation, without taking into account the roles that might be played by interactions among industries via the input-output structure of the economy. One such role arises from the difference between the responses to a devaluation on the part of consumers and firms as demanders. By causing prices and outputs generally to rise, a devaluation will cause an increase in demands for intermediate inputs, whether or not they happen to be tradable. No such increase is likely, however, on the part of consumers, whose total expenditure is more or less held fixed.[5] Thus, we would expect an additional stimulation to output even in nontradable industries, to the extent that they sell a large part of their product to intermediate users. *The EREO, then, should depend negatively on the share of final demand in total demand for an industry.*

The Interindustry Purchases Effect

Just as an industry will benefit, under a devaluation, from sales to other industries, it will also be harmed by the need to purchase inputs itself from these industries. For as the prices of goods generally rise, industries that rely heavily on produced, as opposed to primary, inputs will experience an increase in costs. As long as the wage remains fixed, on the other hand, industries with a low dependence on produced inputs will experience very little increase in costs. *Thus, we would expect the EREO to depend positively on the labor share of valued added in the industry.*

The Expenditure Effect

In general one might expect consumer expenditure to change as a result of a devaluation, so that the intercountry differences in EREOs would depend on the size and direction of that change. However, since our model does not allow for such expenditure effects as they are usually specified, we cannot explore this issue in any detail.[6] What our model does contain is a dependence of expenditure on the economy's tariff revenue. Given the level of tariffs, this revenue depends on import prices and on the quantity of imports, both of which change, but in opposite directions, with a devaluation. It is not clear, a priori, what the net effect on tariff revenue will be. But it should be kept in mind as a possible source of explanation for results of the model that might otherwise be incomprehensible.

Now that we have seen a variety of channels through which exchange rates can affect outputs, it remains to examine the results computed by our model to determine, if possible, which of these channels are most important. Mere inspection of table 7.1 is clearly inadequate for this purpose. Instead, we have tested for the presence of these effects in the industrialized countries

Table 7.2
Rank correlations of exogenous variables with the exchange-rate elasticity of output for the industrialized countries

Exogenous variable	Correlation with EREO
Supply elasticity	0.40*
Share of industry output exported	0.76*
Substitution elasticity between imports and home goods	0.41*
Share of imports in demand	0.67*
Value of production	−0.50*
Final demand share in total demand per good	−0.31*
Labor share of value added	0.28*

*Significant at the .99 level.

by computing rank correlations between the results reported in table 7.1 and the exogenous variables that we found, in the previous discussion, to be likely determinants of the EREO. These rank correlations are reported in table 7.2. It should be made clear that, in spite of their appearance, these correlations are *not* the equivalent of estimating a multiple regression equation, which would be inappropriate here since there was nothing stochastic about the generation of the EREO. They are presented merely as a convenient means of describing how our complicated model works.

All the correlations reported in table 7.2 have the expected sign and are significant. The largest correlations are clearly with respect to the export and import shares, but the results overall serve to confirm our insights into the working of the model. It thus appears that the sensitivity of industrial output to an exchange-rate change can be substantial, and, more important, that there is considerable variation across industries and countries in the size of the response.[7] There are even a number of industries in which output falls. The variations in response will thus make it difficult to offset possible dislocations caused by exchange-rate changes. If all industries of a country were affected identically, then it might be feasible to use macroeconomic policies to anticipate exchange-rate movements and thus to prevent them from having any effect at all. But, in fact, it is likely to be difficult to find a policy that would affect each industry by just the right amount.

Own-Country Price Effects of Uniform Exchange-Rate Changes

Turning now to examination of the price effects of exchange-rate changes, we have used the model as in the preceding section to calculate the effects,

Table 7.3
Percentage change in home-sector price by industry due to 1% devaluation in each country assuming money wages fixed[a]

Industry	(ISIC)	ALA	ATA	BLX	CND	DEN	FIN	FR	GFR	IRE	IT	JPN	NL	NZ*	NOR	SWD	SWZ	UK
Traded goods																		
AGR., FOR., & FISH.	(1)	1.06	0.82	0.82	0.58	1.00	0.86	0.50	0.44	1.02	0.32	0.26	1.17	0.61	0.72	0.69	0.82	0.27
FOOD, BEV., & TOB.	(310)	0.45	0.42	0.43	0.31	0.50	0.43	0.27	0.22	0.56	0.22	0.13	0.71	−2.53	0.38	0.37	0.41	0.16
TEXTILES	(321)	0.63	0.82	0.81	0.41	0.69	0.83	0.48	0.55	0.77	0.64	0.29	0.81	−6.43	0.61	0.69	0.76	0.49
WEARING APPAREL	(322)	0.36	0.57	0.52	0.28	0.43	0.55	0.23	0.31	0.44	0.22	0.20	0.48	−5.56	0.48	0.51	0.50	0.20
LEATHER PROD.	(323)	0.41	0.58	0.61	0.38	0.67	0.58	0.38	0.47	0.63	0.68	0.24	0.59	−10.25	0.46	0.51	0.49	0.45
FOOTWEAR	(324)	0.32	0.44	0.30	0.33	0.46	0.41	0.23	0.33	0.37	0.29	0.19	0.38	−12.16	0.38	0.40	0.41	0.23
WOOD PROD.	(331)	0.36	0.74	0.81	0.54	0.70	0.83	0.32	0.51	0.55	0.68	0.25	0.57	−4.16	0.60	0.78	0.63	0.36
FURN. & FIXT.	(332)	0.24	0.41	0.57	0.27	0.50	0.38	0.25	0.33	0.38	0.31	0.15	0.43	−5.34	0.37	0.40	0.37	0.27
PAPER & PAPER PROD.	(341)	0.31	0.58	0.67	0.44	0.51	0.68	0.29	0.49	0.54	0.42	0.25	0.51	−4.18	0.52	0.61	0.46	0.35
PRINT. & PUBL.	(342)	0.18	0.32	0.46	0.20	0.32	0.26	0.19	0.20	0.37	0.23	0.12	0.34	−3.64	0.23	0.24	0.27	0.22
CHEMICALS	(35A)	0.58	0.76	0.78	0.53	0.71	0.75	0.47	0.54	0.76	0.50	0.50	0.80	−10.12	0.70	0.70	0.79	0.48
PETROL. & REL. PROD.	(35B)	0.86	0.74	0.64	0.88	0.64	0.73	0.42	0.44	0.79	0.76	0.39	0.82	−11.14	0.94	0.83	0.77	0.44
RUBBER PROD.	(355)	0.41	0.57	0.72	0.40	0.82	0.57	0.52	0.55	0.61	0.43	0.27	0.58	−6.91	0.54	0.56	0.56	0.33
NONMETAL. MIN. PROD.	(36A)	0.29	0.41	0.45	0.37	0.38	0.36	0.27	0.34	0.51	0.32	0.17	0.48	−4.67	0.42	0.40	0.44	0.25
GLASS & GLASS PROD.	(362)	0.30	0.45	0.49	0.33	0.34	0.43	0.26	0.29	0.49	0.31	0.16	0.54	−4.57	0.41	0.45	0.45	0.23
IRON & STEEL	(371)	0.36	0.56	0.84	0.43	0.77	0.49	0.40	0.57	0.57	0.51	0.53	0.63	−10.92	0.60	0.57	0.57	0.36
NONFERROUS METALS	(372)	0.72	0.68	0.73	0.72	0.64	0.66	0.42	0.59	0.68	0.53	0.51	0.70	−9.64	0.84	0.79	0.67	0.41
METAL PROD.	(381)	0.28	0.47	0.43	0.36	0.56	0.45	0.25	0.34	0.61	0.36	0.21	0.46	−10.20	0.53	0.49	0.50	0.29
NONELEC. MACH.	(382)	0.26	0.43	0.45	0.34	0.39	0.37	0.24	0.26	0.46	0.31	0.16	0.44	−9.87	0.42	0.43	0.44	0.28
ELEC. MACH.	(383)	0.27	0.42	0.52	0.30	0.56	0.39	0.26	0.29	0.62	0.33	0.17	0.56	−7.63	0.43	0.46	0.42	0.35
TRANSP. EQUIP.	(384)	0.32	0.56	0.81	0.44	0.59	0.55	0.36	0.42	0.56	0.29	0.19	0.65	−12.56	0.65	0.56	0.57	0.29
MISC. MANUF.	(38A)	0.39	0.64	0.72	0.45	0.52	0.59	0.28	0.47	0.75	0.38	0.28	0.64	−9.31	0.56	0.61	0.63	0.43
Average		0.53	0.59	0.61	0.45	0.62	0.64	0.35	0.39	0.64	0.38	0.26	0.72	−4.86	0.57	0.55	0.56	0.32
Nontraded goods																		
MIN. & QUARRY.	(2)	1.50	1.20	1.20	1.53	0.59	1.17	0.84	0.91	0.63	1.02	0.33	1.26	−3.25	1.60	1.40	1.26	0.60
ELEC., GAS, & WATER	(4)	0.44	0.54	0.36	0.45	0.22	0.56	0.28	0.42	0.24	0.35	0.16	0.44	−4.83	0.57	0.52	0.48	0.32
CONSTRUCTION	(5)	0.19	0.29	0.29	0.23	0.23	0.27	0.14	0.15	0.30	0.15	0.12	0.34	−5.69	0.29	0.27	0.26	0.17
WHOLE. & RET. TRADE	(6)	0.10	0.14	0.12	0.10	0.12	0.15	0.07	0.15	0.11	0.12	0.04	0.13	−2.34	0.13	0.13	0.13	0.11
TRANSP., STOR., & COMM.	(7)	0.16	0.28	0.21	0.19	0.17	0.29	0.13	0.17	0.19	0.17	0.07	0.18	−3.75	0.25	0.26	0.25	0.21
FIN., INS., & REAL EST.	(8)	0.18	0.25	0.11	0.18	0.08	0.26	0.09	0.08	0.13	0.14	0.03	0.09	−3.86	0.25	0.21	0.25	0.33
COMM., SOC., & PERS. SERV.	(9)	0.06	0.09	0.08	0.07	0.07	0.09	0.06	0.06	0.08	0.07	0.05	0.07	−1.92	0.09	0.08	0.08	0.07
Average		0.22	0.24	0.17	0.22	0.13	0.21	0.11	0.14	0.15	0.16	0.07	0.16	−3.36	0.29	0.19	0.21	0.17
Overall average		0.32	0.39	0.34	0.29	0.33	0.41	0.21	0.26	0.34	0.26	0.16	0.40	−3.85	0.39	0.34	0.38	0.23

Table 7.3 (continued)

Industry	(ISIC)	US	ARG*	BRZ*	CHL*	COL*	GRC*	HK	IND*	ISR	SK*	MEX	POR*	SNG	SP*	TWN*	TRK*	YUG
Traded goods																		
AGR., FOR., & FISH.	(1)	0.31	0.05	-0.12	2.16	-0.15	-0.30	0.59	-0.10	0.30	-1.50	0.07	-0.41	0.63	-0.32	-2.02	-0.15	0.21
FOOD, BEV., & TOB.	(310)	0.15	-0.12	-0.15	1.67	-0.16	-0.29	0.42	-0.15	0.21	-1.33	0.07	-0.40	0.45	-0.29	-2.10	-0.15	0.14
TEXTILES	(321)	0.17	-2.48	-0.20	1.57	-0.09	-0.17	0.97	-0.11	0.46	-1.25	0.20	-0.14	0.79	-0.34	-1.28	-0.07	0.44
WEARING APPAREL	(322)	0.10	-1.60	-0.18	1.46	-0.16	-0.35	0.69	-1.34	0.21	-3.15	0.12	-0.46	0.70	-0.35	-4.05	-0.14	0.19
LEATHER PROD.	(323)	0.14	-2.49	-0.21	1.61	-0.17	-0.80	0.87	-1.38	0.51	-4.66	0.19	-0.34	0.85	-0.28	-9.15	-0.25	0.37
FOOTWEAR	(324)	0.12	-2.35	-0.18	1.36	-0.16	-0.76	0.63	-1.37	0.33	-4.37	0.11	-0.32	0.61	-0.22	-7.14	-0.21	0.25
WOOD PROD.	(331)	0.20	0.15	-0.15	1.91	-0.10	-0.65	0.78	-0.09	0.45	-5.62	0.38	-0.33	0.82	-1.09	-2.94	-0.19	0.32
FURN. & FIXT.	(332)	0.10	-1.05	-0.19	1.52	-0.15	-0.54	0.65	-0.25	0.41	-3.93	0.31	-0.36	0.68	-0.79	-3.90	-0.19	0.27
PAPER & PAPER PROD.	(341)	0.13	-0.24	-0.26	1.67	-0.25	-0.63	0.66	-0.38	0.43	-1.99	0.27	-0.18	0.64	-0.34	-2.04	-0.25	0.29
PRINT. & PUBL.	(342)	0.06	-0.16	-0.20	1.52	-0.26	-0.43	0.19	-0.21	0.15	-1.38	0.08	-0.37	0.49	-0.28	-1.94	-0.19	0.09
CHEMICALS	(35A)	0.20	-0.35	-0.80	1.86	-0.51	-0.85	0.91	-0.41	0.79	-2.81	0.59	-0.75	0.81	-0.62	-3.14	-0.71	0.64
PETROL. & REL. PROD.	(35B)	0.22	0.39	0.63	0.99	0.94	0.80	0.28	0.42	0.97	0.55	0.94	0.76	1.00	0.74	0.52	0.57	0.90
RUBBER PROD.	(355)	0.15	-0.35	-0.42	1.95	-0.51	-0.98	0.83	-0.20	0.68	-1.84	0.58	-0.72	0.93	-0.59	-3.25	-0.55	0.71
NONMETAL. MIN. PROD.	(36A)	0.11	-0.13	-0.11	1.73	-0.14	-0.40	0.70	-0.37	0.31	-1.27	0.25	-0.31	0.69	-0.26	-1.98	-0.15	0.28
GLASS & GLASS PROD.	(362)	0.11	-0.09	-0.20	1.36	-0.23	-0.65	0.70	-0.18	0.46	-1.40	0.23	-0.28	0.71	-0.35	-2.78	-0.16	0.34
IRON & STEEL	(371)	0.14	-0.91	-0.50	1.32	-1.14	-1.09	0.81	-0.52	0.73	-3.99	0.46	-1.88	0.84	-0.49	-8.18	-1.12	0.55
NONFERROUS METALS	(372)	0.20	-2.01	-0.56	-23.32	-1.98	-0.60	0.84	-4.68	0.73	-9.12	0.70	-3.54	0.87	-1.03	-6.33	-0.65	0.62
METAL PROD.	(381)	0.13	-0.49	-0.30	0.52	-0.44	-0.56	0.61	-0.45	0.40	-2.61	0.39	-0.83	0.71	-0.35	-6.91	-0.45	0.31
NONELEC. MACH.	(382)	0.11	-0.68	-0.39	1.39	-0.44	-0.71	0.39	-0.43	0.21	-2.40	0.22	-0.66	0.28	-0.70	-3.70	-0.38	0.28
ELEC. MACH.	(383)	0.12	-0.76	-0.57	0.51	-0.59	-0.75	0.70	-0.59	0.37	-4.66	0.56	-0.87	0.61	-0.54	-5.88	-0.44	0.32
TRANSP. EQUIP.	(384)	0.17	-0.26	-0.39	1.74	-0.63	-1.28	0.62	-0.34	0.55	-3.09	0.51	-0.80	0.75	-0.46	-4.21	-0.48	0.42
MISC. MANUF.	(38A)	0.18	-0.46	-0.41	1.51	-0.32	-0.55	0.72	-1.75	0.63	-4.86	0.29	-0.65	0.63	-0.60	-6.12	-0.36	0.47
Average		0.17	-0.29	-0.21	-1.96	-0.20	-0.38	0.74	-0.18	0.40	-1.81	0.32	-0.45	0.79	-0.36	-2.76	-0.19	0.33
Nontraded goods																		
MIN. & QUARRY.	(2)	0.36	0.52	0.84	1.08	1.17	1.16	0.22	0.63	1.14	0.95	1.11	1.06	1.16	0.99	1.07	0.74	1.04
ELEC., GAS, & WATER	(4)	0.13	-0.09	-0.11	1.28	-0.11	-0.25	0.11	-0.09	0.06	-0.91	0.07	-0.25	0.10	-0.17	-1.42	-0.11	0.14
CONSTRUCTION	(5)	0.07	-0.17	-0.17	1.17	-0.20	-0.38	0.25	-0.19	0.17	-1.50	0.15	-0.41	0.26	-0.27	-2.31	-0.20	0.13
WHOLE. & RET. TRADE	(6)	0.04	-0.07	-0.11	1.31	-0.11	-0.25	0.13	-0.06	0.03	-0.78	0.02	-0.23	0.06	-0.17	-1.23	-0.11	0.05
TRANSP., STOR., & COMM.	(7)	0.06	-0.09	-0.10	1.05	-0.10	-0.28	0.12	-0.09	0.09	-0.82	0.09	-0.25	0.15	-0.15	-1.32	-0.11	0.09
FIN., INS., & REAL EST.	(8)	0.06	-0.07	-0.09	0.91	-0.09	-0.21	0.01	-0.07	0.01	-0.66	0.00	-0.19	0.02	-0.13	-1.04	-0.09	0.01
COMM., SOC., & PERS. SERV.	(9)	0.02	-0.32	-0.22	1.01	-0.24	-0.39	0.24	-0.23	0.16	-1.39	0.18	-0.36	0.25	-0.34	-2.05	-0.22	0.16
Average		0.06	-0.13	-0.12	1.10	-0.11	-0.26	0.14	-0.10	0.11	-0.99	0.13	-0.26	0.12	-0.20	-1.52	-0.10	0.17
Overall average		0.09	-0.22	-0.16	0.00	-0.16	-0.32	0.35	-0.15	0.23	-1.47	0.21	-0.36	0.38	-0.27	-2.21	-0.15	0.26

a. Countries assumed to use import licensing are marked with an asterisk. Averages are weighted using value of production.

within each country, of a 1% devaluation of its own currency. The results are recorded in table 7.3 for each of the 34 countries and 29 industries of the model. The numbers record percentage changes in home-sector prices in each case. The prices of exports and imports, as we have explained, are more directly tied to world prices in most cases and are therefore less interesting at the disaggregated level.

The results in table 7.3 are very much as we would expect from the theoretical discussion earlier in the chapter. That is, in all countries without import licensing, home-sector prices rise in response to a devaluation, and they virtually always do so by a percentage that is less than the devaluation itself. Likewise, in countries like New Zealand and many of the less developed countries (LDCs), where there is import licensing, home-sector prices fall, often by large amounts.

In the non-import-licensing countries, while prices generally rise by less than the devaluation, it is possible for the secondary shifts of supply and demand to raise the price beyond 1%. This appears to have happened for a few industries in table 7.3 but it does not happen often. A good example is agriculture (ISIC 1), whose demand and therefore price rises substantially in some countries, presumably because it is such an important intermediate input into the production of food (ISIC 310). Similarly, though prices of most nontraded goods rise by only a small amount, the mining and quarrying industry (ISIC 2) posts a large price increase in many countries, apparently because it is a large provider of inputs especially to the (tradable) petroleum and related products industry (ISIC 35B).

All of the effects just described are dampened somewhat if export and import prices do not rise by the full amount of the devaluation. This is most true for large countries, especially the United States, where increased net supply to world markets drives down the world price. Home-price effects are also made even smaller in the United States by the relatively small size of trade relative to the domestic economy. This reduces the scope for all of the effects mentioned.

On turning to the countries with import licensing, the results in table 7.3 provide some indication of how drastic such a licensing policy can be. The price effects recorded for some of these countries in table 7.3 are many times larger than the devaluation that caused them.

Actually, the import-licensing scheme could conceivably turn out to work perversely, and this appears to have happened in our results for one country, Chile. If domestic prices are very sensitive to the scarcity of foreign exchange, then the costs of inputs to the export sectors may be raised so much that exports and export revenues are reduced still further, and the process of finding an equilibrium level of licensing can be unstable. In such a case, the equations of our model will find an equilibrium in the other direction. As seems to have happened in the anomalous case of Chile, the additional export revenues that are provided by a devaluation permit tighter rationing of foreign exchange so as to raise prices and thus costs of producing for export.[8]

The results in table 7.3 are calculated assuming that money wages remain constant in all industries and countries. To test the importance of this assumption, we reran the experiment twice, first allowing wages to adjust to clear the national labor markets in each country, and second allowing wages in each industry to adjust independently to equate labor supply and demand industry by industry within each country. The results do not differ substantially from those in table 7.3, except in one respect, and we therefore do not report the disaggregated results here. The one exception, which will be clear in the price indices to be reported, was the following: When wages adjust industry by industry, the price effects of a devaluation on nontradable industries essentially disappear. The reason is that wage increases in tradables eliminate any net expansion of output there, and thus obviate any increase in demand for nontradables as intermediate inputs. As the same time, wages change in nontradable industries to offset any other cost increases there, thus keeping output and employment in nontradables constant as well. Accordingly, in figure 7.3, we can say that both the supply and demand curves return essentially to their initial positions.

To summarize the role of wage flexibility in determining the price effects of a devaluation, we report in table 7.4 the effects on several price indices that we have calculated in each of the runs. An index of consumer prices is reported, column (1), assuming first that wages are fixed and second and third that wages are flexible by country and by industry, respectively. Column (2) reports an index of producer prices in tradable industries only for each of these three assumptions. Column (3) does the same for nontradable industries. Several conclusions can be derived by examining this table.

First, as our earlier discussion suggested, prices in tradable industries tend always to rise more than in nontradables. This is true regardless of the assumption about wages, but becomes most pronounced when industry wages are flexible. As already explained, prices of nontradables change hardly at all when industry wages adjust.

The effect of allowing the country wages to adjust is, in most countries, to cause prices to rise by more than when wages are fixed. The reason is, of course, that the devaluation tends to raise the overall demand for labor, especially in tradable industries, and the wage must rise to restore equilib-

Table 7.4
Effects of 1% devaluation by country on various price indices in devaluing country[a]

Country	(1) Consumer prices			(2) Producer prices: tradable			(3) Producer prices: nontradable		
	Wages fixed	Country wages flexible	Industry wages flexible	Wages fixed	Country wages flexible	Industry wages flexible	Wages fixed	Country wages flexible	Industry wages flexible
Industrialized countries									
Australia	0.35	0.49	0.22	0.58	0.64	0.69	0.22	0.41	−0.01
Austria	0.45	0.65	0.35	0.71	0.76	0.81	0.24	0.56	0.00
Belgium-Luxembourg	0.41	0.59	0.33	0.80	0.83	0.86	0.17	0.43	0.01
Canada	0.32	0.49	0.22	0.55	0.62	0.73	0.22	0.43	−0.01
Denmark	0.39	0.54	0.33	0.78	0.80	0.84	0.13	0.38	0.01
Finland	0.45	0.62	0.35	0.72	0.70	0.75	0.21	0.55	0.00
France	0.25	0.39	0.24	0.46	0.52	0.63	0.11	0.31	−0.02
German Federal Republic	0.31	0.46	0.31	0.54	0.61	0.68	0.14	0.36	−0.01
Ireland	0.38	0.56	0.32	0.76	0.78	0.82	0.15	0.42	0.01
Italy	0.30	0.45	0.29	0.49	0.57	0.65	0.16	0.36	−0.01
Japan	0.18	0.23	0.21	0.35	0.37	0.51	0.07	0.15	−0.04
Netherlands	0.45	0.58	0.38	0.83	0.85	0.89	0.16	0.38	0.01
New Zealand*	−4.78	−21.43	−0.55	−3.77	−16.96	−0.04	−3.36	−16.35	−0.62
Norway	0.43	0.59	0.27	0.67	0.69	0.77	0.29	0.53	−0.00
Sweden	0.39	0.60	0.34	0.70	0.75	0.80	0.19	0.50	−0.00
Switzerland	0.45	0.65	0.38	0.69	0.76	0.80	0.21	0.55	−0.02
United Kingdom	0.26	0.44	0.25	0.41	0.53	0.66	0.17	0.39	−0.00
United States	0.11	0.19	0.12	0.21	0.27	0.38	0.06	0.15	−0.00

Developing countries									
Argentina*	−0.28	−0.19	−0.59	−0.18	−0.12	−0.60	−0.13	−0.03	−0.32
Brazil*	−0.21	−0.22	−0.17	−0.12	−0.13	−0.06	−0.12	−0.14	−0.16
Chile*	−0.67	0.08	−0.04	1.48	0.89	0.96	1.10	0.95	0.84
Colombia*	−0.19	−0.19	−0.46	−0.06	−0.06	−0.37	−0.11	−0.11	−0.35
Greece*	−0.37	−0.39	−0.31	−0.21	−0.21	−0.09	−0.26	−0.29	−0.34
Hong Kong	0.42	0.62	0.33	0.91	0.92	0.92	0.14	0.44	−0.00
India*	−0.21	−0.19	−0.09	−0.09	−0.08	−0.02	−0.10	−0.08	−0.04
Israel	0.30	0.34	0.25	0.53	0.55	0.62	0.11	0.17	−0.03
South Korea*	−1.73	−2.38	−0.53	−1.20	−1.61	−0.20	−0.99	−1.62	−0.51
Mexico	0.23	0.28	0.11	0.39	0.42	0.48	0.13	0.20	−0.12
Portugal*	−0.44	−0.45	−0.39	−0.24	−0.25	−0.12	−0.26	−0.27	−0.41
Singapore	0.45	0.52	0.38	0.95	0.95	0.97	0.12	0.24	−0.00
Spain*	−0.34	−0.36	−0.26	−0.20	−0.22	−0.05	−0.20	−0.23	−0.25
Taiwan*	−2.72	−4.63	−0.91	−1.28	−2.31	−0.14	−1.52	−3.02	−0.90
Turkey*	−0.18	−0.20	−0.41	−0.14	−0.15	−0.47	−0.10	−0.13	−0.23
Yugoslavia	0.29	0.35	0.19	0.39	0.41	0.48	0.17	0.28	−0.16

a. Countries assumed to use import licensing are marked by an asterisk.

rium. The wage increase in turn raises costs in all industries and these costs are passed through to prices. Industry wage flexibility, in the rightmost subcolumns of columns (1)–(3) in table 7.4, has the same effect but only in the tradable industries.

All of these results apply, incidentally, only to the countries, most of them industrialized, in which imports are modeled as responding freely to world prices. In contrast, in countries with import licensing, prices generally fall, and the price decreases tend to be smaller when wages adjust. The reason for this damping of the price changes is that devaluations still stimulate production and employment in export sectors and thus require upward adjustment of wages.

For some purposes it is convenient to summarize the combined effects of exchange-rate and price changes by looking at a measure of the "real exchange rate." This term has been used with several different meanings in the literature, and we therefore report effects on two different measures of real exchange rates in table 7.5.

The usual concept of the real exchange rate consists of the nominal exchange rate corrected for inflation. If, for example, the dollar were to depreciate by 10%, but prices were also to rise in the United States by 10% more than abroad, then we would say that no *real* change in the exchange rate had taken place. We account for this in the "World-domestic" real exchange-rate changes that are reported in table 7.5. These are calculated as changes in the ratio of an index of prices on world markets, valued in domestic currency at the nominal exchange rate, to an index of domestic producer prices. The latter includes prices in both home and export sectors and in both tradable and nontradable industries. The real exchange rate by this definition indicates to what extent nominal exchange-rate changes are offset by price increases at home and by price decreases abroad. It may loosely be thought of as indicating the competitive edge that a devaluation provides.

A second concept of the real exchange rate is also sometimes used in the literature. This is the ratio of the prices of traded to nontraded goods, and is reported in table 7.5 as the "Traded-nontraded" real exchange rate. The purpose of this measure is to indicate, in broad terms, the extent to which a devaluation provides incentives for resource reallocation within the domestic economy. A large change in the real exchange rate in this sense suggests a strong incentive for labor and capital to move out of nontraded industries into the now more lucrative tradable industries. The traded-nontraded exchange-rate changes in table 7.5 are calculated as the difference between the changes in the prices of traded and nontraded goods in table 7.4.

Table 7.5
Effects of 1% nominal devaluation by country on own-country real exchange rates[a]

	World-domestic real exchange rate			Trade-nontraded real exchange rate		
Country	Wages fixed	Country wages flexible	Industry wages flexible	Wages fixed	Country wages flexible	Industry wages flexible
Industrialized countries						
Australia	0.62	0.48	0.76	0.36	0.22	0.70
Austria	0.54	0.34	0.64	0.46	0.19	0.80
Belgium-Luxembourg	0.56	0.39	0.64	0.63	0.40	0.85
Canada	0.60	0.44	0.73	0.33	0.18	0.74
Denmark	0.60	0.44	0.65	0.66	0.43	0.83
Finland	0.53	0.36	0.64	0.51	0.15	0.74
France	0.65	0.51	0.65	0.36	0.22	0.65
German Federal Republic	0.55	0.41	0.57	0.40	0.26	0.69
Ireland	0.60	0.43	0.67	0.61	0.36	0.82
Italy	0.63	0.49	0.65	0.33	0.21	0.66
Japan	0.73	0.67	0.71	0.29	0.22	0.55
Netherlands	0.52	0.38	0.58	0.68	0.47	0.88
New Zealand*	4.47	17.44	1.43	−0.41	−0.61	0.58
Norway	0.56	0.40	0.72	0.38	0.16	0.77
Sweden	0.56	0.37	0.65	0.51	0.25	0.80
Switzerland	0.53	0.33	0.60	0.48	0.21	0.81
United Kingdom	0.64	0.47	0.69	0.24	0.14	0.67
United States	0.57	0.47	0.48	0.15	0.11	0.39
Developing countries						
Argentina*	1.16	1.08	1.47	−0.05	−0.10	−0.28
Brazil*	1.12	1.13	1.12	−0.00	0.01	0.10
Chile*	−0.24	0.07	0.11	0.38	−0.06	0.12
Colombia*	1.08	1.08	1.36	0.05	0.05	−0.02
Greece*	1.24	1.26	1.22	0.06	0.08	0.25
Hong Kong	0.59	0.39	0.67	0.77	0.48	0.92
India*	1.10	1.09	1.03	0.02	−0.00	0.02
Israel	0.71	0.67	0.75	0.43	0.38	0.65
South Korea*	2.11	2.61	1.33	−0.21	0.01	0.31
Mexico	0.75	0.70	0.88	0.26	0.21	0.60
Portugal*	1.25	1.26	1.26	0.01	0.02	0.29
Singapore	0.55	0.48	0.62	0.83	0.71	0.97
Spain*	1.20	1.23	1.16	−0.01	0.01	0.20
Taiwan*	2.38	3.62	1.47	0.23	0.72	0.76
Turkey*	1.12	1.14	1.36	−0.04	−0.02	−0.24
Yugoslavia	0.70	0.64	0.80	0.22	0.13	0.64

a. Countries assumed to use import licensing are marked by an asterisk.

The results in table 7.5 indicate that, in the industrialized countries, something like one-half of a nominal exchange-rate change shows up as a change in real exchange rates by either definition, and thus only a fraction of the nominal change is offset by price changes, according to our model. Generally speaking, the world-domestic exchange-rate changes are somewhat larger than the changes in the traded-nontraded version, but the difference here is not substantial. Also, wage flexibility matters for determining the real exchange-rate effects of a devaluation, but not as much as one might have expected. Wage flexibility at the country level reduces the real exchange-rate effect of a devaluation, but it continues to be substantial. Wage flexibility at the industry level actually seems to *increase* the real exchange-rate effects, especially by the traded-nontraded definition. The reason for this is the insulation that this form of wage flexibility provides to nontraded industries from the effects of a devaluation.

In countries with import licensing, except for the anomalous case of Chile, the world-domestic real exchange-rate effects turn out to be actually *larger* than the 1% of the nominal devaluation. The reason is that domestic prices fall in these countries, as explained earlier. However, in the presence of the amount of market interference that import licensing represents, it is not clear just what the significance of the real exchange rate by this definition really is. The meaning of the traded-nontraded exchange rate is clearer, and this, it appears, changes very little in these countries. Apparently, by keeping exports and imports balanced in these countries, import licensing leaves little scope for resource reallocation into or out of nontraded goods.

Cross-Country Price Effects of Uniform Exchange-Rate Changes

In the preceding section, we examined only the effects of devaluations on prices within the devaluing country. It was possible to do this for all 34 countries simultaneously due to a feature of our solution program that permits solution for the effects of own-country exogenous variables only. But it does mean that these runs of the model did not tell us the extent to which countries are dependent on the values of particular foreign currencies. It is to this subject that we now turn.

We ran the model three more times, now looking at the effects in all countries of a devaluation by only one. We chose to look, in the three runs, at devaluations by the United States, the United Kingdom, and Japan. In all cases we held money wages fixed, so that the own-country results are the same as were reported in table 7.3. These three countries were chosen primarily because of their importance in world markets and because our model currently includes separate input-output tables for each of them. We thought that there might be some differences in the international effects of devaluations based upon differences in these input-output tables.

A comparison of own and cross-country home-price effects is reported in table 7.6. Column (1) shows, for example, how the United States is affected by 1% devaluations in each of the three countries. Naturally, the United States is affected by devaluations abroad in the direction opposite to those at home, since devaluations of the pound or yen amount to partial appreciations of the dollar. It is evident that the effects of these foreign devaluations on the United States are comparatively small. In contrast, a US devaluation has a sizable impact on home prices in both the Unied Kingdom and Japan.

Effects on countries other than these three are shown in table 7.7. Here, however, we combine the effects on prices and exchange rates by again reporting changes in a measure of real exchange rates. This time, because our solutions of the model include both own and cross-country effects, we are able to calculate a real exchange rate that accounts for domestic prices in all countries. The procedure was as follows. For each country we first calculated a bilateral real exchange-rate change with respect to each of the other countries in the model. This was done using the bilateral nominal exchange rates and the indices of producer prices in each country. Then, these bilateral real exchange-rate changes were averaged, using bilateral exports plus imports as weights, to obtain the real effective exchange rates reported in the table. The signs of these changes are defined so as to indicate what happens to the value of the country's own currency. Thus, a negative number now indicates a devaluation.

Perhaps the most interesting feature of the results reported in table 7.7 is the relatively large effect that devaluation by a large country can have on the real values of the currencies of certain of its trading partners. For example, Canada is so dependent on trade with the United States that a 1% devaluation by the United States causes a real appreciation of the Canadian dollar by more than 0.5%. And Japan too shows a rather substantial dependence on the value of the US dollar. Similar effects can be found in the table for the effect of the United Kingdom on Ireland and for the effect of Japan on Australia. Large effects are also reported for many of the countries with import licensing, though here the effect is artificially exaggerated, as we saw in connection with table 7.5, and it is not clear in any case what the significance is of real exchange rates for such countries.

It may be noted also that the own effects for the three devaluing countries are somewhat larger here than they were in the analogous column of table 7.5. The reason is a difference in the definition of the real exchange rate in

Table 7.6
Own- and cross-country home price effects due to 1% devaluations by the United States, the United Kingdom, and Japan[a]

Industry	(ISIC)	(1) Effects on US home prices due to devaluation by			(2) Effects on UK home prices due to devaluation by			(3) Effects on Japanese home prices due to devaluation by		
		US	UK	JPN	US	UK	JPN	US	UK	JPN
Traded goods										
AGR., FOR., & FISH.	(1)	0.31	−0.03	−0.02	−0.08	0.27	−0.02	−0.08	−0.02	0.26
FOOD, BEV., & TOB.	(310)	0.15	−0.02	−0.01	−0.05	0.16	−0.01	−0.03	−0.01	0.13
TEXTILES	(321)	0.17	−0.02	−0.02	−0.16	0.49	−0.05	−0.09	−0.03	0.29
WEARING APPAREL	(322)	0.10	−0.01	−0.01	−0.06	0.20	−0.01	−0.06	−0.02	0.20
LEATHER PROD.	(323)	0.14	−0.01	−0.01	−0.15	0.45	−0.02	−0.07	−0.02	0.24
FOOTWEAR	(324)	0.12	−0.01	−0.01	−0.07	0.23	−0.01	−0.06	−0.02	0.19
WOOD PROD.	(331)	0.20	−0.02	−0.02	−0.12	0.36	−0.03	−0.08	−0.02	0.25
FURN. & FIXT.	(332)	0.10	−0.01	−0.01	−0.09	0.27	−0.02	−0.05	−0.02	0.15
PAPER & PAPER PROD.	(341)	0.13	−0.01	−0.01	−0.10	0.35	−0.02	−0.07	−0.02	0.25
PRINT. & PUBL.	(342)	0.06	−0.01	−0.00	−0.07	0.22	−0.01	−0.03	−0.01	0.12
CHEMICALS	(35A)	0.20	−0.03	−0.02	−0.15	0.48	−0.04	−0.16	−0.05	0.50
PETROL. & REL. PROD.	(35B)	0.22	−0.03	−0.02	−0.21	0.44	−0.03	−0.14	−0.04	0.39
RUBBER PROD.	(355)	0.15	−0.02	−0.02	−0.10	0.33	−0.03	−0.08	−0.03	0.27
NONMETAL. MIN. PROD.	(36A)	0.11	−0.02	−0.01	−0.08	0.25	−0.02	−0.04	−0.02	0.17
GLASS & GLASS PROD.	(362)	0.11	−0.02	−0.01	−0.07	0.23	−0.02	−0.04	−0.02	0.16
IRON & STEEL	(371)	0.14	−0.02	−0.01	−0.12	0.36	−0.03	−0.13	−0.07	0.53
NONFERROUS METALS	(372)	0.20	−0.03	−0.02	−0.14	0.41	−0.03	−0.17	−0.05	0.51
METAL PROD.	(381)	0.13	−0.02	−0.01	−0.09	0.29	−0.02	−0.05	−0.02	0.21
NONELEC. MACH.	(382)	0.11	−0.02	−0.01	−0.09	0.28	−0.02	−0.04	−0.02	0.16
ELEC. MACH.	(383)	0.12	−0.02	−0.01	−0.11	0.35	−0.03	−0.04	−0.02	0.17
TRANSP. EQUIP.	(384)	0.17	−0.02	−0.02	−0.09	0.29	−0.02	−0.05	−0.02	0.19
MISC. MANUF.	(38A)	0.18	−0.03	−0.02	−0.13	0.43	−0.04	−0.08	−0.04	0.28
Average		0.17	−0.02	−0.02	−0.10	0.32	−0.02	−0.07	−0.03	0.26

Nontraded goods										
MIN. & QUARRY.	(2)	0.36	−0.06	−0.04	−0.20	0.60	−0.04	−0.11	−0.04	0.33
ELEC., GAS, & WATER	(4)	0.13	−0.02	−0.01	−0.11	0.32	−0.02	−0.05	−0.02	0.16
CONSTRUCTION	(5)	0.07	−0.01	−0.01	−0.06	0.17	−0.01	−0.03	−0.01	0.12
WHOLE. & RET. TRADE	(6)	0.04	−0.00	−0.00	−0.04	0.11	−0.01	−0.01	−0.01	0.04
TRANSP., STOR., & COMM.	(7)	0.06	−0.01	−0.01	−0.07	0.21	−0.02	−0.02	−0.01	0.07
FIN., INS., & REAL EST.	(8)	0.06	−0.01	−0.01	−0.10	0.33	−0.03	−0.00	−0.00	0.03
COMM., SOC., & PERS. SERV.	(9)	0.02	−0.00	−0.00	−0.02	0.07	−0.01	−0.01	−0.01	0.05
Average		0.06	−0.01	−0.00	−0.06	0.17	−0.01	−0.02	−0.01	0.07
Overall average		0.09	−0.01	−0.01	−0.07	0.23	−0.02	−0.04	−0.02	0.16

a. Averages are weighted using value of production.

Table 7.7
Own- and cross-country real effective exchange-rate effects of 1% devaluations by the United States, the United Kingdom, and Japan[a]

Country	US	UK	JPN
Industrialized countries			
Australia	0.02	0.05	0.26
Austria	−0.01	0.03	0.00
Belgium-Luxembourg	0.03	0.05	0.00
Canada	0.55	0.02	0.04
Denmark	0.05	0.09	0.02
Finland	0.01	0.11	0.01
France	0.08	0.06	0.02
German Federal Republic	0.06	0.03	0.01
Ireland	0.04	0.39	0.01
Italy	0.08	0.04	0.01
Japan	0.28	0.00	−0.80
Netherlands	0.00	0.06	0.01
New Zealand*	1.25	0.37	0.35
Norway	0.02	0.09	0.04
Sweden	0.04	0.09	0.01
Switzerland	0.02	0.06	0.01
United Kingdom	0.10	−0.71	0.02
United States	−0.83	0.04	0.13
Developing countries			
Argentina*	0.30	0.08	0.09
Brazil*	0.37	0.06	0.10
Chile*	−0.58	−0.09	0.05
Colombia*	0.47	0.06	0.08
Greece*	0.15	0.07	0.11
Hong Kong	0.16	0.04	0.11
India*	0.35	0.13	0.15
Israel	0.22	0.12	0.03
South Korea*	0.68	0.11	0.37
Mexico	0.54	0.01	0.04
Portugal*	0.16	0.13	0.04
Singapore	0.07	0.02	0.19
Spain*	0.26	0.09	0.06
Taiwan*	0.83	0.16	0.33
Turkey*	0.20	0.10	0.06
Yugoslavia	0.09	0.04	0.01

a. Countries assumed to use import licensing are marked by an asterisk.

the two tables. Here we are able to use domestic prices to deflate exchange rates in all countries, whereas in table 7.5 we had to use changes in prices on world markets as a proxy for foreign prices. Since world price changes are only partially passed through to domestic prices, the latter offset less of the effect of a nominal exchange-rate change than do the former, and the real exchange-rate effect is therefore larger.

8 Effects of Nonuniform Exchange-Rate Changes over Time

In the preceding chapter, we reviewed several of the channels by which uniform exchange-rate changes affect an economy in the short to intermediate run. Actual exchange-rate changes are seldom uniform, especially in today's environment of flexible exchange rates. In addition, the extreme assumptions that we have made so far—that nominal wages are either completely fixed or adjust fully to labor-market equilibrium, and that nominal expenditure is also largely fixed—seem inappropriate for the analysis of exchange-rate changes as they occur in the real world. Therefore in this chapter we drop these assumptions in an analysis of an example of certain actual exchange-rate changes. The changes we examine are those that occurred between the second quarters of 1980 and 1981, when the US dollar appreciated substantially, but unevenly, with respect to the other major currencies of the world.[1]

In place of our earlier assumptions of either fixed or flexible money wages and expenditure, the model of this chapter is based on the assumption that these variables respond gradually over time to market conditions, and in particular to changes in prices. This adjustment is implemented in our model by a procedure that we describe later, and that is admittedly quite ad hoc. Nonetheless there are reasons to believe that such an adjustment process occurs, even if the pseudodynamic analysis we shall be using fails to capture it perfectly, and we feel that this analysis gives us an improved flavor of how the effects of exchange-rate changes may be felt over time.

The exchange-rate changes we examine are taken to be exogenous. What this really means in the context of our model is that they are not themselves a result of changes in trade or production, since if they were, there would be no further need to examine their real effects. However, this leaves open a number of possibilities for causes of the exchange-rate changes.

For example, it may be that the exchange rates were determined by official intervention in exchange markets and that the parities set by this intervention have changed. Or, more plausibly under flexible exchange rates, changes may have occurred in response to capital flows that in turn were a response to changes in interest rates and thus monetary policies. They may even be a reflection of changes in expectations about the relative soundness of various currencies, which in turn have led to incipient speculative capital transactions that have changed exchange rates. Regardless of which of these possibilities obtains, the exchange-rate changes that result may be expected to have real effects on trade, output, and employment, unless and until the exchange-rate changes can be passed through completely and evenly to equivalent changes in all prices, wages, and other nominal amounts. Thus there is scope for an analysis of the sort to come.

It must be admitted, however, that whatever the original cause of an exchange-rate change, there may well be further effects that will be felt and that are not accounted for in our model of the real side of the economy. Payments imbalances may lead to international flows of reserves. Capital flows may alter portfolios. And expectations may change. These and other changes may cause a reversal in the change of the exchange rate itself, or they may lead to other changes in behavior that will eventually impinge on goods markets. Yet none of them is included in our model. Thus our analysis must be taken to represent the effects of exchange-rate changes only under the assumptions that they (a) were not themselves the result of changes in the real side of the economy[2] (b) will not be undone by later exchange-rate changes in the opposite direction, and (c) will not lead to further changes in government policy and/or financial markets that will cause changes in real behavior. This is a tall order, but we continue to feel that the results of such an analysis are of interest.

We begin the chapter by describing how we have adapted our model to analyze the effects of changes in exchange rates in the very short run. We then use this version of the model to calculate the effects on domestic prices, trade, and employment in the Unied States, the EEC, and Japan due to the actual changes in exchange rates that occurred between the second quarters of 1980 and 1981.

Since this particular period is only one of many in which exchange rates have changed substantially over time, the question also arises as to whether it is possible to develop some "rule of thumb" that would provide reasonable estimates of the overall and sectoral impacts of any given exchange-rate changes for individual countries and regions. For this purpose, we have in addition selected a *uniform* 1% devaluation for the United States, the EEC, and Japan, which is analogous to what was done in chapter 7. In order to determine whether these uniform results could provide the basis for a rule of thumb, we multiplied them by the actual changes in exchange rates that had occurred from 1980 to 1981. These scaled results are then compared with the results based on the *nonuniform* changes in exchange rates, and an assessment is made of the usefulness of a rule of thumb in terms of uniform changes in exchange rates.

Adaptation of the Model for Very Short-Run Analysis

It will be recalled that exchange rafes are represented in our model under both fixed and flexible exchange-rate regimes, and a system of import licensing is assumed when relevant. Since our present focus is on exogenous changes in exchange rates, we rely on the fixed exchange-rate version of the model that is applicable to the United States and the other major industrialized countries.

Exchange rates can have real effects in our model to the extent that other nominal variables are fixed. In any given solution of the model, the values of each country's nominal wages and nominal expenditure are specified exogenously in units of local currency. Thus changes in exchange rates cause changes in relative wages and expenditure levels, and it is these relative changes that in turn cause the real effects we shall be reporting. As prices feed back into changes in nominal wages and expenditure over time, in the manner to be described, these real effects of exchange-rate changes may be expected eventually to wash out. It appears, however, that the time horizon of our analysis is too short to exhibit this tendency.

The model as we have described it in chapters 2 and 3 and as we have used it in our earlier work is designed for short-to-intermediate run analysis. Because capital stocks are held constant in each sector and industry, the results of the model cannot be regarded as meaningful for a period of more than a few years. On the other hand, the elasticities of supply and demand that are incorporated into the model are derived from studies that measure relatively long-run adjustments that would require at least several quarters to complete. In view especially of the fact that shocks due to exchange-rate changes may be regarded as temporary, there is good reason to believe that our model as we have used it earlier will overstate the effects of exchange-rate changes, especially in the first few quarters after they occur. We have therefore modified some of the parameters of the model, in ways that we shall describe shortly, in order to reflect more accurately the sluggishness of adjustment in the very short run.

In addition, our experience with the model's behavior when exchange rates change has suggested one feature of the model that would be a source of difficulty. In recognition of the relatively low elasticities of demand for imports that many investigators have found, we long ago introduced into the model the assumption of less-than-perfect substitutability between imports and home goods. The tractability of the solution procedure has forced us to assume that imports from various foreign sources are perfect substitutes among themselves. This was not much of a problem so long as we were dealing with tariff reductions, as was the case in much of our earlier analysis. However, in examining the effects of exchange-rate changes that may be quite different for different countries, this assumption leads to changes in exports that are unreasonably large in the short run. To eliminate this effect from the current runs of the model, we have used estimates of export-demand elasticities to dampen the price responsiveness of exports in the model. The precise calculation will be described later.

Finally, as we began to consider variations in the responsiveness of supplies and demands that are appropriate for different short-run horizons, we also thought it appropriate to consider the extent to which, in a dynamic model, exchange-rate changes and their resulting price changes are reflected later in changes in nominal wages and expenditures. We therefore have altered our application of the model to incorporate such an effect.

To deal with all of these issues we used the model to calculate effects of exchange-rate changes by solving it not once, but 12 times. Each solution is intended to measure the cumulative effects of the changes after different periods of time, running from 1 quarter to 12 quarters subsequent to the exchange-rate shocks. In each quarter, different elasticities of supply and demand are assumed throughout the model, appropriate to the period of time being analyzed. Also in each period after the first, the price-index changes from the preceding periods are used to calculate changes in exogenous wages and expenditure, so that the price effects of exchange-rate changes are gradually spread throughout the economies involved.[3]

The parameter changes that were used for the foregoing purposes are shown in table 8.1. Partial elasticities of labor demand with respect to changes in outputs were multiplied by the fractions indicated in column (1). In the model, labor demand is determined by output in the home and export sectors. Thus, when output changes due to an exchange-rate change, firms will alter their demand for labor. They will not do so instantaneously, however. There is reason to believe that, in the short run, firms will retain some excess capacity in terms of labor. If output is to be expanded by some percentage, the demand for labor will rise by only some fraction of this percentage. Similarly, if firms experience a decline in output, they will reduce their demand for labor less than proportionately. Since the production

Table 8.1
Elasticity-damping and lagged-price parameters

Quarter	Damping coefficients (1) Labor demand[a]	(2) Output supply[a]	(3) Import demand[b]	(4) Average export elasticity[b]	(5) Lagged-price coefficient for wages[c]
1	0.51	0.73	0.42	0.025	0.190
2	0.76	0.80	0.58	0.048	0.190
3	0.88	0.85	0.71	0.066	0.112
4	0.94	0.90	0.81	0.079	0.089
5	0.97	0.93	0.89	0.087	0.072
6	0.99	0.95	0.95	0.090	0.057
7	0.99	0.97	0.98	0.088	0.047
8	1.00	0.98	1.00	0.080	0.037
9	1.00	0.99	1.00	0.068	0.029
10	1.00	0.99	1.00	0.050	0.023
11	1.00	0.99	1.00	0.028	0.000
12	1.00	1.00	1.00	0.000	0.000

a. Based on Dhrymes (1969) as reported in Hamermesh (1976, pp. 512 and 516).
b. Based on elasticities for US aggregate nonoil imports and nonagricultural exports calculated in the Federal Reserve Multicountry model (MCM), in November 1981. Personal communication from Peter Hooper.
c. Based on Belton, Hymans, and Lown (1981).

function requires that firms must eventually adjust their input demands fully in response to changes in output, the partial responses will then become complete at some point. This is evident in column (1), where the labor demand responds by 0.51 in quarter 1, rises to 1.00 in quarter 8, and remains at this level thereafter. The fractions indicated are based on estimates by Dhrymes (1969) of one-quarter and long-run employment-output elasticities, with values for quarters other than the first interpolated assuming a geometric lag structure.

Dhrymes also reported elasticities of employment with respect to wages. In our model, labor is the only variable component of value added, and these elasticities can therefore be derived from the price elasticities of output supply together with the output elasticities of labor demand. The point involved here is that, when the demand for output increases, firms may not respond fully because there may be costs entailed in searching out and training additional workers. In a sense, the shadow price of labor is increased so that output is not expanded as much as it might have been otherwise. Firms may wish to wait to determine whether the change in the demand for output is permanent. By the same token, if demand falls, the cost to the firm of keeping workers on hand becomes lower than the wage, and output may not be reduced as much as otherwise. Since, in our model, labor is the only variable factor, output and labor demand are determined simultaneously in response to changes in wages. Thus, there may be an additional damping mechanism at work in the short run. Accordingly, we multiplied all the output supply elasticities for the sectors in the model by the fractions in column (2) of table 8.1, so that together with column (1) they imply the lag structure reported by Dhrymes.

Import demands were similarly damped, using the coefficients in column (3). Again, the long-run elasticities are maintained as in our existing model and are different across commodities. However, all are damped in the short run to give the same pattern over time as has been measured for aggregate US import-demand elasticities in the Federal Reserve Multicountry model (MCM). Thus, the damping coefficients in column (3) are intended to reflect time lags due to existing contractual obligations, the diffusion of information on price changes, habit persistence, and the like.

Column (4) of table 8.1 differs from the first three in that it reports actual elasticities, rather than fractions by which existing elasticities in the model have been multiplied. This column contains elasticities of demand for aggregate exports with respect to current and lagged prices as measured in the Federal Reserve MCM. Their cumulative value is only 0.7 and is persuasive evidence against the assumption made in our model that US exports compete on world markets as perfect substitutes for the exports of other countries. We therefore chose to reduce the price responsiveness of exports in the model to reflect this. Because the structure of our model does not permit independent import- and export-demand elasticities, we have followed the almost equivalent procedure of scaling down our export-supply elasticities.[4] In each quarter the export-supply elasticities are all reduced by some fraction in such a way that they equal, on average, the accumulated values of the elasticities reported in column (4) of table 8.1.

Finally, for quarters beyond the first, we wished to capture the effect that changing prices have on the nominal wages that are set in subsequent periods. This is a familiar feature of the wage equations of most macroeconometric models. It reflects such features of the economy as automatic and negotiated cost-of-living adjustments in labor contracts and the formation of expectations of inflation that in turn influence the wages that employers will offer and that workers will accept. To incorporate such effects into our model, we used the wage equation reported by Belton, Hymans, and Lown (1981) for the Michigan Quarterly Econometric Model of the US Economy. From it we calculated the coefficients shown in the last column of table 8.1. These are used as follows. In each quarter after the first, changes in the exogenous wage, W, and in expenditure, E, are calculated from the following formula:

$$\Delta \ln E_t = \Delta \ln W_t = \sum_{i=1}^{t-1} k_{t-1} \Delta \ln p_i^I,$$

where p_i^I is the price index in period i and k_j is the coefficient in the jth row, last column, of table 8.1. While the coefficients k_j come only from a wage equation, we assume that exogenous expenditure also changes by the same amount as wages, to reflect the role of both prices and wages in determining nominal incomes.[5] Thus, in each successive quarter, these exogenous wage and expenditure changes will incorporate, in a partial way, the price changes that have occurred in previous quarters in the model.

In the context of an exogenous dollar appreciation, which tends to lower domestic prices, these coefficients will capture the extent to which the price reductions will in turn be reflected in subsequent reductions in wages. Thus, as wages fall and themselves cause still further price reductions, the initial cost-price disadvantages that firms experience due to the appreciation will be eroded.

Results of Nonuniform Exchange-Rate Changes

Having reviewed briefly the transmission and impact of changes in exchange rates and the adaptation of our model for short-run analysis, we can turn to our results. In table 8.2, we list in columns (1) and (2) the bilateral US dollar exchange rates for each country in the model grouped according to the breakdown into six country/regions used to summarize the calculations.[6] These exchange rates are averages for the second quarters of 1980 and 1981 and were the latest available when the calculations were done. The changes in these bilateral rates are given in column (3). We then report in column (4) the percentage change in the consumer price index in each country for this same period. The differences between the changes in exchange rates and changes in consumer prices provide an approximation of the changes in real exchange rates that occurred over the period. These real bilateral exchange-rate changes vis-a-vis the United States are shown in column (5). These are the exchange-rate changes that were entered into our model as exogenous changes. Finally, as an aid in interpreting these bilateral changes, we report in column (6) the changes in the trade-weighted, real *effective* exchange rates that the bilateral changes imply, based on our classification of six country/regions.

Table 8.2
Changes in nominal and real exchange rates, 1980:II–1981:II

Region/country	Exchange rate[a] (1) 1980:II	(2) 1981:II	(3) %Δ[e]	(4) Change in consumer price index 1980:II–1981:II (%)	(5) Change in bilateral real exchange rate vis-a-vis US (%)[e]	(6) Change in trade-weighted effective exchange rate (%)[f]
U.S.	—	—	—	9.8	—	6.9
EEC					22.2	−15.4
Belgium-Luxembourg	29.055	37.184	28.0	7.2	30.6	
Denmark	5.6398	7.1497	26.8	12.2	24.4	
France	4.2121	5.4185	28.6	12.8	25.6	
German Federal Republic	1.8105	2.2758	25.7	5.6	29.9	
Ireland	2.0612[b]	1.6077[b]	22.0	17.1[c]	14.7	
Italy	851.46	1134.09	33.2	20.6	22.4	
Netherlands	1.9904	2.5265	26.9	6.5	30.2	
United Kingdom	2.2849[b]	2.0813	8.9	11.7	7.0	
Japan	232.69	220.00	−5.5	5.3	−1.0	6.2
Other Europe					16.5	0.7
Austria	12.911	16.092	24.6	6.8	27.6	
Finland	3.7250	4.3067	15.6	12.6	12.8	
Norway	4.9425	5.6836	15.0	14.2	10.6	
Sweden	4.2481	4.8769	14.8	13.1	11.5	
Switzerland	1.6828	2.0342	20.9	6.0	24.7	
Other developed countries					0.5	4.0
Australia	1.1248[b]	1.445[b]	−1.8	8.8	−0.8	
Canada	1.1703	1.1986	2.4	12.5	−0.3	
New Zealand	0.9681[b]	0.8818[b]	8.9	15.0	3.7	

Less developed countries					4.5	5.5
Argentina	1803.5	3760.5	108.5	89.2	29.1	
Brazil	49.825	83.892	68.4	105.5	−27.3	
Chile	51.651[d]	44.873[d]	0.0	22.8	−13.0	
Colombia	46.456	53.286	14.7	27.0	−2.5	
Greece	42.965	55.480	29.1	24.0	14.9	
Hong Kong	4.942	5.435	10.0	15.3	4.5	
India	7.921	8.410	6.2	13.6	2.4	
Israel	4.510	10.270	127.7	124.0	13.5	
South Korea	594.07	682.60	14.9	24.9	−0.2	
Mexico	22.848	24.091	5.4	28.3	−13.1	
Portugal	49.509	60.591	22.4	17.7	14.5	
Singapore	2.1742	2.1341	−1.8	7.7	0.3	
Spain	70.819	91.142	28.7	14.9	23.6	
Taiwan	36.047	36.382	0.9	19.3	−8.6	
Turkey	75.529	102.914	36.3	30.6	15.5	
Yugoslavia	23.070	33.421	44.9	43.0	11.7	

a. Domestic currency per US dollar, except for those marked with a dash.
b. US dollar per domestic currency unit.
c. Estimated.
d. Pegged to US dollar in terms of pesos per SDR (Special Drawing Right).
e. Positive %Δ means depreciation vis-a-vis US dollar; negative %Δ means appreciation vis-a-vis US dollar.
f. Positive %Δ means real effective appreciation vis-a-vis a basket of trading-partner currencies. Calculated from preceding column.

Source: Exchange rates are quarterly averages from country tables in IMF (International Monetary Fund), *International Financial Statistics*, line rf, and change in consumer price indexes from same source, table 64x. Data for Taiwan from personal communication with IMF and for Hong Kong from Federal Reserve Board.

Some discussion may be in order regarding our particular selection of exchange-rate changes. We chose them originally as the latest available at the time we began our research. Had we chosen a different period of time, either earlier or later, the changes themselves and their implications would both be quite different, since exchange rates are changing all the time. We are not therefore looking at an isolated historical event whose ramifications need to be understood in order to assess the future. Instead, we are looking at a more or less arbitrary example of the kind of exchange-rate realignment that occurs quite frequently in today's world and asking what its real effects would be if it *were* to occur in isolation. Naturally, to the extent that exchange rates have instead moved farther in the same direction, or have reversed themselves, the real adjustments required of the world's economies will be a complicated mixture of the lagged effects of many recent changes.

As mentioned, the procedure followed in calculating the effects of the exchange-rate changes was to solve the model quarter by quarter, for a total of 12 times. Each solution was designed to measure the cumulative effects through time subsequent to the exogenous changes in exchange rates. At each time, the supply and demand elasticities in the model were adjusted based on the damping coefficients and export elasticities noted in table 8.1. Further, after each period, the price-inxdex changes from the preceding periods were used to calculate changes in exogenous wages and expenditure, which then provided the basis for still further effects of the exchange-rate changes on prices in subsequent periods. We should also note that we abstract throughout our analysis from any changes in monetary and fiscal policies that might be introduced for macro-stabilization purposes and from any feedback effects on the exchange rate itself. In effect, we are assuming that the authorities intervene to peg the exchange rate and use open market operations to maintain aggregate nominal expenditure in fixed proportion to wages.

The overall results for the United States are indicated on a cumulative quarterly basis in table 8.3. As can be seen, the effects of the real effective US appreciation of approximately 7% are felt only gradually over time. They build to a maximum in about the third year and then begin to reverse themselves. This pattern is the result of the combined effects of the low but growing elasticities that determine supplies and demands for output, labor, and traded goods, plus, acting in the opposite direction, the gradual feedback of prices on wages that eventually begins to erode the effects of the appreciation.

Looking at the individual variables, we see first that the appreciation causes prices to fall in the United States. The change is quite small, however,

Table 8.3
Summary of effects of actual exchange-rate changes, 1980:II–1981:II, on prices, trade, and employment in the United States by quarter

Quarter	(1) Price index (%Δ)	Trade changes ($ × 10⁶) (2) Exports	(3) Imports	(4) Balance	Employment change (5) Man-years × 10³	(6) %
1	−0.39	−218.4	4,640.5	−4,858.9	157.4	0.18
2	−0.57	−664.0	7,889.3	−8,553.2	39.4	0.05
3	−0.75	−1,256.9	10,230.9	−11,487.9	−78.3	−0.09
4	−0.91	−1,939.0	11,904.8	−13,843.8	−185.5	−0.21
5	−1.06	−2,646.3	13,024.4	−15,670.7	−277.9	−0.32
6	−1.21	−3,336.4	13,699.5	−17,035.8	−354.2	−0.40
7	−1.34	−3,963.0	14,017.2	−17,980.2	−413.6	−0.47
8	−1.47	−4,489.1	14,048.5	−18,537.6	−456.2	−0.52
9	−1.59	−4,885.9	13,849.9	−18,735.8	−482.4	−0.55
10	−1.69	−5,121.7	13,471.5	−18,593.2	−492.0	−0.56
11	−1.79	−5,182.6	13,106.9	−18,289.5	−492.1	−0.56
12	−1.88	−5,050.1	12,790.9	−17,841.1	−482.0	−0.55

being only 0.4% in the first quarter and growing to only 1.9% after 3 years. From the structure of the model we would expect this change to continue in quarters still further in the future, but it will never become very large.

These price changes are similar to, though somewhat smaller than, estimates that have been made with other models. Some estimates have been made in Hooper (1982) of the impact of the recent dollar appreciation, using various features of the Federal Reserve MCM. In particular, based on the partial-equilibrium US International Accounts model, the dollar appreciation between 1980:III and 1981:III, as measured by the Federal Reserve Board 10-country weighted average exchange-rate index, suggests a cumulative decline in the US consumer price index of 1% in 1981, 2.4% in 1982, and 3.1% in 1983. Comparable calculations based on the US Sector model component of the MCM, in which GNP (gross national product) and many other domestic and external variables are endogenous, suggest a decline in US consumer prices of 1% in 1981, 2.7% in 1982, and 4.1% in 1983.

As one might expect from an appreciation, table 8.3 indicates that it is trade that responds most noticeably, though even here the changes are quite small in the first quarters due to the very low short-run elasticities of demand for exports and imports. The 7% appreciation causes exports to decline by $218 million in the first quarter, which is a negligible percentage of total production.[7] The extent of the decline in exports rises, however, to a peak of

$5.2 billion in quarter 11, which is 0.4% of the total production of tradable goods. In quarter 12 this decline falls off somewhat as falling wages restore some of the lost competitiveness, and presumably this reversal would continue in quarters beyond the third year.

Imports respond positively to the appreciation, of course, and in the case of the United States, the changes are larger than the changes in exports. Imports rise by $4.6 billion, which is 0.3% of total domestic demand for tradables, in the first quarter, and the increase grows to $14.0 billion, or 1.0% of domestic demand, in quarter 8. Imports decline thereafter, but only moderately so by the end of the third year. This larger response of imports than of exports, which we shall see happening in the other direction for the European Economic Community, is a result of the fact that export elasticities are lower than can be explained solely by import-demand elasticities, presumably due to country-of-origin product differentiation. This prevents a country's exchange rate from having a dramatic effect on its exports, which depend somewhat more on world market demand than on relative prices. As a result, countries that appreciate and depreciate the most relative to the world experience greater swings in their imports than in their exports.

Changes in the trade balance are reported in column (4) of table 8.3 and are just the differences between the changes in exports and imports in the preceding columns. Thus, the US trade balance worsens due to the 7% appreciation by $4.9 billion in the first quarter, and this decline grows to a maximum of $18.7 billion in quarter 9. About two-thirds of this change is due to imports, in the later quarters, and even more early on.

It will be noted that our results for the trade balance do not display the phenomenon of the "J-curve." That is, we do not find the appreciation of the dollar causing the US trade balance first to improve and then to worsen. This result should not be taken too seriously, however, since the way that we have modeled the inflexibility of exports more or less assures it. For determining the trade balance, the valuation of exports is important, and as mentioned, by modeling export inflexibility from the supply side rather than the demand side we have produced incorrect responses for export prices. Low elasticities of export *demand* could quite possibly result in a J-curve response of the trade balance in the short run, but low elasticities of export *supplies* cannot. This is of course a drawback of our model, but it does not interfere with the validity of our calculation of sectoral trade and employment responses, which are the primary focus of the model and of this book.

Turning now to the aggregate employment changes, we find a somewhat surprising result in table 8.3. The appreciation of the US dollar is estimated to *increase* US employment during the first two quarters after the appreciation.

The change is small—only 157 thousand man-years or 0.2% of the labor force in the first quarter—and it is reversed in the later quarters. The reason for this short-run increase in employment can be found in the small short-run elasticities throughout the model, together with the fact that the appreciation does have some negative impact on prices. An exchange-rate appreciation in general exerts two offsetting forces on employment: it causes substitution in demand away from domestic products but also reduces prices of imported inputs. In the short run as low elasticities limit the significance of the former substitution effect, the latter import-price effect dominates and employment goes up. Only later, as elasticities become larger, does the substitution effect come to play a more important role and employment declines. Thus, beginning in the third quarter, US employment is reduced below its level prior to the appreciation, and the reduction grows to a peak of 492 thousand man-years in the eleventh quarter. Even then, though, the change is only 0.6% of the US labor force.

These aggregate changes mask much industry detail, which can be found reported in tables 8.4–8.9. Sectoral changes in exports are reported in millions of US dollars in table 8.4, with the corresponding changes as a percentage of production shown in table 8.5. Changes in sectoral imports are similarly shown in absolute terms in table 8.6 and as a percentage of domestic demand in table 8.7. And finally, changes in sectoral levels of employment are shown in thousands of man-years in table 8.8 and in percentage terms in table 8.9. Rather than discussing the results of these tables in detail, we shall only comment on a few of the patterns that seem to emerge.

On looking first at exports, the greatest percentage declines in table 8.5 seem to occur in leather products, nonelectric machinery, textiles, and electric machinery. The greatest percentage increases in imports can be seen in table 8.7 to occur in rubber products, transport equipment, miscellaneous manufactures, footwear, and leather products.

One special feature of tables 8.6 and 8.7 should be noted, however, and that is the small and generally negative response of US imports of petroleum and related products. This is a result of our having essentially fixed the price of oil expressed in US dollars. With this assumption, the appreciation of the dollar has no effect on the dollar price at which oil can be obtained from the world market, and there is therefore no reason for the quantity of oil imports into the United States to increase. On the contrary, there is some small decline in the domestic demand for oil, for use as an intermediate input, as the domestic economy contracts. Thus, oil imports tend to follow employment and decline after the first two quarters.

Table 8.4
Change in value of exports, in millions of US dollars, due to actual exchange-rate changes, 1980:II–1981:II, for the United States

Industry	(ISIC)	Quarter 1	2	3	4	5	6	7	8	9	10	11	12
AGR., FOR., & FISH.	(1)	−4.5	−13.9	−26.4	−40.7	−55.5	−70.2	−83.7	−95.2	−104.1	−109.8	−111.7	−109.4
FOOD, BEV., & TOB.	(310)	−11.6	−37.3	−73.2	−115.7	−160.7	−205.1	−245.7	−280.1	−306.1	−321.8	−326.6	−319.3
TEXTILES	(321)	−15.9	−47.9	−91.8	−143.4	−197.9	−252.0	−301.7	−343.9	−376.4	−396.5	−403.4	−395.3
WEARING APPAREL	(322)	−5.5	−17.0	−32.8	−51.6	−71.6	−91.6	−110.0	−125.8	−137.8	−145.2	−147.5	−144.1
LEATHER PROD.	(323)	−7.8	−22.7	−42.2	−64.3	−87.1	−109.2	−129.1	−145.8	−158.4	−166.0	−168.3	−164.6
FOOTWEAR	(324)	−0.4	−1.3	−2.6	−4.1	−5.7	−7.3	−8.7	−10.0	−11.0	−11.6	−11.8	−11.5
WOOD PROD.	(331)	−2.7	−8.1	−15.1	−23.2	−31.6	−40.0	−47.7	−54.2	−59.4	−62.6	−63.8	−62.6
FURN. & FIXT.	(332)	−1.3	−4.0	−7.7	−12.0	−16.5	−20.9	−25.0	−28.5	−31.2	−32.9	−33.4	−32.6
PAPER & PAPER PROD.	(341)	−13.0	−38.3	−70.7	−106.8	−143.6	−178.9	−210.7	−237.2	−257.3	−269.4	−273.1	−267.4
PRINT. & PUBL.	(342)	−2.5	−7.6	−14.3	−22.0	−30.1	−38.1	−45.5	−51.8	−56.6	−59.6	−60.5	−59.2
CHEMICALS	(35A)	−20.2	−60.6	−113.8	−175.0	−238.9	−302.0	−360.3	−410.2	−449.0	−473.4	−481.7	−471.4
PETROL. & REL. PROD.	(35B)	−0.1	2.2	9.4	22.4	41.7	66.9	96.9	129.8	163.1	193.7	219.3	234.8
RUBBER PROD.	(355)	−1.8	−5.6	−10.8	−16.7	−23.0	−29.2	−35.0	−39.9	−43.8	−46.2	−47.0	−46.0
NONMETAL. MIN. PROD.	(36A)	−2.1	−6.7	−13.0	−20.4	−28.4	−36.3	−43.6	−49.9	−54.8	−57.9	−58.9	−57.6
GLASS & GLASS PROD.	(362)	−1.3	−4.2	−8.3	−13.1	−18.3	−23.5	−28.3	−32.5	−35.7	−37.7	−38.4	−37.5
IRON & STEEL	(371)	−9.0	−30.1	−60.8	−98.1	−138.3	−178.6	−216.2	−248.5	−273.5	−289.2	−294.4	−287.9
NONFERROUS METALS	(372)	−8.0	−23.2	−43.7	−67.5	−92.7	−117.8	−141.1	−161.2	−176.8	−186.8	−190.5	−186.8
METAL PROD.	(381)	−9.2	−28.2	−53.3	−82.1	−112.1	−141.6	−168.6	−191.7	−209.4	−220.4	−223.7	−218.6
NONELEC. MACH.	(382)	−52.6	−163.7	−312.7	−484.2	−661.8	−835.1	−992.8	−1,125.9	−1,227.3	−1,289.2	−1,308.4	−1,279.9
ELEC. MACH.	(383)	−18.9	−57.7	−109.2	−168.7	−230.8	−291.9	−348.1	−395.9	−432.8	−455.6	−462.9	−452.8
TRANSP. EQUIP.	(384)	−20.8	−62.6	−117.4	−180.5	−246.4	−311.6	−371.9	−423.7	−464.2	−489.9	−498.3	−487.1
MISC. MANUF.	(38A)	−9.0	−25.5	−46.8	−71.2	−96.8	−122.4	−146.3	−167.1	−183.4	−194.0	−197.6	−193.3
Total traded		−218.4	−664.0	−1,256.9	−1,939.0	−2,646.3	−3,336.4	−3,963.0	−4,489.1	−4,885.9	−5,121.7	−5,182.6	−5,050.1

Table 8.5
Change in value of exports as percentage of production due to actual exchange-rate changes, 1980:II–1981:II, for the United States

Industry	(ISIC)	Quarter 1	2	3	4	5	6	7	8	9	10	11	12
Traded goods													
AGR., FOR., & FISH.	(1)	−0.0	−0.0	−0.0	−0.0	−0.0	−0.1	−0.1	−0.1	−0.1	−0.1	−0.1	−0.1
FOOD, BEV., & TOB.	(310)	−0.0	−0.0	−0.0	−0.1	−0.1	−0.1	−0.1	−0.1	−0.1	−0.1	−0.2	−0.1
TEXTILES	(321)	−0.0	−0.1	−0.2	−0.3	−0.5	−0.6	−0.7	−0.8	−0.9	−0.9	−0.9	−0.9
WEARING APPAREL	(322)	−0.0	−0.1	−0.1	−0.2	−0.2	−0.3	−0.4	−0.4	−0.5	−0.5	−0.5	−0.5
LEATHER PROD.	(323)	−0.3	−0.7	−1.4	−2.1	−2.9	−3.6	−4.2	−4.8	−5.2	−5.4	−5.5	−5.4
FOOTWEAR	(324)	−0.0	−0.0	−0.0	−0.1	−0.1	−0.1	−0.1	−0.2	−0.2	−0.2	−0.2	−0.2
WOOD PROD.	(331)	−0.0	−0.0	−0.1	−0.1	−0.1	−0.2	−0.2	−0.2	−0.2	−0.2	−0.3	−0.2
FURN. & FIXT.	(332)	−0.0	−0.0	−0.1	−0.1	−0.1	−0.2	−0.2	−0.2	−0.3	−0.3	−0.3	−0.3
PAPER & PAPER PROD.	(341)	−0.0	−0.1	−0.1	−0.2	−0.3	−0.3	−0.4	−0.4	−0.5	−0.5	−0.5	−0.5
PRINT. & PUBL.	(342)	−0.0	−0.0	−0.0	−0.0	−0.1	−0.1	−0.1	−0.1	−0.1	−0.1	−0.1	−0.1
CHEMICALS	(35A)	−0.0	−0.1	−0.1	−0.2	−0.2	−0.3	−0.3	−0.4	−0.4	−0.4	−0.4	−0.4
PETROL. & REL. PROD.	(35B)	−0.0	0.0	0.0	0.0	0.0	0.1	0.1	0.1	0.2	0.2	0.2	0.3
RUBBER PROD.	(355)	−0.0	−0.0	−0.1	−0.1	−0.1	−0.2	−0.2	−0.2	−0.3	−0.3	−0.3	−0.3
NONMETAL. MIN. PROD.	(36A)	−0.0	−0.0	−0.1	−0.1	−0.1	−0.2	−0.2	−0.2	−0.2	−0.3	−0.3	−0.3
GLASS & GLASS PROD.	(362)	−0.0	−0.1	−0.1	−0.2	−0.2	−0.3	−0.3	−0.4	−0.4	−0.5	−0.5	−0.5
IRON & STEEL	(371)	−0.0	−0.0	−0.1	−0.1	−0.2	−0.2	−0.3	−0.3	−0.4	−0.4	−0.4	−0.4
NONFERROUS METALS	(372)	−0.0	−0.1	−0.1	−0.2	−0.2	−0.3	−0.3	−0.4	−0.4	−0.4	−0.5	−0.4
METAL PROD.	(381)	−0.0	−0.0	−0.1	−0.1	−0.2	−0.2	−0.2	−0.3	−0.3	−0.3	−0.3	−0.3
NONELEC. MACH.	(382)	−0.0	−0.1	−0.3	−0.4	−0.6	−0.7	−0.9	−1.0	−1.1	−1.1	−1.2	−1.1
ELEC. MACH.	(383)	−0.0	−0.1	−0.1	−0.2	−0.3	−0.4	−0.5	−0.5	−0.6	−0.6	−0.6	−0.6
TRANSP. EQUIP.	(384)	−0.0	−0.0	−0.1	−0.1	−0.2	−0.2	−0.3	−0.3	−0.3	−0.3	−0.4	−0.3
MISC. MANUF.	(38A)	−0.0	−0.0	−0.1	−0.1	−0.2	−0.2	−0.3	−0.3	−0.3	−0.4	−0.4	−0.4
Total traded		−0.0	−0.0	−0.1	−0.1	−0.2	−0.2	−0.3	−0.3	−0.3	−0.4	−0.4	−0.4

Table 8.6
Change in value of imports, in millions of US dollars, due to actual exchange-rate changes, 1980:II–1981:II, for the United States

Industry	(ISIC)	Quarter 1	2	3	4	5	6	7	8	9	10	11	12
Traded goods													
AGR., FOR., & FISH.	(1)	255.5	462.3	611.7	717.5	787.7	829.6	849.3	851.5	840.1	818.3	798.2	781.8
FOOD, BEV., & TOB.	(310)	123.1	207.4	264.0	301.0	323.5	335.4	339.6	338.3	332.7	324.1	315.9	308.9
TEXTILES	(321)	37.2	54.3	65.7	72.9	77.0	78.7	78.8	77.6	75.6	73.1	71.0	69.6
WEARING APPAREL	(322)	203.7	295.2	347.2	378.0	395.0	402.7	404.0	400.5	393.5	384.0	374.6	366.2
LEATHER PROD.	(323)	31.7	43.8	52.7	59.0	63.0	65.0	65.5	64.8	63.2	61.0	59.2	58.0
FOOTWEAR	(324)	99.2	137.4	161.7	177.7	187.5	192.9	194.8	194.2	191.5	187.2	182.6	178.4
WOOD PROD.	(331)	61.3	104.7	137.2	160.9	177.1	187.0	191.9	192.7	190.2	185.3	181.0	177.5
FURN. & FIXT.	(332)	48.1	89.4	122.2	147.2	165.2	177.1	183.7	185.8	184.4	179.9	175.4	171.4
PAPER & PAPER PROD.	(341)	123.5	217.5	285.1	332.3	362.6	379.5	386.0	384.2	376.3	363.8	353.5	346.2
PRINT. & PUBL.	(342)	20.4	31.6	37.5	40.8	42.5	43.2	43.2	42.8	42.0	40.9	39.9	39.1
CHEMICALS	(35A)	350.4	631.2	841.7	996.7	1,104.0	1,171.6	1,206.6	1,215.1	1,202.1	1,172.2	1,144.0	1,120.2
PETROL. & REL. PROD.	(35B)	30.0	3.5	−38.2	−83.5	−130.0	−175.4	−218.4	−258.0	−293.6	−324.6	−353.8	−379.4
RUBBER PROD.	(355)	161.4	296.6	400.5	478.2	532.9	568.3	587.8	594.2	589.8	576.7	563.7	552.0
NONMETAL. MIN. PROD.	(36A)	67.1	132.1	184.9	226.0	256.0	276.3	288.0	292.6	291.1	284.7	278.2	272.1
GLASS & GLASS PROD.	(362)	14.9	29.0	40.7	49.8	56.6	61.2	63.8	64.8	64.5	63.0	61.5	60.2
IRON & STEEL	(371)	123.1	229.6	319.7	390.2	440.6	473.3	491.0	496.2	491.6	479.2	467.3	457.1
NONFERROUS METALS	(372)	98.5	152.8	192.9	221.6	240.3	250.7	254.2	252.3	246.3	237.6	230.8	226.7
METAL PROD.	(381)	222.8	418.9	567.6	678.4	756.1	805.8	832.1	839.2	830.4	809.0	788.3	770.6
NONELEC. MACH.	(382)	281.2	487.2	644.7	760.0	837.9	884.9	907.0	909.2	895.5	869.7	846.6	828.4
ELEC. MACH.	(383)	408.3	708.0	926.8	1,084.3	1,190.6	1,255.6	1,287.3	1,292.4	1,276.1	1,243.2	1,212.1	1,185.9
TRANSP. EQUIP.	(384)	1,308.7	2,274.7	2,965.8	3,462.1	3,799.6	4,011.4	4,122.0	4,150.7	4,112.4	4,020.0	3,925.7	3,838.9
MISC. MANUF.	(38A)	570.2	882.0	1,098.8	1,253.4	1,358.6	1,424.7	1,459.1	1,467.5	1,454.3	1,423.3	1,391.3	1,361.5
Total traded		4,640.5	7,889.3	10,230.9	11,904.8	13,024.4	13,699.5	14,017.2	14,048.5	13,849.9	13,471.5	13,106.9	12,790.9

Table 8.7
Change in value of imports as percentage of domestic demand due to actual exchange-rate changes, 1980:II–1981:II, for the United States

		Quarter											
Industry	(ISIC)	1	2	3	4	5	6	7	8	9	10	11	12
Traded goods													
AGR., FOR., & FISH.	(1)	0.2	0.4	0.5	0.6	0.6	0.7	0.7	0.7	0.7	0.6	0.6	0.6
FOOD, BEV., & TOB.	(310)	0.1	0.1	0.1	0.1	0.1	0.2	0.2	0.2	0.2	0.2	0.1	0.1
TEXTILES	(321)	0.1	0.1	0.2	0.2	0.2	0.2	0.2	0.2	0.2	0.2	0.2	0.2
WEARING APPAREL	(322)	0.6	0.9	1.1	1.2	1.2	1.2	1.2	1.2	1.2	1.2	1.2	1.1
LEATHER PROD.	(323)	1.1	1.5	1.8	2.0	2.2	2.2	2.3	2.2	2.2	2.1	2.0	2.0
FOOTWEAR	(324)	1.3	1.8	2.1	2.3	2.4	2.5	2.5	2.5	2.5	2.4	2.4	2.3
WOOD PROD.	(331)	0.2	0.4	0.5	0.6	0.7	0.7	0.8	0.8	0.8	0.7	0.7	0.7
FURN. & FIXT.	(332)	0.4	0.7	1.0	1.2	1.3	1.4	1.5	1.5	1.5	1.4	1.4	1.4
PAPER & PAPER PROD.	(341)	0.2	0.4	0.5	0.6	0.6	0.7	0.7	0.7	0.7	0.6	0.6	0.6
PRINT. & PUBL.	(342)	0.0	0.1	0.1	0.1	0.1	0.1	0.1	0.1	0.1	0.1	0.1	0.1
CHEMICALS	(35A)	0.3	0.6	0.8	1.0	1.1	1.1	1.2	1.2	1.2	1.1	1.1	1.1
PETROL. & REL. PROD.	(35B)	0.0	0.0	−0.0	−0.1	−0.1	−0.1	−0.2	−0.2	−0.2	−0.3	−0.3	−0.3
RUBBER PROD.	(355)	0.9	1.7	2.3	2.8	3.1	3.3	3.4	3.5	3.5	3.4	3.3	3.2
NONMETAL. MIN. PROD.	(36A)	0.3	0.6	0.8	1.0	1.1	1.2	1.3	1.3	1.3	1.2	1.2	1.2
GLASS & GLASS PROD.	(362)	0.2	0.4	0.5	0.6	0.7	0.8	0.8	0.8	0.8	0.8	0.8	0.7
IRON & STEEL	(371)	0.2	0.3	0.4	0.5	0.5	0.6	0.6	0.6	0.6	0.6	0.6	0.6
NONFERROUS METALS	(372)	0.2	0.3	0.4	0.5	0.5	0.6	0.6	0.6	0.5	0.5	0.5	0.5
METAL PROD.	(381)	0.3	0.6	0.8	0.9	1.0	1.1	1.1	1.2	1.1	1.1	1.1	1.1
NONELEC. MACH.	(382)	0.3	0.5	0.7	0.8	0.9	0.9	0.9	0.9	0.9	0.9	0.9	0.8
ELEC. MACH.	(383)	0.5	0.9	1.2	1.4	1.6	1.7	1.7	1.7	1.7	1.7	1.6	1.6
TRANSP. EQUIP.	(384)	1.0	1.7	2.2	2.5	2.8	2.9	3.0	3.0	3.0	2.9	2.9	2.8
MISC. MANUF.	(38A)	1.0	1.6	2.0	2.3	2.4	2.6	2.6	2.6	2.6	2.6	2.5	2.5
Total traded		0.3	0.6	0.7	0.8	0.9	1.0	1.0	1.0	1.0	1.0	0.9	0.9

Table 8.8
Change in employment, in thousands of man-years, due to actual exchange-rate changes, 1980:II–1981:II, for the United States

		Quarter											
Industry	(ISIC)	1	2	3	4	5	6	7	8	9	10	11	12
Traded goods													
AGR., FOR., & FISH.	(1)	14.1	−6.1	−25.3	−41.9	−55.6	−66.3	−74.2	−79.6	−82.4	−83.0	−82.5	−81.0
FOOD, BEV., & TOB.	(310)	13.2	16.3	17.7	18.2	18.2	17.7	17.0	16.3	15.5	14.7	14.1	13.8
TEXTILES	(321)	3.3	−1.9	−7.1	−12.0	−16.6	−20.7	−24.2	−26.9	−28.9	−29.9	−30.1	−29.5
WEARING APPAREL	(322)	4.8	−1.0	−5.1	−8.2	−10.5	−12.3	−13.7	−14.7	−15.3	−15.5	−15.4	−15.1
LEATHER PROD.	(323)	0.5	−0.7	−1.9	−3.1	−4.2	−5.2	−6.1	−6.7	−7.2	−7.4	−7.5	−7.3
FOOTWEAR	(324)	2.5	1.1	0.1	−0.7	−1.2	−1.6	−1.8	−2.0	−2.0	−2.0	−2.0	−2.0
WOOD PROD.	(331)	−0.4	−3.3	−5.7	−7.9	−9.6	−10.9	−11.9	−12.5	−12.8	−12.9	−12.8	−12.5
FURN. & FIXT.	(332)	2.6	1.3	0.1	−0.9	−1.8	−2.5	−3.0	−3.4	−3.5	−3.6	−3.5	−3.5
PAPER & PAPER PROD.	(341)	−0.4	−3.9	−7.2	−10.0	−12.3	−14.2	−15.6	−16.6	−17.1	−17.3	−17.2	−16.8
PRINT. & PUBL.	(342)	2.0	1.6	1.1	0.6	0.2	−0.3	−0.7	−1.1	−1.3	−1.5	−1.6	−1.6
CHEMICALS	(35A)	−1.7	−10.5	−18.3	−25.1	−30.6	−35.0	−38.2	−40.4	−41.6	−41.7	−41.4	−40.5
PETROL. & REL. PROD.	(35B)	0.4	0.5	0.6	0.8	1.0	1.2	1.5	1.7	2.0	2.2	2.4	2.5
RUBBER PROD.	(355)	−1.8	−5.4	−8.4	−10.9	−12.7	−14.0	−14.9	−15.3	−15.4	−15.2	−15.0	−14.7
NONMETAL. MIN. PROD.	(36A)	−0.5	−2.7	−4.8	−6.5	−8.0	−9.1	−9.9	−10.3	−10.6	−10.5	−10.4	−10.2
GLASS & GLASS PROD.	(362)	0.2	−0.6	−1.4	−2.2	−2.8	−3.3	−3.8	−4.0	−4.2	−4.3	−4.3	−4.2
IRON & STEEL	(371)	−0.3	−6.0	−11.4	−16.1	−20.1	−23.3	−25.7	−27.4	−28.3	−28.5	−28.2	−27.6
NONFERROUS METALS	(372)	−0.8	−3.6	−6.1	−8.3	−10.1	−11.6	−12.7	−13.4	−13.9	−13.9	−13.8	−13.6
METAL PROD.	(381)	−0.6	−9.2	−16.8	−23.2	−28.3	−32.3	−35.1	−36.9	−37.7	−37.7	−37.2	−36.4
NONELEC. MACH.	(382)	13.2	5.7	−3.4	−12.8	−21.5	−29.3	−35.7	−40.8	−44.2	−46.0	−46.5	−45.5
ELEC. MACH.	(383)	7.3	−2.7	−12.1	−20.3	−27.1	−32.5	−36.5	−39.2	−40.8	−41.1	−40.9	−40.0
TRANSP. EQUIP.	(384)	5.1	−7.5	−18.4	−27.2	−34.1	−39.3	−42.8	−45.0	−45.9	−45.6	−45.0	−44.1
MISC. MANUF.	(38A)	4.5	−10.6	−22.7	−32.5	−40.1	−45.9	−49.9	−52.5	−53.7	−53.6	−53.0	−51.9
Total traded		67.3	−49.2	−156.5	−250.0	−328.0	−390.6	−438.0	−470.7	−489.4	−494.4	−491.9	−481.6

Nontraded goods													
MIN. & QUARRY.	(2)	1.4	−0.6	−2.4	−3.8	−4.8	−5.4	−5.6	−5.4	−5.0	−4.3	−3.5	−2.7
ELEC., GAS, & WATER	(4)	1.2	0.1	−1.0	−2.1	−3.1	−4.0	−4.6	−5.1	−5.4	−5.6	−5.6	−5.5
CONSTRUCTION	(5)	12.0	14.8	16.4	17.4	18.0	18.2	18.1	17.9	17.6	17.1	16.7	16.2
WHOLE. & RET. TRADE	(6)	30.7	29.0	24.3	18.7	12.9	7.4	2.6	−1.4	−4.4	−6.4	−7.6	−7.8
TRANSP., STOR., & COMM.	(7)	5.5	2.3	−1.1	−4.3	−7.1	−9.4	−11.3	−12.6	−13.4	−13.7	−13.7	−13.4
FIN., INS., & REAL EST.	(8)	11.5	7.9	3.3	−1.4	−5.9	−9.8	−13.0	−15.4	−17.1	−17.8	−18.1	−17.7
COMM., SOC., & PERS. SERV.	(9)	27.8	35.0	38.5	39.9	40.1	39.3	38.1	36.6	34.9	33.2	31.7	30.6
Total nontraded		90.1	88.5	78.1	64.5	50.1	36.4	24.4	14.5	7.1	2.4	−0.2	−0.4
Total, all industries		157.4	39.4	−78.3	−185.5	−277.9	−354.2	−413.6	−456.2	−482.4	−492.0	−492.1	−482.0

Table 8.9
Percentage change in employment due to actual exchange-rate changes, 1980:II–1981:II, for the United States

Industry	(ISIC)	Quarter 1	2	3	4	5	6	7	8	9	10	11	12
Traded goods													
AGR., FOR., & FISH.	(1)	0.4	−0.2	−0.8	−1.3	−1.7	−2.0	−2.2	−2.4	−2.5	−2.5	−2.5	−2.4
FOOD, BEV., & TOB.	(310)	0.8	0.9	1.0	1.1	1.0	1.0	1.0	0.9	0.9	0.8	0.8	0.8
TEXTILES	(321)	0.3	−0.2	−0.6	−1.0	−1.4	−1.7	−2.0	−2.3	−2.4	−2.5	−2.5	−2.5
WEARING APPAREL	(322)	0.4	−0.1	−0.4	−0.7	−0.9	−1.1	−1.2	−1.3	−1.3	−1.3	−1.3	−1.3
LEATHER PROD.	(323)	0.5	−0.7	−2.1	−3.4	−4.6	−5.7	−6.5	−7.2	−7.7	−7.9	−8.0	−7.8
FOOTWEAR	(324)	1.4	0.6	0.0	−0.4	−0.7	−0.9	−1.0	−1.1	−1.2	−1.2	−1.1	−1.1
WOOD PROD.	(331)	−0.1	−0.6	−1.1	−1.5	−1.8	−2.0	−2.2	−2.3	−2.4	−2.4	−2.4	−2.3
FURN. & FIXT.	(332)	0.6	0.3	0.0	−0.2	−0.5	−0.6	−0.8	−0.8	−0.9	−0.9	−0.9	−0.9
PAPER & PAPER PROD.	(341)	−0.1	−0.6	−1.1	−1.5	−1.8	−2.1	−2.3	−2.5	−2.5	−2.6	−2.5	−2.5
PRINT. & PUBL.	(342)	0.2	0.2	0.1	0.1	0.0	−0.0	−0.1	−0.1	−0.1	−0.1	−0.1	−0.1
CHEMICALS	(35A)	−0.2	−1.0	−1.7	−2.3	−2.8	−3.2	−3.5	−3.7	−3.8	−3.8	−3.7	−3.7
PETROL. & REL. PROD.	(35B)	0.2	0.3	0.4	0.5	0.6	0.7	0.8	1.0	1.1	1.2	1.4	1.4
RUBBER PROD.	(355)	−0.7	−2.0	−3.2	−4.1	−4.7	−5.2	−5.5	−5.7	−5.7	−5.7	−5.6	−5.5
NONMETAL. MIN. PROD.	(36A)	−0.1	−0.6	−1.1	−1.5	−1.8	−2.0	−2.2	−2.3	−2.4	−2.4	−2.3	−2.3
GLASS & GLASS PROD.	(362)	0.1	−0.3	−0.8	−1.2	−1.6	−1.9	−2.1	−2.3	−2.4	−2.4	−2.4	−2.3
IRON & STEEL	(371)	−0.0	−0.8	−1.4	−2.0	−2.5	−2.9	−3.2	−3.4	−3.6	−3.6	−3.6	−3.5
NONFERROUS METALS	(372)	−0.3	−1.2	−2.0	−2.7	−3.3	−3.7	−4.1	−4.3	−4.4	−4.5	−4.4	−4.3
METAL PROD.	(381)	−0.0	−0.6	−1.1	−1.5	−1.8	−2.1	−2.3	−2.4	−2.4	−2.4	−2.4	−2.3
NONELEC. MACH.	(382)	0.6	0.3	−0.2	−0.6	−0.9	−1.3	−1.6	−1.8	−1.9	−2.0	−2.0	−2.0
ELEC. MACH.	(383)	0.4	−0.1	−0.7	−1.1	−1.5	−1.8	−2.0	−2.1	−2.2	−2.2	−2.2	−2.2
TRANSP. EQUIP.	(384)	0.3	−0.4	−1.0	−1.5	−1.9	−2.2	−2.4	−2.5	−2.5	−2.5	−2.5	−2.4
MISC. MANUF.	(38A)	0.4	−0.8	−1.8	−2.5	−3.1	−3.5	−3.8	−4.0	−4.1	−4.1	−4.0	−4.0
Total traded		0.3	−0.2	−0.7	−1.1	−1.5	−1.7	−1.9	−2.1	−2.2	−2.2	−2.2	−2.1

Nontraded goods													
MIN. & QUARRY.	(2)	0.2	−0.1	−0.3	−0.5	−0.6	−0.7	−0.7	−0.7	−0.6	−0.5	−0.4	−0.3
ELEC., GAS, & WATER	(4)	0.2	0.0	−0.1	−0.3	−0.4	−0.5	−0.6	−0.7	−0.7	−0.8	−0.8	−0.7
CONSTRUCTION	(5)	0.3	0.4	0.5	0.5	0.5	0.5	0.5	0.5	0.5	0.5	0.5	0.5
WHOLE. & RET. TRADE	(6)	0.1	0.1	0.1	0.1	0.1	0.0	0.0	−0.0	−0.0	−0.0	−0.0	−0.0
TRANSP., STOR., & COMM.	(7)	0.2	0.1	−0.0	−0.1	−0.2	−0.3	−0.3	−0.3	−0.4	−0.4	−0.4	−0.4
FIN., INS., & REAL EST.	(8)	0.1	0.1	0.0	−0.0	−0.1	−0.1	−0.2	−0.2	−0.2	−0.2	−0.2	−0.2
COMM., SOC., & PERS. SERV.	(9)	0.1	0.1	0.1	0.1	0.1	0.1	0.1	0.1	0.1	0.1	0.1	0.1
Total nontraded		0.1	0.1	0.1	0.1	0.1	0.1	0.0	0.0	0.0	0.0	−0.0	−0.0
Total, all industries		0.2	0.0	−0.1	−0.2	−0.3	−0.4	−0.5	−0.5	−0.5	−0.6	−0.6	−0.5

Table 8.10
Summary of effects of actual exchange-rate changes, 1980:II–1981:II, on prices, trade, and employment in the United States by quarter, assuming doubling of export elasticities

Quarter	Price index (%Δ)	Trade changes ($ × 10^6) Exports	Imports	Balance	Employment change Man-years × 10^3	%
1	−0.39	−438.6	4,658.5	−5,097.2	150.1	0.17
2	−0.59	−1,333.3	7,926.5	−9,259.8	10.1	0.01
3	−0.78	−2,519.1	10,269.0	−12,788.0	−139.6	−0.16
4	−0.96	−3,875.4	11,923.0	−15,798.4	−284.2	−0.32
5	−1.13	−5,272.1	13,005.6	−18,277.7	−415.0	−0.47
6	−1.29	−6,624.8	13,631.3	−20,256.1	−528.0	−0.60
7	−1.44	−7,842.5	13,893.3	−21,735.8	−620.1	−0.71
8	−1.59	−8,854.1	13,868.6	−22,722.7	−689.4	−0.78
9	−1.72	−9,606.3	13,619.2	−23,225.5	−735.3	−0.84
10	−1.84	−10,041.3	13,200.3	−23,241.6	−756.2	−0.86
11	−1.95	−10,134.5	12,806.0	−22,940.4	−758.5	−0.86
12	−2.05	−9,854.2	12,474.1	−22,328.3	−740.9	−0.84

Turning finally to the disaggregated results for employment in tables 8.8 and 8.9, we see that the small percentage decline in aggregate employment after the first two quarters is borne disproportionately by most of the tradable industries. The largest numbers of workers are unemployed in large tradable industries such as agriculture (81 thousand), miscellaneous manufactures (52 thousand), nonelectrical machinery (46 thousand), and transport equipment (44 thousand). But the greatest percentage declines are in other industries where we already saw large percentage changes in either exports or imports (for example, leather products and rubber products). Employment in nontradable industries changes by only fractions of a percent, and actually rises in construction (16 thousand man-years) and community, social, and personal services (31 thousand man-years). The reason that nontraded industries may expand is that they enjoy the benefits of cheaper imported inputs without the disadvantage of having to compete with them. Indeed, if a nontraded industry declines due to an appreciation, it must be because it depends on the tradable sectors more for demand than for supply.

In order to test the sensitivity of our calculations, we doubled the export elasticities noted in table 8.1 in order to make export supply more responsive. We focused on the export elasticities because they appeared to us to be on the low side.[8] All the damping and lagged-price coefficients noted in table 8.1 were assumed unchanged. A summary of the results obtained by doubling the export elasticities is given in table 8.10. Comparing table 8.10

Table 8.11
Summary of effects of actual exchange-rate changes, 1980:II–1981:II, on prices, trade, and employment in the European Economic Community by quarter

Quarter	Price index (%Δ)	Trade changes ($ × 10⁶) Exports	Imports	Balance	Employment change: Man-years × 10³	%
1	1.98	646.7	−19,580.9	20,227.6	−1,023.6	−1.01
2	2.43	1,691.5	−24,881.2	26,572.7	−592.7	−0.59
3	2.94	2,960.5	−27,991.2	30,951.8	−256.7	−0.25
4	3.37	4,359.2	−29,874.9	34,234.2	17.3	0.02
5	3.78	5,773.8	−30,846.6	36,620.4	242.0	0.24
6	4.17	7,134.6	−31,155.4	38,290.0	423.0	0.42
7	4.54	8,359.0	−30,979.4	39,338.5	563.3	0.56
8	4.90	9,381.7	−30,452.8	39,834.6	664.7	0.66
9	5.24	10,152.5	−29,675.1	39,827.6	729.3	0.73
10	5.56	10,614.2	−28,734.6	39,348.8	757.3	0.76
11	5.86	10,733.3	−27,912.1	38,645.4	761.9	0.76
12	6.11	10,479.1	−27,297.4	37,776.5	741.6	0.74

with table 8.3 shows that the percentage decline in the US price index changes from 1.9 to 2.0% in quarter 12, exports fall by $9.9 billion as compared with $5.1 billion, imports rise by $12.5 billion as compared with $12.8 billion, the trade-balance decline is $22.3 billion as compared with $17.8 billion, and the decline in overall employment is 741 thousand as compared with 482 thousand man-years. The percentage decline in overall employment is 0.8% compared with 0.6%.

In short, doubling the export elasticities approximately doubles the response of exports, leaves imports more or less unchanged, and causes only a fractional increase in the changes in prices and employment. It may be wondered how it can be that exports become more responsive to exchange-rate changes and imports do not. The answer is that by increasing the export elasticities we make it possible for the purchasers of a given quantity of imports to substitute more in favor of lower cost sources of supply. Thus, exports can rise by more in depreciating countries and fall by more in appreciating countries, without imports anywhere changing by much at all.

It may be of interest finally to examine the effects of the exchange-rate changes on the EEC and Japan. The EEC experienced an effective depreciation of 15.4% from 1980:II to 1981:II according to the calculation noted in table 8.2. The effects of this depreciation are summarized in table 8.11 and have been calculated simultaneously with the results in table 8.3 using the various coefficients and elasticities recorded in table 8.1. Prices in the

Table 8.12
Summary of effects of actual exchange-rate changes, 1980:II–1981:II, on prices, trade, and employment in Japan by quarter

Quarter	Price index (%Δ)	Trade changes ($ × 10^6)			Employment change	
		Exports	Imports	Balance	Man-years × 10^3	%
1	−0.58	−77.4	1,375.9	−1,453.4	277.0	0.53
2	−0.84	−235.6	2,193.5	−2,429.0	223.7	0.43
3	−1.11	−447.6	2,728.8	−3,176.3	160.3	0.30
4	−1.35	−692.6	3,079.9	−3,772.5	97.2	0.18
5	−1.58	−947.5	3,291.2	−4,238.7	38.3	0.07
6	−1.80	−1,196.5	3,397.5	−4,593.9	−14.2	−0.03
7	−2.01	−1,422.6	3,424.2	−4,846.8	−58.6	−0.11
8	−2.20	−1,612.2	3,390.9	−5,003.1	−94.1	−0.18
9	−2.39	−1,755.1	3,312.2	−5,067.3	−120.2	−0.23
10	−2.56	−1,840.0	3,200.7	−5,040.7	−136.3	−0.26
11	−2.71	−1,861.7	3,097.1	−4,958.9	−145.1	−0.27
12	−2.85	−1,813.7	3,010.9	−4,824.6	−145.4	−0.28

EEC rise by an estimated 6.1% by quarter 12, exports rise by $10.5 billion, imports fall by $27.3 billion, the trade balance increases by $37.8 billion, and employment increases by 742 thousand man-years, which is 0.7% of aggregate EEC employment. According to the detailed results, which are not reported here, the largest increases in exports as a percentage of production are in petroleum and related products, leather products, nonferrous metals, wearing apparel, footwear, textiles, and miscellaneous manufactures. The largest declines in imports as a percentage of domestic demand are in petroleum and related products, rubber products, miscellaneous manufactures, wearing apparel, transport equipment, footwear, leather products, and wood products.[9] The greatest percentage increases in employment are concentrated in petroleum and related products, mining and quarrying, leather products, nonferrous metals, textiles and wearing apparel, rubber products, and miscellaneous manufactures.

According to table 8.2, Japan experienced an effective exchange-rate appreciation of 6.2% from 1980:II to 1981:II. The estimated effects of this appreciation are summarized in table 8.12. By quarter 12, prices fall by an estimated 2.8%, exports fall by $1.8 billion, imports rise by $3.0 billion, the trade balance declines by $4.8 billion, and employment declines by 145 thousand man-years. Employment in Japan rises in quarter 1 apparently because of the input-cost effects of the appreciation that we noted earlier in the case of the United States. But in Japan these effects persist for a somewhat longer time, with the change in employment turning negative only by quarter 6. It is possible that the damping, elasticities, and price-wage-feedback coefficients based on US experience may not be applicable to Japan. This would be worth investigating at some later time.

Comparison of Effects of Nonuniform and Uniform Exchange-Rate Changes

The preceding results were based on the actual exchange-rate changes that occurred between the second quarters of 1980 and 1981. However, since exchange rates can change continuously and substantially over time, the question arises as to whether it is possible to develop some "rules of thumb" that would provide reasonable estimates of the overall and sectoral impacts of arbitrary exchange-rate changes for individual countries and regions. Since our model is suited to handle any variety of such changes, we thought that it would be interesting and potentially useful to undertake some experimentation based on the model. Thus, we first assumed a one percent devaluation for the United States, the European Economic Community (EEC), and Japan. In each case, the own-country/region exchange rate was changed, holding all other rates constant. In order then to determine whether these *uniform* 1% results could be used as rules of thumb, we multiplied them by the actual changes in real exchange rates that occurred between the second quarters of 1980 and 1981. These scaled calculations were then compared with our preceding results based upon the *nonuniform* changes in exchange rates that in fact occurred.

The overall results of a *uniform*, 1% devaluation for the United States, the EEC, and Japan individually, holding all other exchange rates constant, are given in tables 8.13–8.15. The procedure followed was the same as previously; that is, the model was solved quarter by quarter for a total of 12 times. Each solution was designed to measure the cumulative effects through time subsequent to the assumed exogenous change in exchange rates. At each time, the various dampened elasticities and price-index changes noted previously were applied. Space does not permit discussion of the detailed results, but the changes can be interpreted along the same lines already indicated in the preceding discussion.

The question now arises as to whether these results of a uniform, 1% change in exchange rates can be used to approximate the effects of actual (nonuniform) exchange-rate changes that may occur. For this purpose, we scaled the above results for a 1% devaluation by the real effective exchange-rate changes analyzed previously. We then compared these scaled calcu-

Table 8.13
Summary of effects of 1% devaluation on prices, trade, and employment in the United States by quarter

Quarter	Price index (%Δ)	Trade changes ($ × 10⁶) Exports	Imports	Balance	Employment change Man-years × 10³	%
1	0.02	13.1	−280.2	293.3	−9.4	−0.01
2	0.03	40.6	−486.4	527.0	−2.4	−0.00
3	0.05	78.5	−646.1	724.7	5.0	0.01
4	0.06	123.7	−768.0	891.8	11.9	0.01
5	0.07	172.4	−858.0	1,030.4	18.2	0.02
6	0.08	221.7	−921.0	1,142.8	23.6	0.03
7	0.09	268.6	−961.1	1,229.8	28.1	0.03
8	0.10	310.1	−981.9	1,292.0	31.6	0.04
9	0.11	343.8	−986.1	1,329.9	34.0	0.04
10	0.12	366.8	−976.6	1,343.4	35.3	0.04
11	0.12	377.4	−966.6	1,343.9	35.8	0.04
12	0.13	372.6	−956.7	1,329.3	35.6	0.04

Table 8.14
Summary of effects of 1% devaluation on prices, trade, and employment in the European Economic Community by quarter

Quarter	Price index (%Δ)	Trade changes ($ × 10⁶) Exports	Imports	Balance	Employment change Man-years × 10³	%
1	0.10	32.4	−971.1	1,003.6	−50.2	−0.05
2	0.12	85.7	−1,242.7	1,328.4	−28.5	−0.03
3	0.15	151.3	−1,406.7	1,558.0	−11.3	−0.01
4	0.17	224.5	−1,510.2	1,734.7	3.1	0.00
5	0.19	299.6	−1,568.2	1,867.9	15.0	0.01
6	0.21	372.9	−1,592.8	1,965.7	24.8	0.02
7	0.23	439.9	−1,592.4	2,032.3	32.6	0.03
8	0.25	497.0	−1,573.3	2,070.3	38.4	0.04
9	0.27	541.2	−1,540.5	2,081.6	42.3	0.04
10	0.28	569.0	−1,498.1	2,067.1	44.2	0.04
11	0.30	578.3	−1,460.8	2,039.1	44.8	0.04
12	0.31	566.7	−1,432.7	1,999.5	43.9	0.04

Table 8.15
Summary of effects of 1% devaluation on prices, trade, and employment in Japan by quarter

		Trade changes ($ × 10⁶)			Employment change	
Quarter	Price index (%Δ)	Exports	Imports	Balance	Man-years × 10³	%
1	0.04	6.5	−143.6	150.1	−37.7	−0.07
2	0.06	18.6	−206.3	224.9	−33.9	−0.06
3	0.08	34.6	−248.1	282.7	−29.7	−0.06
4	0.09	53.1	−276.5	329.6	−25.4	−0.05
5	0.11	72.5	−295.1	367.6	−21.3	−0.04
6	0.13	91.8	−306.1	397.9	−17.5	−0.03
7	0.14	109.8	−311.3	421.1	−14.3	−0.03
8	0.16	125.5	−311.9	437.4	−11.5	−0.02
9	0.17	138.0	−308.9	446.9	−9.5	−0.02
10	0.19	146.3	−303.2	449.5	−8.2	−0.02
11	0.20	149.9	−298.0	447.9	−7.4	−0.01
12	0.21	147.7	−293.9	441.6	−7.3	−0.01

lations with the results from tables 8.3, 8.11, and 8.12, which reflect the nonuniform exchange-rate changes from 1980 to 1981, that is, with the United States and Japan appreciating while at the same time the EEC was depreciating. The results are summarized in tables 8.16–8.18. For the United States, the actual effects based on the nonuniform exchange-rate changes were almost exactly twice as large as those estimated by scaling the results of the 1% change using the own-country calculations. The actual effects were also larger for the EEC, but the factor of proportionality was closer to 1.2 than double. For Japan, depending on the variable and quarter, the actual results were larger than the own-country scaled results by a factor ranging from 1.5 to somewhat more than 2.0. The comparisons of the detailed, sectoral results, which are not reported here, generally reflect the differences noted.

It thus apparently makes a considerable difference whether an exchange-rate change is uniform or nonuniform across countries/regions. The reason seems to be a sort of leverage that occurs in the competition for third-country markets. That is, when a country depreciates relative to only one of its trading partners, its trade *with* that partner behaves as one would normally expect. But in addition, third countries—with respect to which it has not depreciated—will substitute in its favor due to its lower relative prices. Thus, the effect of a depreciation tends to be larger when it is uneven.[10]

Between the second quarters of 1980 and 1981, we noted that the United

Table 8.16
Comparison of effects of a 6.9% uniform and nonuniform appreciation by the United States on prices, trade, and employment by quarter[a]

	Price index (%Δ)		Trade changes ($ × 10^9)						Employment change over man-years	
			Uniform			Nonuniform				
Quarter	Uniform	Nonuniform	Exports	Imports	Balance	Exports	Imports	Balance	Uniform	Nonuniform
1	−0.1	−0.4	−0.1	1.9	−2.0	−0.2	4.6	−4.9	64.9	157.4
2	−0.2	−0.6	−0.3	3.4	−3.6	−0.7	7.9	−8.6	16.6	39.4
3	−0.3	−0.8	−0.5	4.5	−5.0	−1.3	10.2	−11.5	−34.5	−78.3
4	−0.4	−0.9	−0.9	5.3	−6.2	−1.9	11.9	−13.8	−82.1	−185.5
5	−0.5	−1.1	−1.2	5.9	−7.1	−2.6	13.0	−15.7	−125.6	−277.9
6	−0.6	−1.2	−1.5	6.4	−7.9	−3.3	13.7	−17.0	−162.8	−354.2
7	−0.6	−1.3	−1.9	6.6	−8.5	−4.0	14.0	−18.0	−193.9	−413.6
8	−0.7	−1.5	−2.1	6.8	−8.9	−4.5	14.0	−18.5	−218.0	−456.2
9	−0.8	−1.6	−2.4	6.8	−9.2	−4.9	13.8	−18.7	−234.6	−482.4
10	−0.8	−1.7	−2.5	6.7	−9.3	−5.1	13.5	−18.6	−243.6	−492.0
11	−0.8	−1.8	−2.6	6.7	−9.3	−5.2	13.1	−18.3	−247.0	−492.1
12	−0.9	−1.9	−2.6	6.6	−9.2	−5.1	12.8	−17.8	−245.6	−482.0

a. Uniform changes have been obtained by multiplying the 1% results in table 8.13 by −6.9. Nonuniform changes are based on model calculations, assuming actual 1980:II–1981:II real exchange-rate changes for all six country/regions of the model. These include, in effective terms, a 6.9% appreciation for the United States, a 15.4% depreciation for the EEC, and a 6.2% appreciation for Japan.

Table 8.17
Comparison of effects of a 15.4% uniform and nonuniform depreciation by the European Economic Community on prices, trade, and employment by quarter[a]

	Price index (%Δ)		Trade changes ($ × 10^9)						Employment change over man-years	
			Uniform			Nonuniform				
Quarter	Uniform	Nonuniform	Exports	Imports	Balance	Exports	Imports	Balance	Uniform	Nonuniform
1	1.5	2.0	0.5	−15.0	15.5	0.6	−19.6	20.2	−773.1	−1,023.6
2	1.8	2.4	1.3	−19.1	20.5	1.7	−24.9	26.6	−438.9	−592.7
3	2.3	2.9	2.3	−21.7	24.0	3.0	−28.0	31.0	−174.0	−256.7
4	2.6	3.4	3.5	−23.3	26.7	4.4	−29.9	34.2	47.7	17.3
5	2.9	3.8	4.6	−24.2	28.8	5.8	−30.8	36.6	231.0	242.0
6	3.2	4.2	5.7	−24.5	30.3	7.1	−31.2	38.3	381.9	423.0
7	3.5	4.5	6.8	−24.5	31.3	8.4	−31.0	39.3	502.0	563.3
8	3.8	4.9	7.7	−24.2	31.9	9.4	−30.5	39.8	591.4	664.7
9	4.2	5.2	8.3	−23.7	32.1	10.2	−29.7	39.8	651.4	729.3
10	4.3	5.6	8.8	−23.1	31.8	10.6	−28.7	39.3	680.7	757.3
11	4.6	5.9	8.9	−22.5	31.4	10.7	−27.9	38.6	689.9	761.9
12	4.8	6.1	8.7	−22.1	30.8	10.5	−27.3	37.8	676.1	741.6

a. Uniform changes have been obtained by multiplying the 1% results in table 8.14 by 15.4. Nonuniform changes are based on model calculations, assuming actual 1980:II–1981:II real exchange-rate changes for all six country/regions of the model. These include, in effective terms, a 6.9% appreciation for the United States, a 15.4% depreciation for the EEC, and a 6.2% appreciation for Japan.

Table 8.18
Comparison of effects of a 6.2% uniform and nonuniform appreciation by Japan on prices, trade, and employment by quarter[a]

	Price index (%Δ)		Trade changes ($\$ \times 10^9$) Uniform			Nonuniform			Employment change over man-years	
Quarter	Uniform	Nonuniform	Exports	Imports	Balance	Exports	Imports	Balance	Uniform	Nonuniform
1	−0.2	−0.6	−0.0	0.9	−0.9	−0.1	1.4	−1.5	233.7	277.0
2	−0.4	−0.8	−0.1	1.3	−1.4	−0.2	2.2	−2.4	210.2	223.7
3	−0.5	−1.1	−0.2	1.5	−1.8	−0.4	2.7	−3.2	184.1	160.3
4	−0.6	−1.4	−0.3	1.7	−2.0	−0.7	3.1	−3.8	157.5	97.2
5	−0.7	−1.6	−0.4	1.8	−2.3	−0.9	3.3	−4.2	132.1	38.3
6	−0.8	−1.8	−0.6	1.9	−2.5	−1.2	3.4	−4.6	108.5	−14.2
7	−0.9	−2.0	−0.7	1.9	−2.6	−1.4	3.4	−4.8	88.7	−58.6
8	−1.0	−2.2	−0.8	1.9	−2.7	−1.6	3.4	−5.0	71.3	−94.1
9	−1.1	−2.4	−0.9	1.9	−2.8	−1.8	3.3	−5.1	58.9	−120.2
10	−1.2	−2.6	−0.9	1.9	−2.8	−1.8	3.2	−5.0	50.8	−136.3
11	−1.2	−2.7	−0.9	1.8	−2.8	−1.9	3.1	−5.0	45.9	−145.1
12	−1.3	−2.9	−0.9	1.8	−2.7	−1.8	3.0	−4.8	45.3	−145.4

a. Uniform changes have been obtained by multiplying the 1% results in table 8.15 by −6.2. Nonuniform changes are based on model calculations, assuming actual 1980:II–1981:II real exchange-rate changes for all six country/regions of the model. These include, in effective terms, a 6.9% appreciation for the United States, a 15.4% depreciation for the EEC, and a 6.2% appreciation for Japan.

States and Japan both appreciated and the EEC depreciated. Since the change for the EEC was more uniform—being about the same relative to both the United States and Japan—its effects are not much underestimated by scaling a uniform 1% devaluation. But for both the United States and Japan, who appreciated significantly relative to Europe but hardly at all relative to each other, these third-country effects become more important and the uniform exchange-rate change provides a poor approximation for evaluating the results involved.

The following implications can be drawn from the foregoing analysis:

1. The effects of actual exchange-rate changes are not well approximated by analyzing a uniform devaluation or appreciation. Nonuniform changes have effects of their own that must be taken into account. This means that it may be risky to use rules of thumb to estimate changes in trade and employment from given changes in exchange rates. If exchange-rate changes are nonuniform, a much more detailed analysis of the specific case at issue will be required, and this may mean using a fairly complicated model such as ours.

2. The information content of an index of effective exchange rates may be somewhat limited. If the impacts of exchange-rate changes in the domestic economy are at all sensitive—as they seem to be—to the way that those changes are distributed across a nation's trading partners, then no simple index can suffice in itself to indicate the significance of the changes. Again, a more detailed analysis is required.

Conclusion

We have investigated in this chapter and the one preceding a variety of important issues involving the sectoral and overall impacts of changes in exchange rates. It is clear that there are sizable intersectoral differences among countries in the responsiveness of industry output to exchange-rate changes. We were also able to assess the impacts on own-country prices under a variety of assumptions as well as the cross-country impacts for the major industrialized and developing countries. Our calculations and analysis thus call attention to the multiplicity of effects of changes in exchange rates and to the orders of magnitude that may be relevant in formulating and evaluating changes in policies that bear upon exchange rates.

Our second major objective was to demonstrate how the appreciation of the dollar and changes in other exchange rates since 1980 have had a significant impact on trade, prices, and employment in the United States and the other major industrialized countries. In this connection, we took the observed changes in exchange rates as exogenous. It would have been ideal if we had been able to model the determinants of exchange-rate movements. But our results are nonetheless useful because they demonstrate that large changes in exchange rates can have sizable impacts on individual sectors and overall in the world's major producing and trading countries. The issue then becomes one of identifying the sources of these changes in exchange rates and seeking to design policies that will promote greater economic stability.

9

Changes in Trade and Employment in the Major Industrialized Countries, 1970–1976

There has been increasing concern in industrial countries in recent years that international trade has a possibly adverse impact on employment in particular sectors of the economy. Imports have accordingly been restricted in such sectors as textiles and wearing apparel, footwear, iron and steel, automobiles, and consumer electronics. At the same time, the expansionary effect that trade through exports may have on employment has not always been duly recognized.

In order to shed some light on these issues, we use our model in this chapter to estimate the effects of trade on employment between 1970 and 1976.[1] We shall also examine the employment effects of projected future increases in trade in manufactures between the major industrial and developing countries.

We first discuss some conceptual issues concerning the effects of trade on employment and the nature of our calculations. In this connection, we used the model to run two basic experiments. The first experiment was to calculate the employment effect that might result if the 1970 pattern of total trade were to be restored in all countries in 1976. The second experiment involved restoring the 1970 pattern of trade in manufactures between the industrialized and developing countries included in the model. The results of these experiments are described in later sections of the chapter. We also ran one further experiment using the projected future increases in trade in manufactures between the industrialized and developing countries based upon World Bank projections as modified and reported by Balassa (1979). These results are presented in the final section of the chapter.

Conceptual Issues in the Effects of Trade on Employment

The question of how trade affects employment poses conceptual difficulties. Part of the problem is that trade is not exogenous, but instead is itself determined by many of the same changes in tastes, technology, and government policy that can be expected to influence employment directly. If trade and employment tend to move together historically, this may only reflect their dependence on the same exogenous forces, and need not indicate that one causes the other. Nonetheless, it does seem likely that the course of employment would have been different if trade had not been permitted to expand. It is this difference that we shall try to assess in what follows.

We proceed by asking this question: Supposing that trade had not been permitted to expand from 1970 to 1976, how would 1976 employment have differed compared with what it actually turned out to be? The difference between the hypothetical and actual employment can then be ascribed to the changes in trade that in fact occurred. To illustrate, if employment in a particular sector grew by 100,000 workers over the 6 years and would have grown by only 40,000 if trade had remained constant, then the difference of 60,000 can be taken as the employment created by the change in trade. Or if employment actually fell by 20,000 when it would have risen by 50,000 with constant trade, then the change in trade can be said to have had a negative effect of 70,000 workers.

To implement this idea using our model, we essentially worked backward. Starting with the data for 1976, we calculated the effect on employment of a return to the 1970 pattern of trade as measured by the ratios of exports and imports to gross domestic product. The change in trade is assumed to be the deliberate result of an increase in tariffs on imports and taxes on exports. In our applications of the model in chapters 4 and 5 involving the evaluation of the effects of tariff reductions, these reductions were taken as exogenous changes and the model was asked to determine what the resulting changes in trade and employment would be. By treating changes in trade as exogenous in the present application, we are making tariffs on imports and taxes on exports endogenous and asking how these tariffs and taxes would have to change in order to attain in 1976 the ratios of trade to GDP (gross domestic product) that were realized in 1970. In the process, we can then determine what the effects on 1976 sectoral employment would be from restoration of the 1970 pattern of trade. The answers, with their signs reversed, then indicate the employment effects of the trade expansion that took place from 1970 to 1976, all other things (for example, population, productivity, and government policy) held constant at their 1976 levels.

Before the foregoing procedure could be implemented, we had to decide what was meant by the "1970 trade pattern." Our trade data for both years were in nominal terms, and this included a good deal of apparent expansion of trade that was only the result of inflation. Obviously, we would not want to analyze a return to the nominal trade levels of 1970, for that would be overdoing it in real terms. But even a return to *real* 1970 trade levels struck us as exaggerating the effects we wished to measure. For one would expect the growth of trade at least to parallel growth in the economy as a whole without there being cause for concern. Presumably, even a staunch protectionist would not argue that trade should be prevented from growing altogether. Rather, a case might be made that trade be prevented from growing faster than the domestic economy. It is this interpretation that we have adopted for purposes of analysis. Therefore, when we speak of restoring the 1970 pattern of trade, we mean it in terms of exports and imports as fractions of total GDP.

Our first step was to take trade and GDP data for 1970 and 1976 and to calculate by how much exports and imports would have had to change in 1976 to restore their relative positions as of 1970. The proportional change in exports for each country i and sector j was calculated from the following formula:

$$\frac{\Delta X_{ij}}{X_{ij}^{76}} = \frac{X_{ij}^{70}\,\mathrm{GDP}_i^{76}}{X_{ij}^{76}\,\mathrm{GDP}_i^{70}} - 1,$$

where X refers to nominal exports in the given year and GDP to the value of total gross domestic product. An analogous calculation was also made to obtain the percentage changes in imports for 1976 based on the 1970 trade patterns for each country and sector.

Taking the foregoing percentage changes in exports and imports as exogenous, we then solved our model for the effects on employment. As mentioned, this required a somewhat different solution procedure for our model than we had previously used, because in the present analysis tariffs and taxes on imports and exports are unknown. It turned out that we could solve the model for present purposes on a country-by-country basis rather than for all countries simultaneously. The reason is that countries depend on each other only through world prices and exchange rates. Since in our model these variables affect a country only through its trade, and trade in the present analysis is exogenous, it follows that there is no mechanism here for countries to affect one another.[2]

This independence of the solutions among countries is also convenient in that it solves another problem that might otherwise have been troubling. With different growth rates of GDP in different countries between 1970 and 1976, there is no reason that restoration of 1970 ratios of trade to GDP should lead to quantities traded that would clear world markets. However, since we solve the model on a country-by-country basis, and never make use of any world-market-clearing equations, this failure poses no difficulty for our solution. It does mean, however, that the experiment that we do is inconsistent for all of the countries together. That is, if all countries were to attempt to restore these 1970 trade ratios, most markets would fail to clear and the effort would fail. This may be viewed as a drawback of our analysis, though we think it is preferable to the only obvious alternative of restoring 1970 ratios of trade to *world* GDP. This would be consistent with world-markets clearing, since it would merely scale all 1970 actual trade volumes by a common percentage. But it would lead to quite uneven results across countries with different growth rates, in terms of the expansion and contraction of the importance of trade in their economies.

One other drawback of our analysis should also be mentioned. Because of data limitations, it is the ratio of *nominal* trade to GDP that we use as the basis of our calculations. To the extent that prices rose differently in different sectors between 1970 and 1976, this means that we are not using the real importance of trade in 1970 as the basis for our experiment. For example, if no real quantities traded or produced had changed over this period but prices had nonetheless changed unevenly, our experiment would require that a country contract its trade in sectors where prices had risen relative to others, and expand its trade elsewhere. If in fact relative price changes have been more significant than changes in quantities over this period, then our results may be quite misleading.

In our judgment, however, while changes in relative prices certainly have occurred, changes in quantities have still been important enough to justify our procedure. The one industry that may be an exception to this is the petroleum industry, and partly for that reason we have elected to exclude it from the analysis in the results to be reported. That is, in the experiments that we report, trade in petroleum has not been returned to 1970 levels, but has been held constant.

Estimated Employment Effects of Restoring the 1970 Pattern of Total Trade

Our procedure was first to calculate the percentage employment changes that could be ascribed to an attempt to return to the trade pattern of 1970 in all industries. The results, which are not reported here, were both negative and positive, with the contraction of trade reducing employment primarily where exports would fall more than imports and expanding employment otherwise. Restoration of the 1970 pattern of trade would also shift employment between tradables and nontradables depending upon changes in relative prices. Thus, for example, if the contraction of trade resulted in a rise in the prices of tradable goods relative to nontradables, there would be a shift in demand and therefore employment away from tradables and into nontradables.

When we examined the results, there were certain percentage employment changes that appeared unusually large and consequently point up a limitation of including all industries in the analysis. These unusual results were concentrated in ISIC 35B, petroleum and other fuel products, where the calculated employment changes were frequently very large, in some cases well in excess of 1,000%. This is not to say, however, that these results are necessarily incorrect. In addition to the price changes already discussed, they reflect the substantial shifts in the pattern of trade in petroleum and other fuel products that occurred so rapidly over the period from 1970 to 1976 and the difficulty that countries would encounter in trying to reverse these changes. In any case, and as noted previously, in view of the special circumstances involving petroleum, we did a second run of the model with the changes in trade in the petroleum sector set at zero. We then multiplied the resulting estimates of percentage changes in employment by the levels of employment in 1976. The results are reported in thousands of workers in table 9.1. These results can be interpreted as the employment changes that can be ascribed to the growth of trade between 1970 and 1976.

For the United States, there were substantial increases in employment for agriculture, textiles, chemicals, and durable manufactures. The largest absolute declines in employment for the United States were in food and kindred products, wearing apparel, footwear, printing and publishing, and the nontradable sectors. Table 9.1 also shows the employment increases and declines by sector for the other industrialized countries in the model. In table 9.2 we show the actual changes in sectoral employment that occurred from 1970 to 1976. By taking both tables together, it is evident that trade has been an important factor in shaping the employment experiences of industries in the world's major producing and trading countries. However, neither the direction nor the relative size of this effect is uniform, and it is necessary to look at the results industry by industry to see what the role of trade has been.

To show more clearly the effects involved, we summarize in table 9.3 the experiences of the United States, the European Economic Community, and Japan in terns of the hypothetical and actual changes in employment that occurred between 1970 and 1976. The largest employment effect that we calculated as resulting from trade for the United States was the increase of 1.4 million workers in agriculture. This reflects of course the marked expansion of US agricultural exports over the period. Actual agricultural employ-

Table 9.1
Estimated changes in employment resulting from growth of trade from 1970 to 1976 in all industries except petroleum refineries, in thousands of man-years

Industry	(ISIC)	ALA	ATA	BLX	CND	DEN	FIN	FR	GFR	IRE	IT	JPN	NL	NZ	NOR	SWD	SWZ	UK	US
Traded goods																			
AGR., FOR., & FISH.	(1)	42.46	0.45	77.66	32.99	−43.14	19.81	153.64	141.32	−109.05	−62.41	−999.00	60.36	−20.98	−15.89	28.59	20.80	−17.31	1,423.20
FOOD, BEV., & TOB.	(310)	−9.99	2.65	19.55	−9.99	−2.29	−2.15	17.25	69.48	4.05	23.68	−19.04	1.62	−13.89	−4.21	−5.31	−11.71	22.80	−33.21
TEXTILES	(321)	−13.05	−0.75	−27.27	−5.92	1.59	4.12	−60.67	21.92	7.85	30.70	−171.21	−23.44	3.68	−0.39	1.57	−0.50	−67.92	73.04
WEARING APPAREL	(322)	−11.92	−16.89	−14.92	−22.49	−8.60	6.45	−7.67	−32.42	−4.81	41.51	−153.73	−12.81	1.68	−3.32	−5.19	−2.88	−53.90	−94.97
LEATHER PROD.	(323)	−0.25	−0.43	−2.37	0.38	0.74	0.53	−4.22	2.27	0.41	−9.17	−7.53	−0.85	0.19	−0.84	−0.01	0.12	3.49	15.58
FOOTWEAR	(324)	−0.75	−0.09	−5.52	1.71	0.67	0.83	−13.04	−7.32	−1.47	62.40	−14.62	−1.96	−0.46	−0.28	0.97	−1.79	−11.06	−17.95
WOOD PROD.	(331)	9.22	−1.47	7.19	−17.14	−0.91	−22.47	−9.03	35.74	−0.51	−15.42	−0.42	1.23	−2.65	4.90	−11.10	8.88	−4.86	13.33
FURN. & FIXT.	(332)	−2.34	4.26	5.65	−5.04	1.72	0.90	−3.88	14.53	0.25	66.91	−12.87	0.30	−0.02	−3.20	4.76	0.17	0.49	−1.21
PAPER & PAPER PROD.	(341)	1.48	0.30	−2.53	−11.23	−0.22	−17.86	−4.67	31.68	−0.75	4.55	−1.20	1.32	2.17	−9.69	5.25	3.96	−27.20	−1.17
PRINT. & PUBL.	(342)	0.33	−1.33	0.03	2.17	−0.66	1.99	0.55	3.77	0.67	−2.63	−8.51	−3.77	−0.30	−1.97	−0.57	−0.24	−9.45	−19.30
CHEMICALS	(35A)	13.83	8.50	45.79	0.31	1.55	5.70	21.83	93.90	6.65	17.73	36.63	35.83	−5.15	−1.29	4.44	12.06	29.29	47.85
PETROL. & REL. PROD.	(35B)	−0.00	0.17	−0.03	−0.14	−0.24	−0.04	−8.01	−0.52	−4.32	−12.69	22.63	−0.66	−0.09	−0.01	−0.62	0.01	−9.26	−4.96
RUBBER PROD.	(355)	−0.41	0.49	3.40	2.14	1.80	1.38	14.18	34.50	0.58	21.71	35.45	0.37	−0.39	−0.20	−0.48	1.19	−4.56	−14.76
NONMETAL. MIN. PROD.	(36A)	0.05	−2.98	−5.77	−3.65	0.39	1.34	−6.43	0.66	0.66	31.93	−3.15	4.84	−0.12	−1.37	−5.84	2.45	−7.40	−5.33
GLASS & GLASS PROD.	(362)	0.35	−0.41	−16.04	−0.91	1.05	1.58	0.63	−1.70	1.20	5.52	1.46	4.99	0.01	0.72	1.23	0.99	−0.54	5.41
IRON & STEEL	(371)	5.99	2.11	−55.68	−1.52	5.03	6.67	10.54	58.87	1.28	91.45	283.60	8.38	0.78	0.80	−1.89	10.61	−43.36	−3.17
NONFERROUS METALS	(372)	0.34	4.66	−33.63	−48.61	1.40	1.38	7.11	50.28	−3.46	35.94	143.53	5.14	2.84	−4.93	1.19	5.98	12.38	−13.18
METAL PROD.	(381)	−1.76	7.01	−6.82	3.80	−6.14	1.90	13.55	36.65	3.00	54.74	−37.87	6.41	−1.52	−8.09	−9.69	7.94	−20.01	26.27
NONELEC. MACH.	(382)	5.24	12.08	11.98	1.82	3.78	14.32	126.74	211.83	4.25	60.76	156.82	13.22	0.27	0.11	5.17	7.52	30.11	198.85
ELEC. MACH.	(383)	−8.55	2.13	6.18	−11.73	−6.69	2.36	38.35	58.72	1.38	4.49	210.07	−3.52	−2.39	−3.03	8.05	17.16	12.25	56.31
TRANSP. EQUIP.	(384)	−2.66	0.08	23.84	−17.03	−8.04	9.19	83.97	150.66	2.53	48.81	497.80	30.29	−1.65	3.65	25.80	1.41	−74.80	96.62
MISC. MANUF.	(38A)	4.41	8.23	13.66	−23.37	11.77	4.05	15.50	63.52	8.00	66.54	54.43	30.74	−2.85	7.03	16.78	19.11	65.85	0.79
Total		32.01	28.76	44.36	−133.46	−45.44	41.98	386.21	1,038.34	−81.63	567.04	13.26	158.05	−40.83	−41.51	63.12	103.22	−174.97	1,748.03
Nontraded goods																			
MIN. & QUARRY.	(2)	3.24	1.44	−8.85	−12.05	1.11	2.30	−3.40	27.94	1.25	55.53	54.27	1.64	1.08	−1.25	−3.48	13.03	−13.14	−25.68
ELEC., GAS, & WATER	(4)	0.63	0.49	−1.49	−5.53	0.02	1.06	−6.01	6.57	−1.19	8.16	20.02	0.47	0.10	−1.40	−2.78	5.88	−25.02	−30.03
CONSTRUCTION	(5)	−7.88	17.36	−6.60	3.53	−8.98	−0.13	−48.97	−113.80	−6.67	−117.22	−316.11	−33.44	−2.26	−12.33	−54.00	−8.98	−69.41	−74.15
WHOLE. & RET. TRADE	(6)	−5.65	3.50	−16.18	−34.57	3.26	6.58	−129.11	−29.10	−21.72	−215.48	−104.73	−20.81	−2.72	−10.89	−34.54	13.68	−265.82	−607.16
TRANSP., STOR., & COMM.	(7)	0.55	3.99	1.49	−16.68	1.28	2.16	−24.09	1.36	−3.53	−4.94	−21.70	−5.85	−1.09	−7.59	−13.78	14.37	−67.57	−65.26
FIN., INS., & REAL EST.	(8)	1.08	1.78	0.08	−15.97	0.09	3.92	−51.45	−42.08	−4.15	−67.27	−24.03	−7.53	−1.69	−4.59	−19.74	18.38	−137.91	−279.36
COMM., SOC., & PERS. SERV.	(9)	−3.42	0.56	−14.71	−46.55	5.52	7.05	−118.78	−118.74	−20.98	−96.80	−203.30	−29.38	−1.87	−8.96	−55.70	14.45	−338.10	−737.71
Total		−11.44	29.13	−46.26	−127.82	2.29	22.94	−381.81	−267.85	−56.99	−438.01	−595.58	−94.91	−8.45	−47.01	−184.01	70.81	−916.97	−1,819.37
Overall total		20.57	57.89	−1.90	−261.28	−43.15	64.91	4.40	770.49	−138.62	129.03	−582.32	63.14	−49.28	−88.51	−120.90	174.04	−1,091.94	−71.33

Table 9.2
Actual changes in employment from 1970 to 1976, in thousands of man-years

Industry	(ISIC)	ALA	ATA	BLX	CND	DEN	FIN	FR	GFR	IRE	IT	JPN	NL	NZ	NOR	SWD	SWZ	UK	US
Traded goods																			
AGR., FOR., & FISH.	(1)	−67.00	−196.00	−48.80	53.00	−43.00	−189.00	−643.00	−519.00	−40.00	−684.00	−2,430.00	−34.00	3.00	−40.00	−60.00	−21.00	−124.00	−165.00
FOOD, BEV., & TOB.	(310)	−10.26	2.03	−21.59	43.16	1.25	7.61	−3.92	−88.52	−3.65	8.19	141.86	−22.18	7.24	−6.30	0.62	−8.44	−55.08	244.78
TEXTILES	(321)	−27.47	−14.95	−28.37	15.79	−5.47	−5.10	−86.71	−214.77	−6.72	−144.43	−401.31	−31.35	−4.23	−3.70	−10.93	−24.10	−137.47	187.37
WEARING APPAREL	(322)	−27.55	−7.05	−24.87	22.16	−5.90	0.54	−21.91	−141.85	−6.02	12.57	155.56	−35.60	−8.15	−4.47	−12.76	−13.12	−37.74	131.11
LEATHER PROD.	(323)	−3.84	0.76	−2.86	1.20	−0.44	−0.47	−2.18	−22.58	−0.19	−5.66	−0.31	−2.20	0.09	−0.10	−1.71	−1.65	−6.55	13.63
FOOTWEAR	(324)	−8.82	0.60	1.45	2.16	−0.77	−2.33	−12.70	−46.69	−2.76	−11.58	−0.19	−4.25	−1.08	−1.22	−1.82	−3.40	−13.11	−6.01
WOOD PROD.	(331)	−9.75	4.20	−10.45	37.70	−2.05	−10.05	2.43	−42.33	−0.14	−30.62	−113.63	−5.89	−1.62	2.09	−3.68	−9.71	−10.77	103.86
FURN. & FIXT.	(332)	0.18	−2.55	−4.01	13.62	1.14	−0.87	12.09	−10.38	−0.43	13.86	2.81	−3.18	−0.84	−0.58	1.11	−5.22	−3.10	88.00
PAPER & PAPER PROD.	(341)	−1.91	−3.86	1.20	31.55	−1.17	5.45	−4.75	−69.92	−0.11	−2.32	−4.85	−4.74	−1.63	−0.34	−0.69	−3.62	−34.65	80.63
PRINT. & PUBL.	(342)	−9.56	2.91	0.42	22.27	−2.33	2.94	−3.69	−62.44	−1.51	12.65	52.53	−5.18	−1.63	7.04	−4.02	−9.62	−42.63	115.58
CHEMICALS	(35A)	−8.72	0.77	12.04	20.39	1.88	5.87	22.37	−72.81	1.44	11.95	−0.18	−3.21	5.56	1.52	2.09	0.70	−40.25	159.48
PETROL. & REL. PROD.	(35B)	0.41	1.15	1.73	3.93	0.11	0.73	−31.20	−7.99	0.56	−1.64	8.79	−1.02	0.0	0.79	0.15	0.10	−0.71	48.58
RUBBER PROD.	(355)	−4.37	−0.46	−2.33	7.56	−0.69	0.52	3.18	−42.06	−0.11	6.57	−19.43	−0.82	0.53	−0.66	−1.39	0.16	−16.00	27.17
NONMETAL. MIN. PROD.	(36A)	−3.45	0.24	9.71	10.94	−2.65	1.81	−6.37	−51.62	2.01	−15.82	−41.37	−7.73	−0.77	0.41	−6.05	−8.30	−35.39	64.46
GLASS & GLASS PROD.	(362)	−2.83	−1.36	0.84	2.93	0.0	0.01	7.38	−15.59	0.69	−12.29	−6.70	−2.43	−0.35	0.51	−0.58	−1.70	−14.35	26.60
IRON & STEEL	(371)	−3.90	2.77	−16.80	11.97	0.66	6.16	5.15	−241.54	1.04	90.85	2.67	−3.62	−0.28	−0.42	8.35	−4.99	−104.95	15.92
NONFERROUS METALS	(372)	0.69	1.23	−3.13	7.20	0.26	1.65	−1.17	−43.24	0.29	−12.28	−2.77	−1.05	2.26	−2.64	3.69	−5.10	−30.64	35.93
METAL PROD.	(381)	−20.97	8.78	43.93	31.51	−2.59	3.69	8.59	−112.62	1.30	−9.66	−53.11	−4.74	1.74	−0.31	6.60	−15.96	−72.38	249.27
NONELEC. MACH.	(382)	−0.79	−0.70	−48.94	21.25	2.16	7.53	29.32	−174.60	1.52	51.79	−121.45	−7.00	−9.78	8.88	8.63	−8.09	−185.56	411.37
ELEC. MACH.	(383)	−18.10	4.52	−2.35	20.56	−5.45	9.36	71.46	−171.30	0.77	197.45	−102.23	−6.40	4.74	4.04	13.29	−7.40	−67.53	245.89
TRANSP. EQUIP.	(384)	−15.20	−20.31	−15.17	47.84	2.38	4.27	57.46	−85.28	−0.52	103.11	201.53	−5.72	3.39	5.75	29.03	−16.18	−104.96	288.74
MISC. MANUF.	(38A)	2.24	4.50	−3.88	12.52	2.27	0.58	21.28	−51.74	3.64	16.43	−18.06	−3.50	−1.08	4.31	5.98	−29.71	−37.06	268.78
Total		−240.97	−212.78	−162.23	441.21	−60.40	−149.10	−576.89	−2,288.87	−48.90	−404.88	−2,749.84	−195.81	−2.89	−25.40	−24.09	−196.35	−1,174.88	2,636.14
Nontraded goods																			
MIN. & QUARRY.	(2)	4.00	−7.00	−16.69	49.80	1.10	0.0	−61.00	34.00	0.0	34.00	−20.00	−0.20	0.0	3.00	0.0	−6.89	−67.00	−214.80
ELEC., GAS, & WATER	(4)	−3.04	0.0	2.46	16.50	1.10	−3.10	17.00	39.00	1.00	12.00	50.00	2.00	2.00	4.00	9.00	−5.38	−47.00	−254.90
CONSTRUCTION	(5)	31.00	8.00	−1.12	−60.50	−56.10	−30.00	−142.00	−138.00	0.0	−200.00	980.00	−68.00	7.00	14.00	−77.00	−75.00	8.00	−3,695.50
WHOLE. & RET. TRADE	(6)	409.00	61.00	21.78	352.60	43.70	91.10	280.00	−283.00	−2.00	108.00	1,390.00	−12.00	54.30	61.00	36.00	−9.70	106.00	7,671.30
TRANSP., STOR., & COMM.	(7)	31.00	9.00	31.90	56.90	8.70	12.00	67.00	14.00	4.00	111.00	170.00	5.00	16.00	4.00	9.00	72.52	−78.00	−3,049.40
FIN., INS., & REAL EST.	(8)	220.00	34.00	50.39	18.50	34.70	31.80	304.00	246.00	5.00	879.59	410.00	85.50	−12.50	46.00	49.00	146.33	186.00	2,867.20
COMM., SOC., & PERS. SERV.	(9)	26.00	84.00	137.83	777.00	112.30	47.80	589.00	764.00	17.00	−123.60	1,570.00	140.70	64.30	186.00	230.00	−186.14	1,069.00	2,897.80
Total		717.96	189.00	226.55	1,210.80	145.50	149.60	1,054.00	676.00	25.00	820.99	4,550.00	153.00	131.10	318.00	256.00	−64.26	1,177.00	6,221.70
Overall total		476.99	−23.78	64.32	1,652.01	85.10	0.50	477.11	−1,612.87	−23.90	416.11	1,800.16	−42.81	128.21	292.60	231.91	−260.61	2.12	8,857.84

Table 9.3
United States, Japan, and the European Economic Community: comparison of estimated changes in employment resulting from the growth of trade (excluding petroleum refineries) with actual changes in employment 1970–1976, in thousands of man-years

Industry	(ISIC)	United States: Change resulting from growth of trade	United States: Actual change	European Economic Community: Change resulting from growth of trade	European Economic Community: Actual change	Japan: Change resulting from growth of trade	Japan: Actual change
Traded goods							
AGR., FOR., & FISH.	(1)	1,423.20	−165.00	201.07	−2,135.80	−999.00	−2,430.00
FOOD, BEV., & TOB.	(310)	−33.21	244.78	156.13	−185.50	−19.04	141.86
TEXTILES	(321)	73.04	187.37	−117.24	−655.29	−171.21	−401.31
WEARING APPAREL	(322)	−94.97	131.11	−93.62	−261.32	−153.73	155.56
LEATHER PROD.	(323)	15.58	13.63	−9.71	−42.66	−7.53	−0.31
FOOTWEAR	(324)	−17.95	−6.01	22.72	−90.41	−14.62	−0.19
WOOD PROD.	(331)	13.33	103.86	13.42	−99.82	−0.42	−113.63
FURN. & FIXT.	(332)	−1.21	88.00	85.97	5.99	−12.87	2.81
PAPER & PAPER PROD.	(341)	−1.17	80.63	2.17	−116.46	−1.20	−4.85
PRINT. & PUBL.	(342)	−19.30	115.58	−11.48	−104.71	−8.51	52.53
CHEMICALS	(35A)	47.85	159.48	252.56	−66.59	36.63	−0.18
PETROL. & REL. PROD.	(35B)	−4.96	48.58	−35.73	−40.16	22.63	8.79
RUBBER PROD.	(355)	−14.76	27.17	71.99	−52.26	35.45	−19.43
NONMETAL. MIN. PROD.	(36A)	−5.33	64.46	18.87	−107.86	−3.15	−41.37
GLASS & GLASS PROD.	(362)	5.41	26.60	−4.89	−35.75	1.46	−6.70
IRON & STEEL	(371)	−3.17	15.92	76.51	−269.21	283.60	2.67
NONFERROUS METALS	(372)	−13.18	35.93	75.16	−90.96	143.53	−2.77
METAL PROD.	(381)	26.27	249.27	81.38	−148.17	−37.87	−53.11
NONELEC. MACH.	(382)	198.85	411.37	462.67	−331.31	156.82	−121.45
ELEC. MACH.	(383)	56.31	245.89	111.17	16.65	210.07	−102.23
TRANSP. EQUIP.	(384)	96.62	288.74	257.26	−48.70	497.80	201.53
MISC. MANUF.	(38A)	0.79	268.78	275.59	−52.56	54.43	−18.06
Total		1,748.03	2,636.14	1,891.96	−4,912.84	13.26	−2,749.84

Nontraded goods							
MIN. & QUARRY.	(2)	−25.68	−214.80	62.07	−75.79	54.27	−20.00
ELEC., GAS, & WATER	(4)	−30.03	−254.90	−18.50	27.56	20.02	50.00
CONSTRUCTION	(5)	−74.15	−3,695.50	−405.09	−597.22	−316.11	980.00
WHOLE. & RET. TRADE	(6)	−607.16	7,671.30	−694.94	262.48	−104.73	1,390.00
TRANSP., STOR., & COMM.	(7)	−65.26	−3,049.40	−101.85	163.60	−21.70	170.00
FIN., INS., & REAL EST.	(8)	−279.36	2,867.20	−310.23	1,791.18	−24.03	410.00
COMM., SOC., & PERS. SERV.	(9)	−737.71	2,897.80	−731.97	2,706.23	−203.30	1,570.00
Total		−1,819.37	6,221.70	−2,200.50	4,278.04	−595.58	4,550.00
Overall total		−71.33	8,857.84	−308.54	−634.80	−582.32	1,800.16

ment fell, however, by 165,000 workers. This means that the employment in US agriculture would have fallen by a good deal more—something like 1.6 million workers—had the increase in agricultural exports not been permitted. Trade in this case provided an outlet for what would have been a substantial surplus of agricultural productivity and permitted the adjustment of the agricultural sector to be more gradual than otherwise. In several instances, notably textiles, chemicals, and durable manufactures, trade evidently contributed substantially to the increase in employment over the period. On the other hand, in several sectors already noted, trade contributed negatively to employment. In the wearing apparel industry, for example, actual employment grew, but would have grown much more had trade been more restricted.

If one examines the detailed results by sector for the European Economic Community (EEC) in tables 9.1 and 9.2, it is evident that there were some important differences in the employment experiences in the individual EEC countries. It may not be altogether meaningful therefore to aggregate these experiences across countries. Nonetheless, it appears from table 9.3 that trade contributed importantly to employment in the EEC in all industries except textiles and wearing apparel, leather products, printing and publishing, fuel products, glass products, and nontradables. The increases were greatest in agriculture and food and kindred products, furniture, chemicals, rubber products, metals and metal products, and durable manufactures.

In Japan, trade was a major factor in increasing employment in chemicals, fuel products, rubber products, metals, and durable manufactures. Trade contributed negatively to employment in Japan especially in agriculture, textiles and wearing apparel, metal products, and several nontradables.

It is apparent from table 9.3 that trade has played a major role in expanding employment, especially in chemicals and the engineering industries, in the major industrialized countries and in reducing employment in the textiles and wearing apparel and leather and footwear industries. Trade in agricultural products has also had an important impact on employment, partially offsetting in the United States and the European Economic Community what would have been an even larger reduction in agricultural employment than actually occurred and, in the case of Japan, apparently contributing to the decline in agricultural employment.

As in most applications of our model, the analysis is best suited for comparisons at the industry level rather than for determining aggregate effects. Had trade been prevented from expanding by means of tariffs and taxes, there is no way of telling how macroeconomic policy would have

Table 9.4
Estimated absolute and percentage changes in aggregate 1976 employment by country due to growth of trade (excluding petroleum refining), 1970–1976, in thousands of man-years

Industrial country	Absolute	%
Australia	20.57	0.35
Austria	57.89	1.96
Canada	−261.28	−2.73
European Economic Community	−308.54	−0.31
Belgium-Luxembourg	−1.90	−0.05
Denmark	−43.15	−1.80
France	4.40	0.02
German Federal Republic	770.49	3.14
Ireland	−138.62	−13.58
Italy	129.03	0.68
Netherlands	63.14	1.39
United Kingdom	−1,091.94	−4.48
Finland	64.91	3.03
Japan	−582.32	−1.10
New Zealand	−49.28	−4.08
Norway	−88.51	4.95
Sweden	120.90	−2.96
Switzerland	174.04	6.18
United States	−71.33	−0.08
Total	−1,164.77	−0.43

differed from what it actually was. In this case, the assumption of essentially constant expenditure that we make in the model might well be unfounded. Still, the net aggregate effects are available from the model and we report them in table 9.4, with the caveat that they are only suggestive and should not be taken literally.

Table 9.4 thus contains both the absolute and percentage employment changes in 1976 for each industrialized country in the aggregate that we attribute to the growth of trade relative to GDP from 1970 to 1976 in all sectors except petroleum and other fuel products. The results suggest that 1976 employment in 10 of the 18 industrialized countries was negatively affected in the aggregate due to the growth of trade. In the United States, employment is calculated as declining in 1976 by 71,000 workers, and there are sizable reductions also in Canada, Denmark, Ireland, the United Kingdom, Japan, New Zealand, and Norway. On the other hand, it should be noted that there are instances among the industrial countries where the changes in trade had a positive effect on aggregate employment. The largest increase was 770,000 workers in West Germany.

Estimated Employment Effects of Restoring the 1970 Pattern of Trade in Manufactures between the Major Industrialized and Developing Countries

Having examined the employment effects of restoring the 1970 pattern of total trade, we shall now consider what the effects would be if only that trade in manufactures between the major advanced and developing countries were restored to its 1970 levels by sector in relation to total GDP.[3] The point of this exercise is to attempt to isolate the intra- from the intertrade employment effects for the two groups of countries. For this purpose, we have ignored changes in trade in agricultural products, food and kindred products, and petroleum and other fuel products.

The procedure followed was the same as before, namely, we first calculated the percentage changes in 1976 exports and imports by sector and country needed to restore trade between the industrialized and developing countries to 1970 levels relative to total GDP. These changes were then introduced as exogenous variables into the model and a solution was obtained country by country. The resulting changes in employment in thousands of man-years are shown by sector and country in table 9.5.

To provide a basis for comparison, we have singled out, as before, the United States, the European Economic Community, and Japan in table 9.6, in which we indicate the changes in employment resulting from the growth in total trade previously calculated (excluding petroleum refining) and the changes in employment resulting from the growth in trade in manufactures (excluding agriculture, food, beverages, and tobacco, and petroleum refining) between the industrialized and developing countries. For the United States, it is evident that trade in manufactures with the developing countries has had substantial and positive effects in textiles, chemicals, metals, and durable manufactures, and negative effects in agriculture, wearing apparel, leather products and footwear, and miscellaneous manufactures. Much the same pattern of positive and negative employment effects is evident for the European Economic Community and Japan, except in miscellaneous manufactures, where the effects are positive rather than negative as in the case of the United States. The effect of trade among the industrialized countries themselves on shaping employment can also be gauged from the two sets of calculations in table 9.6. In several instances, the calculated employment effects are of opposite sign, reflecting differences in the composition of exports and imports between and among the two groups of countries.

Table 9.6 further makes clear the danger of singling out particular sectors where some major developing countries have made inroads in industrial

Table 9.5
Estimated changes in employment due to growth of industrial/developing country trade from 1970 to 1976 in all industries except agriculture, food, beverage, and tobacco, and petroleum refining, in thousands of man-years

Industry	(ISIC)	ALA	ATA	BLX	CND	DEN	FIN	FR	GFR	IRE	IT	JPN	NL	NZ	NOR	SWD	SWZ	UK	US
Traded goods																			
AGR., FOR., & FISH.	(1)	−1.25	−0.21	10.68	−31.74	−0.41	−2.25	−26.97	−38.44	−5.28	−29.94	−107.75	−5.77	2.74	−1.76	−12.54	−0.78	−1.71	−21.88
FOOD, BEV., & TOB.	(310)	−0.51	−0.27	4.65	−7.26	−0.29	−0.40	−3.23	−10.47	−0.45	−4.43	−20.02	−1.11	−0.18	−0.48	−2.35	−0.27	−5.91	−6.17
TEXTILES	(321)	2.49	1.02	6.74	−9.36	3.51	1.35	−19.13	11.28	1.28	−36.44	−88.74	−1.81	4.67	−0.43	0.09	0.34	−4.49	9.19
WEARING APPAREL	(322)	−7.39	−1.62	6.15	−22.13	−1.63	1.40	−19.95	−54.89	−0.53	−15.45	−88.59	−7.14	−0.33	−1.17	−0.58	−2.91	−33.79	−93.68
LEATHER PROD.	(323)	0.07	−0.89	1.10	1.07	0.70	−0.02	−1.52	1.34	0.09	−14.69	5.39	−0.02	0.15	−0.21	0.06	−0.28	−1.01	−5.83
FOOTWEAR	(324)	−0.43	0.62	0.59	−1.23	0.34	1.35	−4.84	−1.66	−0.10	−5.61	−6.25	−1.06	−0.21	−0.29	−0.03	−0.10	−3.78	−25.81
WOOD PROD.	(331)	−1.77	1.30	4.56	−9.23	1.43	−0.23	−4.24	8.80	−0.72	−8.02	3.76	−5.05	−0.12	0.79	0.28	2.07	1.26	−2.62
FURN. & FIXT.	(332)	−0.75	−0.86	0.28	−3.57	0.49	0.36	1.37	2.90	0.05	17.58	−5.85	−0.31	−0.09	−0.36	0.03	0.06	2.29	−0.24
PAPER & PAPER PROD.	(341)	−0.33	0.58	−3.25	1.29	−0.18	1.05	−1.30	9.01	−0.07	0.50	−1.65	−0.37	0.68	−0.43	0.99	0.51	3.80	2.04
PRINT. & PUBL.	(342)	0.04	0.05	3.00	−3.54	−0.07	1.02	1.31	0.81	−0.02	−0.72	−7.15	−1.10	−0.08	0.09	−1.29	0.33	3.66	−3.14
CHEMICALS	(35A)	3.11	5.42	17.29	−6.90	0.82	1.34	11.52	76.11	2.85	31.34	33.49	13.63	1.36	2.21	1.23	7.69	29.94	34.38
PETROL. & REL. PROD.	(35B)	−0.00	−0.04	0.12	−0.80	−0.27	−0.01	−1.96	−0.04	−0.38	0.89	22.78	−0.56	0.01	0.00	−0.40	−0.01	2.02	−0.83
RUBBER PROD.	(355)	−0.21	1.23	0.91	−2.67	0.98	0.60	8.26	21.70	0.03	9.68	18.93	−0.57	−0.03	0.32	1.15	0.37	3.69	2.16
NONMETAL. MIN. PROD.	(36A)	0.26	−0.44	2.92	−5.03	0.94	0.74	0.13	4.12	0.05	11.14	14.43	−0.47	−0.09	0.38	−3.84	−0.14	2.20	−0.64
GLASS & GLASS PROD.	(362)	−0.23	1.46	0.49	−1.18	0.18	−0.23	1.60	0.00	0.37	3.70	0.65	6.40	−0.01	0.22	0.32	0.24	1.88	1.49
IRON & STEEL	(371)	5.03	6.01	−4.65	−9.61	1.86	3.45	19.90	74.50	0.15	52.38	260.82	2.54	0.21	−1.97	−0.88	2.90	14.18	24.98
NONFERROUS METALS	(372)	0.64	3.12	−8.59	−0.77	0.50	0.58	7.72	30.64	−1.60	23.59	119.78	3.21	0.14	−0.05	5.32	2.38	14.78	2.31
METAL PROD.	(381)	−2.34	7.26	8.68	−14.73	0.17	1.25	17.22	52.25	−0.18	41.67	−14.89	4.32	−1.15	0.74	−7.73	2.82	17.20	41.06
NONELEC. MACH.	(382)	0.49	13.53	12.23	−7.80	3.80	12.68	112.29	264.32	1.39	52.51	88.11	17.34	0.08	0.79	4.30	17.90	61.42	138.39
ELEC. MACH.	(383)	−1.77	0.36	1.88	−24.10	0.86	1.00	43.19	55.18	0.28	20.01	71.53	2.96	−0.06	1.57	3.43	12.17	48.60	59.49
TRANSP. EQUIP.	(384)	−4.92	4.21	5.47	−15.59	4.22	5.40	44.16	95.91	0.15	34.63	248.81	12.51	−0.28	11.59	15.70	0.34	26.45	94.08
MISC. MANUF.	(38A)	7.04	−2.55	11.35	−11.31	−0.42	1.08	18.12	53.47	3.72	31.48	34.71	2.64	0.13	3.82	4.95	−21.18	83.18	−55.39
Total		−2.72	39.30	82.61	−186.17	17.52	31.52	203.64	656.83	1.08	215.81	582.28	40.19	7.55	15.36	8.22	24.45	265.85	193.35
Nontraded goods																			
MIN. & QUARRY.	(2)	2.31	0.74	1.11	−12.10	0.47	1.25	4.34	27.59	0.48	37.56	43.05	0.43	0.13	−0.07	−1.50	3.28	16.21	2.98
ELEC., GAS, & WATER	(4)	0.13	0.74	3.57	−8.69	−0.02	0.57	1.04	6.74	−0.19	8.50	16.27	−0.30	0.24	0.26	−1.19	0.89	5.22	−1.15
CONSTRUCTION	(5)	−1.81	−5.97	5.17	−58.51	−3.21	−0.78	−17.08	−69.98	−0.00	−25.91	−182.17	−7.23	−0.00	−0.28	−37.38	−2.80	−8.03	−9.59
WHOLE. & RET. TRADE	(6)	−4.03	1.85	90.45	−72.86	−0.58	1.34	−27.33	−16.32	−3.33	−27.22	−35.87	−15.37	0.47	2.26	−14.77	0.30	14.97	−63.43
TRANSP., STOR., & COMM.	(7)	0.05	2.02	22.19	−35.34	0.15	1.99	1.30	4.38	−0.45	11.75	−0.19	−4.34	0.75	0.80	−7.63	2.44	14.69	0.93
FIN., INS., & REAL EST.	(8)	−1.03	0.98	25.47	−32.94	−0.83	0.80	−6.38	−22.86	−0.68	0.37	−6.27	−5.75	0.41	0.95	−9.20	1.48	20.51	−32.12
COMM., SOC., & PERS. SERV.	(9)	−3.05	0.75	80.53	−91.50	−2.16	−0.33	−27.32	−69.78	−3.56	−6.23	−101.47	−23.02	−0.13	1.31	−23.86	−1.30	−13.99	−118.27
Total		−7.43	1.11	228.50	−311.95	−6.19	4.83	−71.44	−140.23	−7.74	−1.17	−266.65	−55.57	1.86	5.23	−95.54	4.29	49.58	−220.66
Overall total		−10.15	40.41	311.11	−498.12	11.33	36.35	132.19	516.60	−6.66	214.64	315.63	−15.38	9.41	20.59	−87.32	28.75	315.43	−27.31

Table 9.6
United States, Japan, and the European Economic Community: comparison of estimated changes in employment resulting from the growth of industrial/developing country trade (except agriculture, food, beverage, and tobacco, and petroleum refining) with estimated changes due to growth of all trade excluding petroleum refining, in thousands of man-years

		United States: change resulting from growth of		European Economic Community: change resulting from growth of		Japan: change resulting from growth of	
Industry	(ISIC)	Industrial/ developing country trade	All trade	Industrial/ developing country trade	All trade	Industrial/ developing country trade	All trade
Traded goods							
AGR., FOR., & FISH.	(1)	−21.88	1,423.20	−97.84	201.07	−107.75	−999.00
FOOD, BEV., & TOB.	(310)	−6.17	−33.21	−21.26	156.13	−20.02	−19.04
TEXTILES	(321)	9.19	73.04	−39.06	−117.24	−88.74	−171.21
WEARING APPAREL	(322)	−93.68	−94.97	−127.24	−93.62	−88.59	−153.73
LEATHER PROD.	(323)	−5.83	15.58	−14.01	−9.71	5.39	−7.53
FOOTWEAR	(324)	−25.81	−17.95	−16.12	22.72	−6.25	−14.62
WOOD PROD.	(331)	−2.62	13.33	−1.98	13.42	3.76	−0.42
FURN. & FIXT.	(332)	−0.24	−1.21	24.64	85.97	−5.85	−12.87
PAPER & PAPER PROD.	(341)	2.04	−1.17	8.15	2.17	−1.65	−1.20
PRINT. & PUBL.	(342)	−3.14	−19.30	6.87	−11.48	−7.15	−8.51
CHEMICALS	(35A)	34.38	47.85	183.49	252.56	33.49	36.63
PETROL. & REL. PROD.	(35B)	−0.83	−4.96	−0.18	−35.73	22.78	22.63
RUBBER PROD.	(355)	2.16	−14.76	44.68	71.99	18.93	35.45
NONMETAL. MIN. PROD.	(36A)	−0.64	−5.33	21.02	18.87	14.43	−3.15
GLASS & GLASS PROD.	(362)	1.49	5.41	14.63	−4.89	0.65	1.46
IRON & STEEL	(371)	24.98	−3.17	160.86	76.51	260.82	283.60
NONFERROUS METALS	(372)	2.31	−13.18	70.24	75.16	119.78	143.53

METAL PROD.	(381)	41.06	26.27	141.33	81.38	−14.89	−37.87
NONELEC. MACH.	(382)	138.39	198.85	525.28	462.67	88.11	156.82
ELEC. MACH.	(383)	59.49	56.31	172.97	111.17	71.53	210.07
TRANSP. EQUIP.	(384)	94.08	96.62	223.49	257.26	248.81	497.80
MISC. MANUF.	(38A)	−55.39	0.79	203.54	275.59	34.71	54.43
Total		193.35	1,748.03	1,483.53	1,891.96	582.28	13.26
Nontraded goods							
MIN. & QUARRY.	(2)	2.98	−25.68	88.19	62.07	43.05	54.27
ELEC., GAS, & WATER	(4)	−1.15	−30.03	24.56	−18.50	16.27	20.02
CONSTRUCTION	(5)	−9.59	−74.15	−126.27	−405.09	−182.17	−316.11
WHOLE. & RET. TRADE	(6)	−63.43	−607.16	15.25	−694.94	−35.87	−104.73
TRANSP., STOR., & COMM.	(7)	0.93	−65.26	49.68	−101.85	−0.19	−21.70
FIN., INS., & REAL EST.	(8)	−32.12	−279.36	9.87	−310.23	−6.27	−24.03
COMM., SOC., & PERS. SERV.	(9)	−118.27	−737.71	−65.53	−731.97	−101.47	−203.30
Total		−220.66	−1,819.37	−4.25	−2,200.50	−266.65	−595.58
Overall total		−27.31	−71.33	1,479.27	−308.54	315.63	−582.32

Table 9.7
Estimated absolute and percentage changes in aggregate 1976 employment by country resulting from the growth of industrial/developing country trade (excluding agriculture, food, beverage, and tobacco, and petroleum refining), in thousands of man-years

Industrial country	Absolute	%
Australia	−10.15	−0.17
Austria	40.41	1.37
Canada	−498.12	−5.20
European Economic Community	1,479.27	1.47
Belgium-Luxembourg	311.11	8.05
Denmark	11.33	0.47
France	132.19	0.63
German Federal Republic	516.60	2.10
Ireland	−6.66	−0.65
Italy	214.64	1.13
Netherlands	−15.38	−0.34
United Kingdom	315.43	1.29
Finland	36.35	1.70
Japan	315.63	0.60
New Zealand	9.41	0.78
Norway	20.59	1.15
Sweden	−87.32	−2.14
Switzerland	28.75	1.02
United States	−27.31	−0.03
Total	1,307.50	0.48

country markets without also considering how important the major developing countries themselves have become as markets for the industrialized countries. There may nonetheless be some interest in examining the net aggregate employment effects of this trade as we have done previously. The results are shown in table 9.7. The restoration of the 1970 pattern of trade in manufactures between the industrialized and developing countries would have had a detrimental effect on aggregate employment in all the industrial countries except Australia, Canada, Ireland, the Netherlands, Sweden, and the United States.

Estimated Employment Effects of Projected Increases in Trade in Manufactures between the Major Industrialized and Developing Countries

Our final experiment was based on World Bank projections of trade in manufactures between the major industrialized and developing countries, as modified and reported by Balassa (1979).[4] The annual projected increases in

Table 9.8
Projected annual growth rates of exports and imports of manufactures between the major industrial and less developed countries

	Industrial countries	
ISIC	Exports to less developed countries (%)	Imports from less developed countries (%)
321	3.0	6.2
322	3.0	8.3
323	3.0	10.0
324	3.0	10.0
331	3.0	10.0
332	3.0	10.0
341	5.7	10.0
342	5.7	10.0
35A	5.7	13.0
35B	3.0	10.0
355	3.0	10.0
36A	3.0	10.0
362	3.0	10.0
371	3.0	10.7
372	3.0	10.7
381	3.0	10.7
382	7.0	20.3
383	7.0	20.3
384	5.7	20.3
38A	6.5	10.0

Source: Adapted from Balassa (1979).

trade by sector are listed in table 9.8. These increases were treated as changes in exogenous variables in the model, and the same procedure was followed as in the preceding sections. The employment effects by sector and country are recorded in table 9.9.

For the United States, the effects are mostly negative, with the exception of paper and paper products, chemicals, iron and steel, metal products, nonelectrical machinery, and transport equipment. For Japan, there are negative effects especially in agriculture and food and kindred products, wearing apparel, wood products, and nonferrous metals, and positive effects in chemicals, iron and steel, and durable manufactures. The results for the European Economic Community are similar to those for Japan.

The aggregate employment effects of the projected increases in trade are presented in table 9.10. These effects are positive for 8 of the industrialized countries and negative for the remaining 10 countries. In practically all cases though, the changes are relatively very small.[5]

Table 9.9
Estimated changes in employment resulting from projected annual growth in industrial/developing country trade in all industries except agriculture, food, beverage, and tobacco, and petroleum refining, in thousands of man-years

Industry	(ISIC)	ALA	ATA	BLX	CND	DEN	FIN	FR	GFR	IRE	IT	JPN	NL	NZ	NOR	SWD	SWZ	UK	US
Traded goods																			
AGR., FOR., & FISH.	(1)	−0.32	2.05	−1.58	2.11	−0.33	−1.49	−6.49	−6.54	−1.27	−8.25	−55.92	−0.98	−0.10	−0.43	−0.11	−1.04	−2.64	−4.54
FOOD, BEV., & TOB.	(310)	−0.02	0.14	−0.94	0.63	−0.07	−0.10	−0.66	−1.59	−0.09	−1.05	−0.29	−0.20	−0.03	−0.07	−0.03	−0.09	−4.52	−0.90
TEXTILES	(321)	0.09	0.79	1.21	−0.22	0.10	−0.03	−0.61	1.23	−0.11	−2.82	3.08	0.46	0.08	−0.02	−0.05	−0.16	−3.25	−2.15
WEARING APPAREL	(322)	−0.25	−0.19	−0.14	−1.08	−0.21	0.05	−0.96	−4.55	−0.05	−0.14	−3.60	−0.43	0.18	−0.14	−0.38	−0.22	−4.62	−8.45
LEATHER PROD.	(323)	0.01	−0.06	0.03	0.04	0.05	−0.00	−0.41	−0.97	−0.00	−1.90	−0.26	0.04	0.01	0.00	0.02	−0.03	−0.63	−1.16
FOOTWEAR	(324)	0.01	0.15	−0.09	−0.04	−0.01	0.07	−0.03	0.22	−0.01	0.43	−0.21	−0.01	0.12	−0.01	0.03	0.03	−0.30	−1.90
WOOD PROD.	(331)	−0.55	0.08	0.29	0.35	−0.26	−0.35	−2.77	−2.89	−0.15	−4.27	−14.39	−1.82	−0.04	0.01	0.24	−0.07	−2.71	−2.22
FURN. & FIXT.	(332)	0.02	2.40	0.63	0.33	0.12	0.05	0.03	0.34	0.02	1.68	0.32	0.11	0.01	0.02	−0.02	−0.00	0.27	−0.15
PAPER & PAPER PROD.	(341)	0.00	0.98	−0.06	0.82	0.03	1.23	0.15	1.37	−0.05	0.35	2.41	0.09	0.05	0.22	0.86	0.15	−0.49	0.78
PRINT. & PUBL.	(342)	−0.07	0.24	−0.15	0.26	−0.03	0.04	0.32	0.29	−0.04	−0.06	−0.76	−0.16	−0.03	−0.05	−0.00	−0.03	−0.56	−0.62
CHEMICALS	(35A)	0.00	1.24	2.21	0.49	0.39	−0.05	2.53	14.55	0.04	3.10	10.22	1.75	−0.20	−0.22	0.31	2.29	2.15	2.63
PETROL. & REL. PROD.	(35B)	−0.00	0.10	−0.02	0.06	−0.07	−0.01	−0.40	−0.09	−0.11	−0.23	0.45	−0.10	−0.00	−0.00	0.01	−0.00	−0.39	−0.16
RUBBER PROD.	(355)	−0.16	0.10	−0.03	0.01	0.05	−0.02	0.14	1.17	−0.03	0.48	1.48	0.02	−0.04	0.01	0.06	0.01	0.09	−1.09
NONMETAL. MIN. PROD.	(36A)	−0.04	1.29	0.29	0.41	−0.05	−0.05	−0.29	−0.37	−0.02	−0.02	−1.92	−0.05	−0.01	−0.03	0.15	0.01	−0.45	−0.69
GLASS & GLASS PROD.	(362)	−0.05	0.20	0.26	0.04	−0.01	−0.03	0.30	0.17	0.00	0.28	0.36	0.24	−0.01	0.00	0.03	0.01	0.09	−0.05
IRON & STEEL	(371)	0.25	1.86	0.96	0.62	0.09	0.00	2.10	8.84	−0.05	4.07	23.11	0.56	−0.01	0.13	0.76	0.35	1.98	1.76
NONFERROUS METALS	(372)	0.06	−0.19	0.01	0.06	0.04	−0.08	−0.90	−3.05	0.00	−3.77	−16.05	−0.13	−0.00	−0.13	−0.06	0.19	−0.83	−3.61
METAL PROD.	(381)	−0.02	2.41	1.95	1.66	0.10	0.11	1.72	3.87	−0.04	3.30	2.74	0.19	−0.12	0.18	1.20	0.49	0.98	1.45
NONELEC. MACH.	(382)	0.48	2.91	2.71	1.65	2.02	1.35	17.20	46.22	0.11	13.10	27.20	3.63	−0.00	0.31	4.07	4.48	11.89	18.04
ELEC. MACH.	(383)	−0.06	1.34	3.30	2.28	0.34	0.21	7.29	13.79	−0.03	5.78	28.22	1.86	−0.03	0.29	2.97	1.56	7.03	−2.14
TRANSP. EQUIP.	(384)	0.30	0.69	1.17	1.89	1.18	0.74	7.23	14.31	−0.05	6.34	31.98	2.05	−0.10	1.76	3.24	0.01	7.84	9.65
MISC. MANUF.	(38A)	0.36	0.28	2.66	0.35	0.14	−0.08	3.45	16.87	0.40	5.23	10.99	0.80	−0.02	−0.02	0.65	2.99	5.62	−3.06
Total		0.05	18.82	14.67	12.72	3.60	1.59	28.94	103.20	−1.54	21.62	49.16	7.93	−0.30	1.81	13.96	10.94	16.57	1.45
Nontraded goods																			
MIN. & QUARRY.	(2)	0.08	0.59	0.18	0.94	−0.04	−0.08	−0.21	1.77	−0.03	1.32	−2.75	−0.05	−0.01	−0.02	0.14	0.40	−0.46	−1.33
ELEC., GAS, & WATER	(4)	−0.09	0.33	−0.36	0.60	−0.07	−0.05	−0.16	0.50	−0.08	0.49	−1.33	−0.19	−0.04	−0.07	0.04	0.06	−1.09	−1.04
CONSTRUCTION	(5)	0.11	7.82	3.31	5.29	−0.02	−0.02	−1.45	−1.29	0.03	−0.79	−8.06	0.25	−0.02	0.19	1.57	−0.44	−3.27	−0.26
WHOLE. & RET. TRADE	(6)	−0.93	2.37	−14.73	5.04	−0.61	−0.69	−7.62	−3.56	−1.03	−9.23	−32.04	−4.34	−0.23	−0.61	−0.02	−0.51	−14.55	−17.75
TRANSP., STOR., & COMM.	(7)	−0.18	1.83	−2.00	2.77	−0.14	−0.04	−0.73	−0.28	−0.24	0.54	−7.97	−1.22	−0.11	−0.14	0.59	0.29	−3.07	−1.90
FIN., INS., & REAL EST.	(8)	−0.46	1.08	−3.62	2.23	−0.29	−0.36	−2.29	−3.96	−0.23	−2.07	−8.70	−1.54	−0.16	−0.27	0.02	−0.16	−6.56	−9.71
COMM., SOC., & PERS. SERV.	(9)	−0.83	0.28	−14.06	5.63	−1.32	−1.15	−7.65	−15.07	−1.05	−4.35	−28.84	−6.14	−0.26	−1.11	−1.43	−1.07	−21.26	−23.61
Total		−2.30	14.30	−31.28	22.49	−2.50	−2.38	−20.11	−21.90	−2.63	−14.10	−89.69	−13.23	−0.83	−2.03	0.91	−1.43	−50.26	−55.61
Overall total		−2.25	33.12	−16.61	35.21	1.10	−0.80	8.83	81.30	−4.17	7.52	−40.52	−5.30	−1.13	−0.22	14.86	9.51	−33.69	−54.16

Table 9.10
Estimated absolute and percentage changes in aggregate 1976 employment by country resulting from projected annual growth in industrial/developing country trade in all industries except as before, in thousands of man-years

Industrial country	Absolute	%
Australia	−2.25	−0.04
Austria	33.12	1.12
Canada	35.21	0.37
European Economic Community	38.97	0.04
Belgium-Luxembourg	−16.61	−0.43
Denmark	1.10	0.05
France	8.83	0.04
German Federal Republic	81.30	0.33
Ireland	−4.17	−0.41
Italy	7.52	0.04
Netherlands	−5.30	−0.12
United Kingdom	−33.69	−0.14
Finland	−0.80	−0.04
Japan	−40.52	−0.08
New Zealand	−1.13	−0.09
Norway	−0.22	−0.01
Sweden	14.86	0.36
Switzerland	9.51	0.34
United States	−54.16	−0.06
Total	32.59	0.01

Conclusion

Our results suggest that international trade has played a major role in shaping the employment experiences of the major industrialized countries between 1970 and 1976. While we have not dealt with the underlying factor endowments, technology, and government policies that are the main determinants of comparative advantage, the patterns of change that we have calculated seem broadly consistent with prior expectations. In particular, trade appears to have increased employment in the chemical and engineering industries in the United States the European Economic Community, and Japan and to have been an important factor in reducing employment in textiles and wearing apparel, leather products, and footwear. Trade has also had an important influence on employment in agriculture in the industrial countries.

It should be emphasized that in this application of our model the labor markets in individual countries are not permitted to adjust to exogenous changes. As a consequence, the employment effects that we have calculated are in a sense upper bounds on what might in fact occur. Moreover, while discussing a 6-year interval, we are assuming that the changes in employment occur all at once rather than being spread over the entire period. Nonetheless, our results suggest that there have been large and important changes in the allocation of labor among sectors in response to changes in trade. To the extent that labor markets may not always function smoothly, there will accordingly be a continued need for effective policies of domestic adjustment that will enhance the ability of individual sectors to adapt to the currents of change in the world economy.

10 Experience from the Michigan Model and Implications for Research

In the previous chapters, we have set forth the structure of our model of world production and trade and then considered a variety of applications of the model, including changes in tariffs and NTBs, domestic taxes and subsidies, exchange rates, and the effects of trade on employment. It is time now to step back from all of this and ask what we have learned from our efforts and what are the most promising directions for future research.

Lessons from Computer Modeling of Trade[1]

In 1973–1974 the present authors embarked on what has turned out to be a lengthy and time-consuming project, namely, the construction and use of a large computable model of world production and trade. Our object originally was to devise a means of estimating the disaggregated employment effects of a round of multilateral tariff reductions, such as the Tokyo Round, which was then in progress. Analysis of tariff changes has continued to be a major focus of our work with this model, although we have also applied it to a variety of other problems. In the course of this research we have learned a great deal in quantitative terms about these different problems, and we would hope that we have contributed to the level of economic understanding that now informs the conduct of trade policy in the United States and elsewhere. Our quantitative results have already been discussed extensively in earlier chapters of this book. In addition, through the process of building and revising the model, we have also learned some things about trade *theory*, and its relation to empirical reality. Because of the more practical and policy orientation of many of our papers we did not develop these theoretical insights in any detail. Yet it is precisely these insights that have made the whole process of computer modeling worthwhile from the conceptual point of view. In this section we would like to explain how this process has worked—how the building of an empirically based computable model can lead one to learn things about theoretical relations or their importance—and also to lay out what a few of these lessons have been.

We should say immediately that while these lessons were new, or newly appreciated, by ourselves, they are not necessarily new to others. Large computable models never tell one anything about theory that could not have been learned as well or better from a small theoretical model. Indeed, one would not believe a result of a large model if it could not also be understood in simpler terms. Thus we may merely be exposing our ignorance of matters that others more knowledgeable than us have always understood. However, we shall present these lessons as though they were new, for the benefit of others who may have shared our ignorance.

We shall begin by describing our methodology: the curious and cumbersome process of informed trial and error by which we have used numerical models to grope toward an understanding of both theory and reality. We shall then describe several particular problems that we encountered with the model, the ways we dealt with them, and the insights we derived about them from this process. We shall deal with these matters more or less in the order that they arose for us in the decade or so that we have been working with the model.

The first issue to be addressed is the empirical inadequacy of the usual trade-theoretic assumptions that foreign and domestic goods are perfect substitutes in perfectly competitive markets. The second concerns the importance of another familiar trade-theoretic assumption: that tariff revenues are redistributed to consumers. Third, we shall explain why we were led to model import licensing in developing countries and the problems that arose when we did. Finally, we shall pull together briefly several of the general results that we have obtained regarding the effects of tariffs, which were after all the original object of our research.

Methodology

The process of developing our model has included two distinct parts, or phases, which are probably typical of empirical modeling in general. Only the first of these phases, which we shall call the planning phase, shows up clearly in the finished product. Yet it is the second phase, the feedback phase, that yields most of the insights that we shall discuss. These two phases alternated back and forth as the model was being developed, extended, and refined. It is their interaction that we have found fascinating and informative over the years of working with the model, much more so than the ultimate numerical answers to the particular problems we set out to solve.

The planning phase is the aspect of model construction that is most straightforward. We started with a problem we wished to solve: in our case the effect of multilateral tariff reductions on employment. Next we used standard theoretical relations, where these could be found, to specify equations that, if quantified and solved, could solve this problem. If received theory were not sufficient for this purpose, some original theorizing would be needed here, but this was not a problem for the relatively straightforward and familiar problems we have dealt with in our model. Next, the equations had to be quantified. One approach would be to use econometric techniques to estimate various parameters of the equations. In our case, far too many relations were involved for this to be feasible. Instead, we used standard functional forms in our behavioral assumptions (regarding production and utility functions), and derived our equations with parameters that could either be obtained from point estimates of things like trade and factor shares, or inferred from published estimates of behavioral elasticities. Once quantified, the equations were programmed into the computer and solved to yield answers to the questions originally being addressed. This ended the planning phase of the modeling effort, and would seem, on the face of it, to be the end of the process completely.

However it is not the end, for the following reason. What typically happened when we solved the model was that we found something unexpected in the results. Sometimes the results were just nonsense and we had to go back and find out why. More often the results were plausible overall but contained one or two features that we did not expect in terms of either direction or size of an effect. The feedback phase of model construction consists of examining the assumptions of the model carefully until such surprises can be explained, and then either modifying the model or modifying our ideas of what to expect so that the results are no longer surprising. Either way something can be learned in the process.

Thus, in our view, the modeling effort is not complete until it yields only *expected* results—in general terms, of course, since we do not require that specific numerical answers be altogether predictable. To some this may seem to make the whole exercise either pointless or illegitimate. If we keep fiddling with the model until it gives us the answers we want, then what confidence can one have in these answers? Or if we trust our intuition as to what is reasonable, why not bypass the modeling entirely and just let us pull the answers out of our heads? One answer to these questions is that our expectations are only general. We could not predict specific numerical results, such as the effect of the Tokyo Round on employment in the Belgian glass industry, even if we wanted to, and many users of our results do seem to be interested in this kind of detail. But the better answer, from the standpoint of trade theory, is that the feedback phase of modeling is as often as much a process of revising expectations as it is of revising the model itself. And even when we have revised the model, what we have learned about the viability of certain assumptions has been important in itself.

When feedback led us to change our assumptions, then the planning phase began once again. Often we found it necessary to bring into the model new aspects of economic behavior, and these too had to be modeled by finding acceptable assumptions that could generate quantifiable and solvable equations. This led to a new version of the model whose results, once obtained, had also to be evaluated for reasonableness in yet another feedback phase. Thus the development of the model proceeded in a succession of alternating planning and feedback phases until a final set of results was obtained that was no longer surprising. Furthermore, the process began anew each time we extended the model by adding new data or the capability of dealing with new problems.

To some extent this process of continually revising the model was necessary only because we failed initially to understand the world as well as we ultimately had the need to do. A more accomplished theorist, one might argue, would already know and appreciate the importance of all of the issues that we shall describe. Such a theorist would succeed in building the "right" model the first time out, and would go through the planning phase only once. This may be true in part. But it is also true that even the most enlightened thinker may not be able to assess a priori the empirical importance of all the assumptions that might be made, and therefore might not be able to choose among assumptions until their numerical implications have been worked out. This too is a part of the process. Sometimes the feedback phase merely tells us that an aspect of behavior that we knew about, but thought we could ignore, is too important quantitatively to be left out of the analysis.

The Armington Assumption

When we first began our efforts to quantify the effects of multilateral tariff reductions, our analysis paralleled that most commonly found in the textbooks on international trade. In particular, we modeled the demand for imports of a particular product and the supply of exports as excess demands and supplies from the domestic market. This implicitly meant that imported and domestically produced goods were assumed to be perfect substitutes in demand. Our contribution in Deardorff and Stern (1974) was merely to recognize that all of these excess supplies and demands interact on world markets and thus that the tariffs of all countries must be taken into account simultaneously in determining trade and employment in each.

Our procedure for doing this in our 1974 paper was to assume simple functional forms for production and utility functions, use these to derive market supply and demand—and therefore excess supply and demand—functions for each country, and then put these together with tariffs into a single world-market-clearing equation for each good. These were solved to determine the effects of multilateral tariff changes in each industry and country.

As we began to explore this model further, and in particular as we began to use it to look at the trade balance in order to model flexible exchange rates, we found aspects of its behavior unacceptable. Specifically, we found tariff reductions to have a much larger effect on trade and the trade balance than seemed reasonable given what had been found especially in more aggregated studies of trade. Looking at our model more carefully, we found that our assumptions about demand implied elasticities of demand for imports that were much larger than any that had been found in the numerous econometric estimates of import demand equations that appeared in the literature.

This problem has by now become a familiar one in empirical studies of trade such as ours, and may be seen quite simply. If import demand is the excess of domestic demand over supply, then the price elasticity of import demand, η_M, is related to the elasticities of domestic supply, ε, and demand, η, as follows:

$$\eta_M = \frac{1}{\theta_M}\eta + \frac{(1-\theta_M)}{\theta_M}\varepsilon,$$

where θ_M is the share of demand satisfied by imports. In a country like the United States, where these import shares average only 10% this means that import demand elasticities will on the average be at least 10 times as large as domestic demand elasticities, even if domestic supplies are completely inelastic, and considerably larger if not. According to Stern, Francis, and Schumacher (1976), the "best" econometric estimates of import demand elasticities for the United States range around 2, thus implying implausibly small values for elasticities of domestic demand.

Of the several possible ways of resolving this seeming inconsistency, the one we chose, and the one that has been adopted most frequently in empirical trade models, is to assume that imports and domestic goods are not perfect substitutes.[2] Most commonly, following Armington (1969), it is assumed that goods are differentiated by country of origin. While in our model for technical reasons a slightly different assumption is made, the effect is essentially the same as for the Armington assumption.[3]

This, then, is a good example of a case in which our first try at model building led us to implausible results, causing us to reconsider the assumptions on which the model was based. We had ignored the phenomenon of differentiated products initially, assuming, as has traditionally been done in applying economic theory to international trade, that departures from perfect substitution would not be sufficiently pervasive or important to invalidate the results. In practice we found, as have others, that at least for the problem we were dealing with this was not the case. We therefore modified the model in a way that would make it more consistent with empirical appearance.

The use of the Armington assumption has in turn led to other patterns in our results that would not have been predictable from simple traditional theory with its assumption of perfect substitutability, though these patterns are no longer surprising once imperfect substitution is recognized. First, and in rather general terms, imperfect substitution tends to insulate economies from changes abroad. Changes in world prices and/or tariffs cause a country's import prices to change, of course, but this no longer causes domestic prices of otherwise comparable goods to change by the same amount, as they would if they were perfect substitutes for imports. Thus imperfect substitution dampens the changes in the domestic economy compared with what they would otherwise be.

One implication of this insulation that has been a constant theme of our work analyzing the Tokyo Round and other tariff cutting exercises is that such changes have really tiny effects on employment and welfare. While there are several reasons that contribute to this result, the assumption of imperfect substitution is definitely significant.[4]

A second implication, which we noted in chapter 5, concerns effective protection. The simple measure of effective protection derived by Corden (1966) can be generalized and calculated within our model in terms of changes in per unit value added. However, when this is done, the fact that domestic prices are dampened in their response to tariff changes means that the true effective protection provided by a tariff structure is much smaller, by an order of magnitude, than would be calculated from the simple Corden formula.

Tariff Revenue Redistribution

When trade theorists analyze tariffs in a general-equilibrium context, they routinely grapple with the problem of specifying how the tariff revenue is spent. Without that, a general-equilibrium model is indeterminate, since income and expenditure are not equal. A standard solution to this problem that avoids the need to describe government behavior is to assume that tariff revenue is redistributed in some nondistorting fashion to consumers, to be spent like any other income.

When we built our model initially, for reasons discussed in chapter 2, we chose deliberately not to specify it as a full general-equilibrium model. Instead, in part because we wished to analyze effects of tariffs on unemployment in the short run, we allowed disequilibrium in labor markets. Furthermore, because we do not view the Walrasian closure of a general-equilibrium model as necessarily appropriate in this situation, we did not relate expenditure to factor incomes, but instead made it exogenous in nominal terms. Together with a fixed money wage, this left employment and therefore factor incomes to be determined at the disaggregated level by the way that exogenous expenditure found its way into domestic and foreign markets. At the same time, because we did not directly relate income and expenditure, it did not occur to us to do anything special with the tariff revenue. We ignored it, implicitly assuming that it went into government savings.

What we did not anticipate was that this implicit treatment of tariff revenues would bias our results for aggregate employment. When we solved this version of the model for the effects of tariff reductions, we found that aggregate employment went up noticeably in most countries, regardless of the exact nature of the tariff cuts or other assumptions made, for example, about the exchange-rate regime. This was at first a pleasant surprise, since it reinforced our theoretical presumption in favor of free trade, and we were tempted to attribute it to gains in efficiency. But on reflection we realized that this was not the case, that however much allocative efficiency might improve, there was no reason for this improvement to increase employment. Instead what was happening was a direct result of our treatment of tariff revenues.

Given a constant money wage and a constant level of nominal expenditure, employment is determined roughly by the amount of labor that can be paid out of that expenditure, allowing also for a share that must go to capital. However, if taxes are levied and their revenues not redistributed, it is after-tax expenditure that determines employment. Now this is also true in the world economy, and tariffs act as taxes that divert a fraction of expenditure from ever becoming available to pay primary factors. Thus any reduction in these tariffs tends to increase aggregate employment in the world as a whole.

Recognizing this, we then modified our model to require that tariff revenues (as well as the revenues from other kinds of taxes, when these are included) be calculated and added to the otherwise exogenous level of nominal expenditure in each country. This eliminates the bias in our aggregate employment results, and leaves employment to be determined by the composition of demand among supplying countries and among labor- versus capital-intensive industries.

The point of relating this little episode is twofold. First, the treatment of tariff revenues can have economic implications, analogous to taxes, that are usually neglected in trade theory, where the issue is typically only one of model consistency. Second, this provides another example of a case where the feedback phase of model construction mentioned previously led us to change an assumption of the model and at the same time drew our attention to an economic relation we would otherwise have neglected.

Import Licensing

For the first several years during which we used our model, it included only the 18 most industrialized countries of the world. Among these countries we modeled exchange rate relations as either all fixed rates or all flexible rates, depending on which seemed most appropriate for the issue at hand. We did not make any effort to characterize exchange regimes more accurately than this, and since most of these industrialized countries did in fact allow their currencies to float during much of the 1970s, this seemed appropriate.

Beginning in about 1979, however, we undertook to expand the model, incorporating data on production, trade, and employment for an additional 16 developing countries. Because most of these countries peg their currencies to some degree, it no longer seemed appropriate to assume either that all exchange rates were pegged or that all were flexible. Instead, as we expanded the model to include the additional countries, we also included a facility for specifying exchange regimes on a country-by-country basis. Each currency could be set either to float or to be pegged, and, if pegged, it could be pegged either to a particular other currency in the model or to a prespecified basket of currencies. Then when we solved the model, we set each country's exchange regime in accordance with what had been reported to the International Monetary Fund.

When we solved this expanded model, we once again got a surprising result. Even though we had specified the US dollar as one of the floating currencies, the US balance of trade was far from constant in the face of tariff reductions. Part of the reason for this was obvious. Because the dollar was the numeraire in our model, the exchange market equilibrium condition that appeared for other floating currencies was not in fact used for the dollar. But the question remained as to why the market for the dollar had apparently not cleared automatically, as one would expect from Walras's law.[5]

The real reason for the problem turned out to be the following. Exchange rates for the newly added developing countries were mostly pegged, and therefore there was no requirement that trade for these countries be balanced. Furthermore, we had always modeled the financing of trade imbalances as taking place in US dollars. Thus equilibrium required that the US trade balance be the mirror image of the aggregate of those elsewhere. In this case, it meant that the US trade balance would reflect the changing trade imbalances of the pegging LDCs (less developed countries). And this would be true, incidentally, regardless of whether these countries pegged to the dollar itself or to some other currency or currencies.

This was an aspect of economic behavior that we had certainly not anticipated, but that our model had inadvertently brought to light. On reflection it seemed a valid phenomenon. Given the role of the dollar as a vehicle and reserve currency, it is quite correct that the US balance of trade is a reflection of conditions and policies elsewhere. We saw no reason to modify this particular feature of the model.

On the other hand, it did seem implausible for US trade to depend so much on the relatively small and otherwise economically unimportant developing countries. The problem, we decided, was not that US payments depended on theirs, but that theirs were being allowed to vary so widely. Having assumed pegged exchange rates for these developing countries, we naturally found their balances of trade to vary when tariff changes altered conditions in world markets. But was it really reasonable to expect such changes in developing country trade balances? We had noticed the problem as reflected in US trade, but the real anomaly was the result that developing country trade balances would be allowed to worsen or improve substantially.

All of this led us to model what was, if you like, a third kind of exchange regime for these countries. In our model, we do peg their exchange rates to one or more of those in the developed world, but we also model a system of import licensing as controlling trade. Specifically, we calculate each country's earnings of foreign exchange from exports. Imports are then regulated (through endogenous industry-specific tariff equivalents) to just exhaust this foreign exchange. Thus when tariffs in the industrialized countries fall and they import more both from among themselves and from the developing countries, the exchange constraint in the latter is relaxed, tariff equivalents fall, and imports rise. In this way the need for a substantial change in the US trade balance is removed, and at the same time, the modeling of trade in the developing countries is made more realistic in an important and interesting way.

Thus once again, what we learned in the feedback phase of using our model led us to alter the model at the same time that it taught us something—about the operation of the international monetary system—that we had not fully appreciated before. However, this time the process was not yet over. For when we rebuilt the model to include import licensing and solved it, we found yet another surprise.

This time something appeared to have gone terribly wrong. When we solved, as before, for the effect of tariff reductions by the industrialized countries, and looked at the effects on the newly added developing countries, we no longer found the effects to be small, as had always been the case before. Instead, in a handful of the developing countries, we found changes that were much larger than in the industrialized countries. Worse still, in one country, India, results were not only large in size but opposite in sign to those elsewhere. Thus when prices on world markets rose somewhat due to industrialized-country tariff reductions, one expected exports of the developing countries to rise in response. In most of them this happened, but in a few the increases were much larger than could be accounted for by the price changes themselves, given the supply elasticities for exports that we knew were in the model. And most perversely, in India exports fell and by large amounts.

What was happening here was not hard to guess, since this is precisely the pattern of response one expects in comparative static analysis when markets are dynamically unstable or nearly so. In the elasticities approach to the foreign exchange market, for example, when the Marshall-Lerner condition is only barely satisfied, a small shift in supply or demand will cause the equilibrium exchange rate to change in the expected direction but by a much larger amount than if elasticities were comfortably large. If the market is actually unstable, the Marshall-Lerner condition being violated, then the same shifts will cause the equilibrium rate to move in the wrong direction. This, of course, together with the doubt it casts on the usefulness of results of the latter sort, is just the lesson of Samuelson's Correspondence Principle.

In our case, what had happened then was this: By modeling import licensing in what we thought was a simple and straightforward manner, we had come up with a system that could be unstable, and appeared in fact to be so in the case of India. It is easiest to see this instability by example. Suppose that world prices rise, stimulating a country's exports. The addition to export revenue permits the rationing of imports to be relaxed. Thus the shadow prices, or tariff equivalents, on imports are reduced and the prices of both imports and their domestic substitutes both fall. But production for export requires inputs from other sectors, and as prices of imports and domestic goods both fall, this will stimulate production for export, and export revenue, still further. That exports might rise considerably more than can be accounted for by simple export supply elasticities is clear. And one can imagine that this process might fail to converge. If it does not converge, then equilibrium would have to be found in the other direction. A rise in world prices would require tighter rationing of foreign exchange so as to reduce both exports and imports rather than increase them.

Once we recognized the problem, we were even more dismayed. It did seem that we had hit upon what could be a serious problem in the real world. The error seemed to lie with the institution of import licensing itself, rather than with our modeling of it. However, in an equilibrium, comparative-static model like ours, one could not legitimately proceed if the equilibria one was studying were unstable. In view of the relative economic unimportance of the developing countries in our model, it would not be too much of an error, perhaps, to retain the results for countries that appeared stable, and simply dismiss those for India as anomalies. But even the near instability in several other LDCs made us uncomfortable.

At about this time we were fortunate to be visited at Michigan by T. N. Srinivasan, with whom we discussed this problem. He too felt that this source of instability might be a real problem. But with his help we realized that a sensible import-licensing scheme would be run somewhat differently than we had modeled it, and so possibly avoid this instability. Given the importance placed on exports, one would expect those who allocate scarce foreign exchange to favor exporters who require imported inputs in order to produce. Thus foreign exchange would not be allocated among importers solely in proportion to, say, existing imports as we modeled it, but preference would instead be given to producers for export who would be able to buy all they needed at the market rate. In terms of our model, imported inputs to the export sectors would be exempted from the tariff equivalents that were used to regulate other imports.

So once again we embarked on a revision of the model. This time we added a rebate facility, whereby producers in export sectors had any tariff equivalents that they paid returned to them. Decisions to produce in these sectors were therefore responsive directly to world prices and exchange rates, but not to the state of the balance of payments. The new model was run, and indeed the apparent instability did disappear, as did most of the cases in which developing countries appeared to be overresponsive to export prices.

The potential for instability, by the way, is still present. Even though exporters are no longer rationed in the model, they must still purchase inputs that are produced domestically and the prices of these are also raised by the rationing of scarce foreign exchange. It is still possible, therefore, that import licensing might worsen the balance of trade rather than improve it, through its effects on domestic prices and costs. Based on our rather crude data for some developing countries, this does not appear to be the case empirically, but there is some evidence of a tendency in this direction in certain countries.[6]

Tariffs

We have focused thus far on some lessons we have learned essentially by accident, as by-products of our efforts to model the effects of tariffs and trade. Lest the reader be left with the impression that these were the only things we learned from our model, we shall conclude by mentioning a few things we have learned about the effects of tariffs, since this, after all, was what we set out to study in the first place.

We have already mentioned the conclusion that permeates our results regarding the overall magnitude of the effects of tariff reductions. We have consistently found, as have other investigators, that tariff reductions such as those of the Tokyo Round will have effects on trade, employment, and welfare that are so small as to be negligible among all the other changes that continually occur in the world. A major reason for this, technically, is the Armington assumption that domestic and foreign goods are imperfect substitutes, but the ultimate justification for both the assumption and the conclusion lies in the relatively low elasticities of import demand that have been estimated repeatedly by many authors.

Our model is intended not only to calculate the overall effects of tariff changes, but even more so the disaggregated effects among industries. Here another pattern has consistently emerged and provides a second theme throughout our work on tariff reductions. Tariff reductions tend to stimulate output and employment worldwide in those industries where tariffs are reduced, at the expense of those industries where they are not. Since the latter include primarily the nontraded sectors, this means that trade liberalization generally shifts resources away from nontraded goods and toward traded goods. The reason for this result is that tariffs, viewed from the perspective of the world rather than of any particular country, constitute simply a tax on traded goods. When tariffs are reduced multilaterally, this tax falls and the prices of traded goods facing consumers fall relative to those of nontraded goods. They therefore substitute toward the goods with the lower prices. There are numerous exceptions to this pattern, of course, for nontraded goods that interact heavily with traded goods and for traded goods that are exempt from tariff reductions or are insulated from them by NTBs. But the overall pattern stands out clearly.

Finally, we can mention a possibility that arises in our model, and that is not surprising in context, but is not what one normally expects. Unilateral tariff reduction or elimination may, particularly in small countries, cause an improvement in their balance of trade. We found this to be the case for the Netherlands when we examined the structure of protection, as in chapter 5. The reason for this possibility is similar to the problem noted earlier for import licensing, and arises only in a model where interindustry flows are important. Tariff reduction reduces the domestic prices of imported inputs to the export sectors. If export producers depend heavily on imported inputs, as they must in a very small country, then exports may be stimulated more than imports. Again this possibility would be precluded if exporters were exempt from paying tariffs, but this is probably not generally the case.

Directions for Future Research

It should be evident from the preceding discussion that our modeling efforts have evolved in a variety of interesting ways. We are currently pursuing several new directions for research, and it may be useful therefore to conclude this volume by discussing briefly our agenda for future research. This agenda includes (1) development and implementation of a model in which traded goods are distinguished by country of origin, (2) more accurate measurement and representation of NTBs, (3) incorporation of macroeconomic relations and development of alternative methods for macroeconomic closure of the model, (4) further disaggregation, and (5) incorporation of trade in services.

As mentioned previously, we allowed for imperfect substitution between imports and home goods and separated production for export from production for the home market. This enabled us to capture the essence of the Armington assumption and at the same time to solve simultaneously for equilibrium in as many world markets as there are goods. The complete implementation of the Armington assumption requires that goods be differentiated by country of origin. In terms of the present country and commodity coverage of our model, this would mean 748 separate world markets since we have 34 countries and 22 tradable goods. A revised version of our model that incorporates the full Armington assumption has been completed by Brown (1984). The data and parameter requirements of Brown's model are clearly much greater than our model in its present form, and the solution is more costly because there are so many more markets being considered. Nonetheless, this new model will be useful because it will permit analysis of changes in bilateral trade and commercial policies. This is something that we have not been able to do with the current model because it has world markets that treat goods homogeneously no matter where produced. Brown's model can thus be used to analyze a variety of changes in preferential arrangements such as, for example, the impact of the Tokyo Round negotiations on the EEC and the effects of GSP (generalized system of preferences).

We described earlier the representation of NTBs in our model in terms of the fraction of trade in individual sectors subject to NTBs of any kind. This is a rather crude way to capture the effects of NTBs. We are now engaged accordingly in research that is designed to measure the effects of different kinds of NTBs directly in terms of their impact on the price and/or the volume of imports in the individual countries in our model. Once these measures of NTBs are complete, they will be incorporated into the model. This will permit calculations to be made of the effects of reducing or removing NTBs by sector and country, which is something that cannot be done with the present version of our model. Such analysis is especially important in light of the increased use of NTBs in the advanced industrialized countries especially as existing nominal tariffs have been lowered or removed in the course of the Tokyo Round and previous multilateral negotiations.

We purposely abstracted from macroeconomic relations and policies in our model in order to concentrate attention on the intersectoral effects on production, trade, and employment of changes in tariffs and other variables involving relative prices. By severing the link between expenditure and income, the model is thus not closed satisfactorily from the macroeconomic standpoint. We plan therefore to address these macroeconomic deficiencies in order to design more appropriate rules for closure of the model. Once accomplished, this will enable us to analyze more fully the micro-macro effects of changes in a variety of variables, including exchange rates, domestic taxes/subsidies, and monetary and fiscal policies.

In choosing the sectoral coverage of our model, we were constrained by the availability of data for individual sectors across all the countries included in the model. As mentioned, the most feasible disaggregation was to the 3-digit ISIC level for tradable goods in agriculture and manufacturing and the 1-digit level for private sector and government services. This has the drawback that we cannot readily analyze changes that affect more detailed industry categories. It is with this point in mind that we plan to explore the development of an input-output submodel for the United States that will be tied into our present multilateral model with its more highly aggregated sectors. This does not appear to present any unusual conceptual difficulties, though it does involve a potentially large increase in data requirements. A detailed submodel will nonetheless be useful because it will enable us to break down the effects of changes in different variables for many additional sectors beyond what can be done at present.

Finally, our model covers only merchandise trade and not trade in services. There is considerable interest especially in the United States in assessing the importance of trade in services and the various barriers that serve as impediments to this trade. We plan accordingly to make an effort to incorporate services into our model. This will involve estimating the portions of existing trade flows that may be attributed to services of various kinds as well as taking into account services trade not included currently in our trade measures. It will further require estimates of the barriers to trade in services as well as a more careful elaboration of how trade in services is represented in our industry categories in national input-output tables. It will no doubt be difficult to expand our model to include trade in services, but the effort may be worthwhile in terms of the computational assessments of service-related issues that will be made possible.

Technical Appendix: Derivation of Explicit Functional Forms

In this appendix, which is adapted from Deardorff, Stern, and Baum (1976), we derive the equations of the model with explicit functional forms, based upon profit and utility maximization. In section 1 we examine production decisions of a typical firm. In section 2 we turn to final demands of consumers, which are assumed to derive from a single but perfectly competitive utility-maximizing consumer. In section 3 we aggregate the demands from these two sources, and in section 4 we put it all together, listing the explicit, differentiated equations of the complete Michigan model.

Throughout this appendix we use the following notation to represent proportional differentiation: For any variable, x,

$$ex = d(\ln x) = dx/x.$$

1 Production

To characterize the output supply and input demand functions of the model, we look first at the behavior of a typical firm in any industry and country. For convenience we omit the industry and country subscripts. They will be reintroduced when the results are incorporated into the larger model in sections 3 and 4.

Consider a firm that produces an output, Q, using inputs of capital, K, labor, L, and intermediate inputs that it purchases from other industries, including its own. Its technology distinguishes between imported and home-produced intermediate inputs, which we therefore denote respectively, by Z_j^M for $j = 1, \ldots, n$ and by Z_j^H for $j = 1, \ldots, n'$. The production function, including all of these inputs as arguments, is assumed to be weakly separable in the sense that it takes the following form:

$$Q = F[V(K,L), A^1(Z_1^H, Z_1^M), \ldots, A^n(Z_n^H, Z_n^M), Z_{n+1}^H, \ldots, Z_{n'}^H], \tag{A.1.1}$$

where the functions V and A^j, $j = 1, \ldots, n$, each take the form of familiar linearly homogenous production functions with constant elasticities of substitution. The function F is assumed here to require fixed proportions among its arguments.

The firm is constrained to the use of a fixed capital stock, $K = \bar{K}$, but it may choose the levels of all other inputs. It is a perfect competitor, receiving a price p^0 for its output and paying a wage, w, for labor, prices $p_j^H, j = 1, \ldots, n'$, for home-produced inputs, and prices $p_j^M, j = 1, \ldots, n$, for imported inputs. On taking all of this into account, the firm's profit maximization problem is therefore the following:

$$\text{maximize} \quad \pi = p^0 Q - wL - \sum_{j=1}^{n'} p_j^H Z_j^H - \sum_{j=1}^{n} p_j^M Z_j^M \tag{A.1.2}$$

$$\text{subject to} \quad a_0 Q = V(\bar{K}, L), \tag{A.1.3}$$

$$a_j Q = A^j(Z_j^H, Z_j^M), \qquad j = 1, \ldots, n, \tag{A.1.4}$$

$$a_j Q = Z_j^H, \qquad j = n + 1, \ldots, n'. \tag{A.1.5}$$

Here a_j, $j = 0, 1, \ldots, n'$, are the (fixed) requirements of each of the aggregated inputs per unit of output and π is the firm's profit.

First-order conditions for this maximization problem with respect to Q, L, Z_j^M, and Z_j^H give us the following:

$$p^0 = \sum_{j=0}^{n'} \lambda_j a_j, \tag{A.1.6}$$

$$\lambda_0 V_L = w, \tag{A.1.7}$$

$$\lambda_j A_M^j = p_j^M, \qquad j = 1, \ldots, n, \tag{A.1.8}$$

$$\lambda_j A_H^j = p_j^H, \qquad j = 1, \ldots, n, \tag{A.1.9}$$

$$\lambda_j = p_j^H, \qquad j = n + 1, \ldots, n', \tag{A.1.10}$$

where λ_0 and λ_j are Lagrange multipliers for the constraints (A.1.3) and (A.1.4)–(A.1.5), respectively.

Before we differentiate these equations, it is useful to characterize how the partial derivatives, V_L, A_M^j, and A_H^j in (A.1.7)–(A.1.9) vary with their arguments. This is given by the elasticities of substitution, $\bar{\sigma}$, between capital and labor, and σ_j between home and imported inputs. These are given implicitly by the following equations:

$$eK - eL = \bar{\sigma}[eV_L - eV_K], \tag{A.1.11}$$

$$eZ_j^H - eZ_j^M = \sigma_j[eA_M^j - eA_H^j], \qquad j = 1, \ldots, n. \tag{A.1.12}$$

We now differentiate the constraints (A.1.3)–(A.1.5) and the first-order conditions (A.1.6)–(A.1.10):

$$eQ = \theta_K e\bar{K} + \theta_L eL, \tag{A.1.13}$$

$$eQ = \theta_H^j eZ_j^H + \theta_M^j eZ_j^M, \qquad j = 1, \ldots, n, \tag{A.1.14}$$

$$eQ = eZ_j^H, \qquad j = n + 1, \ldots, n', \tag{A.1.15}$$

$$ep^0 = \sum_{j=0}^{n'} \frac{\lambda_j a_j}{p^0} e\lambda_j, \tag{A.1.16}$$

$$e\lambda_0 + eV_L = ew, \tag{A.1.17}$$

$$e\lambda_j + eA_M^j = ep_j^M, \qquad j = 1, \ldots, n, \tag{A.1.18}$$

$$e\lambda_j + eA_H^j = ep_j^H, \qquad j = 1, \ldots, n, \tag{A.1.19}$$

$$e\lambda_j = ep_j^H, \qquad j = n + 1, \ldots, n', \tag{A.1.20}$$

where

$$\theta_L = \frac{L}{V} V_L = 1 - \theta_K, \tag{A.1.21}$$

$$\theta_H^j = \frac{Z_j^H}{A^j} A_H^j = 1 - \theta_M^j, \qquad j = 1, \ldots, n. \tag{A.1.22}$$

Equations (A.1.11)–(A.1.20), together with Euler's theorem, constitute a system of as many linear equations as unknowns, the unknowns being the proportional differentials of the firm's decision variables. The solution of this system will be somewhat simplified if we first introduce some additional notation. Let

$$b_j = \frac{\lambda_j a_j}{p^0}, \qquad j = 0, \ldots, n', \tag{A.1.23}$$

which we shall interpret later, and note from (A.1.6) that

$$\sum_{j=0}^{n'} b_j = 1. \tag{A.1.24}$$

Also let

$$\varepsilon = \frac{\theta_L \bar{\sigma}}{\theta_K b_0}. \tag{A.1.25}$$

Then the system can be solved for the following supply function of the firm:

$$eQ = \varepsilon ep^0 - \varepsilon \sum_{j=1}^{n} b_j[\theta_H^j ep_j^H + \theta_M^j ep_j^M] \\ - \varepsilon \sum_{j=n+1}^{n'} b_j ep_j^H - \varepsilon b_0 ew + e\bar{K}. \tag{A.1.26}$$

Changes in the firm's demands for inputs can be expressed simply in terms of eQ. Demand for labor is obtained directly from (A.1.13):

$$eL = \frac{1}{\theta_L} eQ - \frac{\theta_K}{\theta_L} e\bar{K}. \tag{A.1.27}$$

Demands for tradable inputs are obtained with a bit more effort as follows:

$$eZ_j^H = eQ + \theta_M^j \sigma_j [ep_j^M - ep_j^H], \qquad j = 1, \ldots, n, \tag{A.1.28}$$

$$eZ_j^M = eQ - \theta_H^j \sigma_j [ep_j^M - ep_j^H], \qquad j = 1, \ldots, n. \tag{A.1.29}$$

Finally, demand for nontradables is given directly by (A.1.15).

We have now derived, in (A.1.26)–(A.1.29), the complete output supply and input demand functions of the firm. It remains to show that the b and θ values in these solutions can be expressed as observable shares of firm expenditure or revenue. For nontradables such an interpretation of b_j is trivial. Substituting (A.1.5) and (A.1.10) into (A.1.23), we get immediately

$$b_j = \frac{p_j^H Z_j^H}{p^0 Q}, \qquad j = n+1, \ldots, n'. \tag{A.1.30}$$

Thus b_j is expenditure on input j as a fraction of revenue. The same interpretation obtains for tradables, though a bit more effort is required to derive it. We substitute (A.1.4) into (A.1.23), then apply Euler's theorem to A^j, and finally use (A.1.8) and (A.1.9):

$$b_j = \frac{\lambda_j A^j}{p^0 Q} = \frac{\lambda_j (A_H^j Z_j^H + A_M^j Z_j^M)}{p^0 Q} \\ = \frac{p_j^H Z_j^H + p_j^M Z_j^M}{p^0 Q}, \qquad j = 1, \ldots, n. \tag{A.1.31}$$

Finally, for b_0, one can use (A.1.30) and (A.1.31) in (A.1.24), together with (A.1.2), to get

$$b_0 = \frac{\pi + wL}{p^0 Q}. \tag{A.1.32}$$

Thus b_0 is the firm's value added as a fraction of its revenue.

θ_L and θ_K may be interpreted as the labor and capital shares of value added, respectively. Substitute (A.1.3) and (A.1.7) into (A.1.21), then use (A.1.23) and (A.1.32):

$$\theta_L = \frac{wL}{\lambda_0 a_0 Q} = \frac{wL}{b_0 p^0 Q} = \frac{wL}{\pi + wL}. \tag{A.1.33}$$

θ_H^j and θ_M^j can be similarly interpreted as shares of expenditure on tradable inputs. Starting with (A.1.22), for example, we substitute from (A.1.9), (A.1.4), (A.1.23), and (A.1.31).

$$\theta_H^j = \frac{p_j^H Z_j^H}{p_j^H Z_j^H + p_j^M Z_j^M}, \qquad j = 1, \ldots, n. \tag{A.1.34}$$

2 Consumption

We turn now to the determination of consumer demand. As was done with production, we look here at a typical consumer in any country, but omit in this section the subscripts indicating which country. The consumer maximizes the utility, U, derived from consumption of home-produced goods, C_j^H, and of imports, C_j^M, subject to the constraint of a given level of expenditure, E. We assume that the utility function, rather like the production function in the previous section, is weakly separable into a Cobb-Douglas function whose arguments for each industry are themselves linearly homogenous functions of home and import consumption. Let α_j, $j = 1, \ldots, n'$, with $\sum_{j=1}^{n'} \alpha_j = 1$, be the parameters of the Cobb-Douglas function. Then the consumer's maximization problem is the following:

$$\text{maximize} \quad U = \left\{ \prod_{j=1}^{n} [A^j(C_j^H, C_j^M)]^{\alpha_j} \right\} \prod_{j=n+1}^{n'} (C_j^H)^{\alpha_j} \tag{A.2.1}$$

$$\text{subject to} \quad \sum_{j=1}^{n} [p_j^H C_j^H + p_j^M C_j^M] + \sum_{j=n+1}^{n'} p_j^H C_j^H = E. \tag{A.2.2}$$

Here A^j is assumed to be identical to the A^j function of section 1, so that we can use the property (A.1.12), applied now to C_j^H and C_j^M instead of Z_j^H and Z_j^M.

First-order conditions for this problem are

$$\alpha_j U A_M^j / A^j = \lambda p_j^M, \qquad j = 1, \ldots, n, \tag{A.2.3}$$

$$\alpha_j U A_H^j / A^j = \lambda p_j^H, \qquad j = 1, \ldots, n, \tag{A.2.4}$$

$$\alpha_j U / C_j^H = \lambda p_j^H, \qquad j = n + 1, \ldots, n', \tag{A.2.5}$$

where λ is a Lagrange multiplier. We look first at the elasticities of the A^j functions, θ_H^j and θ_M^j. As with the firm, we can use (A.2.3) and (A.2.4) together with Euler's theorem for A^j to show that these elasticities equal the home and import shares, respectively, of consumer expenditure on each tradable industry. For example,

$$\theta_H^j = \frac{p_j^H C_j^H}{p_j^H C_j^H + p_j^M C_j^M}, \qquad j = 1, \ldots, n. \tag{A.2.6}$$

By proportionally differentiating the first-order conditions and using an equation analogous to (A.1.12), it is straightforward to derive the following differentiated demand functions:

$$\begin{aligned} eC_j^H &= eE - (\theta_H^j + \theta_M^j \sigma_j) ep_j^H \\ &\quad + \theta_M^j(\sigma_j - 1) ep_j^M, \qquad j = 1, \ldots, n, \end{aligned} \tag{A.2.7}$$

$$\begin{aligned} eC_j^M &= eE + \theta_H^j(\sigma_j - 1) ep_j^H \\ &\quad - (\theta_M^j + \theta_H^j \sigma_j) ep_j^M, \qquad j = 1, \ldots, n, \end{aligned} \tag{A.2.8}$$

$$eC_j^H = eE - ep_j^H, \qquad j = n + 1, \ldots, n'. \tag{A.2.9}$$

3 Aggregation

So far we have described behavior only at the level of the individual firm and consumer. In fact, however, all of our results pertain equally well to the aggregate behavior of groups of firms and groups of consumers, so long as all within a group face identical prices and share identical technologies or tastes. For then all of the coefficients in our differentiated supply and demand functions will be identical across members of a group, and the proportional change in any aggregate supply or demand will equal the proportional changes in each individual supply or demand.

For output supplies and labor demands, this is really all that we need to say. Equations (A.1.26) and (A.1.27), with appropriate labels to indicate the country, industry, and sector involved, provide all the information we need about supply functions and labor demand functions. The coefficients in (A.1.26) and (A.1.27) give us the elasticities of these functions with respect to all of their arguments.

Demand functions for goods are somewhat more difficult to obtain in a manageable form, since demands for each good arise both from consumers and from firms in all industries. To simplify the task we make several additional assumptions. First, we assume that all firms within a given industry share identical technologies, whether they are producing for the home market or for export. Second, we assume that home and export producers in a given industry sell their outputs for prices that are *initially* identical (as would have to be the case if the initial position were the result of a long-run adjustment in which capital stocks were variable). From these two assumptions, it follows that home and export sectors of a given industry must initially be behaving identically except for scale. In particular, all primary and intermediate factor shares must initially be identical in the home and export sectors of a given industry to the corresponding factor shares in the industry as a whole. If we further define

$$\gamma_{ik}^{X} = \frac{S_{ik}^{X}}{S_{ik}^{H} + S_{ik}^{X}}, \qquad i = 1, \ldots, m, \quad k = 1, \ldots, n, \tag{A.3.1}$$

as the fraction being exported out of total output of industry k in country i, then the same symbol will also represent the fraction of that industry's total purchases of any input that is being used by its export sector.

Finally, we assume that within each country *all* firms and consumers share identical functions, A^j, for aggregating purchases of home and imported goods from any particular industry. Thus, their expenditure shares, which we shall denote θ_H^{ij} and θ_M^{ij}, on home and imported products of industry j are identical.

With these assumptions we can now derive the total demands for the various goods, D_{ij}^H and D_{ij}^M. The notation becomes unavoidably cumbersome, but only for a moment. Let $C_{ij}^H, j = 1, \ldots, n'$, and $C_{ij}^M, j = 1, \ldots, n$, be the demands for home and imported products of industry j, respectively, by consumers in country $i = 1, \ldots, m$. These will be determined by equations (A.2.7)–(A.2.9) with all variables and parameters carrying an additional sub- or superscript to denote country i. Next let Z_{ijk}^{HX} be the demand for home-produced products of industry $j = 1, \ldots, n'$ for use as inputs to the export sector of industry $k = 1, \ldots, n$, both in country $i = 1, \ldots, m$. Define similarly Z_{ijk}^{MX}, Z_{ijk}^{HH}, and Z_{ijk}^{MH}. These will be determined by equations (A.1.15), (A.1.28), and (A.1.29) with additional sub- and superscripts to indicate the country, industry, and sector that is the source of the demand. Finally let

$$Z_{ijk}^{H\cdot} = Z_{ijk}^{HX} + Z_{ijk}^{HH}, \qquad j = 1, \ldots, n',$$

$$i = 1, \ldots, m, \quad k = 1, \ldots, n, \tag{A.3.2}$$

$$Z_{ijk}^{M\cdot} = Z_{ijk}^{MX} + Z_{ijk}^{MH}, \qquad j = 1, \ldots, n,$$

and define

$$
\begin{aligned}
v_{ij0} &= \frac{C_{ij}^{H}}{D_{ij}^{H}} = \frac{C_{ij}^{M}}{D_{ij}^{M}}, \\
v_{ijk} &= \frac{Z_{ijk}^{H\cdot}}{D_{ij}^{H}} \\
&= \frac{Z_{ijk}^{M\cdot}}{D_{ij}^{M}}, \qquad k = 1, \ldots, n, \quad i = 1, \ldots, m, \quad j = 1, \ldots, n', \\
v_{ijk} &= \frac{Z_{ijk}^{H}}{D_{ij}^{H}} = \frac{Z_{ijk}^{M}}{D_{ij}^{M}}, \qquad k = n + 1, \ldots, n',
\end{aligned}
\tag{A.3.3}
$$

as the consumer and industry shares of demand for good j in country i. The second equality in each case (which is relevant only for $j = 1, \ldots, n$) follows from the third assumption made earlier. That assumption also permits us to measure each v_{ijk} from the total flows of goods among industries and consumers without regard to sectors.

We can now write out and differentiate each demand function. This will be done here only for imports, the results for home goods being obtainable analogously. The demand, D_{ij}^{M}, for imports of good j in country i is

$$
D_{ij}^{M} = C_{ij}^{M} + \sum_{k=1}^{n} (Z_{ijk}^{MX} + Z_{ijk}^{MH}) + \sum_{k=n+1}^{n'} Z_{ijk}^{MH}. \tag{A.3.4}
$$

It follows that

$$
\sum_{k=0}^{n'} v_{ijk} = 1, \qquad i = 1, \ldots, m, \quad j = 1, \ldots, n. \tag{A.3.5}
$$

Recall, also, from the discussion accompanying (A.3.1), that

$$
\gamma_{ik}^{X} = \frac{Z_{ijk}^{MX}}{Z_{ijk}^{MH} + Z_{ijk}^{MX}}, \; i = 1, \ldots, m, \quad j = 1, \ldots, n, \quad k = 1, \ldots, n. \tag{A.3.6}
$$

Then we can differentiate (A.3.4) and use (A.3.3) and (A.3.6) to get

$$
\begin{aligned}
eD_{ij}^{M} = {} & v_{ij0} eC_{ij}^{M} + \sum_{k=1}^{n} v_{ijk} [(1 - \gamma_{ik}^{X}) eZ_{ijk}^{MH} + \gamma_{ik}^{X} eZ_{ijk}^{MX}] \\
& + \sum_{k=n+1}^{n'} v_{ijk} eZ_{ijk}^{MH}, \qquad i = 1, \ldots, m, \quad j = 1, \ldots, n.
\end{aligned}
\tag{A.3.7}
$$

Finally we substitute from (A.2.8) and (A.1.29), factor the common terms involving price changes from the summations, use (A.3.5), and rearrange to get the following final form of the differentiated import demand function:

$$eD_{ij}^{M} = -[v_{ij0} + \theta_H^{ij}(\sigma_{ij} - v_{ij0})]ep_{ij}^{M} + \theta_H^{ij}(\sigma_{ij} - v_{ij0})ep_{ij}^{H} + v_{ij0}eE_i + \sum_{k=1}^{n} v_{ijk}[(1 - \gamma_{ik}^{X})eS_{ik}^{H} + \gamma_{ik}^{X}eS_{ik}^{X}] + \sum_{k=n+1}^{n'} v_{ijk}eS_{ik}^{H}. \tag{A.3.8}$$

4 The Differentiated Model

We can now write down the complete differentiated version of the entire model. Each of the following equations results from differentiation of the corresponding equations (2.1)–(2.17) in chapter 2. The first five incorporate the information accumulated in sections 1–3 of this appendix, while the remaining equations, for the most part, simply apply the standard rules of differentiation. These equations refer only to the fixed-coefficient specification of technology that was analyzed here.

$$eS_{ij}^{X} = \varepsilon_{ij}ep_{ij}^{X} - \varepsilon_{ij}\sum_{k=1}^{n} b_{kj}[\theta_H^{ik}ep_{ik}^{H} + \theta_M^{ik}ep_{ik}^{M}] - \varepsilon_{ij}\sum_{k=n+1}^{n'} b_{kj}ep_{ik}^{H} - \varepsilon_{ij}b_{0j}ew_{ij} + eK_{ij}^{X}, \qquad i = 1, \ldots, m, \quad j = 1, \ldots, n, \tag{A.4.1}$$

$$eS_{ij}^{H} = \varepsilon_{ij}ep_{ij}^{H} - \varepsilon_{ij}\sum_{k=1}^{n} b_{kj}[\theta_H^{ik}ep_{ik}^{H} + \theta_M^{ik}ep_{ik}^{M}] - \varepsilon_{ij}\sum_{k=n+1}^{n'} b_{kj}ep_{ik}^{H} - \varepsilon_{ij}b_{0j}ew_{ij} + eK_{ij}^{H}, \qquad i = 1, \ldots, m, \quad j = 1, \ldots, n', \tag{A.4.2}$$

$$eD_{ij}^{M} = -[v_{ij0} + \theta_H^{ij}(\sigma_{ij} - v_{ij0})]ep_{ij}^{M} + \theta_H^{ij}(\sigma_{ij} - v_{ij0})ep_{ij}^{H} + v_{ij0}eE_i + \sum_{k=1}^{n} v_{ijk}[\gamma_{ik}^{X}eS_{ik}^{X} + (1 - \gamma_{ik}^{X})eS_{ik}^{H}] + \sum_{k=n+1}^{n'} v_{ijk}eS_{ik}^{H}, \qquad i = 1, \ldots, m, \quad j = 1, \ldots, n, \tag{A.4.3}$$

$$eD_{ij}^H = -[v_{ij0} + \theta_M^{ij}(\sigma_{ij} - v_{ij0}]ep_{ij}^H + \theta_M^{ij}(\sigma_{ij} - v_{ij0})ep_{ij}^M + v_{ij0}eE_i + \sum_{k=1}^{n} v_{ijk}[\gamma_{ik}^X eS_{ik}^X + (1 - \gamma_{ik}^X)eS_{ik}^H] + \sum_{k=n+1}^{n'} v_{ijk}eS_{ik}^H, \quad i = 1, \ldots, m, \quad j = 1, \ldots, n, \tag{A.4.4a}$$

$$eD_{ij}^H = -v_{ij0}ep_{ij}^H + v_{ij0}eE_i + \sum_{k=1}^{n} v_{ijk}[\gamma_{ik}^X eS_{ik}^X + (1 - \gamma_{ik}^X)eS_{ik}^H] + \sum_{k=n+1}^{n'} v_{ijk}eS_{ik}^H, \quad i = 1, \ldots, m, \quad j = n+1, \ldots, n', \tag{A.4.4b}$$

$$ep_{ij}^X = et_{ij}^{Xeq} + eR_i + ep_j^W, \quad i = 1, \ldots, m, \quad j = 1, \ldots, n, \tag{A.4.5}$$

$$ep_{ij}^M = et_{ij}^{Meq} + eR_i + ep_j^W, \quad i = 1, \ldots, m, \quad j = 1, \ldots, n, \tag{A.4.6}$$

$$eE_i = \mu_i^0 eE_i^0 + \sum_{j=1}^{n} \mu_{ij}^M et_{ij}^{Meq} + \sum_{j=1}^{n} \mu_{ij}^M \left(\frac{t_{ij}^{Meq} - 1}{t_{ij}^{Meq}}\right)[eR_i + ep_j^W + eD_{ij}^M] - \sum_{j=1}^{n} \mu_{ij}^X et_{ij}^{Xeq} + \sum_{j=1}^{n} \mu_{ij}^X \left(\frac{1 - t_{ij}^{Xeq}}{t_{ij}^{Xeq}}\right)[eR_i + ep_j^W + eS_{ij}^X] - \sum_{j=1}^{n'} \mu_{ij}^H t_{ij}^H et_{ij}^H + \sum_{j=1}^{n'} \mu_{ij}^H(1 - t_{ij}^H)[ep_{ij}^H + eS_{ij}^H], \quad i = 1, \ldots, m, \tag{A.4.7a}$$

or

$$\sum_{j=1}^{n'} \lambda_{ij}eD_{ij}^L = eS_i^{L0}, \quad i = 1, \ldots, m, \tag{A.4.7b}$$

$$eS_{ij}^H = eD_{ij}^H, \quad i = 1, \ldots, m, \quad j = 1, \ldots, n', \tag{A.4.8}$$

$$et_{ij}^{Meq} = et_{ij}^{M} + \left[\frac{\theta_{ij}^{QM}}{\eta_{ij}(1-\theta_{ij}^{QM})}\right] \cdot (eQ_{ij}^{M} - eD_{ij}^{M}), \qquad i = 1,\ldots,m, \quad j = 1,\ldots,n, \tag{A.4.9a}$$

or

$$eD_{ij}^{M} = \frac{1}{M_i}\sum_{k=1}^{n} [X_{ik}eS_{ik}^{X} + (X_{ik} - M_{ik})ep_k^{W} + dB_i^{K0}], \qquad i = 1,\ldots,m, \quad j = 1,\ldots,n, \tag{A.4.9b}$$

or

$$eD_{ij}^{M} = eD_{ij}^{M0}, \qquad i = 1,\ldots,m, \tag{A.4.9c}$$

$$et_{ij}^{Xeq} = et_{ij}^{X} + \left[\frac{\theta_{ij}^{QX}}{\varepsilon_{ij}(1-\theta_{ij}^{QX})}\right] \cdot (eQ_{ij}^{X} - eS_{ij}^{X}), \qquad i = 1,\ldots,m, \quad j = 1,\ldots,n, \tag{A.4.10a}$$

or

$$eS_{ij}^{X} = eS_{ij}^{X0}, \qquad i = 1,\ldots,m, \quad j = 1,\ldots,n, \tag{A.4.10b}$$

$$eL_{ij} = \gamma_{ij}^{X}\left[\frac{1}{\theta_L^{ij}}eS_{ij}^{X} + \frac{\theta_K^{ij}}{\theta_L^{ij}}eK_{ij}^{X}\right] + (1-\gamma_{ij}^{X}) \cdot \left[\frac{1}{\theta_L^{ij}}eS_{ij}^{H} + \frac{\theta_K^{ij}}{\theta_L^{ij}}eK_{ij}^{H}\right], \qquad i = 1,\ldots,m, \quad j = 1,\ldots,n, \tag{A.4.11a}$$

$$eL_{ij} = \frac{1}{\theta_L^{ij}}eS_{ij}^{H} + \frac{\theta_K^{ij}}{\theta_L^{ij}}eK_{ij}^{H}, \qquad i = 1,\ldots,m, \quad j = n+1,\ldots,n', \tag{A.4.11b}$$

$$ew_{ij} = ew_i^{0}, \qquad i = 1,\ldots,m, \quad j = 1,\ldots,n', \tag{A.4.12a}$$

or

$$\sum_{j=1}^{n'} \lambda_{ij}eD_{ij}^{L} = eS_i^{L0},$$
$$ew_{ij} = ew_{ik}, \qquad i = 1,\ldots,m, \quad j \neq k = 1,\ldots,n', \tag{A.4.12b}$$

or

$$eD_{ij}^{L} = eS_{ij}^{L0}, \qquad i = 1, \ldots, m, \quad j = 1, \ldots, n', \tag{A.4.12c}$$

$$dN_{ij}^{X} = X_{ij}eS_{ij}^{X} - M_{ij}eD_{ij}^{M}, \qquad i = 1, \ldots, m, \quad j = 1, \ldots, n, \tag{A.4.13}$$

$$\sum_{i=1}^{m} dN_{ij}^{X} + N_{j}^{\text{row}}eN_{j}^{\text{row}} = 0, \qquad j = 1, \ldots, n, \tag{A.4.14}$$

$$\begin{aligned} dB_{i}^{T} = \sum_{j=1}^{n} [X_{ij}eS_{ij}^{X} &- M_{ij}eD_{ij}^{M} \\ &+ (X_{ij} - M_{ij})ep_{j}^{W}], \qquad i = 1, \ldots, m, \end{aligned} \tag{A.4.15}$$

$$eN_{j}^{\text{row}} = -\left[\sum_{i=1}^{m} (M_{ij} - X_{ij})\right] ep_{j}^{W}, \qquad j = 1, \ldots, n, \tag{A.4.16}$$

$$eR_{i} = \sum_{j \neq i} \theta_{ij}^{R} eR_{j} + eR_{i}^{0}, \qquad i = 1, \ldots, m, \tag{A.4.17a}$$

or

$$dB_{i}^{T} + dB_{i}^{K0} = 0, \qquad eR_{m} = eR_{m}^{0}, \qquad i = 1, \ldots, m - 1. \tag{A.4.17b}$$

Most of the notation in these equations has been previously introduced, either in this appendix or in equations (2.1)–(2.17) in chapter 2. The following, however, are new:

$$\mu_{ij}^{M} = \frac{t_{ij}^{Meq} R_{i} p_{j}^{W} D_{ij}^{M}}{E_{i}}, \qquad i = 1, \ldots, m, \quad j = 1, \ldots, n, \tag{A.4.18}$$

$$\mu_{ij}^{X} = \frac{t_{ij}^{Xeq} R_{i} p_{j}^{W} S_{ij}^{X}}{E_{i}}, \qquad i = 1, \ldots, m, \quad j = 1, \ldots, n, \tag{A.4.19}$$

$$\mu_{ij}^{H} = \frac{p_{ij}^{H} S_{ij}^{H}}{E_{i}}, \qquad i = 1, \ldots, m, \quad j = 1, \ldots, n'. \tag{A.4.20}$$

These represent domestic values bought or sold of each import, export, and home good respectively, all as fractions of total consumer expenditure. In addition:

μ_{i}^{0} = share of expenditure in country *j* not accounted for by tax and tariff revenue.

λ_{ij} = industry *j*'s share in total employment in country *i*.

$\theta_{ij}^{QM}, \theta_{ij}^{QX}$ = shares of imports and exports of industry *j* subject to quantitative restrictions in country *i*.

η_{ij} = price elasticity of demand for imports of good *j* in country *i*.

M_{i} = total imports of country *i*.

X_{ik}, M_{ik} = values of exports and imports of industry k, country i.

Equation (A.4.9a) is derived as follows. Let a typical import demand depend on the tariff equivalent, with elasticity η, and a list, λ, of other variables including price:

$$eD^M = \eta et^{Meq} + \lambda. \tag{A.4.21}$$

Define an implicit tariff, t^{QM}, that would hold imports to a given quantity, Q^M, in (A.4.21),

$$eQ^M = \eta et^{QM} + \lambda, \tag{A.4.22}$$

and define t^{Meq} as the weighted average of t^M and t^{QM}:

$$et^{Meq} = (1 - \theta^{QM})et^M + \theta^{QM}et^{QM}. \tag{A.4.23}$$

By eliminating t^{QM} and λ, (A.4.21)–(A.4.23) can be solved to yield (A.4.9a). Equation (A.4.10a) can be derived similarly.

Most of the coefficients in equations (A.4.1)–(A.4.17) can be calculated in obvious ways from data on trade, tariffs, output, employment, and inter-industry transactions for the countries and industries included in the model. The only exceptions are the substitution elasticities between capital and labor, $\bar{\sigma}_{ij}$ [which enter the calculation of ε_{ij} in (A.1.25)], and between home and imported products, σ_{ij}, for each industry and country. The former can be obtained from published econometric studies of production functions. The latter we derive indirectly from published estimates of price elasticities of demand for imports, $\hat{\eta}_{ij}$. If we substitute (A.4.1) and (A.4.2) into (A.4.3), retaining only the terms involving ep_{ij}^M, the following expression for the own price elasticity of import demand can be derived:

$$\eta_{ij} = \theta_H^{ij}\sigma_{ij} + \theta_M^{ij}[v_{ij0} + \sum_{k=1}^{n'} v_{ijk}\varepsilon_{ik}b_{jk}]. \tag{A.4.24}$$

Equating (A.4.24) to $\hat{\eta}$ and solving for σ_{ij}, we get

$$\sigma_{ij} = \frac{1}{\theta_H^{ij}}[\hat{\eta}_{ij} - \theta_M^{ij}(v_{ij0} + \sum_{k=1}^{n'} v_{ijk}\,\varepsilon_{ik}b_{jk})], \tag{A.4.25}$$

which can be used to provide an estimate of σ_{ij}.

Notes

Chapter 1

1. See, however, Brown (1984), who has gone well beyond the Michigan model in incorporating trade-policy parameters into a computable model of world trade.

2. See, for example, the argument in Deardorff (1984) that Harris gets his results from a questionable combination of two assumptions: free entry and (partial) "focal point" pricing.

Chapter 2

1. Adapted from Deardorff and Stern (1979b, pp. 19–23).

2. This section and those following are adapted from Deardorff and Stern (1981, pp. 128–137; 1984c).

3. As will become clear, the microeconomic focus of our model distinguishes it from the macro-oriented world-linkage systems typified by the LINK, DESMOS, METEOR, and Federal Reserve Multicountry models. These latter models are also highly aggregated in terms of their sectoral coverage within countries.

4. This approximation to the Armington (1969) assumption will be discussed further.

5. Actually, if the tax on home production $(1 - t_{ij}^{H})$ is not zero, producers receive only $t_{ij}^{H} p_{ij}^{H}$.

6. Given that we normally assume fixed money wages, the model would behave in the aggregate in a very simple Keynesian fashion were we to make expenditure a function of income. This would also enable us to "close" the model.

7. For consistency we specify the total value of rest-of-world net supplies as equal to the sum of exogenous capital inflows. If then follows from equations (2.14)–(2.17) that $B_m^T + B_m^{KO} = 0$. This means, as Walras's law would suggest, that equilibrium in all but the mth currency market implies equilibrium in it as well.

8. These elasticities are surveyed in Stern, Francis, and Schumacher (1976). To infer elasticities of substitution from these estimates, we first used our model to derive

import-demand elasticities in terms of substitution elasticities and measurable parameters such as import shares. The result was then solved for the substitution elasticities. Details are contained in Deardorff, Stern, and Baum (1976).

9. Elasticities of substitution between capital and labor were taken from Zarembka and Chernicoff (1971). Shares of value-added and intermediate inputs were obtained from the various national input-output tables.

10. See Dervis, de Melo, and Robinson (1981) for a more extensive analysis of alternative adjustment mechanisms of payments imbalances in developing countries.

11. As, for example, Baldwin (1976) and Cline et al. (1978).

12. If expenditure were positively related to income, as is more conventional in Keynesian models, then this curve would be flatter than a 45° line. Still, the qualitative properties of the model are the same in either case. The main implication of holding expenditure constant is that the Keynesian multiplier is smaller than one normally expects.

13. As noted earlier in this chapter, we never exactly hold expenditure fixed, but instead allow for redistributed tariff revenue, and it might be thought that this should show up in figure 2.4 as a drop in expenditure when tariffs are reduced. In fact, however, the relevant relation in the figure is between real income and real expenditure. When tariff reductions occur, import prices fall and some reduction in nominal expenditure is needed to hold real expenditure constant. Redistributing tariff revenue may not serve exactly to hold real expenditure constant, but it does do so approximately.

14. As usual in models of this sort, it is not difficult to show that the relative slopes of the *IS* and *IS** curves are as drawn, and that their intersection moves up and to the left with a tariff cut.

15. With the many sectors of the Michigan model, on the other hand, income and employment are not uniquely related and some change in national income can occur. This will happen, for example, if tariff reductions shift the composition of national output in favor of less labor-intensive goods. Then a given level of employment will support a larger quantity of output, and national income will rise somewhat.

16. Elasticities of import demand are large enough in the model that the Marshall-Lerner condition is satisfied, so that this is in fact the direction of change that occurs.

17. He also mentions a closure rule associated with Kaldor, which we shall not discuss.

18. The Johansen approach has also been applied by Brown (1984).

19. In this connection see Scarf and Shoven (1984), Shoven and Whalley (1984), and Whalley and Srinivasan (1985).

Chapter 3

1. The reason for this choice was the compilation of detailed information on post-Kennedy Round ad valorem tariffs at the line-item level for these countries in

machine-readable form by the General Agreement on Tariffs and Trade (GATT, 1974). These tariffs were first available based upon 1970 trade. They have since been updated to 1976, which was the reference year for the Tokyo Round.

2. The tradable sectors cover merchandise trade only, and traded services are therefore excluded since the available data are incomplete and do not correspond well to the industry classifications used. We plan to incorporate traded services into the model at a later time. ISIC 2, mining and quarrying, reflects the initial production stage for the petroleum and mineral products involved. When these products are traded, they are included in ISIC 35B, 371, and 372.

3. We are currently analyzing—see Deardorff and Stern (1984a)—the implications of using the US input-output table as compared with the other individual national tables in order to determine how sensitive the model calculations are to alternative representations of technology. For additional research along these lines, see de Melo and Robinson (1982).

4. The basis for this calculation is shown in equation (A.4.25) of the technical appendix, which is derived assuming that intermediate inputs are used in fixed proportions. With the alternative of a Cobb-Douglas technology the calculation should be slightly different, though given the considerable uncertainty that surrounds the original import-demand elasticities, we have not felt it worthwhile to make this alternative calculation.

5. See Shoven and Whalley (1984, pp. 1038–1039) for a summary description of the data sources and elasticities used in the various computational trade models listed in table 2.1.

6. It should be noted, however, that linearization may affect the numerical results from a nonlinear model. For further discussion and comparison of solution methods, see de Melo (1978, 1980).

7. These approximations consisted primarily of using exogenous tariff changes to approximate the change in both expenditure and the prices of intermediate goods, and of ignoring demands for intermediate goods in the demand functions, at certain stages of the solution.

Chapter 4

1. The material in this chapter has been adapted from Deardorff and Stern (1983b,d).

2. These averages are weighted by own-country, 1976 imports, which include, in the case of the European Economic Community (EEC), imports from partner countries.

3. It is evident from tables 4.2 and 4.3 that there were, and will still be, noticeable disparities in tariffs among sectors, particularly in the United States. Much attention was given in the Kennedy Round to tariff disparities between the United States and the EEC. The issue was not settled then, perhaps because the EEC could not demonstrate readily the importance of disparities, and pressures for removing them reemerged in the Tokyo Round. This time agreement was reached on a harmonization formula proposed by the Swiss. In Deardorff and Stern (1979b, p. 48), we

compared the actual tariff reductions negotiated with those based on the Swiss formula. The overall actual depth of cut for the United States was close to the Swiss formula, but depths of cut for the EEC especially were substantially smaller, even though the EEC favored tariff harmonization.

4. As mentioned earlier, we do not have data in our model covering tariffs and NTBs for developing countries. This is not serious for our analysis here, since these countries will make few, if any, changes in policies as a result of the Tokyo Round. We do, however, capture elements of their existing NTBs by modeling a system of import licensing in most of the countries.

5. Our estimates will be somewhat overstated because, due to data limitations, no allowance has been made for existing government imports.

6. The price changes as directly calculated in the model are not used, since government-procurement liberalization implies shifting of demand curves. These measures of consumer and producer surplus, though they have ample precedent, are quite ad hoc. One might prefer a measure of welfare based on a social-utility function, though even the validity of that would be questionable in our model, which allows disequilibrium in labor markets and which, by not equating income and expenditure, implicitly allows for saving. In addition, the calculations here need to evaluate government demand. Given these difficulties, our surplus calculation may be as good as any, but it should not be taken too seriously.

7. These results indicate generally less expansion of trade, employment, and welfare than we report in Deardorff and Stern (1979b). The reason is an improved method of calculating weights on tariff revenues as they affect welfare. It turns out that we underestimated the importance of lost tariff revenue in our previous calculations.

8. In earlier calculations, when we kept expenditure essentially fixed and aggregate employment was therefore variable, the changes were still never more than a fraction of 1% in any country.

9. Like most developing countries, Chile is assumed to use import licensing to manage its balance of payments. In this case, however, the process of adjustment is unstable, or nearly so, so that unusually large changes are needed to clear the market. Whether this instability is a real problem for the Chilean economy or is an accident of our applying the Brazilian input-output table to Chile, we have thus far not been able to determine. In this connection, Brown (1984) does not obtain anomalous results for Chile in her analysis of the Tokyo Round, so that the clue may lie in our implementation of the Armington assumption. Whatever the explanation may turn out to be, it is best to regard the results for Chile as anomalies and discount them.

10. Note that exchange rates here depend solely on trade, and not on macro and monetary determinants. Frenkel (1981) discusses the latter and empirical evidence relating to them.

11. The large absolute increase in employment in agriculture reflects the NTB concessions obtained by the United States. Negative employment effects in non-tradable sectors are common and reflect substitution toward tradables as tariff reduction reduces their relative prices.

12. This conclusion might perhaps be qualified to the extent that our model does not

capture the effects of intraindustry specialization and scale economies and possible dynamic changes that may occur as the result of increased competitive pressures and innovation. These considerations have been stressed by Cline et al. (1978), Harris and Cox (1984), and others, but given the structure of our model, we cannot assess how important they may be in the context of the trade liberalization achieved by the Tokyo Round.

13. Kreinin and Officer (1979) reach a similar conclusion in their survey of studies of the effects of the Tokyo Round.

14. An exception here is that our model tends to overstate the changes in trade for the European Economic Community and other preferential arrangements because we do not account explicitly for the trade creation and diversion that may occur when tariffs are reduced. Brown is able to distinguish bilateral commercial policies, including customs unions and selective preferences, and thus avoids the overstatement that we find in our model.

15. Cline (1984) has estimated a logit model for NTB protection for the United States, Canada, the United Kingdom, France, and West Germany, using data for the late 1970s. The model that fit best for the United States related NTB protection to import penetration and the sector share in total manufacturing labor.

16. As noted, the Tokyo Round reductions in tariffs and selected NTBs, chiefly government procurement and certain agricultural concessions, were estimated to increase exports by about $13 billion for all the countries. For the United States, exports were estimated to rise by $2.9 billion and imports by $2.4 billion.

17. The estimated gross changes in employment attributed to the Tokyo Round were 123 thousand workers for the United States, 342 thousand workers for the EEC, and 36 thousand workers for Japan.

18. The welfare effects attributed to the Tokyo Round, which included both tariff reductions and the liberalization of government procurement and some agricultural concessions, were positive for all the industrialized countries except Australia, Austria, Denmark, and New Zealand.

19. The estimated changes in exchange rates due to the Tokyo Round were all relatively small in comparison.

20. All the price reductions due to the Tokyo Round were less than 1% except for Belgium-Luxembourg (−1.06%).

21. It is noteworthy that the net percentage changes in employment across sectors due to the Tokyo Round were generally fairly small in comparison with the results obtained here for tariff elimination. This suggests that the Tokyo Round negotiations were orchestrated so as to minimize possible disruptive effects in labor and product markets in certain participating countries.

Chapter 5

1. Taylor and Black (1974) seem to have been the first to use a general-equilibrium model—of the Johansen type—to evaluate protection, and de Melo (1978) fol-

lowed using a Walrasian model. Both made comparisons of their results with those based on an effective protection calculation. Both used single-country models, however.

2. The material in this chapter is adapted from Deardorff and Stern (1983c, 1984c).

3. The role of imperfect substitutability in trade modeling has been addressed also in de Melo and Robinson (1981).

4. Corden (1971) has gone well beyond the simple formula of equation (5.5) in considering many of the general-equilibrium complications that our model is designed to incorporate. We shall associate the simple formula with his name only for ease of reference.

5. It is also common to assume fixed production coefficients. Our model is capable of handling either fixed or variable coefficients, and, as will be noted, we have done the calculations both ways.

6. We explore the sectoral impact of exchange-rate changes in chapters 7 and 8.

7. Results for the remaining industrialized countries are available, but are not reported here.

8. It should be noted that we have not attempted to make adjustments in the underlying input-output relations in order to correct for any biases resulting from using actual rather than free trade conditions.

9. In order to make the reporting of our results somewhat less burdensome, we decided to concentrate only on the United States, the EEC, and Japan. For this purpose, the EEC member countries have been combined using weighted averages for the particular measures noted. It should be noted, however, that all of our calculations have been done using the full 34-country model and that detailed results are available for each country.

10. It is noteworthy that this is not the case in Japan, where the correlation between own-country and all-country protection measures is not significant, and New Zealand, where the correlation is negative. In correlations run between pairs of developed-country vectors of tariff reductions, these two countries stand out as unusual.

11. It should be noted that our model is not able currently to incorporate differences between the capital-to-intermediate good elasticity on the one hand and the labor-to-intermediate good elasticity on the other. Our experiment using Cobb-Douglas technology should thus be interpreted with this limitation in mind.

12. This finding was least true for Japan, where neither simple nor rank correlations, though negative, were significant. Since our data on tariff offers reflected the unilateral tariff reductions made by Japan prior to the conclusion of the Tokyo Round negotiations, our comparisons for Japan may not reflect accurately the forces involved there.

13. de Melo and Robinson (1981) showed that across-the-board tariff changes are likely to have different effects on resource allocation than tariffs changed indivi-

dually by sector. Our results, which involve comparisons of across-the-board tariff changes for the individual measures noted, are in agreement with their conclusion but show it to be the case even more strongly. de Melo (1978, 1980) has also demonstrated that partial-equilibrium estimates of effective rates of protection do not conform well to general-equilibrium estimates.

14. With only 22 tradable industries in our model, it is certainly possible that harmonization did occur but is obscured by our level of aggregation. Since we did find evidence of harmonization of nominal tariffs, however, such harmonization of true protection must have been relatively weak.

15. As pointed out in the preceding chapter, the Tokyo Round tariff reductions will be beneficial to some developing countries involved currently in the exports of manufactures. But since many existing NTBs affecting a variety of manufactured exports from developing countries were left intact (for example, textiles and apparel, and footwear), the Tokyo Round may be of limited consequence for these countries.

Chapter 6

1. This chapter has been adapted from Deardorff and Stern (1983e).

2. As will be noted below, data on domestic subsidies were available for the United Kingdom but not for the United States and Japan.

3. The removal of NTBs was not considered because of inadequate data availability.

4. In the preliminary version of our analysis, we used the detailed estimates for Japan underlying Whalley's 5-sector aggregation. However, when Whalley's estimates were compared with the data in the original sources, there were some important discrepancies. In particular, for labor taxes, the government mandated premiums to be paid by private firms for health and welfare programs and labor costs included premiums for old age, invalidity, death, sickness, maternity, work injury, unemployment, and family allowances. Whalley's estimates of labor taxes covered only the first five of these items and then apparently only partially. His estimates of Japan's capital taxes also had to be revised to use data from the unincorporated-enterprise survey to supplement the results for corporations. Whalley based his calculations upon a survey of small and medium enterprises that apparently included only firms that were already covered in the stratified sample for all corporations.

5. According to Whalley (1980, p. 1199), "The corporate tax and property tax are treated as taxes on capital use by industry. Social security taxes are treated as taxes on labor use by industry. For the other taxes, the broadly based value-added taxes, commodity taxes, and retail sales taxes are treated as consumer taxes on products purchased as are the selective excise taxes on drink, tobacco, hydrocarbon oil, and other specific products." It should be noted that no provision for subsidies was made in calculating the tax rates because of the lack of data. Also, personal income taxes are treated as taxes on incomes received by households and are therefore excluded. Whalley calculated excise taxes on intermediate goods by sector, but we have excluded them because they could not be readily accommodated in our input-output representation. In any event, most sectors were not subject to these taxes.

6. Weighted averages were used when Whalley's sectors were more detailed than ours. The same rates were applied when two or more of our sectors were included in one of Whalley's sectors.

7. Whalley (1980) used tax rates for the EEC in the aggregate. In our model, we include each of the EEC countries separately and take intra-EEC member-country trade into account. Time and resources did not permit us to aggregate the EEC, and Whalley's data were not readily accessible for the individual countries. We therefore chose only to analyze the United Kingdom and to leave the remaining EEC countries for future consideration.

8. Thus, for example, a 50% tax on a gross basis is equivalent to a 100% tax on a net basis.

9. UK tax rates on capital for 1973 apparently reflect the influence of the taxation of inflationary capital gains arising especially from the historical cost valuation of inventories. This feature of the tax law was changed in 1974. The 1973 rates are accordingly somewhat overstated for particular sectors, but for our purposes the variations across sectors may nonetheless be representative.

10. Ideally, it would be preferable to use marginal rather than average effective tax rates and to provide some measure of the benefits associated with the taxes/subsidies involved. To do so would go far beyond the scope of our present effort, however.

11. The net tax rates in table 6.1 were first converted to gross tax rates by dividing by one plus the net tax rates.

12. Thus, supply prices in each sector were reduced by the product of the gross-capital-tax rates implied by table 6.1 and the share of capital in total value of output.

13. Whalley (1980) modeled tax reductions as replaced by a uniform sales tax of equal revenue. The two approaches are equivalent, except that prices in his model are higher than in ours by the amount of the uniform tax.

14. These are again obtained from table 6.1 by dividing each net tax rate reported there by one plus itself.

15. The formula for the rate of protection afforded industry j is therefore

$$P_j = -\frac{\widetilde{\mathrm{NVA}}_j - \mathrm{NVA}_j}{\mathrm{NVA}_j}$$

$$= 1 - \exp\left(\frac{\hat{p}_j - \sum_{i=1}^{n} b_{ij}\hat{p}_i}{1 - \sum_{i=1}^{n} b_{ij}}\right)\left[\frac{1 - \theta_j^L \tilde{\tau}_j^L - \theta_j^K \tilde{\tau}_j^K}{1 - \theta_j^L \tau_j^L - \theta_j^K \tau_j^K}\right],$$

where a tilde (˜) indicates new values after taxes are removed, a circumflex (ˆ) indicates the change in the log of a variable, and $b_{ij} = p_i a_{ij}/p_j$ is the share of input i in the value of the output of good j. For analyzing simultaneous removal of both labor and capital taxes, the numerator in square brackets reduces to one, since both

$\tilde{\tau}$s are zero. If, on the other hand, neither tax is altered, then τs and $\tilde{\tau}$s are identical and the entire term in square brackets reduces to one. The formula then yields essentially the conventional measure of effective protection.

16. Besides the effects on net value added, domestic taxes and tariffs influence many other endogenous variables in the individual countries and industries in the model. However, in themselves, the orders of magnitude of changes in these other variables are not of interest since, as noted, it is their variation across industries that matters. We have chosen therefore not to report these details, but they are available on request. It might also be interesting to determine how much of our results stems from foreign rather than strictly domestic influences. We have not attempted such calculations in the present chapter, but we have done this for tariffs in chapter 5.

17. It bears repeating that we have not considered the protective effects of NTBs because of the lack of data.

18. Some might prefer that capital taxes be modeled competitively. If this were done, since capital stocks are assumed in the model to be fixed and industry specific in the relevant short run, the owners of capital would bear the whole incidence of the taxes and there would be no effects at all on prices or other variables in the model. The tax rates themselves, together with capital shares, would then directly measure their effects on net value added, and there would be no need for general-equilibrium calculations.

Chapter 7

1. Tariff revenues are still assumed to be redistributed to consumers, so that changes in these revenues still cause nominal expenditure to change. But since we now hold tariffs themselves constant, these changes arise only from changes in the revenues from existing tariffs and from changes in the tariff equivalents of nontariff barriers, and thus tend to be relatively minor.

2. The material in this and the following two sections is adapted from Deardorff, Stern, and Greene (1979b) and Deardorff and Stern (1982b).

3. This, of course, is not a test of theoretical hypotheses, since the numbers we are using were derived from the model rather than observed in the real world. Our purpose is rather to evaluate the quantitative importance of various theoretical mechanisms by which exchange rates can affect output and employment.

4. Regarding the determinants of the EREO that were mentioned in the preceding paragraph, it is clear that they can also influence, in a more limited way, the extent to which the exchange rate can affect output through the home sector. A large supply elasticity will again contribute positively to the effect, while a large export share of production will limit the influence of the home sector on the total industry. The second of these effects can be neglected, however, since the expansion of the home sector can never be greater, in percentage terms, than the expansion of the export sector. Thus, we continue to expect both the supply elasticity and the export share to play positive roles in determining the EREO.

5. Actually, expenditure, in our model, does depend slightly on the exchange rate through the redistribution of tariff revenue, the amount of which changes in response to a devaluation. See the "expenditure effect," to be discussed. Tariffs are too small for this expenditure effect to upset the conclusion that intermediate demands are more responsive than final demands to a devaluation.

6. The possibility that the exchange rate may affect expenditure, through its effect on the terms of trade, has been discussed extensively in the literature of international macroeconomics, beginning with the classic papers of Harberger (1950) and Laursen and Metzler (1950). The evidence for this effect, both theoretical and econometric, is limited and mixed. See Deardorff and Stern (1978).

7. A good example of this variation can be found in the leather products industry (ISIC 323). The values reported for its EREO in table 7.1 are unusually large in all of the countries for which we have used the US input-output table to characterize technology. This is largely because the supply elasticity implied by that input-output table is larger than in other countries. This, combined with the great importance of the footwear industry (ISIC 324) as a demander for leather, seems to account for this large and varying degree of sensitivity to exchange-rate changes.

8. This effect is of course contingent upon our modeling of Chile as having a system of import licensing, which applied during much of the 1970s, but has since been liberalized at least until 1983.

Chapter 8

1. The material in this chapter is based on Deardorff and Stern (1982a,c).

2. Thus, for example, if dollar appreciation were the result of a sudden large improvement in productivity in the United States or some other change affecting the goods market, our analysis of its effects would be completely off the mark.

3. Thus in each period we assume market equilibrium in all goods markets, and we change the equilibrium from period to period by changing the elasticities of supply and demand. An alternative approach would be to permit disequilibrium in each period, with prices moving sluggishly in response to excess supplies and demands. The latter approach would require explicit modeling of the behavior of suppliers and demanders whose desires are unfulfilled and would therefore entail modifying our model substantially and in ways that are not well understood.

4. Consider the familiar partial-equilibrium model of a market for exports, $X = D(p^*) = S(ep^*)$, where X is the quantity of exports, and D and S are their supplies and demands as functions of the foreign price, p^*, and the exchange rate, e. Letting the elasticities of supply and demand be ε and η, respectively, this implies the following expression for the change in exports, $\hat{X}$, due to a change in the exchange rate, $\hat{e}$:

$$\hat{X} = \frac{\varepsilon\eta}{\varepsilon + \eta}\hat{e}.$$

It is because of the symmetry of ε and η in this expression that we can approximate a reduction in η by reducing ε instead. This symmetry does not extend to the effects on prices, but since export prices do not play much of a role in our model beyond determining exports, this is not a problem.

5. This is necessary since, with expenditure exogenous in the model, there is no automatic mechanism for factor income to be reflected in expenditure.

6. The model was also solved in terms of all 34 countries and the results were then aggregated, but they are not reported here. Generally, the more detailed model yielded somewhat smaller effects than those indicated in the text.

7. It should be noted that all trade in our model is merchandise trade. We have not yet been able to incorporate trade in services into the model.

8. More recent estimation of the US export elasticities in the Federal Reserve MCM tends to bear this out according to a personal communication from Peter Hooper.

9. Fixing the US dollar price of oil almost eliminates, as we have seen, any change in US trade in that industry. But it increases the oil-trade response in the EEC, which devalues even more relative to the dollar than it does relative to a trade-weighted basket of currencies.

10. Recall that our analysis of this effect has only been approximate, since we were unable to use the full Armington assumption of product differentiation by country of origin in our model. Our damping of export-supply elasticities is intended to achieve similar results, but is necessarily somewhat inaccurate.

Chapter 9

1. The material in this chapter is adapted from Deardorff and Stern (1983a). The choice of 1970 and 1976 was dictated by the data base constructed for our model in connection with our previous research on the effects of tariff reductions and changes in exchange rates on employment; see chapters 4, 7, and 8.

2. One technical problem did arise, however, that required attention. Our model consists of a large number of equations that have been differentiated, to be solved therefore for the differentials of the variables. Stated as proportions of their corresponding levels, these differentials can be interpreted as percentage changes so long as the changes involved are small. This has been our procedure in much of our work with the model. For present purposes, however, the exogenous changes in trade are quite substantial and our usual procedure is inappropriate. Instead we assume that our model, prior to differentiation, is linear in the logarithms of its variables. This is equivalent to assuming constant elasticities for the functions involved in the model. And it permits us to use logarithmic and exponential transformations to transform variables into percentage changes that are valid even when large.

Specifically, the variables of the model are proportional differentials of the form (dx/x). For inputs to the model, these are calculated from discrete changes, Δx (such as that defined above for exports), as follows:

$$\frac{dx}{x} = \log\left(\frac{\Delta x}{x} + 1\right).$$

For outputs, the transformation is reversed to get percentage changes from proportional differentials as follows:

$$\frac{\Delta x}{x} = \exp\left(\frac{dx}{x}\right) - 1.$$

3. Balassa (1979) has calculated the employment effects resulting from the expansion of industrial countries' trade in manufactured goods with the developing countries on the alternative assumptions of a balanced increase in 1976 trade and a proportional increase in 1976 trade. His results are not directly comparable with ours since we are asking what the effects would be of restoring the observed 1970 pattern of trade in 1976. Balassa also reviewed previous studies of the employment effects of trade in manufactures between developed and developing countries. For another review of these studies, see OECD (Organization for Economic Cooperation and Development) (1979).

4. Balassa (1979) presents calculations of the employment effects by sector of the projected increases in trade for the Organization for Economic Cooperation and Development countries combined for the period 1976–1986. Our results reflect only the annual rates of increase. He shows overall negative employment effects in the industrial countries for textiles and clothing, leather and leather products, lumber and wood products, furniture and fixtures, rubber and plastics, electrical equipment and supplies, and miscellaneous manufactures. It is difficult to make precise comparisons between our results and his because he uses more disaggregated data and our aggregate industry classifications do not quite match his; we treat Greece, Spain, and Turkey as developing countries; and our model contains more explicit industry behavior and interindustry reactions. The main differences in our results compared with his appear in agriculture, nonferrous metals, electrical machinery, and miscellaneous manufactures. We also account for employment effects in nontradable industries, which he does not consider. Finally, because our model is disaggregated by country, we can estimate employment effects for each of the world's major trading countries.

5. Our results for the industrial countries combined indicate an estimated overall expansion of employment of 32,600 workers annually, whereas Balassa estimates that the net employment effects would be approximately zero.

Chapter 10

1. The material in this section is adapted from Deardorff (1982).

2. An alternative approach, which can actually be complementary to the differentiated products assumption, is that markets are monopolistically, rather than perfectly, competitive. See Harris and Cox (1984) for an effort to incorporate such a departure from perfect competition into a computable, empirically based model.

3. We assume that demanders differentiate between domestic and imported goods, but that all imports are perfect substitutes. We also assume that producers cannot shift freely between production for the home market and production for export. Together these two assumptions mimic the effects of the full Armington assumption, but permit us to solve simultaneously for equilibrium in only as many world markets as there are goods, rather than having a world market for each good-and-country combination.

4. Other reasons for the small effects of tariff cuts are detailed in chapter 4. They include the small size of the tariffs themselves, the fact that tariffs are generally reduced in many countries at once and may be partly offset by exchange rate changes, and the off-setting effects of tariffs on prices of outputs and inputs.

5. In the earlier 18-country version of the model when all exchange rates were flexible, Walras's law had been seen to be valid for combined world goods and exchange markets, and indeed we had successfully used the US trade balance as a ready indicator of whether our solution program was working correctly.

6. As noted in chapter 4, for example, we found such a tendency especially in Chile, where the effects of the Tokyo Round cuts in tariffs and selected NTBs were found to be an order of magnitude larger than in other developing countries.

References

Armington, P. S. (1969). "A Theory of Demand for Products Distinguished by Place of Production," *IMF Staff Papers* 16.

Balassa, B. (1979). "The Changing International Division of Labor in Manufactured Goods," Banca Nazionale del Lavoro, *Quarterly Review* 130.

Baldwin, R. E. (1976). "Trade and Employment Effects in the United States of Multilateral Tariff Reductions," *American Economic Review* (Papers and Proceedings) 66.

Baldwin, R. E. (1981). *The Political Economy of U.S. Import Policy,* in process.

Baldwin, R. E., J. H. Mutti, and J. D. Richardson (1980). "Welfare Effects on the United States of a Significant Multilateral Tariff Reduction," *Journal of International Economics* 10.

Belton, T., S. H. Hymans, and C. Lown (1981). "The Dynamics of the Michigan Quarterly Econometric Model of the U.S. Economy," Research Seminar in Quantitative Economics, The University of Michigan, R-108.81, December.

Boadway, R. W., and J. M. Treddenick (1978). "A General Equilibrium Computation of the Effects of the Canadian Tariff Structure," *Canadian Journal of Economics* 11.

Brown, D. K. (1984). "The Economic Effects of the Tokyo Round, Using a Computational Model with Bilateral Trade Flows and Commercial Policies," Ph.D. Dissertation, The University of Michigan.

Brown, D. K. (1985). "A Theoretical and Computational Evaluation of Commercial Policies in a Model in Which Imports Are Disaggregated by Place of Production," in process.

Brown, F., and J. Whalley (1980). "General Equilibrium Evaluations of Tariff-Cutting Proposals in the Tokyo Round and Comparisons to More Extensive Liberalization of Trade," *Economic Journal* 90.

Cline, W. R. (1984). *Exports of Manufactures from Developing Countries: Performance and Prospects for Market Access.* Washington: The Brookings Institution.

Cline, W. R., N. Kawanabe, T. O. M. Kronso, and T. Williams (1978). *Trade Negotiations in the Tokyo Round: A Quantitative Assessment.* Washington: The Brookings Institution.

Corden, W. M. (1966). "The Structure of a Tariff System and the Effective Protective Rate," *Journal of Political Economy* 74.

Corden, W. M. (1971). *The Theory of Protection.* London: Oxford University Press.

Deardorff, A. V. (1982). "Lessons from Computer Modeling of Trade," presented at Summer Institute in International Studies, National Bureau of Economic Research, Cambridge, MA, August.

Deardorff, A. V. (1984). "Essential Features of the Harris and Keyzer Models," in Whalley and Srinivasan (1985).

Deardorff, A. V., and R. M. Stern (1974). "Partial Equilibrium Estimation of the Effects of Trade Liberalization," presented at the Winter Meeting of the Econometric Society, San Francisco, December.

Deardorff, A. V., and R. M. Stern (1978). "The Terms-of-Trade Effect on Expenditure: Some Evidence from Econometric Models," *Journal of International Economics* 8.

Deardorff, A. V., and R. M. Stern (1979a). "American Labor's Stake in International Trade," in Institute for Contemporary Studies, *Tariffs, Quotas, and Trade: The Politics of Protectionism.* San Francisco: Institute for Contemporary Studies.

Deardorff, A. V., and R. M. Stern (1979b). *An Economic Analysis of the Effects of the Tokyo Round of Multilateral Trade Negotiations on the United States and the Other Major Industrialized Countries.* MTN Studies 5. Washington: U.S. Government Printing Office.

Deardorff, A. V., and R. M. Stern (1981). "A Disaggregated Model of World Production and Trade: An Estimate of the Impact of the Tokyo Round," *Journal of Policy Modeling* 3.

Deardorff, A. V., and R. M. Stern (1982a). "The Effects of Exchange-Rate Changes on Domestic Prices, Trade, and Employment in the U.S., European Community, and Japan," International Economic Association Conference, "Structural Adjustment in Trade Dependent Advanced Economies," Yxtaholm, Sweden, August, in process.

Deardorff, A. V., and R. M. Stern (1982b). "The Role of Exchange Rates in the Michigan Computational Model of World Production and Trade," *Tijdschrift voor Economie en Management* 27.

Deardorff, A. V., and R. M. Stern (1982c). "The Sectoral Impact of the Recent Appreciation of the U.S. Dollar," a report to the Office of the U.S. Trade Representative, unpublished.

Deardorff, A. V., and R. M. Stern (1983a). "Changes in Trade and Employment in the Major Industrialized Countries, 1970–76," in B. Weisbrod and H. Hughes (eds.), *The Problems of Developed Countries and the International Economy.* London: Macmillan Press.

Deardorff, A. V., and R. M. Stern (1983b). "Economic Effects of the Tokyo Round," *Southern Economic Journal* 49. [Reprinted in *PORTFOLIO: International Economic Perspectives* 10 (1984).]

Deardorff, A. V., and R. M. Stern (1983c). "Tariff and Exchange-Rate Protection under Fixed and Flexible Exchange Rates in the Major Industrialized Countries," in J. S. Bhandari and B. P. Putnam (eds.), *Economic Interdependence and Flexible Exchange Rates*. Cambridge: MIT Press.

Deardorff, A. V., and R. M. Stern (1983d). "The Economic Effects of Complete Elimination of Post-Tokyo Round Tariffs on the Major Industrialized and Developing Countries," in W. R. Cline (ed.), *Trade Policy in the 1980s*. Washington: Institute for International Economics.

Deardorff, A. V., and R. M. Stern (1983e). "The Effects of Domestic Tax/Subsidies and Import Tariffs on the Structure of Protection in the United States, United Kingdom, and Japan," in J. Black and A. L. Winters (eds.), *Policy and Performance in International Trade*. London: Macmillan Press.

Deardorff, A. V., and R. M. Stern (1984a). "Input-Output Technologies and the Effects of Tariff Reductions," *Journal of Policy Modeling*, forthcoming.

Deardorff, A. V., and R. M. Stern (1984b). "The Effects of the Tokyo Round on the Structure of Protection," in R. E. Baldwin and A. O. Krueger (eds.), *The Structure and Evolution of Recent U.S. Trade Policy*. Chicago: University of Chicago Press for the National Bureau of Economic Research.

Deardorff, A. V., and R. M. Stern (1984c). "The Structure and Sample Results of the Michigan Computational Model of World Production and Trade," in Whalley and Srinivasan (1985).

Deardorff, A. V., and R. M. Stern (1984d). "The Structure of Tariff Protection: Effects of Foreign Tariffs and Existing NTBs," *Review of Economics and Statistics*, forthcoming.

Deardorff, A. V., and R. M. Stern (1985). "Neighborhood Effects of Developing Country Protection," *Journal of Development Economics*, forthcoming.

Deardorff, A. V., R. M. Stern, and C. F. Baum (1976). "A Simulation Model of World Production and Trade," unpublished manuscript.

Deardorff, A. V., R. M. Stern, and C. F. Baum (1977). "A Multi-Country Simulation of the Employment and Exchange-Rate Effects of Post-Kennedy Round Tariff Reductions," in N. Akrasanee et al. (eds.), *Trade and Employment in Asia and the Pacific*. Honolulu: University Press of Hawaii.

Deardorff, A. V., R. M. Stern, and M. N. Greene (1979a). "The Implications of Alternative Trade Strategies for the United States," in D. B. H. Denoon (ed.), *The New International Economic Order: A U.S. Response*. New York: New York University Press. [Original-unrevised version reprinted in *The 1978 Midyear Review of the Economy*, Hearings before the Joint Economic Committee, 95th Congress, Second Session, Part 2, Washington: U.S. Government Printing Office.]

Deardorff, A. V., R. M. Stern, and M. N. Greene (1979b). "The Sensitivity of Industrial Output and Employment to Exchange-Rate Changes in the Major Industrialized Countries," in J. P. Martin and M. A. M. Smith (eds.), *Trade and Payments Adjustment under Flexible Exchange Rates*. London: Macmillan Press.

de Melo, J. (1978). "Protection and Resource Allocation in a Walrasian Trade Model," *International Economic Review* 19.

de Melo, J. (1980). "Tariffs and Resource Allocation in Partial and in General Equilibrium," *Weltwirtschaftliches Archiv* 116.

de Melo, J., and S. Robinson (1981). "Trade Policy and Resource Allocation in the Presence of Product Differentiation," *Review of Economics and Statistics* 63.

de Melo, J., and S. Robinson (1982). "Trade Adjustment Policies and Income Distribution in Three Archetype Developing Economies," *Journal of Development Economics* 10.

Dervis, K., J. de Melo, and S. Robinson (1981). "A General Equilibrium Analysis of Foreign Exchange Shortages in a Developing Economy," *Economic Journal* 91.

Dervis, K., J. de Melo, and S. Robinson (1982). *General Equilibrium Models for Development Policy*. New York: Cambridge University Press.

Dhrymes, P. (1969). "A Model of Short-Run Labor Adjustment," in J. Duesenberry et al. (eds.), *The Brookings Model: Some Further Results.* Chicago: Rand McNally.

Dixon, P. B., B. R. Parmenter, J. Sutton, and D. P. Vincent (1982). *ORANI: A Multisectoral Model of the Australian Economy.* Amsterdam: North-Holland.

Dornbusch, R. (1980). *Open Economy Macroeconomics.* New York: Basic Books.

Frenkel, J. A. (1981). "Flexible Exchange Rates, Prices, and the Role of 'News': Lessons from the 1970s," *Journal of Political Economy* 89.

GATT (General Agreement on Tariffs and Trade) (1974). *Basic Documentation for the Tariff Study*. Geneva: GATT.

Ginsburgh, V., and J. Waelbroeck (1981). *Activity Analysis and General Equilibrium Modeling.* Amsterdam: North-Holland.

Gunning, J. W., G. Carrin, and J. Waelbroeck (1982). "Growth and Trade of Developing Countries: A General Equilibrium Analysis," Discussion Paper 8210, Centre d'Economie Mathématique et d'Econometrie, Université Libre de Bruxelles.

Hamermesh, D. S. (1976). "Econometric Studies of Labor Demand and Their Application to Policy Analysis," *Journal of Human Resources* 11.

Harberger, A. C. (1950). "Currency Depreciation, Income and the Balance of Trade," *Journal of Political Economy* 58.

Harris, R. G., and D. Cox (1984). *Trade, Industrial Policy, and Canadian Manufacturing.* Toronto: Ontario Economic Council.

Hooper, P. (1982). "Estimated Impacts of Recent Movements in the Dollar Based on Simulations with the MCM," Quantitative Studies Section, U.S. Federal Reserve Board, Washington D.C., February, mimeo.

Johansen, L. (1960). *A Multi-Sectoral Study of Economic Growth.* Amsterdam: North-Holland.

Kreinin, M. E., and L. H. Officer (1979). "Tariff Reductions under the Tokyo Round: A Review of Their Effects on Trade Flows, Employment, and Welfare," *Weltwirtschaftliches Archiv* 115.

Laursen, S., and L. A. Metzler (1950). "Flexible Exchange Rates and the Theory of Employment," *Review of Economics and Statistics* 32.

Leamer, E. E., R. M. Stern, and C. F. Baum (1977). "An Empirical Analysis of the Composition of Manufacturing Employment in the Industrialized Countries," *European Economic Review* 17.

Lysy, F. J. (1983). "The Character of General Equilibrium Models under Alternative Closures," in process.

Manne, A. S., and P. Preckel (1983). "A Three-Region Intertemporal Model of Energy, International Trade, and Capital Flows," Operations Research, Stanford University.

Melvin, J. R. (1979). "Short-Run Price Effects of the Corporate Income Tax and Implications for International Trade," *American Economic Review* 69.

Miller, M. H., and J. E. Spencer (1977). "The Static Economic Effects of the U.K. Joining the EEC: A General Equilibrium Approach," *Review of Economic Studies* 44.

Murray, T., and I. Walter (1978). "Special and Differential Liberalization of Quantitative Restrictions on Imports from Developing Countries," in L. Perez (ed.), *Trade Policies toward Developing Countries: The Multilateral Trade Negotiations*. Washington: Agency for International Development.

Neumann, G. R. (1979). "Adjustment Assistance for Trade-Displaced Workers," in D. B. H. Denoon (ed.), *The New International Economic Order: A U.S. Response*. New York: New York University Press.

OECD (Organization for Economic Cooperation and Development) (1979). "The Impact of the Newly Industrialized Countries on Production and Trade in Manufactures," Report by the Secretary-General, Paris.

Piggott, J. R., and J. Whalley (1981). *Economic Effects of U.K. Tax-Subsidy Policies: A General Equilibrium Appraisal*, in process.

Scarf, H. E. (1967). "On the Computation of Equilibrium Prices," in W. J. Fellner (ed.), *Ten Economic Studies in the Tradition of Irving Fisher*. New York: Wiley.

Scarf, H. E., and J. F. Shoven (1984). *Applied General Equilibrium Analysis*. New York: Cambridge University Press.

Shoven, J. B., and J. Whalley (1984). "Applied General Equilibrium Models of Taxation and International Trade: An Introduction and Survey," *Journal of Economic Literature* 22.

Srinivasan, T. N., and J. Whalley, eds. (1986). *General Equilibrium Trade Policy Modeling*. Cambridge: MIT Press.

Staiger, R. W., A. V. Deardorff, and R. M. Stern (1985a). "An Evaluation of Factor Endowments and Protection as Determinants of Japanese and American Foreign Trade," in process.

Staiger, R. W., A. V. Deardorff, and R. M. Stern (1985b). "The Effects of Protection on the Factor Content of Japanese and American Foreign Trade," in process.

Stern, R. M. (1979). "Evaluating the Consequences of Alternative Policies for Trade Liberalization in the MTN," in G. and V. Curzon (eds.), *Commercial Policy Issues 3,4: Evaluating the Effects of Trade Liberalization.* Leiden: Sijthoff.

Stern, R. M., J. F. Francis, and B. F. Schumacher (1976). *Price Elasticities in International Trade: An Annotated Bibliography.* London: Macmillan Press.

Taylor, L., and S. L. Black (1974). "Practical General Equilibrium Estimation of Resource Pulls under Trade Liberalization," *Journal of International Economics* 4.

Whalley, J. (1980). "Discriminatory Features of Domestic Factor Tax Systems in a Good Mobile-Factors Immobile Trade Model: An Empirical General Equilibrium Approach," *Journal of Political Economy* 88.

Whalley, J. (1982). "An Evaluation of the Tokyo Round Agreement Using General Equilibrium Computational Methods," *Journal of Policy Modeling* 4.

Whalley, J. (1984). *Trade Liberalization among Major World Trading Areas.* Cambridge: MIT Press.

Zarembka, P., and H. B. Chernicoff (1971). "Further Results on the Empirical Relevance of the CES Production Function," *Review of Economics and Statistics* 53.

Index